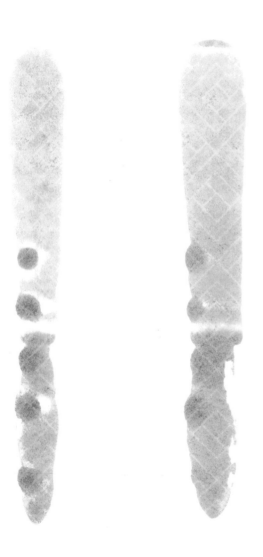

The Israeli Economy

The situation of Israel is in many ways unique. No other country has absorbed so many immigrants in relation to its size. Few other countries have been able to grow so fast, modernise so extensively and maintain a free society and a republican democracy. Israel has achieved this despite the active hostility of many of its neighbours, and whilst undertaking enormous military, political and social commitments. However, its economy has been undergoing a crisis phase. Its rate of economic growth has slowed drastically and there are now serious doubts about whether it can continue to finance such extensive commitments.

Yair Aharoni discusses how the economy has reached its current state and assesses its future prospects. The early fathers of the Israeli state envisaged a sovereign Jewish state that was independent, socially just and economically prosperous. And yet their dreams have been consistently compromised. Persistent and high levels of capital imports have helped supply the capital necessary for rapid modernisation, but they have also helped to finance consumption. Israel holds the record for the highest rate of foreign debt per capita (actually higher than its equivalent rate of GDP), and also for the largest trade deficit per capita. Throughout recent years, successive governments have struggled to control massive inflationary pressures within the economy. An enormous defence budget places a further strain on the economy. However, given the realities of Israel's recent past and its immediate situation, it is difficult to see how this burden is going to be eased substantially in the near future. Aharoni analyses the possible consequences of this predicament.

Throughout, Aharoni measures the economic problems Israel endures against the social and economic successes it has been able to achieve. He highlights the incongruities of the aspirations of Israel's founders and supporters and the actual reality, and the interplay of economic and political forces that have shaped this reality.

Yair Aharoni is currently J. Paul Sticht Visiting Professor of International Business at the Fuqua School of Business, Duke University. He is also the Issacher Haimovic Professor of Business Policy at the Leon Racanati Graduate School of Business Administration, Tel-Aviv University. He has published extensively, and his publications include more than twenty books and numerous scholarly articles.

Frontispiece The economy of Israel 1950-1989

	1950	1960	1965	1967	1970	1975	1980	1985	1987	1988	1989
Population (1,000s)	1,370	2,150	2,598	2,776	3,022	3,493	3,922	4,266	4,406	4,477	4,556
% annual increase		4.6	3.8	3.3	2.9	2.1	2.2	1.8	1.7	1.6	1.8
Labor force participation rate											
Men		78.1	76.1	72.1	69.2	64.9	63.7	63.6	62.4	63.2	63.0
Women		27.3	29.4	28.6	29.3	31.9	35.7	38.2	38.9	40.0	41.3
Unemployment rate (men)		4.5	3.4	10.0	3.4	2.5	4.1	6.3	5.2	5.7	7.9
% Annual change[a]											
GNP		10.8	9.7	1.5	12.0	3.5	2.8	4.8	6.0	2.9	1.3
Per capita GNP		5.1	5.5	-1.4	8.6	1.2	0.4	0.3	1.4	0.5	
Per capita											
consumption		4.4	5.4	-0.9	5.5	-2.0	-5.2	3.3[b]	6.7	1.4	-2.7
Real wages						-2.2	-3.3	-9.0	8.0	5.9	-1.8
Ratios to GNP											
Private consumption	74.1	70.4	68.1	68.0	61.2	60.3	61.5	64.3	63.9	65.0	63.1
Government consumption	18.6	18.7	20.7	30.2	36.3	44.2	36.1	36.5	35.2	34.3	31.7
Gross domestic capital formation	31.0	27.5	30.0	17.4	29.0	32.1	23.6	18.5	19.8	18.8	16.9
Import surplus	23.9	16.7	19.2	15.7	26.6	36.7	21.3	15.1	21.5	15.3	
Imports ($ mill.)	330	682	1,234	1,447	2,664	7,536	13,567	15,092	20,095	20,982	20,877
Exports ($ mill.)	45	336	711	911	1,402	3,687	9,795	11,245	14,288	15,656	17,151
Transfers ($ mill.)	114	311	321	521	650	1,770	2,966	4,997	4,839	4,651	
Net foreign debt ($ mill.)		676	979	1,144	2,261	6,315	12,010	19,397	18,246	18,602	16,400
Consumer price index (1973 = 1.0)	0.1	0.4	0.5	0.6	0.7	1.9	21.3	48.01	85.2	99.1	119.1
Inflation rate[a]		12.7	7.1	4.8	3.6	39.2	41.6	193[b]	21[c]	16[d]	21[d]
Savings/disposal income							33.0	29.0	20.5	21.4	

Source: CBS, Statistical Abstracts, various years.
Notes: [a]Calculated relative to 1970. [b]1981-4. [c]August 1985-7. [d]Relative to previous years.

The Israeli Economy
Dreams and Realities

Yair Aharoni

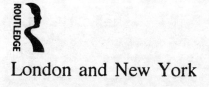

London and New York

First published in 1991
by Routledge
11 New Fetter Lane, London EC4P 4EE

Simultaneously published in the USA and Canada
by Routledge
a division of Routledge, Chapman and Hall Inc.
29 West 35th Street, New York, NY 10001

Printed and bound in Great Britain by Mackays of Chatham PLC, Kent

British Library Cataloguing in Publication Data
Aharoni, Yair
    The Israeli economy.
    1. Israel. Economic. Conditions
    I. Title
    330.95694
    ISBN 0-415-02192-8

Library of Congress Cataloging in Publication Data
has been applied for

Contents

Contents

Tables

Tables

Acknowledgements

I am indebted to many organizations and individuals for assistance throughout the long months of collecting and organizing the material for this book. In Israel, Doron Shavit made many valuable comments on earlier drafts, and Ruth Dagan spent many long hours typing and reading proofs. The Leon Recanati Graduate School of Business provided a convenient environment for research.

Most of the book was prepared at the Fuqua School of Business, Duke University. The library here provided exemplary service, without which the book would not have been written, and several drafts were typed by Vivian Hawkins. I owe a deep sense of gratitude to San McGraw, who typed and retyped many drafts and spent long hours reading proofs and checking data.

The critical comments of several reviewers greatly improved the book. I am especially thankful to Yaakov Amihud for many insightful comments and to Ohad Bar-Ephrat for checking data. Monty Graham read several chapters and made important comments. John Lynch devoted many hours to correcting the English in the manuscript.

I would like to thank my editor at Routledge, Mr Peter Sowden, for his help and encouragement during the development of the manuscript and for acting as a valuable stimulus throughout its many revisions. For the successful metamorphosis of the book as a whole, I am grateful to the entire staff at Routledge. Copy editing was done by Graeme Leonard, and the index was prepared by John Tooke. Jennifer Binnie provided important editorial help. My sincere thanks to all of them.

Finally, my wife and two daughters allowed me to spent my evenings writing and made my task easy in every way. I would like to express utmost appreciation for their patience, support, understanding and love.

Introduction: the dreams and the realities

This book attempts to explain the major economic and political changes that have occurred in Israel and to examine the impact of these changes on the country and its people. The time scale adopted is predominantly that of the last forty years or so, that is, since Israel was established in May 1948. However, reference is made to longer historical perspectives, without which it is difficult to understand the main forces that have stamped Israel.

I have chosen to focus on what I believe to be the key political and economic influences, but also to highlight the major incongruities of the aspirations, dreams, hopes and the actual reality. In analyzing these forces, my approach is deliberately eclectic, drawing not only on economics but also on sociology, on organization theory and on political science.

Israel is a land of many contrasts. It is one of the oldest countries in the world, and Jews were exiled from it for two thousand years before they returned to it in the relatively recent past. It was established as a homeland and a safe haven for the Jews, yet has been unable to attract most of the Jews to live in it: at the end of 1988, only 28 per cent of the Jewish population lived in Israel, while 44 per cent of world Jews live in the USA In fact, the number of Jews living in New York, New Jersey, California and Florida alone (3,665,000) was larger by the end of 1986 than that of Jews living in Israel (3,561,000). To be sure, when the pioneers of the Zionist movement started the modern return to Zion in 1882, only 0.3 per cent of the Jewish population lived in Israel. As late as 1939, after five waves of Jewish immigration to Palestine, only 449,000 Jews out of 16 million (or 3 per cent of total world Jewry) lived in the Holy Land. Even after 6 million Jews were massacred in the Holocaust, only 650,000 out of the remaining 11.5 million world Jewry (5.7 per cent) lived in Israel when the state was declared on May 14, 1948.

While during almost all the British Mandate period there were various restrictions on Jewish immigration, the State of

Israel made Jewish immigration one of its major political aims. The Law of the Return guarantees irrevocably every Jew (except those fleeing criminal prosecution) the right to immigrate to Israel and become her citizen. Israel did significantly increase the share of Jews living within its borders. However, those immigrating were mainly Jews living in distressed conditions in their country of origin. Jews coming from Europe or the United States are known as Ashkenazim. Those coming from Asian and African countries are Sephardim. Of the total world Jewry about 85 per cent are Ashkenazim. Today, only about 10 per cent of the Ashkenazim Jews compared to about two-thirds of the Sephardim live in Israel. In short, the dream of the return of the people to its old homeland did not fully materialize. Despite many calls of Zionist leaders, most of the Jews did not return to the promised land although many of them continued to pray for such a return three times a day. At the same time, Israel's ethnic composition has materially changed.

Most Israelis still believe their country has a major task of providing a refuge for any non-criminal Jew. Jews, on their part, show anxiety, concern, pride, even yearning toward Israel but to a large extent see it as an insurance for shelter if hard times come. The relations between Israeli Jews and those in the Diaspora are very complex. Most Jews may help Israel financially, but do not choose to live within its borders. Only those ideologically or religiously inclined made the actual move to try and immigrate to Israel. Many of those later decided to emigrate. From 1988, the accumulated migration balance was negative, but became positive in 1989 and 1990.

In 1990 Israel made strenuous efforts to absorb a new wave of immigrants. In the first eight months of the year, almost 100,000 new immigrants arrived — mainly as a result of a change in the immigration policy of the USSR that allowed a large number of Jews to emigrate. This was coupled by the unwillingness of the United States to allow these immigrants to enter the US.

The ideology of the Zionist leaders, in particular (though not exclusively) of its Socialist leaders, called for the restratification of the Jewish occupational structure — as a vital part of the normalization of the Jews and their state. The creation of a Jewish proletariat, predominantly in agriculture, was seen as being of paramount importance. The dreamers of the First immigration waves (called in Hebrew *Aliya* — literally 'ascent') regarded the occupational structure of the Jews in the Diaspora as a deplorable abnormality. They aspired to remedy this structure in the new Jewish state by becoming farmers, making the return to the land an ideological norm, equal to a religious dictate. The symbolic value of agriculture was deemed so important that David Ben Gurion, Israel's first prime minister, insisted on registering his occupation at the population census as a farmer, although he had been in public life and lived in cities for more than thirty years by the time this specific census was taken.

By the end of 1989, only 4.7 per cent of the total employed persons worked in agriculture, forestry and fishing. More than half were employed in services. In fact, based on its occupational structure Israel may be seen as a post-industrial society, although based on GNP per capita, Israel is much less developed than that.

Israel holds the world record for the number of scientific papers published per capita, and in some agricultural production levels, but also holds records for foreign debt per capita ($7,440 by the end of 1987, compared to GNP per capita of $6,810) and in the size of trade deficit. It was established by ideologists who hoped to create a new and just society that could be seen as a 'light to the gentiles.' Its founders pursued a Utopian dream of a kingdom of saints and a world purged of sin and suffering. After several generations of a life of interminable emergency more and more persons react with cynicism if not despair. The sheer problems of survival as a mini-state in a very disturbed part of the world reduce the desirability of living within its borders. The majority of its elite is still composed of Jews of Eastern European origin, although the majority of its citizens are of Afro-Asian origin. To be sure, this is changing. In 1989, 9 out of 26 government ministers were Sephardim. In the local councils, Sephardim are about 50 per cent of the elected dignitaries. Its occupational structure resembles that of the most developed post-industrial societies of the world, but its GNP per capita is about 35 per cent of that of the United States, and has declined relative to the United States since 1974. Its two major departments of economics, at the Hebrew University and Tel Aviv University, have been ranked according to the rate of publications in the first league of world economics departments, but its economic policies are often perceived as leaving a lot to be desired. Certainly, Israel was never able to put its economic house in order completely. It always needed a large influx of capital imports, used most of the time to finance investments but under some less responsible governments — also to finance rising consumption.

When the State of Israel was declared in 1948, its currency, the Israeli lira (IL) was equal to US $4. Since then, the lira has been replaced by the shekel, and the shekel by the new shekel.

Each new shekel is equivalent to IL10,000 and to less than US ¢50. In other words, the Israeli currency was devalued in forty years by 80,000 per cent. Between May 1948 and January 1959, the cost of living index rose by 308 per cent. From then to December 1976 it increased by 685.16 per cent. From 1977 to 1987, it zoomed by 333,439 per cent.

While for years the image of the Jews was one of brilliant merchants but not very courageous individuals, Israel gained a very high reputation for having one of the best armies in the world, but also as a country with very weak international marketing. Many Israelis — only two generations away from the Nazi Holocaust — still doubt the country's military strength and are constantly worried that the country, still besieged by enemies, might be wiped out by a surprise attack initiated by its neighbors.

The Zionist settlement in Israel opposed the so-called 'Haluka' ('distribution') system, by which pious Jews in Eretz Israel lived on money raised among Diaspora Jews and allocated among the Jews in the Holy Cities. The socialist pioneers at the turn of the century also despised the farmers who had immigrated to Israel previously and who had found it necessary to ask Baron Rothschild to help them. Yet since then Zionist leaders continued to raise — even demand — money from their brethren abroad. Despite pious talks about the need for economic independence, Israel continues to consume much more than it produces, increasing dependence on those giving grants and loans. In 1988, forty years after independence, Israel received $4.5 billion in unilateral transfers, $2.8 billion of which came from the US government and a few hundred millions came from Jewish donations. Its import surplus was 14.8 per cent of GDP. Having learned to get funds from abroad, the Israelis may have made less effort to produce. The product per employed person grew for the decade 1974-84 by 4.6 per cent. Japan at the same time increased product per employed person by 40.5 per cent.

Israel is also a very small country in world terms, located at quite a distance from its major markets. Israel's total size is about 1/7,000 of the world's territory and its population is less than 1/1,000 of that of the world. The ability of such a mini-state to survive despite the animosity and active trade blocks of its immediate neighbors and the constant attacks of infiltrators, some of which are willing to commit suicide attacks, has been a major challenge to the State of Israel.

While tiny, and relatively new, Israel is also very old, permeated by a strong consciousness of its long and cherished history. The acknowledgement of the historical connection between the Jews and their land has been crucial in achieving world reaffirmation of the right to rebuild a Jewish national home. The indomitable loyalty and dedication of the Jews to their religion, and therefore the land of their fathers, has created an inseparable link between the present and the past. Amidst the turbulence of riots, attack by violent mobs, exiles and persecutions, the faith in the Ingathering of the Exiles remained with undiminished power for generations. Yet, the modern return to Zion was started by secular Jews.

When the Jews began to return to their ancient land, they did not realize Arabs occupied a part of that land. The Founding Fathers believed that Israel's ability to raise the material standard of living would make Arabs hospitable to Jewish immigration. Indeed, Jewish immigrants materially raised the standard of living of all — and many Arabs came to Palestine to share the prosperity. The rate of natural increase among Arabs also accelerated. Between 1919 and 1947, the Jewish population of Palestine grew ten fold — the Arab population doubled. Arabs treated Jewish immigration with animosity, jealousy and anxiety; and it has been the seed of a long, bitter and seemingly insolvable and never ending conflict between Arabs and Jews. Non-Jews consisted of 90 per cent of the population in 1919, but only two-thirds in December 1947. The Arabs were adamant in their opposition to a Jewish state even on a tiny part of Palestine. Arabs fought against Jews in 1920, 1929, 1936-9, and again in attempting to stop the creation of an independent state in 1948. Since then, Arab atrocities have made entire lifetimes seem like an interminable emergency. In 1956, Israel participated in the Suez War, alongside Britain and France. For Israel, defense has always been a first priority and a costly burden that could have caused the economy to sink under its weight.

In 1967, Israel was forced into yet another war. Brilliantly fought, the war resulted in conquering of the West Bank, Gaza Strip, the Sinai Peninsula and part of the Golan Heights. It also resulted in having 1.5 million Palestinians living under military rule. The whole of the Sinai Peninsula, an area of 23,622 square miles, was returned to Egypt as part of a peace treaty signed between Israel and Egypt in 1979. The other territories, a total area of 2,986 square miles, are still under Israel's military rule. Israel extended its sovereignty over all of Jerusalem, Israel's eternal capital, in 1980. Members of ultra-nationalistic parties repeatedly introduce laws extending Israel's sovereignty over all captured territories.

The Palestinian uprising (Intifada) in these areas had caused Israel much embarrassment by the end of the 1980s. It was increasingly seen by more and more Israelis as a sign of Israeli mistakes and the need to negotiate peace. Other Israelis believed the uprising must be ended — even by harsh methods. They did not see any peaceful solution of the Arab-Israeli conflict. Each of the opposite groups fear that the policy advocated by the other will lead to the destruction of the state.

The events which led to the resurrection of a Jewish state almost two thousand years after it was destroyed by the Roman legions are often perceived as unique and unprecedented. For two thousand years the Jews, despite their dispersal in different parts of the world, retained strong religious and emotional bonds to the old land. In their prayers, they faithfully turned three times a day towards Jerusalem, recalling the memory of the days of a sovereign state and praying for the return to Zion. In these prayers and thinking, Jews have been waiting for the Messiah to bring them back to the Holy Land, and only a handful of them actually lived there. In the modern period many Jews attempted to assimilate. These Jews were obsessed with a sense of inferiority, unceasingly denying themselves and regarding their heritage with shame, exerting themselves frantically to efface their own identity.

Although religion created the bonds to the old state, and the continued hope for the return and the Ingathering of the Exiles, the world Zionist movement, officially founded at an international congress in Basle in 1897, was led mainly by the non-religious, some of them even assimilated, Jews. They were able to awaken the energies of many Jews. Theodor Herzl, who inspired, created and led the new movement, believed in getting the Jewish state through political means. His obstinacy and persistence in the face of enormous odds, as that of those who sowed the first seeds of Zionism before him, cannot be understood except in terms of faith.

Many religious leaders in Herzl's time were opposed to Jewish immigration to Israel. Not waiting for the Messiah to arrive was considered a sin. For some ultra-orthodox Jews, this is still true: they see the existence of the State of Israel as blasphemy and refuse to recognize its laws. Yet most coalition governments in Israel were at the mercy of orthodox mini-parties. At least one of these parties was willing to vote for the government in return for funds transferred to its institutions but refused to allow its representatives to become ministers and an integral part of the government.

Israelis like to claim that they are different. Most of the country's Founding Fathers believed that economic laws and evaluations were irrelevant to the special needs of constructing a new sovereign Jewish state. They were convinced that their sheer will would be enough to create a new, independent, socially just and economically prosperous state. Israel, however, is a very small country, highly dependent on foreign trade for its survival. It imports 83 per cent of its GNP and must export enough to finance this import. The reality, therefore, is not only that economic laws cannot be disregarded, but that even the economic environment of other countries is of crucial importance to Israel.

In some senses Israel is certainly unique. No other country has absorbed so many immigrants relative to its size. Very few countries were able to grow very fast and modernize themselves while maintaining a free society and a republican democracy. Israel was able to revive its ancient language to a viable modern one. The number of books published per capita and the reading figures for daily newspapers and periodicals are amongst the highest in the world. In 1987, about half of the Jewish population aged 14 and over read at least one book during the month and 81 per cent read a daily newspaper at least once a week. Israel undertook enormous commitments in economic, military, political, and social dimensions. The relations between the relatively large military establishment and its civilian masters are also described as exceptional (Perlmutter, 1969).

Despite very low salaries, Israel has one of the highest ratio of medical doctors to population in the world and thousands of candidates attempt to enter its world-renowned medical faculties. Its agriculture is among the most developed in the world, its manufacturing industry produces some very sophisticated Israeli-developed products. It awarded, in 1982, 16.9 bachelor's degrees in natural sciences and engineering (and 5.5 advanced degrees) per 10,000 participants in the labor force compared to 17.0 and 4.6 in the USA or 10.8 and 1.3 in the Federal Republic of Germany. Yet, it has severe economic problems.

From 1922 until the 1973 Yom Kippur War, Israel enjoyed one of the highest rates of growth per capita in the world. In 1974, the world entered into recession and since then, Israel has 'managed' to grow less than most countries and to achieve almost a world record in annual inflation. It also achieved one of the highest levels of defense cost as per cent of GNP and a world record of import surplus per capita. By the end of the third decade of its independent existence, one economist believed that Israel faced a somber choice: 'The next decade will tell whether the proper reference group in a future international comparison will be Scandinavia, as long-term trends indicate, or South America, as the recent past suggests' (Moshe Syrquin in Y.

Ben-Porath (1986) p. 74). By the end of the fourth decade of Israel's existence, the answer was still not clear. Israel was able to reduce inflation dramatically, but was still far from being able to implement major necessary changes in its economic structure. It is now inhabited by a third generation led mainly by a second generation of political leaders and has not yet solved the problems of transition from the generation of the great dreamers to those who accept the very existence of the state as a normal course of life, not as a miracle or even as the fulfillment of lifetime dreams.

Although the young generation accepts its existence as the most natural thing, its neighboring countries still challenge its right of existence and the basis of its legitimacy. One result is the high cost of defense, estimated by US sources to have reached 30 per cent of GNP, compared to 3.45 per cent for Germany or 3.3 per cent for Sweden. Israeli military personnel, according to US sources, make up almost 50 per 1,000 in the population compared to 5.9 per cent in the UK or 9.5 in the USA. Unfortunately, Isaiah's prophecy 'and that they shall beat their swords into plowshares and their spears into pruning hooks, nations shall not lift up sword against nation neither shall they learn war anymore' (2:4) is far from reality. Despite many problems, however, Israelis strongly adhere to democratic beliefs, cherish their freedom and seek peace, while forging a new nation from immigrants arriving from more than one hundred countries in the four corners of the earth. Israel also jealously guards the independence of its judiciary, the freedom of its press, and the plurality of its society.

How can a country maintain such a high level of defense preparedness, high social welfare costs, and full employment? The answer is that the country must achieve a very rapid rate of economic growth, that will enable it to augment the available resources. To do that, the country must have a large influx of resources — mainly financial but also human.

Israeli Founding Fathers hoped to create a socialist state and aspired for national control over natural resources and for public ownership of most means of production. Their pragmatism and strong sense of national responsibility led them to accept compromises on their ideological beliefs. The Israeli government has always attempted to mobilize more capital, even to attempt to attract private direct foreign investment. It encouraged private investment, often by large infusions of public funds. It has sometimes looked as if Israel is aspiring for a unique regime in which profits belong to the private sector and losses are covered by the public sector. While Socialists believe in planning, Israel has been unable to have any orderly economic plan. Instead, it has relied on *ad hoc*, often paternalistic and certainly opportunistic, government intervention — with perhaps the highest rate of intervention in the Western world in individual business decisions. By the end of the 1980s, a Labor Finance Minister was trying to reduce this rate of intervention and to sell many state-owned enterprises to private individuals.

The successes, failures, aspirations and tribulations of Israel are of interest since despite many mistakes and the burden of an enormous defense budget, it was able to achieve a major transformation of its economy and its society. To be sure, many of the dreams of its Founding Fathers were not turned into a reality. Economic laws seem to have shown that they do work even though the leaders wished many times that these laws could be ignored. Still, the successes have been quite impressive and the methods of their achievements can often be generally applied to other small countries.

This book describes the achievements of Israel in the face of persistent problems, but also its failures. It starts with a short description of Israel's history, geography, political system, economic structure and ideology. The next chapter is a bird's-eye view of the history of Israel's economic and political institutions and ideological beliefs from the beginning of the period of the pre-state major waves of Jewish immigration to Palestine to date. Chapter 3 analyzes the major trends in Israel's population, immigration and emigration, labor force, labor institutions as well as education and wages. The structure of Israel's economy and its unique ownership patterns are the topic of chapter 4 and the role of the government in different economic branches is evaluated in chapter 5. This chapter also shows the structure of different economic branches and the capital markets. Chapter 6 highlights the impact of defense and the role of the military-industrial complex, while chapter 7 analyzes foreign trade and the balance of payments. The major conclusions and lessons of Israel's experience are drawn in chapter 8. This last chapter also recapitulates some of the recurring themes in the book, as they explain some major clashes between belief systems and realities.

1 Israel: some descriptive data

Introduction

The State of Israel was founded on May 14, 1948, following a decision by the United Nations to partition Palestine at the end of the British Mandate. On that day, there were about about 800,000 inhabitants in Palestine, out of which about 650,000 were Jews, and a fairly well-developed economic base. Developments after the establishment of the state were to some extent a continuation of trends of earlier periods, but also a product of new economic policies and different priorities. As one example, both the earlier and the state period are characterized by a large influx of immigration, causing both a high rate of population growth and a rapid increase in national product. The creation of the state represented the fulfillment of a religious, and national goal: the return to the promised land after two thousand years of exile and of Jewish statelessness. It was also the practical expression of the Zionist campaign to find a national solution to the Jewish problem as it re-emerged in the 19th and 20th centuries.

Israel is the outcome of a revolutionary movement aimed at colonizing an old-new country. The status of its leaders was not based on land ownership, aristocracy, heredity or feudal rights. It was a result of their ability to transform themselves and the country to which they came. These early pioneers have become the rulers of the new state. They aspired to become a center of cultural creativity and scientific endeavor of universal importance. This generation was not always very successful in transmitting its beliefs and aspirations to the new generation, for which the idea of pioneering is much less predominant.

The Zionist movement started in the mid-19th century with some forerunners calling for Jewish redemption. It began to crystallize, from about 1870, in the groups of Hovevei Zion ('the lovers of Zion') created principally in Russia. It gathered momentum following the pogroms (known as 'storms in the south') in the early 1880s, one result of which was the start of the new settlements in Eretz Israel. It blossomed into a political movement, the World Zionist Organization, with the first Zionist Congress in Basle, Switzerland (1897) organized by Theodor Herzl (1869-1904). Herzl's tract — *Der Judensterat* (the Jewish state) — came like a bolt from the blue. By that time, the first settlers already created fourteen villages in Eretz Israel. Since then, but mainly after World War I, the settlement continued under the aegis of the World Zionist Organization. Most immigrants to Eretz Israel went to the cities. They created, in 1909, the first Jewish city — Tel Aviv. Labor pioneers, agitating for productivization of the Jews, went mainly to rural areas. The first kibbutz was also established in 1909.

The Zionist movement negated the Diaspora and stressed Jewish nationalism. It was a revolutionary movement, believing Jews must be transformed and create their own nation-state. It preached that neither Jewish survival nor meaningful Jewish life was possible unless Jews create their own state in the land of their forefathers, in which Jews could develop normal political and economic institutions, revive their ancient language and establish a new center of cultural and social creativity. The vision called also for the creation of 'the new Jew' and the normalization of the Jewish occupational structure from a nation of small merchants to one of farmers settling on their land. It was also generally believed that only in Eretz Israel, the Land of Israel, historical cradle of the Jewish nation, the site of the first two commonwealths of Israel and the land God promised the Patriarchs, could Jews become again a normal, productive community responsible for its own destiny. Herzl was willing to settle at a certain point for Uganda as a palliative measure instead of Palestine, misunderstanding the deep commitment to the old homeland. Most Jews were incapable of transferring their longings, dreams, and bonds of affection from the land of their forefathers to another territory. Zionist beliefs were perceived as alien by the major religious Jewish establishment and were adhered to by only a small minority.

Zionist leaders came from different parts of Europe and from varied backgrounds. They thus naturally emphasized different orientations. Herzl, an assimilationist Western European Jew, believed in political work that would lead to the receipt of a charter on the state. Ahad Ha'am ('one of the people,' the pseudonym of Asher Ginsberg, 1856—1927) opposed Herzl's political emphasis. For him, Zionism did not mean Jews cannot live in the Diaspora. Instead, he advocated the creation of a spiritual center in Eretz Israel to avoid assimilation ('the spiritual

Zionism'). The so-called 'practical Zionists' stressed the actual colonization of Eretz Israel. Chaim Weizmann, an East European who later became the president of the World Zionist Organization, preached for a synthesis, emphasizing both political and practical work. For this reason, he cooperated with pioneer labor leaders, who also stressed egalitarian, community life and a socialist vision. These socialists were ready to settle on the land. Jabotinsky, who later created the New Zionist Organization (Revisionist), attempted to develop a national home through political means. More local, 'bourgeois' leaders represented the nationalist point of view, and preferred the urban colonization.

Much of the history leading up to the birth of the State of Israel is the saga of conflicts and cooperation among different groups, and the clash between the visions and the concrete problems faced by the new settlers. A glimpse into these conflicts is postponed to the second chapter. The new settlers refused to become an upper class colonial society in an Arab peasant economy. They consciously opted for an independent Jewish economy, even though this decision meant the new settlers would face many problems in the process of realizing their vision.

The Jewish attempts to rebuild the land of their ancestors have been long and arduous. The Jewish population in Palestine started to grow rapidly in a series of immigration waves (in Hebrew, the term for immigration is *Aliyah*, plural *Aliyoth*), each one of which doubled the population. The first of these waves came between 1882 and 1903. In 1882, there were about 24,000 Jews in Palestine. Between then and 1903, 20,000 to 30,000 more immigrated to the country. Until 1920, the total number of Jewish immigrants was less than 100,000. These persons were trail blazers who created a new society in Eretz Israel. They came to a poor and neglected country, full of swamps, with primitive agriculture. By sheer will and capital investments, they transformed the place to a middle-income country, enjoying a high level of cultural activities. The few dreamers refused to compromise themselves. They preached, organized, hoped and suffered. Through tedious labor, winning every step by sweat and blood, they were fortunate to have come to see the final phase of their struggle — witnessing the creation of the Third Commonwealth of Israel.

The genocide of six million Jews during World War II highlighted the need for a national homeland. Israel thus came into existence as a result of both the arduous struggle and as the fulfillment of the dreams of the Jews. Second, as a reaction to the suffering imposed on Jews by the Nazis, who murdered a third of the Jews with the rest of the world not doing much to stop the massacre, coupled with a hard necessity for pragmatic policy. A wave of rejoicing and elation spread through the Jewish world. Within hours of its creation, Israel was *de facto* recognized by the USA and three days later was formally recognized by the USSR, Poland and several other countries of Eastern Europe, South America and South Africa. (But later, when it realized Israel was not going to be part of the Socialist camp, the USSR shifted to a pro-Arab policy.) Israel joined the United Nations on May 11, 1949.

On the very first day after the Declaration of Independence, the armies of the five Arab neighboring states (Egypt, Iraq, Transjordan, Lebanon, and Syria) invaded Israel, aided by the army of Saudi Arabia. This war was fought intermittently until January 1949, when armistice agreements were signed with the neighboring states. (Iraq never signed such an agreement. To this date, it is still in a state of war with Israel.) Israel was able to repel the military onslaught. It was left with an area of 7,992 square miles (20,770 square kilometers), while 2,270 square miles of the predominantly Arab West Bank including East Jerusalem were taken and later annexed by Transjordan (which changed its name to Jordan). The 145 square mile Gaza Strip was seized by Egypt. Over 60 per cent of the state's total area was the virtually unpopulated Negev desert extending from Beersheva to Eilat, on the Red Sea. During the War of Independence, a full 1 per cent of Israel's population was killed.

The confrontation between the neighboring Arab states and Israel did not cease in 1949. All Arab states, with the exception of Egypt, still reject Israel's right to exist. Since 1949, Israel has fought five more wars against the Arab States and has been subjected to constant terrorism. In the 1950s, there were numerous attacks on Israeli territory by Fedayeen ('martyrs'), recruited and trained by Syrian army intelligence. In 1964, Syria created *Al-Fatah* ('conquest') as a principal guerrilla movement to fight Israel. Egyptian president Gamal Abdel Nasser created the Palestinian Liberation Organization (PLO) in 1964. These organizations were designed to nip any aspirations for a quiet life for Jews in Israel in the bud. Egypt also barred Israeli shipping from crossing the Suez Canal. In May 1967, President Nasser asked the UN to withdraw its emergency force stationed in Sinai; Egyptian forces reoccupied Sharm esh Sheikh and closed the Straits of Tiran, barring Israeli ships from entering the Red Sea and effectively blockading the Israeli port of Eilat, situated at the Gulf of Aquaba. In retaliation, Israel launched an attack on Egypt. The Six Days War, as it is known, in June, 1967, left

Israel in control of the Golan Heights, the West Bank of the River Jordan, the Gaza Strip and the Sinai desert. East Jerusalem was almost immediately annexed to Israel to make its capital unified again. The rest of the territories are administered under military rule.

President Anwar El Sadat of Egypt was the first (and still the only) Arab leader to pierce the barrier of hatred and ostracism against Israel. He went to Jerusalem (in November 1977) and after long negotiations the Camp David accords culminated with the signature of the March 26, 1979 Peace Treaty between Egypt and Israel. As an integral part of that agreement, Israel relinquished the Sinai Peninsula. It also dismantled the towns, villages and sophisticated air and naval bases built in the Sinai Desert and gave back to Egypt the rich oil wells developed there. The total cost of that withdrawal was estimated at $20 billion — the equivalent of Israel's total gross foreign debt. In retaliation for signing a peace treaty, the League of Arab Nations withdrew Arab Ambassadors from Egypt, moved the headquarters of the league from Cairo to Tunis, halted all bank loans, guarantees, financial and technical aid to Egypt, suspended Egypt's membership in the league and prohibited trade exchange with Egypt and with private establishments dealing with Israel.

Major characteristics of Israel's political economy

Thus, one major characteristic of modern Israel, setting it apart from other nations since its inception, is the enormity of the defense burden. After more than four decades of existence, Israel is still a nation under siege, reviled as an alien wedge in the Arab heartland, and constantly threatened with terrorism and invasion, to which she must respond by constant vigilance. Defense costs have a significant impact on the structure of the economy, manpower allocation, technology policy and the balance of payments (see chapter 6).

Another characteristic of Israel is its small size. By the end of 1989, Israel's total population was 4,560,500 — living in a country about the size of Wales or of the state of New Jersey. Israel had fewer inhabitants than metropolitan areas such as Tokyo (18.8 million in 1985), New York, (15.6 million in 1985), or London, (10.4 million in 1985). In fact, comparing the population of Israel to those of the world's 100 largest urban areas, Israel would have been 35th in 1985, between Baghdad, Iraq (4.4 million) and Philadelphia, Pa. (4.2 million). The majority of Israeli population at the end of 1989 were Jews (3,688,100 or 80.9 per cent) and there were 830,100 non-Jews. In 1988, non-Jews were 634,600 Moslems (14.2 per cent), about 105,000 Christians (2.4 per cent) and 78,000 others (1.7 per cent), mostly Druze.

For readers living in countries with vast land, it may be hard to imagine how tiny Israel is or how short are the distances. Thus, the distance between the major population center in Tel Aviv and the armistice line — where Judea and Samaria (the West Bank) starts — is about 10 km. The area of the whole of Judea and Samaria is 5,575 square kilometers (2,152 square miles). Its width is almost 40 kilometers (25 miles) and its length — 130 km (81 miles). The Gaza Strip lies on an area of 300 sq km (116 sq miles). The distance between Tel Aviv and Jerusalem is merely 63 km (38.7 miles) and the total length of Israel from Metula in the north to Eilat in the south is only 420 kilometers (258 miles).

Israel absorbed a very large number of immigrants compared to its original size. To the Israelis, the first task was the 'Ingathering of the Exiles.' In its first four years of existence Israel absorbed and integrated 1.2 million immigrants, thus tripling its original population. Most of these immigrants were Jews from Arab countries, but some were survivors of the Holocaust. The composition of immigration, as we shall see in greater detail in chapter 3, changed the demographic characteristics of Israel. The Holocaust also deprived Israel of its major reservoir of ideologically motivated manpower.

Despite the never-ending state of belligerence, Israel has constantly maintained its democratic heritage. Its judiciary is beyond reproach, highly regarded and totally independent. A large majority — 70 to 80 per cent — of its citizens participate in elections held every four years, demonstrating an incredible diversity of opinions. The Israeli Arabs are the only Arabs in the Middle East who can vote freely for a representative democratic government. They, as well as the Christians and the Jews, are all equal before the law and enjoy freedom of movement and of expression.

Israel's declaration of independence emphasized the ideal of providing a haven for any Jew who wanted it. It also stressed the ideal of Israel as a spiritual fountainhead and emotional magnet for all Jews. And it called for a peace with the Arab neighbors. It said, in part:

The land of Israel was the birthplace of the Jewish People. Here their spiritual, religious, and political identity was formed. Here they first achieved statehood, created a culture of national and universal significance, and gave to the world the eternal Book of Books.

Exiled forcibly from its land, the people remained faithful to it in all the countries of the dispersion, never ceasing to pray and hope for return and restoration in it of their political freedom.

Impelled by this historic and traditional attachment, Jews strove throughout every generation to re-establish themselves in their ancient homeland. In recent decades they returned in their masses . . . They reclaimed the wilderness, revived the Hebrew language, built villages and cities, and established a vigorous and ever-growing community, with its own economic and cultural life, loving peace but knowing how to defend itself, bringing the blessing of progress to all the country's inhabitants, and aspiring toward independent statehood . . .

Accordingly, we, members of the People's Council, representatives of the Jewish people in the Land of Israel and of the Zionist movement . . . by virtue of our natural and historic right and on the strength of the resolution of the General Assembly of the United Nations, proclaim the establishment of a Jewish state in the Land of Israel, to be known as the State of Israel.

Another major characteristic of Israeli economy is the degree of government intervention in the economy. Unlike most Western countries, the Israeli government intervenes in the economy not only through monetary, fiscal or exchange rate policies, but also by a direct intervention in many business decisions, by the use of discriminating interest rates and by many other means. In fact, the degree of government intervention in Israel is higher than in many less developed countries (see chapter 5).

The high degree of government intervention stems partially from the Socialist tradition of many pioneers of the first generation. These pioneers believed with special ferocity in the public weal as much superior to individual wants. To date, Israeli society is characterized by a prevalence of a collectivist orientation, not by an individualistic orientation as in the United States or Western Europe. Later, they also barricaded much of the economy behind protective ramparts of customs and administrative means of banning imports.

To some extent, the intervention has also been a result of the prophetic message of Judaism — inspired to achieve social justice, human equality, brotherhood and mutual responsibility and a high level of education. Moreover, the objective needs of a small, underdeveloped land with very high defense expenditures and a large-scale immigration made government intervention necessary to take care of these needs.

A final characteristic of Israel is that its land is holy to three major religions of the world: Christianity, Islam and Judaism, as well as to some other religions. Perhaps for this reason, there is a great world interest in the affairs of the State of Israel. This chapter contains some background information on the state and its people.

A short history

The origins of civilization in Israel reach to the mists of antiquity. Perhaps because of the intensive archaeological excavations carried out in Israel, there have been many traces of ancient human activities uncovered. The most ancient of these is about one million years old. It was discovered in the Jordan Valley. Neanderthal human skeletons were discovered in a cave in Mount Carmel. Israel is also the site of the most ancient city uncovered in the world: a fortressed settlement in Jericho — determined by radio carbon test to be from around 6850 BC.

In ancient times, the two strong centers of economic and political power were Aram Naharayim (Mesopotamia) and Egypt. Israel and Syria were in between the two and both saw many conquerors. Israel has also always been a major throughway for caravans plying trade routes between Egypt and other empires. The rugged slopes of the Judea and Samaria mountains forced most roads to be parallel to the Mediterranean, moving then through the different valleys in the north. The route was named by the Romans 'Via Marris.' Around 3300 B.C. the people of Israel had extensive agricultural and manufacturing activities. In the early bronze age, Israel probably exported olive oil, wine, and dried fig.

The tumultuous history of the Jews in Israel starts from the life of the Patriarchs. Abraham was ordered by God, the Bible tells us, to leave Aram Naharayim. He paid 'four hundred shekels of silver' to acquire a burial site of Machpela (Genesis 23:4-20) in Hebron. Isaac built an altar in Beersheva (Hebrew for 'the well of oath') — the place in which his father and Abimelech made their covenant (Genesis 21:27-31). Jacob pitched his tent in several places of Israel. Joshua's conquest of the country, in the 13th century BC, brought the Jews back to the land of their Patriarchs. The detailed description of the tribal allocations of the land is a rich source of information on the country's geography.

The God of Judaism was, of course, the Creator of the world. This God made a covenant with Abraham, promising him the land of Israel. Since then, Jews have been always admonished to remember, to recall and to recognize that God brought them out of the house of bondage in Egypt. Since the days of Abraham, with a missionary zeal Jews have held an unparalleled attachment to their land, carrying out their longings for and passionate memories of their ancient place through many centuries of exile and desperate struggle to maintain their identity. To the Jew, revering God has always meant also remembering his Covenant with Abraham.

The biblical period starts at the iron age. The Israelites conquered the hills and mountain areas, and the Philistines conquered the Southern Coastal Plains around 1200 BC, inhabiting it until the Persians conquered the area during the 6th century BC.

While much of the history of Israel reflects military considerations and economic reality, it cannot be fully understood without taking into account the cultural and religious significance of its holy shrines. One example is Jerusalem, the capital of the land since the Israelite King David conquered this city from the Jebusites in the 10th century BC, and made it the capital of his kingdom. Jerusalem is blessed with neither strategic nor special economic favors. Economic reason alone cannot explain why this city did not long ago vanish as did many other towns or villages. In fact, Jerusalem was off the main caravan routes. Its importance is only the product of spiritual heritage of the prophets who made it their center.

After David's successful assault on the city, he brought into it the sacred Ark and erected sumptuous public buildings. The Ark was the most important religious symbol. It was moved constantly because no one center was generally accepted. David's move made Jerusalem that center. Since then, Jerusalem has become the eternal spiritual capital of the Jewish people. David's son, Solomon, built in it the first temple, using the leading artists of the time for the ornamental decorations and bringing the finest materials available from all over the Middle East. Master craftsmen from all over labored to create most impressive buildings with exquisite workmanship.

Solomon's son, Rehoboam, was unable to keep the unity of the nation. Ten tribes went their own way, creating the Kingdom of Israel. In 722 BC, the Assyrians conquered this kingdom. Shalman-esser exiled the ten tribes to Assyria and replaced them with the Shomronites. These exiled ten tribes disappeared, never to be found again. Only the tribes of Judea and Benjamin remained in the Kingdom of Judea, and they were exiled to Babylon in 587 BC, by Nebuchadnezzar, King of Babylon. The King also destroyed the temple, hoping to wipe out any future prospect of Jerusalem becoming a center of Jewish life and a cause of rebellion.

Less than fifty years later, the Great Babylonian empire fell, overwhelmed by Cyrus, the founder of the New Persian empire. Having just vanquished Babylon, Cyrus was kind to his victims, allowing the Jews to return to Jerusalem and rebuild the temple. The second temple was indeed rebuilt and completed in 515 BC. Jerusalem was again the center of Jewish life. The Jews who came back then settled mainly around Jerusalem.

The Persian empire collapsed in 332 BC to the stronger might of Alexander the Great. After Alexander's death, his generals fought for control, dividing the empire. Ptolemy took Egypt, and Israel came for the next 120 years under the authority of his dynasty (Alexandria). The Seleucids of Syria ended this highly benevolent rule, conquering Israel in 198 BC. In 175 BC, the Seleucid King Antiochus IV ascended the throne. He sought passionately to Hellenize the provinces of his empire in order to impose a standard pattern of life upon his varied vassals. The Holy Temple was defiled — Greek soldiers sacrificed a swine on its altar. Jews were punished by death for any failure to respect new regulations or for refusing to bow down to Greek images.

In 167 BC, the Jews revolted, led by a family of priests of the House of Hason. The son of the first leader, Judah the Maccabee, developed a national liberation army, drove out the Greeks (167-141 BC) and restored Jewish independence. The *Hasmonean* rebellion against the Greek hegemony created an independent state — that reached its summit in the period of Alexander Iannai who ruled Israel 103-76 BC). The Negev, however, was not part of that Kingdom. It was inhabited by the Nebateans, who prospered from international trade.

The Nebateans came from Arabia and carved out for themselves an extensive kingdom whose capital was Petra, east of the River Jordan. In the period of their glory around 400 BC they built different cities to guard their wide-ranging caravan routes. They also conceived ingenious devices to trap water to nourish the soil they reclaimed from the desert. They began to settle in the Negev toward the end of the 4th century BC. Their cities were conquered by the Romans in AD 106.

The *Hasmonean* Kingdom lasted until 63 BC, when Jerusalem was conquered by the Romans. By that time, many Jews lived in

Babylon and Alexandria and the Jewish communities outside Israel were much richer than those within Israel itself. This was a period of growing international trade and many cities were built. Some Jews admired the Greeks. Others clung to the old traditions. A relentless tug of war between the Jewish and Hellenistic ways of life continued for centuries. The traditionalists reacted violently to Hellenistic influence, fighting the corruption, the decadence and the profligacy that were threatening to overwhelm religious traditions and moral standards.

Roman influence became more pervasive, and various struggles among the *Hasmoneans* led to Rome giving the crown in 37 BC to an Idumaean Jewish convert, Herod. Herod was spurned by most Jews, although he tried to please them by reconstructing the Temple. The celebrated Wailing Wall is the sole relic of Herod's Temple. After Herod's death, his surviving sons lost the favor of the Romans. In AD 6, Eretz Israel was proclaimed a Roman Province and remained this way — until the Roman empire was divided in the beginning of the 4th century (except during the short reform of Agripas — AD 35-44 — and the various rebellions). The Romans did not allow religious freedom — but many new religions flourished, some of them near the Dead Sea.

During Herod's period, a child was born in Bethlehem and grew to manhood in Nazareth. Shortly after Herod's death, Pontius Pilatus, Roman Procurator of Judea, ordered the crucifixion in Jerusalem of Jesus of Nazareth. Unknowingly, he started a chain of events leading to a major religious change.

Despite frail chances for success, the Jews revolted against *de facto* Roman rule in AD 66. In AD 70, Titus conquered Jerusalem and its temple was burnt. Many Jews were carried off into captivity. A few managed to carry on the struggle from Massada rock, at the edge of the Judea plateau. With the fall of Massada, in AD 73, the Jews lost their nominally independent state, and Jewish Israel ceased to exist until its rebirth in 1948. Massada has become a symbol for generations of Israelis, who are said to demonstrate a 'Massada complex' — that Massada will never fall again.

Bar Kochva's revolt did give a fleeting moment of Jewish sovereignty from AD 132 to 135. The Romans crushed the rebellion with the full might of their military machine. The revolt resulted in destroying almost any Jewish life in Eretz Israel. Emperor Hadrian ordered Jerusalem to be razed and a new city to be built on its site — Aelia Capitolina, where the Romans erected a shrine to Venus. Hadrian then issued an edict forbidding Jews on pain of death from setting foot in Jerusalem. He also ordered the name of the country to be changed to Syria Palestina — hence Palestine. The name 'Palestine' related to a land of the Philistines (who conquered the shores of Eretz Israel at the time of the biblical Judges).

Jews were left mainly in Galilee — at the north of the land of Israel (Eretz Israel). Non-Jews in Eretz Israel (mainly Greeks and Syrians) cooperated willfully with the Roman governors. This population flourished as a result of the growing international trade under the Pax Romana. The Romans also built infrastructure services, mainly roads and bridges.

After the Roman empire was divided, Eretz Israel became a part of the Byzantine Kingdom. It helped international trade to grow and the population increased in reaction to the economic boom. In 325, during the reign of the Caesar Constantinus (Constantine the Great, AD 306-337), Christianity became the official religion of the Roman Empire and its capital moved to Byzantium — whose name was changed in honor of the Caesar to Constantinopolis. Eretz Israel was elevated from just another province to a preferred area, being the cradle of Christianity. Constantine's mother, Helena, visited the Holy Land in AD 326. She, aided by several church leaders, determined the location of the crucifixion, the burial of Jesus and other sites associated with his life. In each of these places, Constantine erected shrines, the most sacred of which was the Church of the Holy Sepulchre. A series of internal religious and political disputes reduced the power of the Byzantine Empire in the 6th century. The Jews once again attempted to rebel, lost and as a result their number dwindled even further. A period of hope ensued when the Persians reconquered Eretz Israel in 614. It was crushed when the Byzantines reconquered the country in 629.

The Byzantine rule of Palestine was interrupted with the Persian invasion, in 614, and ended by the Moslem conquest between 636 and 640. After that, Moslem Caliphs ruled the country. They erected several Moslem Sanctuaries, among them the Dome of the Rock and the Mosque of Eksa, which stands on the Temple Mount in Jerusalem. Jerusalem for Moslems is the place from which Mohammed ascended to heaven. It is the Third Holy City after Mecca and Medina.

One result of the change of regime was that the Mediterranean, a link in the major trade route for a thousand years by Greeks, Romans and Byzantines, became enemy territory. Thus most of the international trade under Moslem rule was carried out over land routes. The port cities lost their importance as did the major Negev cities.

21

Eretz Israel over the years moved from being domain of one Arab part to another. It was controlled from Damascus (661-750) then from Baghdad (750-969) and then from Egypt (999-1098). There were also some periods of Egyptian control in the Abas (Baghdad) period, and it was under Turkish control between 1071-1098. The Crusaders, who came to save the Holy Land from the Turks (1071) conquered Jerusalem in 1099. However, a reunited Moslem force led by Salah-A-Din defeated the Crusaders in the Horns of Hittin battle of 1187. The third crusade was not very successful and the Crusaders and Salah-A-Din finally signed an armistice agreement. By the 11th century, Eretz Israel had become an agricultural country with a smaller and poorer population. Moslems were not allowed to drink wine. As a result, the cultivation of its major agricultural product — grapes — declined and lost its economic importance.

The next power to govern Eretz Israel was the Mamelukes. They ruled from 1250 until 1517. They were ousted by the Ottoman Turks, who conquered the country in 1517, and ruled it for exactly 400 years, until it was conquered by General Allenby of Great Britain in 1917. By the end of the 16th century there were about 300,000 inhabitants of Eretz Israel, 50,000 of them Jews, mostly in Safed.

The discovery of America affected naval travel routes and made the Middle East much less important. The Turks became occupied with wars in the Balkans (beginning in the 17th century) and neglected the southern part of the empire. Eretz Israel became a dangerous place, with little law and order, and many of its citizens left. By the middle of the 19th century, the country was extremely poor and neglected. Most of its inhabitants were nomads. The opening of the Suez Canal (in November 1869) helped to re-establish the area as an important part of sea routes. A few Jews at that time decided to try and rebuild the land of their fathers.

The Palestine exploration fund financed the first scientific survey of Eretz Israel during 1871-8. They found the population at the time to be 450,000, of which only 24,000 were Jewish and 45,000 Christians. Only 125,000 persons lived in towns, while the majority of the population lived on farms. The exploration identified 700 villages, 600 of them in the mountain regions. Both the valley of Jisreel and the valley of Bethsean were full of marshes and uninhabited. There was some olive production and wine was produced only in monasteries. Jews during the time of the survey lived mainly in the four holy cities — Jerusalem, Safed, Tiberias and Hebron — and were extremely poor. In fact, Jews were the majority population in Jerusalem. Most of them pursued religious studies and were supported by donations from abroad.

In 1869, the Austrian Kaiser Franz Joseph visited the country and a special road was built for this visit from Jaffa to Jerusalem. The road was not maintained and was totally destroyed. In the same years the Templars — Christian Germans — established the first German colony in Haifa. In 1870, the French Jews established the first agricultural school (Mikve Israel), Jews from Jersualem established the first Jewish village — Petah Tiqva (1878).

The British replaced the Ottoman rule in Palestine following their victory in World War I. Jewish aspirations to rebuild their homeland received a tremendous boost by the Balfour Declaration of November 1917. On November 2, 1917, Lord Balfour issued a letter addressed to Lord Rothschild. In this letter he declared that:

His Majesty's Government view with favour the establishment in Palestine of a National Home for the Jewish people, and will use their best endeavours to facilitate the achievement of this object, it being clearly understood that nothing shall be done which may prejudice the civil and religious rights of the existing non-Jewish communities in Palestine or the rights and political status enjoyed by Jews in any other country.

This declaration was seen by Zionists as a recognition of the Jewish right to work out their own salvation and build up a new focus of national life. The dream of returning to the old homeland had received an official legitimation. The Zionists hoped the Jews would respond to the opportunity afforded them and emigrate so as to create a Jewish majority in Palestine. In July 1922, the British Mandate on Palestine was ratified, but its main provisions had *de facto* been applied since the summer of 1920, when a civil administration replaced the military rule in Palestine. The Jews considered the Balfour Declaration as a clear commitment to develop a Jewish homeland. The British attempted a more even-handed policy. In May 1921, the British moved to an 'equality of obligation' (between Jews and Arabs) principle. Later, in 1922, Winston Churchill created Transjordan, partitioning Eretz Israel. The area east of the River Jordan, about 77 per cent of the total mandatory Palestine, was made a separate state, in which Jews were not allowed to settle: the British declared Transjordan excluded from the Jewish homeland under the Balfour Declaration. The original British mandate covered an area of approximately 126,000 square km. The area east of Jordan was 97,740 square km (37,738 square miles). The British were caught with conflicting promises given during World War I. They promised the Jews a national home in the Balfour Declaration; they agreed with the French (Sykes–Picot agreement) that the French would get both Lebanon and Syria. They also promised Hussein ibn Ali, the Sharif of Mecca, to make his two sons kings as a reward for Hussein's cooperation in World War I. Hussein had proclaimed himself, in 1916, King of Hejas (now part of Saudi Arabia). His son Faisal was made King of Iraq. His other son Abdullah was made King of Transjordan. To defend the new Kingdom, the British created, financed and equipped the Arab Legion (Transjordanian Arab forces). Transjordan was changed to Jordan in 1950, when Abdulla annexed the West Bank part of Palestine he had conquered in 1948-9. Jordan is now led by Abdulla's grandson, Hussein. King Hussein dismissed Lieutenant General John Glubb (Glubb Pasha) the chief of staff of the Arab Legion in 1956. He joined Egypt in the 1967 war, in which he lost the West Bank.

In 1939, the British government issued a White Paper which the Jews saw as a death statement to the national home promise since it virtually stopped new immigration. The Zionists were extremely worried by the gap they saw between the enormous need of the Jewish immigrants and the slow pace of activities. The hopes raised by the Balfour Declaration and by the British conquest of Eretz Israel were not fulfilled. Most Jewish immigrants did not come to Eretz Israel. In 1920, the Zionists agreed on the creation of a Foundation Fund (*Keren Hayesod*) that was expected to collect within a year £25,000,000 for the creation of infrastructure. The debate on the use of national capital revealed many attitudal differences, mainly between Brandeis and Weizmann. These will be detailed in later chapters. By August 1921, the fund had collected only £192,000 — far less than expected. Both monetary and human resources were scarce, and an Arab National movement opposing Jewish settlement had started.

Under Article IV of the Mandate, the Zionist Organization was recognized:

> an appropriate Jewish agency shall be recognized as a public body for the purpose of advising and co-operating with the administration of Palestine in such economic, social and other matters as may affect the establishment of the Jewish National Home.

A sense of urgency led Weizmann to propose participation of non-Zionists in a Jewish Agency, allowing them to contribute funds towards the building of the homeland. Despite opposition of those who feared 'the assimilationists' would have a controlling voice in the affairs of the Jewish homeland, the so-called 'enlarged Jewish Agency' was created in August 1929. The labor parties decided to support the new organization in order to be able to increase the available budget. At that time, several leaders argued that the World Zionist Organization had erred in aiding the labor pioneers and neglecting the middle-class majority. This perceived threat made labor agree to support Weizmann (Goldstein, 1975). In 1930, the labor parties merged and were able to gain hegemony in the Zionist movement.

Throughout the British Mandate, there had been increasing conflicts between the rival claims of the Jews and of the Arabs in the country. Arabs attempted to derail Jewish plans for more immigration. Jews attempted to reach a majority. The unrest had been intensified; anti-Jewish rioting occurring in 1920, 1929 and 1937-9. The massacre of a third of the Jewish nation by the Nazis during World War II increased international sympathy to the moral right of granting Jews their own home.

In the spring of 1947, the British decided to refer the whole problem of Palestine to the United Nations. A UN Special Committee proceeded to that country in the summer of 1947. On November 29, 1947, the UN General Assembly voted by a majority of 37 to 13 to terminate the British Mandate and create independent Arab and Jewish states. For the Jews, this was a compromise that they accepted. The Arabs rejected it.

The stormy history of war and peace of Eretz Israel is thus not only a story of economics, but of spiritual importance. In the succession of conquerors — Egyptians, Assyrians, Babylonians, Persians, Ptolemies, Seleucids, Romans, Moslem Arabs, Seljuks, Crusaders, Saracens, Mamelukes, Ottomans, British — each left some remnants of splendour and squalor. The land of Israel was destroyed in long centuries of decline and during the wars. The country was certainly not one of milk and honey. It was turned from a weary and neglected place, infested by swamps and eroded by sand and wars, by the pioneers of the first, second and third Aliyoth. These pioneers revived the land, drained the marshes and created a tapestry of vineyards and orchards, fields of wheat, corn, barley, alfalfa and clover. The valleys were made fertile again, regaining the tones of green and gold. These pioneers came inspired with a burning desire to rebuild the land and recast a new type of Jew. They rebelled against the realities of Jewish life, mainly in Eastern Europe.

The Jews and Eretz Israel

The relationship of the Jews to Israel has been an extremely important factor in the rebuilding of the country. It is impossible in this short treatise to narrate Jewish history, but a few background facts might be helpful. Throughout all the centuries, the attachment of Jews to Zion remained unbroken and their stirrings for redemption and return to the land of their Fathers never ceased. Whatever corner of the earth they were in, the Jews always designed their synagogues so that the Ark of Law would be oriented toward Jerusalem. Their love of the ancient land and the longing to return to it from exile passionately permeated most Jewish prayers, rituals and literatures. Wherever they arrived throughout generations of wandering, religious Jews continued to pray three times a day, uttering the hope that God will return them to Zion. In daily life, however, most of them did very little to achieve this dream, waiting instead for the Messiah to arrive and lead them back to the land of their ancestors.

Jewish history started sometime in the second millennium BC. The Bible tells us about the covenant between Abraham and God and the conquest of the land of Canaan by the twelve tribes of Israel, led by Joshua. Jewish life outside Eretz Israel started when the First Commonwealth was destroyed and Jews were taken into exile. When Cyrus conquered Babylon (550-530), some of the Jews returned. Later, under the leadership of Ezra and Nehemia, they reconstructed the temple, starting the second Commonwealth of Israel. Yet even then, many of the Jews remained in Babylon and in Egypt. Since then, there were multiple centers of Jewish life outside Israel, known as the Diaspora. In each, the major institutions were the family, the synagogue and the communal organizations.

From the destruction of the second Temple, Jewish life centered around religious activities. The religion continually forged a set of rules to be followed, covering all aspects of life. Jews were a political minority, existing by the grace of their rulers. They continuously migrated because of persecution. They suffered from riots and expulsions. In some countries, Jews were burned at the stake for rejecting the dubious opportunity offered them to convert to Christianity. They were lured to a country by those who needed their money and their skills to establish a middle class of bankers, physicians, craftsmen and men of commerce — trades in which Jews were known to excel. Later, general discontent was often turned into venom against Jews. Kings and noblemen periodically unleashed a series of blood orgies against Jews. Jews were also banned from ownership of lands and were excluded from many professions.

Jews moved from one country to another because of the behavior of their hosts and the vicissitudes of dispersion and persecution. Thus, Jews prospered under the Moslem rule of Spain, but were exiled by the Christian rulers in 1492. Jews developed: the rule of closing ranks in face of external threat; the strong belief in martyrology to maintain religious devotion (*Kidush Hashem*); Jewish solidarity; a high level of internal cohesion; and the patience to wait for the Messiah who has yet to come at the end of the days. Their precarious kind of existence made Jews stick to each other and maintain their unique institutions — thus continuing their existence despite lack of political independence.

The life of the various Jewish communities was thus shaped to a large extent by the environment in which they lived and the attitudes of their host rulers. At the same time, the Jews maintained a high level of autonomy within their communities. More and more, the Jewish religion was molded under the rules of the *Halakha* as interpreted by the great Rabbis. To be sure, kernels of heterogeneity did exist. Thus, the Karaites who appeared in Eretz Israel and the Near East in the second half of the eighth century recognized only the written law of the Torah but not the Oral Law developed by the Rabbis. Rabbi Isaac Luria (1534-72) developed the mystical Kabbala movement. After the pogroms in Poland led by Chmelnitzki in 1648, Messianic hopes erupted under Shabbetai Zevi's (1626-76) leadership. He finally converted to Islam in 1666. Yet most Jewish communities followed the Orthodox rule, as articulated by the codification of Joseph Caro (1488-1575) in his *Shulkhan Arukh*. The Hassidic (pietism) movement stressed love of God — and the others, learning of Talmud.

By the end of the 19th century, about 90 per cent of all Jews lived in Europe, mainly in Poland and Russia but also in Western Europe. In Russia, by the end of the 19th century, Jews were legally confined to the Pale of Settlement. They were oppressed by the Czarist Russian government, faced with a constant barrage of suppressive laws, banned from higher education by a strict *nomerus clausus* of not more than 3 per cent Jewish students, and boycotted from most professions.

The shifts in the basic premises of European civilization from the emphasis of religious identity to the belief in universal membership of persons in the human race, epitomized in the 1789 French Declaration of Rights of Man and Citizen, affected also the Jews. Many Jews believed they should be defined as only a religious group, not as a national community. This new definition was perceived as allowing a total assimilation among the nation in which they lived. A similar attitude was also manifested among the rulers. Thus, Joseph II of Austria abolished the corporate status of the Jewish communities but recognized Jews as legitimate domiciled subjects.

The number of Jews in Europe constantly expanded. Since 1830, many of them migrated, lured by the promise of better life in distant lands, mainly to the United States. Between 1840 and 1880, about a quarter of a million Jews, mainly from Germany and Austro-Hungary, emigrated to the United States. After the 1882 pogroms the emigration accelerated. Between 1881 and 1914, about three million East European Jews migrated. Two-thirds of them went to the United States; 400,000 to South Africa; 350,000 to Germany and France; 200,000 to England (tripling the Jewish population there, established in 1664 when Cromwell formally allowed Jews to be readmitted); and 100,000 to Canada. The Jewish communities in the Middle East and North Africa — about 500,000 strong — have also undergone far-reaching changes, away from tradition toward modernization. Only 4 per cent of the Jewish emigrants went to Eretz Israel, and many of those despaired and left.

The beginning of the rebuilding of Eretz Israel is generally considered to be the First Aliyah that also started in 1882. Zionists began to organize Jews to go to Palestine, despite the fact that the Turkish law forbade the acquisition of land by Jews. Jews used infinite varieties of subterfuges to create the first new colonies in the old land. The Zionists were convinced there must be a new way of life for Jews. Other Jews tended to assimilate. Others became revolutionaries or anarchists.

The belief that Jews could be assimilated within European nations was shattered by the Nazi Holocaust. The universal liberal message of the Jewish intellectuals did remain, mainly in Western Europe and more so in the United States. American Jews in particular molded new institutions and did not feel they should emigrate to Israel.

Table 1.1 Rates of growth of Jewish population, product and capital 1922-89 (percentages)

Interval	Jewish population	GNP[a]	Per capita GNP[a]	Capital stock Total	Capital stock Dwelling	Capital stock Non-dwelling	Consumption per capita
1922-32	8.0	17.6	7.8	13.7	–	–	–
1932-47	8.4	11.2	3.0	9.8	–	–	–
1947-50	21.9	–	–	–	–	–	–
1950-1	20.0	29.7	10.0	–	–	–	–
1951-64	4.0	9.1	4.9	12.3	11.6	12.8	5.1
1972-82	2.1	3.2	0.8	6.7	7.7	6.1	3.2
1981-9	1.4	3.2	2.6	3.5	3.4	3.7	2.9

Sources: Ben Porath (ed.) (1986), *The Israeli Economy: Maturing Through Crises*, Cambridge, Mass.: Harvard University Press. Bank of Israel, *Annual Report*, 1988, p. 14.

Notes: [a] Refers to the Jewish economy in Palestine until 1947 and in Israel since 1950.

Growth, resources, and uses

From the 1920s until 1947, the country enjoyed an annual rate of economic growth of 13.7 per cent (Table 1.1). The high rate of growth continued in the period 1950-72, during which the Israeli economy grew by 10.7 per cent per annum. This growth was fuelled by the increase in population and the labor force and by large investments, sometimes without due caution or selectivity. Product per employee increased by 3.3 per cent in the pre-State period and 6.0 per cent annually in the period 1950-1972 (Table 1.2).

Population growth provided a source of demand for housing and a range of other commodities. On the supply side it increased the labor force and the potential for economic adaptation and integration of newcomers. Population growth has decelerated since the 1970s, largely as a result of the decline in immigration.

Until the early 1970s, growth was sufficient to increase living standards without recourse to short term international borrowing. Between 1974 and 1988, in contrast, Israel's rate of growth has been less than 4 per cent per annum and the growth per capita has been close to zero. The arrest of economic growth was caused

Table 1.2 Growth of GDP and GDP per capita at 1986 prices (NIS millions)

Year	GDP		GDP per capita	
1950	3,421		2,701	
1955	6,191		3,537	
1960	8,846		4,454	
1965	15,086		5,887	
1970	21,940		15,246	
1975	31,567		9,152	
1980	36,904		9,561	
1981	38,454		9,790	
1982	38,839		9,705	
1983	39,849		9,776	
1984	40,805		9,813	
1985	42,315		9,999	
1986	43,711		10,169	
1987	45,979		10,532	
1987	46,157	(55,337[a])	10,565	(12,675[a])
1988	46,903	(66,958[a])	10,565	(15,076[a])
1989	47,412	(82,410[a])	10,406	(18,088[a])

Source: Central Bureau of Statistics, *Statistical Abstract of Israel*, 1988, pp. 178-9.
Note: [a]At current prices.

by the combined effects of a sharp increase in oil prices and high public spending, mainly for defense purposes and for social causes. Oil imports increased from 1.5 per cent of GNP to a peak of 10 per cent of GNP in 1980-1. The oil price increases of 1973-4 and 1979-80 cost Israel $12.6 billion between 1973 and 1982 (equal to one year's GNP). The Yom Kippur War in 1973, and much higher levels of defense spending ever since, have cost much more.

One way to get a general bird's-eye view of an economy is by looking at the total resources at the disposal of that economy and their uses. Resources are the gross national product, or the total product of the country, plus the imports. Uses are general government consumption expenditures, private consumption expenditures, gross domestic capital formation (investment in fixed assets and inventory) less exports of goods and services. An analysis of these uses tells us who gets the resources.

Israel's GNP per capita was about $8,100 in 1988. About a third of this amount was spent on defense expenditures and another 18.3 per cent on investments. Yet private consumption was 63.2 per cent as can be seen from Table 1.3.

Several special characteristics of Israel can be seen from the analysis of its resources and uses. First, Israeli GNP is larger than that of many countries of the world, but not that of the rich countries. Second, Israel has always used more resources than it produces. GNP has been equal to only two-thirds of total resources: the total resources at its disposal have always been much higher than the Gross Domestic Product. In other words, the country had a relatively large international trade deficit, or import surplus, financed partially by unilateral transfers, partially by increasing debt. Israel's trade deficit/GDP ratio has remained almost constant since 1955 (Table 1.3). Unilateral transfers financed only part of the import surplus and the cumulative debt resulting from the loans taken to finance the remaining import surplus has become increasingly onerous. Israel has the highest debt per capita in the world. Another result was that Israel has become very much dependent on the United States. Without aid from the United States, Israel could not have avoided cuts in real living standards if it wanted to continue the same level of defense expenditure. The forging of the special relations between Israel and the United States took a long time. Many Israelis are concerned that American friendship should not be taken for granted. They are disturbed by the probability — however slight — of a major and sudden cut in US aid. More generally, the possible future decline in unilateral transfers has been a reason for anxiety.

31

Table 1.3 Resources and their uses (%)

	1950	1955	1960	1965	1970	1975	1980	1985	1987	1988	1989
GDP in NIS current prices						8,180	111,539	28,084	55,640	66,958	84,071
Resources											
GDP	100	100	100	100	100	100	100	100	100	100	100
Imports	26.9	39.3	33.4	38.8	55.2						
Defense						16.5	9.6	9.4	8.5	6.0	3.4
Other						47.3	52.5	53.8	49.9	44.9	42.6
	126.9	139.3	133.4	138.8	155.2	163.8	162.1	163.2	158.4	150.9	146.0
Uses											
Private consumption	74.1	74.0	70.4	68.6	61.2	58.3	59.1	63.8	64.0	63.2	61.5
Public consumption											
Civilian	18.7	19.9	18.7	20.9	10.6	10.1	11.8	10.9	16.2	16.7}	30.9
Defense					25.7	32.6	22.8	22.3	19.0	16.6}	
Gross investment											
in fixed assets	31.1	33.2	27.6	29.0	29.0	29.0	22.3	19.1	19.7	18.4	16.5
in inventory						2.0	0.8	-0.8	0.0	0.0	0.0
Export	3.0	12.2	16.7	20.3	28.7	31.8	45.3	47.9	39.5	36.1	37.2

Source: Bank of Israel, *Annual Report*, 1957, p.1; 1988, p.45; 1989, p.15.
Note: Public consumption includes that of the Jewish Agency, the Jewish National Fund and Keren Hayesod.

Table 1.4 Imports, exports and import surplus

Period	% of real growth p.a.		% of GDP in current prices		
	Imports	Exports	Imports	Exports	Deficit
1950-5	3.5	26.8	33.6	10.2	23.4
1956-60	9.8	20.4	34.6	14.4	20.2
1961-5	11.8	12.4	41.0	20.7	20.3
1966-70	14.2	13.0	45.2	26.2	19.0
1971-5	10.0	9.6	62.0	31.0	31.0
1976-81	2.2	7.7	69.1	43.1	21.1
1981-5	3.4	4.9	60.7	42.6	18.1
1986-7	13.0	7.8	67.4	47.9	19.5
1988	2.7	-2.3	42.0	35.3	6.7
1989	-2.6	4.3	38.9	36.2	2.7

Sources: Z. Zussman (1978), 'Exchange Rate Elasticity, Inflation, Structural Changes,' *Economic Quarterly*, (Hebrew) 99:270-294.
CBS Monthly Bulletin of Statistics, Supplement, 5/1982, 5/1986.
CBS Statistical Abstract.
Note: Excluding imports and exports of factors of production.

Despite the large trade deficit (Table 1.4), there has been no increase in the real exchange rate since 1955. Particularly in the 1970s, the constancy of the exchange rate has been a 'result of government policy aimed at artificially isolating the structure of employment and production from external pressure' (Klinov-Malul, 1984, p. 4). The economic developments of Israel are summarized in chapter 2.

Geography

Until 1967, Israel's borders were those established as a part of the armistice agreements that came after the War of Independence. Israel's area within the 1949 armistice line extends over 7,992 miles. It covers an area less than 20 per cent of the original Palestine area as it was envisaged in November 1917, the time of the Balfour Declaration. This original area was first divided, in 1922, between Transjordan and Palestine to solve what turned out were conflicting promises that had been given by the British government during World War I. On November 29, 1947, the United Nations decided on a further division, between a Jewish state, officially declared on May 14, 1948, and an Arab one that the Arabs chose not to create, hoping (and attempting) to annihilate the State of Israel.

The State of Israel is part of a much larger geographic region, known as the Fertile Crescent. The crescent extends between the Mediterranean and the two extensions of the Indian Ocean — the Red Sea and the Persian Gulf. In the southwest portion of the crescent one finds the African depression that created the Eilat Bay and the valleys of Jordan and the Arava. At the Dead Sea level, this depression creates the lowest point on the Earth (392 m below sea level). To the north, a natural border would have been the Lebanon Mountains, while in the south there is no topographic line that could signify a natural border. Borders in this region, however, were rarely a result of any topographic considerations, but a consequence of contests among big powers over control of the Fertile Crescent. In more recent history, the border between Israel and Egypt is that negotiated in 1906 as a border between the then Ottoman and the British empires. This border was drawn from Eilat in the Gulf of Aquaba to the Mediterranean (Rafiah). Its definition became important in decisions on territorial conflicts between Israel and Egypt in the 1980s. The northern border was negotiated in the 1920s between the French (who controlled Lebanon) and the British.

The State of Israel and the land of Israel are far from being the same in the eyes of many individuals. One of the major political rifts that has polarized Israeli society is that of the proper borders. In fact, the political map of Israel reflects more different points of view on the borders question than on economic, social or other political aspects. For some extremists, the only proper borders are those contained in God's promise to Abraham (Genesis 15:18) as repeated to others (Genesis 26:2, 28:3-4; Exodus 6:3; Joshua 1:3,4, 13:5,6). At the other side are those emphasizing the need for a Jewish state, and therefore willing to give up territories heavily populated by non-Jews. In between are those emphasizing security needs for defensible borders.

Certainly, the borders of Israel are still not fully a settled issue. Israel today shares a border with Lebanon on the north and with Syria and Jordan on the west. On the south, it has a narrow strip of coast line on the Gulf of Aquaba and a long border (already mentioned) with Egypt. Except for Egypt, with which Israel signed a peace treaty in 1979, all Arab nations are formally at war with the state.

Geographically, Israel is a country of fringes. Standing at the edge of southwest Asia and the northern edge of the Red Sea and at the edge of the Mediterranean, the country has always been a bridge between Africa and Asia and a major route of merchants as well as of military conquerors. As shown above, most of the ancient empires of early times — Assyria, Babylon, Greece and Rome — at some point conquered this land and each left in it some important traces.

The country landscape is quite varied. The country lies on the eastern cost of the Mediterranean Sea, and most of its population resides in the coastal region. A few miles further east the terrain is hilly and sometimes mountainous with a few inland valleys — and further east lies the Jordan rift and the Arava. At the southern tip of the country there is a very short strip of coastline on the Gulf of Aquaba, where Eilat is situated.

From a climatic point of view, Israel is also a country of transition. Its climate in most areas is Mediterranean. The main characteristic of a Mediterranean climate is its two well-defined seasons, hot and dry summers and cool and rainy winters. The large deserts engulfing Israel from the east, south and southeast bring to it dry air and the transition to the Mediterranean climate is quite sudden. The border of the arid regions is not fixed: it moves every year by the quantity of rain. Thus, most of the country is arid much of the year, but with a rainy season beginning generally in October and ending in May although a possible early shower can come in September. Seventy per cent of all rain falls in the three months of December, January and February. Most days during the rainy season are clear. The long-term average number of rainy days during this season ranges from 4.6 days in Eilat with an average long-term precipitation of 25 mm per annum, 60.6 rainy days in Mount Kenaan in the north, with 718 mm of precipitation per annum, 46.4 rainy days in Tel Aviv with 539 mm of percipitation and 59 rainy days in Jerusalem with around 571 mm of rain per year. The scarcity of water is a major problem in Israel. Only about 20 per cent of the water resources are used for domestic purposes. Industry uses only 5-6 per cent. The lion's share of water is used by agriculture. Water shortage puts a major limit on the potential increase in agricultural production. Israel has developed many techniques to save precious water, for example, to drop irrigation.

During the summer there are almost no clouds, and the sun is very strong. The annual number of sunny days in Israel is one of the highest in the world: about 75 per cent of all daytime during the year (3,200-3,300 hours out of 4,400 total daytime). This compares to 900 hours in Manchester and 2,200 hours in the Swiss Alps. In addition, the sun comes at an angle of up to 80 degrees above the horizon, and the intensity of its radiation is very high. This high radiation intensity causes a high evaporation level, but also allows the growing of winter vegetables — in particular at the southern part of the Arava. It also provides thermal energy for different needs.

Snow is extremely rare, except on Mount Hermon in the north. There may be 2 or 3 days of light snow in Mount Kenaan or in Jerusalem. The mean daily relative humidity in Eilat ranges from 24 per cent in June to 47 per cent in December. The long-term mean relative humidity in the coastal region ranges from 66 to 74 per cent; for Mount Kenaan in the north, from 45 to 78 per cent; and for Be'er Sheva in the Negev, from 53 to 67 per cent. Monthly mean temperatures in Eilat range from a minimum of 10.7°C to 39°C, in Mount Kenaan from 41°C to 29.4°C, in Tel Aviv from 9.0°C to 29.3°C, and in Jerusalem from 4°C to 28.0°C. Extreme temperatures have reached a high of 45.3°C in Eilat and 44.1°C in the Jordan rift. There are also a few days of hail, thunder, gales or fog during the winter.

The soil in Israel reflects both the climate conditions and the types of rocks on which the soils were developed. Much of the arid regions in Israel do not have any soil coverage. Twenty-three per cent of the non-desert land in Israel is Northern Negev sand, 41 per cent is in hills and mountains and 36 per cent in the valleys and in the coastal plain.

Almost 40 per cent of the country used to be forests — mainly of common oak and of terebinth trees. Almost all of these forests have been destroyed, largely by allowing the goats of nomads to graze them, but also by cutting the trees for firewood. In some plain areas they were replaced by agriculture, oil trees, grapes and other fruits. The majority of the forest trees were used as a source of energy, mainly during World War I. Once destroyed, the remnants of the forests could not recover, in particular since the growth of young trees was prevented by goats grazing. Forests were preserved only in places deemed holy. One part of the movement of Jews back to agriculture was a widespread effort to revitalize the forests. The new trees planted in the 20th century were mainly Jerusalem pine, stone pine, and eucalyptus and cypress. In 1948-9, the natural forests were on 350,000 dunams, and the afforested area was 53,000 dunams. (One dunam is 1,000 square metres of land — about ¼ of an acre.) By the end of 1987, the natural forest remained the same, while the afforested area was 790,000 dunams, of which 495,000 dunams was coniferous, 128,000 — eucalyptus, 23,000 — tamarisk and the rest acacia, carobs, mixed and others.

Israel does not have many natural resources. The major natural resources are concentrated in the Dead Sea brine, in which there is a very high concentration of potash, bromine, magnesium, and other salts. A few areas of low grade phosphate rock have been found in the Negev desert. Israel does have deposits of oil shales and lignite, but is highly dependent on imported energy, largely oil. Despite much investment in exploration, almost no oil or gas have been found. The total production of crude oil in Israel in 1987 was negligible (17 million litres). Israel also produced small quantities of natural gas (45 million cubic meters). The country makes extensive use of sun energy, mainly for private consumption (for example water heaters). The total yearly use of this source is at an equivalent of 250,000 tons of crude oil. Israel imports about 9 million tons of crude oil a year. Egypt provides about 25 per cent of this amount to recompense Israel for the loss of the Sinai oil-field under the Camp David Peace Agreement. Another 2.5 million tons come from Mexico and the rest is purchased on the spot market. Israel's energy use has grown rapidly. Its per capita energy consumption in 1960 was 13.8 per cent of that of the USA and by 1980 — 24.9 per cent (Barkai in Ben Porath, 1986, p. 266). Israel also imports other minerals, including coal and iron. The only minerals produced in Israel are potash (2 million tons), phosphate rock (2.7 million tons), quartz sand (87,000 tons) and bail and fire clay (130,000 tons).

The need for high imports means that the country must export a high per cent of its GNP. This has been found to be a quite difficult task. The combination of high defense burden, the poor availability of natural resources, the costs of absorbing new immigrants, the large public sector and the relatively low worker productivity cause many serious economic problems, discussed in subsequent chapters.

While Israel is a very tiny country, its population has been growing relatively fast since the first wave of Jewish immigration and in particular since the state was born. The main reason for this rapid population growth has been immigration. A second reason was the natural increase. Immigration during the pre-state period was not only of Jews, but also of Arabs. The prosperity in the country served as a magnet for Arabs to come from neighboring countries to Palestine.

The political system

Israel is a parliamentary democratic republic. The population elects a single chamber parliament (Knesset: 'assembly') of 120 members that is the repository of state sovereignty. The Knesset is elected at least once in four years. In some cases, the Knesset is dissolved earlier. Voters vote for a list of candidates usually submitted by political parties — not directly for the candidates — under a 100 per cent proportional representation system, in which the entire country is considered a single constituency. The candidates lists are submitted in rank orders, and voters cast their vote for an entire party list. Each candidates list is awarded the number of Knesset seats equivalent to its percentage of total valid votes, with two caveats. First, the candidates list must receive a minimum, very low, percentage of total votes. Second, the excess votes above the number required per seat are allocated by a formula designed to increase the probability of these seats being distributed to the large political parties.

Theoretically, this method — modelled after the electoral system of the Kerensky regime in Russia — allows a greater democracy in the purest sense. Indeed, the method does allow the whole spectrum of ideologies and interests among the electorate to be represented: almost any small fraction of the population may be able to have representatives elected. However, this pure form of democracy also allows a situation of a flourishing number of political parties, none of which can ever achieve a majority and thus create a government on its own. Israeli elections (and the elections during the Yishuv period before them) have never accorded one political party a clear majority. As a result, Israel has always been governed by coalition governments. Each of the large political parties are forced to maneuver and negotiate the participation of several small parties in order to form a governing coalition. The price for such participation has grown higher the more the large parties have tried to outfox and outbid each other. These coalitions have been inherently unstable, and generally dependent for their survival on the small parties and special interest groups. This guarantees a tyranny of the minorities. Small parties hold much greater power than that granted to them by the electorate since without their support a government cannot be established. Some of these small parties represent religious voters, who have enjoyed a disproportionate amount of political power in Israel.

The government is responsible to the Knesset and must enjoy the confidence of the Knesset. Ministers do not have to be Knesset members (MKs); only the Prime Minister must be one. The Knesset also elects a President for a six-year term. The President is the official head of state, but his powers are very limited.

Many in Israel believe the proportional representation system is carried out to an extreme and must be changed. The large political parties have an interest in such a change. Yet the basic flaw of the system was not solved even when the results of the Israeli elections forced the two large bloc parties to form a grand coalition between the two of them in 1984. Most people believed that this national unity government would change the election system to reduce the power of the small parties. However, each one of the large blocs was concerned that the other one might go to one of the small religious parties and form a narrow coalition with it. As a result, each continued to maintain cordial relations with the small parties. The basic change in the elections law that most Israelis have been hoping for never came to pass.

After the 1988 elections, both large blocs were fed up with the experience of attempting to run a joint cabinet and the political paralysis that resulted. Still, after fifty-two days of intrigues and negotiations, the two blocs again joined in a grand coalition. This, for the first time in Israeli history, came about largely because of the unprecedented vehement tones of the US Jews in their protest against any attempts to give in to the religious parties on the definition of the word Jew in the Law of the Return, recognizing only Orthodox Jewish conversion.

Most Israeli politicians are dependent on the party and its institutions not only for influence but even for livelihood. Politicians are considered a relatively low prestige occupation. In the late 1970s, Knesset member was ranked 64 out of 90 preferred occupations.

The independence of Israel's judiciary is jealously guarded. Formally, the Supreme Court does not have any power of judicial review over the Knesset acts. The Supreme Court actually extended its power in sitting as a High Court of Justice, ruling legislation unenforceable because of procedural inadequacies. Legal inquiry commissions enjoy an extremely high status, and some of them had far-reaching effects on political life (for example the Agranat Commission, established in 1974 to inquire into the Yom Kippur War, and the Kahan Commission, established in 1983 to inquire into the Sabra and Shatila massacres in Lebanon). Israel does not have a written constitution. The religious parties strongly opposed a proclamation of a constitution claiming the Torah (and the *Halakha*) were the only possible constitution. Since 1964, however, the Knesset has chosen a piecemeal approach, enacting a series of basic constitutional laws. These basic laws require an approval by a minimum of sixty-one members of the Knesset.

Israel is, to a large extent, still an emergent society. Her political culture is still in a state of flux. In 1985, the electoral system for mayors of cities was modified to a direct election independent of city councils. This radical departure gave mayors more veto power over council actions and a high degree of independence from party machinery. The influence of the mass media (and through it, that of the state controller) has been growing, weakening the central power of the state.

Political parties

As a direct result of the proportional method of elections, Israel has a few dozen candidates lists in each general national election. By 1981, there were thirty-one different lists; in 1984, twenty-six; and in 1988, 34. Some of these were never able to have even one member of Knesset elected, others have been able to have one, two or three members. These tiny parties may be extremely important in becoming a vital component of a coalition allowing one or other of the major political blocs to formulate a government. The two major blocs are clearly the Labor Alignment and the parties of the Likud. A third major compound of political parties are the Orthodox, or religious parties, that may or may not bloc vote the same way. Each one of the two (or three, if Orthodox parties are included) blocs is composed of many parties, often antagonistic toward one another. Further, these blocs are relatively new. Other federations of political parties existed before.

The Labor Alignment is often referred to as the 'left' and the Likud as the 'right.' These terms are not very accurate. The Likud often represents blue-collar workers. The dividing line is much more on questions related to foreign and defense policies than on the traditional economic issues separating 'right' from 'left' in other countries.

Up to 1977, Israel was ruled largely by a dominant party (Mapai, now part of the Alignment). From 1977 to 1984, the Likud formed the government and in 1984 and 1988, a national unity government was formed, composed of the two blocs. Mapai in its different faces has been the dominant party since its creation in 1930 as an amalgamation of Ahdut Ha'avoda (established in 1919) and Hapoel Ha'tzair (established in 1906). Both parties were composed of militant socialists, who believed in clashes of classes and the need to achieve social justice. They were also well-organized, and created economic institutions closely tied to their political organization. By 1935, the leader of the combined party, David Ben Gurion (later the first Prime Minister of Israel) became Chairman of the World Zionist Organization Executive — the highest position of leadership of the Jews in Eretz Israel. From that time until 1977, Mapai leaders controlled the governing bodies of the Jews (and later the State of Israel). This was achieved by the so-called 'historical partnership' (or coalition) with the National Religious Party (previously Hamizrahi and Hapoel Hamizrahi).

In 1965, Ben Gurion left his own party, creating Rafi: largely because of disagreements on the way to handle a certain affair, known as 'the Lavon affair'. The 'young turks' he nourished left with him to create Rafi. The old guard continued in Mapai, and the leadership moved to the Third Aliyah chieftains. Later Rafi returned to Mapai. In fact, some of its masters became leaders in Mapai — Shimon Peres became Prime Minister, and Yitzhak Navon and Haim Hertzog were to become Presidents of Israel.

The second challenge to Mapai's dominance came when many intellectuals became fed up with the old guard leaders of Mapai. They believed the party had become corrupt and that there was no way for them to ascend up the ladder of political power inside the party. The Democratic Movement for Change (DMC) was created in 1977. The DMC was largely a result of a wave of discontent and frustration stemming from the degree of incompetence and lack of preparedness demonstrated in the first days of the Yom Kippur War. The DMC was able to win 15 seats in 1977, on an appeal to 'throw the rascals out.' One result was that the Likud was able to form a coalition headed by Menachem Begin without the DMC. The DMC decided later to join the government despite the realization that they did not hold the balance of power. The decision caused the new party to splinter; some of its members refused to join and remained in opposition. With time, the party disintegrated. The hopes of the young generation to reinvigorate the political system were shattered.

The Likud ('unity' in Hebrew) was formed in July 1973, as a result of the initiating efforts of former general Ariel Sharon. Sharon proposed to include all center-right groups in one party, thus hoping to change the image of these parties as doomed to be a permanent opposition. The different parties refused to merge. Each one of them kept its central organization. Later, cabinet ministries and other top positions were assigned to each party according to a factional 'key.' The Likud was composed of the '*Herut*' ('Freedom') party and the Liberals — both had formed a bloc already in 1965, known by its Hebrew acronym *Gahal*. In 1973, they were joined by several small parties. One was *Shlomzion* (The peace of Zion) created by Sharon, another was *La'am* ('for the nation'), itself a merger of small parties; Rafi, composed of those who did not return to Mapai after the majority of that party came back to their original party. The

41

Greater Israel party was another.

Herut was a direct descendant of the Revisionist party created by Jabotinsky. It was created when the military arm — Irgun — ceased to operate once independence was achieved. Many of its leaders were members of the so called 'fighting family' or the leaders of the Irgun. From its creation in 1948, Herut was headed by Menachem Begin, who led it to several electoral defeats but also to its victories in 1977 and in 1981. Begin's leadership was charismatic and largely undisputed. When he was challenged by Shmuel Tamir in the 1960s, this pretender to the throne was defeated and his attempt to rejoin the party a decade later was flatly refused. Begin himself resigned after the Lebanon war, and was replaced by Yitzhak Shamir, a veteran of the Lehi faction (that had defected to the Irgun during World War II, believing the war was no reason to stop the fighting against the British).

The Revisionist Party was created in 1925 by Zeev Jabotinsky, who preached for revision of the policies of the World Zionist Organization (WZO), advocated militancy in achieving the national goals, and did not believe in the effectiveness of the patient accumulation of land and persons advocated by the labor parties. The Revisionists won 21 per cent of the delegates to the Zionist Congress in 1931 compared to Mapai's 20 per cent. Later, partially as a result of the allegations that their members murdered the young Labor leader Haim Arlozoroff on June 16, 1933, they dropped to 14 per cent. Jabotinsky decided to leave the WZO, in which Mapai consolidated power. He created a new Zionist Organization — an act that made Ben Gurion extremely angry. The organized Yishuv stigmatized the Revisionists, ostracized them and denied their legitimacy. This attitude continued after the state was born. Ben Gurion singled out the Herut and Maki (communists) parties as the two parties he refused to consider as candidates for his coalition government.

In the period of anxiety before the Six Days War, then Prime Minister Levi Eshkol invited the Herut to join a national unity government. Even before this, Eshkol had decided to initiate a government resolution on the burial of Jabotinsky in Israel (Jabotinsky died in the United States and wrote in his will that he should be reburied in the Jewish state if the government agreed). All of these moves increased the legitimacy of Herut.

The Liberals — a party of the middle-class shopowners and merchants — is a descendant of the General Zionists (those in the Zionist organization not affiliated with other parties, mainly labor ones). In the 1920s, the General Zionists split into faction

A, that later became the Progressive party, and faction B, that remained the General Zionists. Faction A received its power mainly from German immigrants; faction B — from the middle class. The two merged and chose the name Liberals, only to split again when the Progressives refused the creation of a bloc with Herut in 1965. The Liberals suffered from repeated strife among their leaders and were relegated to second place after Herut. Herut repeatedly argued the Liberals received more seats than their real electoral power deserved.

The religious parties' power is much greater than their strength among voters in the country, simply because each of the big blocs needs them as a partner to create a coalition. There are several religious parties, such as the National Religious Party, TAMI, Agudat Israel, Poalei Agudat Israel, Shas, Morasha, and Degel Hatorah. They are different in their degree of Zionism (some of them are anti-Zionist), in the extremity of their orthodoxy and in the Rabbis who lead them. More extreme religious persons refuse even to vote for a secular organization such as the Knesset. The secular Israelis are accused of blasphemous behavior.

Between 1928 and 1977, one bedrock of Israeli politics was that the National Religious Party (NRP), a descendant of Mizrahi (founded in 1902) and Hapoel Hamizrahi — both representing Zionist parties — and Labor would create a coalition. After 1967, the Young Guard faction of the NRP became less willing to accept Labor, since the party was suspected of being willing to accept territorial compromise. By 1977, the Young Guard led the NRP to a coalition with the Likud. Oriental religious Jews felt deprived by the NRP. NRP Minister of Religions, Abu Hatzeira left the NRP and created Tami (the movement of traditional Israel) to appeal to North African Jews. Ultra-orthodox Sephardim Jews created Shas, splitting from Ashkenati-dominated Agudat Israel.

Israelis tend to have a high turnout in the elections, with more than 80 per cent of the eligible voters casting their vote. In the first election of 1949, elated by the prospect of choosing the first Jewish parliament for two thousand years — 86.6 per cent voted.

Table 1.5 shows the election results for the twelve different Knessets. It can be seen that the Alignment has been losing power — first to the DMC in 1977, and later to Likud and religious parties.

The fundamental change in the composition of the population in terms of ethnic origin has had enormous impact on the political, cultural and social life of Israel. The dichotomy

Table 1.5 Knesset election results (120 seats)

Election year	1949	1951	1955	1959	1961	1965	1969	1973	1977	1981	1984	1988
Alignment												
Mapai[a]	46	45	40	47	42	45	56	51	32	47	44	39
Ahdut Haavoda[b]			10	7	8							
Rafi[c]				–	–	10						
Mapam[d]	19	15	9	9	9	8						3
Likud												40
Liberals[e]	7	20	13	8	17							
Herut[f]	14	8	15	17	17							
Religious												
NRP	16	10	11	12	12	11	12	10	12	6	4	5
Aguda parties[g]		5	6	6	6	6	6	5	5	4	8[l]	13[o]

Other												
Arab lists	2	1	4	5	4	4	4	3	1	–	2^m	1
DMC	–	–	–	–	–	–	–	–	15	–	–	–
Independent Liberals[h]	5	4	5	6	–	4	5	4	1	–	–	–
Communist	4	5	6	3	5	4	4	5	5	4	4	4
Others	7	7	1	–	–	8^i	1	3	6^j	11^k	17^n	15^p

Source: Election results as published in *Yalkut Ha'Pirsumim*, various issues.

Notes:
[a] Joined with Ahdut Haavoda in 1965 and the other labor parties in 1969. [b] See note a. [c] Ben-Gurion's party; joined the Labor Alignment in 1969 minus the State List. [d] Ahdut Haavoda included Mapam in 1949 and 1951. [e] Until 1959 known as General Zionists, joined Herut to form Gahal in 1965, and part of the Likud in 1973. [f] Jointly with the Liberals since 1965 and part of the Likud in 1973. [g] Poalei Agudat Israel and Agudat Israel. [h] Included in Liberal party in 1961 and independent again since 1965. In 1984, part of Alignment. [i] Includes the State List (4 members), the Free Center (2 members), and Haolam Haze (2 members). The first two joined Herut and the Liberals in 1973. [j] Includes Shlomzion (2 members), which joined the Likud after the elections, Shelli (2 members), the Citizen's Rights Movement (1 member), and Flatto Sharon (1 member). [k] Includes Tehiya (3 members), Tami (3 members), Telem (2 members), Shinui (2 members), and the Civil Rights Movement (1 member). [l] Including Shas (4 members) Aguda (2 members), and Morasha (partly Poalei Agudat Israel, 2 members). [m] Progressive List for Peace. [n] Including Tehiya (5 members), Shinui (3 members), Civil Rights Movement (3 members), Yahad (3 members), Tami (1 member), Hurewitz (1 member), and Kach (1 member). [o] Including Shas (6 members), Aguda (5), Degel Hatora (2). [p] Shinui – 2, Civil Rights Movement – 5, Tehiya – 3, Moledat – 2, Zunit – 2, Advanud for Peace – 1.

between Sephardim and Ashkenazim is extremely significant. Sephardim are Jews coming from Asian and African countries while Ashkenazim immigrated mainly from European countries or the USA, most of whom speak a hybrid language called Yiddish. The newcomers often felt they were discriminated against. They also perceived the ruling elite during the first years of the state as attempting to erase what they saw as their cherished and great traditional values and mold them into the pattern of the Eastern Europe Jewish culture and modes of behavior. With time, these people developed a strong feeling of resentment against the political party they saw as representing the 'establishment.' This feeling caused them to cast their votes mainly for what they saw as the opposition. This pattern of voting continues, although the Likud has been the power in government since 1977. In addition, in terms of attitudes towards issues such as the future of the territories conquered in the 1967 Six Days War, the Israeli voters are incessantly moving to the right. Since the 1977 elections, when for the first time since the 1930s the right was able to create a coalition government, Labor has been drifting. The Alignment voters are older, more educated and of European background. The Likud is much more heavily supported by the young and by voters of Asian and African background. It is thus generally agreed among political observers that the Likud will gain even more votes from the Alignment in future elections.

In the elections of 1984 and 1988, the results were largely inconclusive with none of the large blocs able to achieve more than an extremely narrow, fragile and unstable coalition, and then only by paying high prices to the religious parties. In both years, the two blocs reluctantly agreed to create a national unity government. In 1988, to make sure that each would not have too strong an incentive to break the coalition that almost no one wanted, both blocs agreed that a new election would follow any pullout by the other party. The more the Likud leadership found itself having to give in to pressure of hard liners within its bloc, the harder if not impossible it became for the Labor party to remain a partner in the national unity government. In 1990, Labour left the government. Shimon Peres attempted to create a narrow coalition and failed. Yitzhak Shamir created a government of Lukud, religious parties and right-wing small parties.

International Relations

Israel's international diplomatic situation has always been precarious. To date, more than forty years after it was officially accepted as a member of the United Nations, many countries refuse to accept its very right to exist. Israel has been unable to sign a peace treaty with any of its neighboring countries, except Egypt (with whom a peace treaty was signed in 1979). Many other countries refuse to recognize Israel.

In the first twenty years of its existence, Israel enjoyed a relatively benign international atmosphere. To be sure, the neighboring countries maintained a constant state of belligerency against the new state, attempted to obliterate it by force and to choke it economically by boycotting it. Yet the state was recognized *de facto* by dozens of nations; it was admitted to the United Nations, and enjoyed the political and moral support of other countries. Some felt they had to pay for the Nazi atrocities and the near extinction of Jews in Europe. Others saw Israel as a democratic bastion in the stormy Middle East. Most perceived the country as a small David having to face a semi-siege by a mammoth Goliath.

The swift Israeli victory in the 1967 Six Days War paradoxically changed this attitude. Israel was no longer perceived as a potential victim of persecution. Instead, it was seen as a politically inflexible, aggressive conquerer of other lands. Its standing in the international arena had deteriorated. There were many attempts to introduce anti-Israel resolutions in the United Nations, or to expel Israel from international organizations.

Israel has special relationships with the United States. There is no official treaty codifying the USA-Israel relations. However, the USA aids Israel, particularly to cover its defense costs. The United States was the first country to recognize Israel *de facto* in 1948. Relations between Israel and the USA have become closer since 1967, and they have been built up over the ensuing decades. In 1981, a memorandum on strategic cooperation was signed between the two countries. The forging of these special relations, especially in matters of defense, have been generally continuous. The United States has attempted to help obtain a settlement between Israel and the Arabs. The two nations do not always agree on the shape this peace should take or the means of achieving it, but the United States has generally been successful in playing the role of an honest broker.

The USSR initially was one of the first countries to extend diplomatic recognition to Israel. But after learning that Israel was not going to be part of their camp, the Russians moved towards a pro-Arab policy. In 1955, President Nasser of Egypt began to acquire arms from Czechoslovakia. The USSR was instrumental in this agreement and also armed Syria. Soviet 'advisory' officers were sent to Egypt and Syria. The USSR and its satellites severed diplomatic relations with Israel after Israel's victory in 1967. In the mid-1980s there have been some changes: Poland has reinstated diplomatic relations and the Soviet Union sent a temporary Consular mission to Tel Aviv.

Israel signed in May 1975 an agreement with the European Economic Community that sets forth the parties' mutual desire to strengthen economic links and continue eliminating obstacles to trade. The agreement forbids the imposition of new duties on imports and aims at a gradual tariff reduction, leading to an elimination of tariffs. The deadlines for tariff reduction were subsequently extended twice with the complete abolition of tariffs postponed. Israel also signed and ratified an agreement with the United States for the creation of a Free Trade Area. Duties are expected to be fully eliminated by January 1, 1995. The existence of these two agreements may allow, subject to rule of origins, some trade through Israel between firms from the USA interested in exports to the European Community.

New Asian and African countries, as well as Latin America, attempted to learn from the rich Israeli experience in building a new nation. The high level of determination in Israel, the ability to maintain democracy, the outstanding achievements in economic and social fields as well as her unique organizations — all attracted interest among developing nations. Despite the desire to learn from her success, the deterioration of Israel's image also affected its relationships with the Third World nations. After the Yom Kippur war, most African nations severed diplomatic relations with Israel. To be sure, the economic ties continued and sometimes even expanded. By the end of the 1980s, a few African countries have also reestablished diplomatic ties.

Ideology

The political system in Israel is hierarchical. The top leaders decide on a party line, and subordinate groups fit into the line. The hierarchy is facilitated by the dependency of individuals on the government — or on appropriation and appointment made by political leaders.

Party life is also strongly based on ideological rhetoric and symbols. After all, only those who tenaciously adhered to the

Zionist ideology came to Israel in the first place, and only those who believed passionately were able to endure throughout years of difficulties. The ideology was reinforced through the schools, the youth movements, and the peer groups. Most Israelis were brought up with the belief that they are to serve their country (first to work to bring about a independent state, and later to maintain it) as a matter of course, and that national needs take precedence over individual feelings. This normative ideological belief is a basis of action, from volunteer participation in underground pseudo-military organizations to work for the national goals.

On a routine basis, politicians have typically been pragmatic, even though they have often used ideological symbols. Yet, on questions such as the right of Jews to immigrate to Israel, the importance of defense, or the importance of social justice, ideology has been paramount, and ideological hair splitting was very common.

Because of its ideological proclivities, the government of Israel has always helped agriculture more than any other sector of the Israeli economy. Since the mid-1950s, the manufacturing industry has also been aided. Throughout the four decades of the state's existence, services were considered 'non-productive' and even parasitic. The only service industry to receive some, albeit often half-hearted, government encouragement has been tourism. This industry has complained it received far fewer incentives than the manufacturing sector. Their fate, however, was much better than that of 'non-productive' consultants or retailers. Thus, when manufacturers received a premium on the value added they brought to the country because the official rate of interest was deemed too low, writers, consultants or universities were compelled to sell their hard-earned foreign exchange to the Bank of Israel at the artificially maintained low rate of exchange.

After a few decades of Israel's existence it has been found that many Israeli-born persons have been lured to the United States by professional and career building opportunities. These Israelis tend to have rather shallow roots in their new communities, often remaining largely tourists in the places they call home. However, they cling to the opportunities found in the new land, and are thus not drawn to return to their own state. They may still claim that Israel is their homeland; but in their pursuit of happiness and opportunity, they do not return to Israel.

The world view of the first generation was molded by the Russian political culture of that period. Unlike the Western civilization's ideological beliefs in the superiority of the individual, the importance of the competitive markets and the preference to a decentralized economic system; the Russians believed in an absolutist point of view, and having the regime intervene in every decision. Further, Karl Marx certainly did not believe the invisible hand allows allocative efficiency. For him (and for most socialists) it led to anarchy and exploitation, leaving individuals devoid of control of their future. Thus, both the political culture of Czarist Russia and the socialist beliefs led to an emphasis on community values. These were reinforced by the need for cooperation to survive in the harsh conditions of Eretz Israel and to gain employment. The third Aliyah pioneers had already witnessed the operations of the Soviets — and copied this system in the organization of their own political system. Most importantly, the socialist leaders of that period clearly believed that economic institutions should be managed and controlled by political leaders. Both in the Yishuv period and after the state was born, the political party was an owner of economic enterprises, supplier of jobs, educator, and a major center of social life.

The leaders of the first generation did not rely on ideology alone. They were sure there was not a way to create a new Jewish state or to achieve the objectives of the state without public regulation and organization from the top down. They were able to create in the beginning period of the country a political and economic system upon which many citizens were dependent. This structure is not very much liked by the young generation. This generation is open to many ideas coming from outside and refuses to accept the strong communitarian beliefs of the earlier period. One challenge for the leaders in the 1980s and mainly in the 1990s is to create the vision of Israel that will appeal to its young generation.

During the Yishuv period, there were no legal sanctions. It was necessary to create a strong moral suasion system, that served to make individual citizens work to achieve national goals. At the same time only those who 'belonged' received employment and social status. The political system made sure that those who preferred to be dissidents would be left outside and be morally and socially banned. The system developed made joining a political party the first step for potential new immigrants (even before they immigrated, the party ensured the immigration certificate). The party helped in the absorption process, in the achieving of employment, in a sick fund, and in organized culture. The worker-member of the party subscribed to its daily newspaper, his children were educated in its schools, his wife belonged to its women's organization, and he may have played or at least watched sports in politically organized groups. If the citizen chose not to belong, he denied himself work opportunities, sports, culture, education and the social support of extremely cohesive groups. In return for being part of the consensus, the citizen received all the services but also learned to follow the directives of the leaders.

To maintain all these economic, cultural, spiritual, health and sports institutions, the political party needed funds. These funds came from the National Institutions budget. Controlling the resource allocation process of these institutions was therefore very important to ensure an appropriate allocation from the public capital.

Generally, the connection between consumption or benefit and the need for payment was becoming weaker and weaker. Many Israelis began to expect their government to solve all their problems. Many see a *quid pro quo*: individuals give the state service in the army. In return, they deserve high wages, subsidies to goods deemed essential, excellent schools, university education, nice (and subsidized) housing with extended mortgages carrying a low interest rate, and even happiness. Many Israelis believe the government, not themselves, has to solve each and every problem — be it clean streets or hours of opening of stores. This belief system means an increasing role for government.

It sometimes seems as if there is no limit to what politicians may demand from the government. Defense costs are considered a 'holy cow' and the extremely heavy defense burden is rarely questioned. The social lobby continuously demands more and more benefits and an increasing array of laws benefitting one group or another — from minimum wages to payments to widows of those killed in military action or housing for the needy. The economic lobby demands import protection, reduced prices for water, electricity, interest costs or land prices, or tax exemption of different activities. Very few except the economists believe wholeheartedly in the virtues of an unfettered market system. Many government economists also do not trust the market to achieve economic growth.

The development of a welfare state

Jews since the time of the Bible have always endeavored in their quest for social justice. The creation and maintenance of a just and humane society has been one of the major tenets of Israeli policy. It manifested itself, first and foremost, in the strong belief that the government should do almost anything to avoid mass unemployment. A second manifestation has been large expenditures on social services, and a third, in a very high level of sensitivity for 'gaps' in income, wealth or status distribution and their avoidance. Israeli policy makers have always been proud of the relatively egalitarian income distribution and very sensitive to any increase in the level of the Gini coefficient (measuring income inequality).

The government of Israel strongly believes that few things are as demoralizing as a prolonged idleness and protracted unemployment. When it could not supply the masses of new immigrants with productive employment, it sent them to plant trees on the side of the major highways. It also attempted to expand employment with every means at its disposal, including protection of local firms from foreign competition.

The development of a welfare state in Israel prevented political shocks and enabled the young state to avoid many frictions. Israel announced its commitment to a welfare state as early as 1948, in the midst of the War of Independence. The law creating the National Insurance system was enacted in 1953. In comparison, the Bank of Israel — the Central Bank — came into being only in 1954. Many interest groups, speaking in the name of one or another ideal, were able to receive benefits from the public purse. This system was one of the prices for the coalition government. It also allowed wide consensus. In addition, Israelis volunteered to many public calls — from the underground or the illegal immigration during the British Mandate — to all kinds of risky operations after the state was born. The wide consensus was possible to some extent because the government was able to confer largesse on many and avoid difficult decisions on priorities. The largesse was bestowed not only through direct budget allocations, but also through a wide and varied number of tools at the disposal of the government: in addition to revenues, taxes, budget and rate of exchange, there were the composition of taxes, transfer prices, subsidies, direct purchases of products and services, licenses and cross-subsidies. The result has been a blurring of the distinction between the private and the public sector. Thus a direct budgetary loan is counted as an increase in the size of the public sector. The same loan, if it is granted by a state-owned bank, appears as a private-sector operation.

Conclusions

After many generations of state-less situation, the Jews were able to create their own, tiny state. This state was established as a result of a transformation achieved by a few vanguard pioneers, who came to Eretz Israel to build a new country, conquer a wasteland, and create a new Jew. They believed in the supremacy of collective needs over individual desires. They were ready to deprive themselves of material comforts, to perform tasks for the benefit of a future collectivity of all the Jewish nation, not only those living in the country. The Yishuv was not built for itself but for the whole Jewish people. The Holocaust seemingly vindicated the Zionist claim that it was impossible for Jews to survive without their own state. The pioneers in the Yishuv also believed in an egalitarian society and in a pluralistic form of a political economy. In 1948, they became the rulers of a new state. They had to redefine many roles, including that of Zionism, to transform many institutions, to mold into one nation immigrants from a hundred countries, to forge a new culture and social life based on the tradition of the past and to achieve an economic independence based on an increased standard of living. During the whole period, many beliefs were shattered in the face of cruel and bitter reality. The Jews did not come to their homeland, and the Arabs saw Israel as a continual transgressor of their rights, rejecting with implacable hostility her right to exist. This chapter has given a short glimpse of the necessary background — before moving to analyze the development of Israel's political economy.

2 A history of Israel's economy

Introduction

This chapter is intended to give the reader a general overview of the political economy before starting with a detailed analysis of various issues. We shall, therefore, start with a short description of the political economy in the pre-state period and then describe chronologically the major events during the state period.

The buds of the relationship between economic and political structures in Israel came in the period immediately after World War I. The world views about what Zionism should be and the kind of society that members wanted to create in Israel influenced the economic strategy of the Zionist organization and contributed to the creation of the unique political, social and economic structure of the Jewish Yishuv of Eretz Israel. In this structure there was (and still is) a very strong interrelationship between politics and economics that was based on corporatist institutional conglomerates and at the same time on very strong ideological rhetoric. Earlier, there was a very close identity if not total congruence between operations of political parties, social interactions, economic operations, and cultural activities. Little by little a regime was created in the Yishuv based on political party key, by which all public capital resources were allocated. Under the political party key system, budgets, immigration certificates, settlement sites, administrative jobs and other employment were allocated in proportion to the relative strength of the parties and other political groups in the representative bodies of the central National Institutions. By these kinds of agreements, the outcome of political elections had an impact on many spheres of life which are not considered political in the narrow sense of the word. The system was similar to that found in small European countries such as Austria or the Netherlands: under this system, consociational segments of the population divide among themselves the access to major centers of power proportionally to the political power of the different segments sharing in the system. This has become known as *Proportz-*

democratie. In the case of the Yishuv, participants in the key system were only those parties considered part of the 'Organized Yishuv': dissident groups such as the Revisionists were subjected to various social, economic and political sanctions.

The Zionist vision called for the creation of a modern Jewish state, the renaissance of the Hebrew language, and the recreation of a normal occupational structure. The so-called productivization of occupations was stressed in negation of the Jewish concentration of small trade in the Diaspora. The Labor Zionists also stressed the need for the creation of an egalitarian society, non-exploitative structure and subservience of the individual to communal needs and national objectives. These revolutionary ideas were to be enforced in a voluntary society, lacking the tools of a sovereign state. After the state came into being, some of the institutions forged during the Yishuv period may have become redundant. However, most of the institutions continued to exist. With time, a society that was far less ideologically oriented found it increasingly more difficult to continue the legacy of the Yishuv period, and the symbols of collective identity. The reality of a small country surrounded by belligerent neighbors was not easy to reconcile with the aspirations of becoming a social and cultural center for all Jews.

The Zionists came to a land in which a Jewish community which long antedated them was composed mainly of pious and Orthodox Jews who devoted their life to sacred study, prayers and good deeds. These persons lived immured behind the walls of a medieval ghetto of their own making. For many generations, they had been supported by charitable contributions of religious Jews outside Palestine in a system of distribution (Halukha) that the new pioneers regarded with contempt, looking at the 'old' Yishuv with much indignation. The new settlers were also completely ignorant of the existence of another small community of old timers — those that were the ancestors of the Spanish Jews. They refused to turn to urban industrial development as a major means of absorbing a considerable number of people. For them, the type of professions in which Jews were forced to specialize in the Diaspora were not only anathema but were looked at with indignation. They rebelled against all that was even remotely connected to the ghetto type of life, which they deplored. They became atheistic and their new religion was that of work on the land.

The pre-state political economy

The roots of the unique structure of Israeli economy are to be found in the pre-state, Yishuv (meaning Jewish community) period, the ideologies of that time and the political structure then developed. The Jewish economy of Palestine during that time was characterized by sharp swings from prosperity to recession. A major factor explaining these swings was the immigration waves. These waves, in turn, were largely influenced by the economic and political conditions of the Jews in the various countries in which they lived, as well as by changes in ideological proclivities and shifts in immigration policies of the various countries. The early immigration waves consisted mainly of youth that joined (or at least wanted to join) the economic labor force. They were also accompanied by a large influx of both human and physical capital. The economic business cycles in Jewish Palestine can be explained by the immigration waves more than they can be attributed to developments in the world economy. The only exception is the period 1942-5, in which the prosperity was caused mainly by the impact of the military demand during World War II.

Between 1830 and 1870, the winds of change began to blow in Eretz Israel (the Land of Israel). Sir Moses Montefiore from the UK attempted to make Jews more productive (for example by setting up a flour mill). French Jews created an agricultural school near Jaffa. Jews went out of the walls of the old city of Jerusalem. There were several modern educational institutions and two Hebrew periodicals in Jerusalem, and Orthodox Jews from Jerusalem established, in 1878, the first Jewish village — Petah Tiqva.

These small-scale attempts at modernization were accelerated by the influx of new immigrants coming in waves. These waves comprised less than 4 per cent of the total Jewish migration. Only those ideologically inclined migrated to Eretz Israel and disassociated themselves sharply from their earlier environment — against which they rebelled. These few were also selected by the various Zionist movements — and again by their ability to withstand the difficulties of the conditions in Eretz Israel. All saw land settlement as a necessary condition for Jewish rejuvenation.

The first Aliyah, mainly from Russia and Romania, consisted of 'Lovers of Zion' pioneers. This wave doubled the number of Jews in Palestine between 1882 and 1884, during which period between 20,000 and 30,000 Jews emigrated to Palestine. A series of pogroms in 1881-4 shocked the Jews in the Pale of Settlement.

They felt a physical danger to their very existence. The result was a variety of new ideological and political movements — one of which was the Zionist one. The adherents to the Zionist ideals returned to the land of their forefathers not simply to create another nation-state. The dreamers who started this movement had a much more important vision. They were attempting to transform the Jews. Some of them believed in a secular ideology, more of a national type, others were believers in national-religious resurrection. All of them believed Jews should come back to Israel and build themselves on the basis of agricultural settlement. The dreams of most of these new immigrants were shattered because they lacked agricultural experience. In addition, they found themselves faced with a harsh reality of a nearly-desert country and a barren land.

The new immigrants came to a country that was part of the Ottoman Empire, in which about 120,000 non-Jews of which 55,000 were Christians lived mainly in small villages (Simon, 1989, p. 18). The economy was based on primitive agriculture and was controlled by the Effendis (absentee landowners). The government administration was lazy and largely corrupt. The problems of settling in an arid land turned out to be more difficult than most of the new immigrants anticipated. The new experiment for agriculture settlement in Israel might have been an ignominious failure except for the fact that Baron Edmond de Rothschild came to the aid of the new settlers. He bought the land for them, imported agricultural experts from France to help them, and promised the new settlers a minimum income. From 1884 to 1900, Baron Rothschild spent about £1,600,000 on land acquisition and building for the settlements (Ulitzur, 1939, p. 222). He invested also in the building of the winery, silk manufacturing plant, glass, water enterprises and many others. By 1914, the Baron-acquired land was 58 per cent of the land owned by Jews in Israel (compared to 4 per cent bought by the Zionist organizations) and by that time his total expenditures to aid the settlements have been estimated at £10,000,000 (Elon, 1971, p. 98).

While the help of the Baron rescued the new settlers, they also became totally dependent on his bureaucracy, and many problems arose. In the meantime, the World Zionist Organization was established in 1897. It created, in 1899, a Zionist Bank (Jewish Colonial Trust). In 1901, it established the Jewish National Fund (*Keren Kayemet*) for land purchases.

Both in the time before and during the first Aliyah, the economy was based mainly on private capital investment in a free market system and on aid from a private individual, Baron

Rothschild. The first settlers did not receive any subsidies of national or public capital. The first Aliyah immigrants did not create a central institution for the whole settlement. Each one of the villages was organized separately. As a result, farmers of these villages had difficulty in influencing the political system in the Zionist organizations.

These farmers managed their affairs by economic criteria only, based on return on investment. One result was that they preferred the Arab worker who was both much cheaper and much more docile than the Jewish one. Two hundred settlers in Zichron Ya'akov employed 1,200 Arabs, and 40 families in Rishon Le'Zion employed 300 Arab families. To be sure, some settlers learned to rely solely on the Baron's aid, showing apathy and irresponsibility. However, many were successful in creating very profitable private agricultural villages. By 1920, there were about 12,000 people living in 22 villages.

Thus, as the new immigrants became more and more established, they turned into colonizers, using cheap Arab labor. This trend was bitterly opposed by the second wave of immigrants who came to Israel from Russia after the revolution there failed in 1905. Between 1905 and 1913, about 35,000 Jews came to Eretz Israel, mainly from Russia. This second wave consisted mainly of young pioneers, many of whom were embedded in the socialist ideology. The newcomers found it hard to gain employment — and fought for a priority to be given to Jewish workers. For them, the continual threat of the much cheaper Arab labor was enough of a reason to reject competitive and unified labor markets. They also believed passionately in socialist ideals. To achieve the ideological goals but also to make sure they had employment, they created political instruments that helped them later gain prominence and change the whole structure of the Jewish community. These young idealists were great believers in the need to create a personal transformation in order to become farmers. They believed in a total overlap of economic, political, social, and cultural aspects of life. During the same period, the World Zionist Organization started operating in Eretz Israel (1908). In 1909, the foundations of the first all-Jewish city — Tel Aviv — were laid. In the same year, the first kibbutz was established.

The symbiotic process between Zionist ideals and Socialist beliefs led to the desire to create a model society. Part of the mythos was the belief that a process of productivization and normalization of the Jewish nation is crucial for its survival in a world to be characterized by a class struggle. This normalization could be achieved only in Eretz Israel. It necessitated a transformation of the individual. Part of this transformation was the need to move to manual work to cultivate the soil. Manual labor had to be achieved without exploitation of others, with self-sacrifice and self-realization.

When the second Aliyah pioneers came to Eretz Israel, they found they could not create a new proletariat — because the rich did not come and did not colonize the land. Eretz Israel was far from a capitalist country that needed the Jewish manual worker. The economic infrastructure required to absorb the immigrants did not exist. Slowly, the pioneers moved their ideology from seeing themselves as creators of the Jewish working class to that of being responsible for the build-up of the economy and the design of the society. The doctrine of 'Hebrew Labor' came to ensure the creation of a self-sufficient Jewish economy that would not have to compete against the much cheaper, docile, and skilled Arab workers. The other doctrine was the creation of collective frameworks to help create the new society.

By the end of World War I, the Jewish population of Palestine dwindled to about 56,000 — roughly the same number as in the turn of the century. This was caused by Turkish expulsion of Jews and by the hunger and other problems of the war period. After the war, a third wave of Jewish immigration came to Palestine, mainly from Russia. This third Aliyah (1917-23) brought 35,000 young pioneers, most of whom were trained by the *Halutz* (pioneer) organization in special *Hachshara* (preparation). They were ready for any job. Conditions, however, were difficult and economic growth did not occur steadily. Those arriving on the third Aliyah found themselves without jobs, and had to organize themselves in cooperatives to work on public works. A severe depression, in 1927, after the initial surge of the fourth wave of immigration, in 1924-5, (that consisted mainly of middle-class Jews from Poland) caused many to leave. By late 1928, the economy began to pick up again, but in 1929, Arab terrorism caused another setback. By that time the basic tenets of the economic and political structure of the Jewish economy had been established — as had the social characteristics and the structure of the regime. These characteristics continued to be the same until at least the third decade of the existence of Israel (and in most cases, until today). A fifth wave of immigration started in 1929, and peaked in 1932. It consisted mainly of Jews from Germany who came with capital and energy. From 1936 on, Jewish immigration was severely limited by the British government. Arabs continued to arrive from neighboring countries as before.

Labor leaders aspired to build in Israel a new and just

society. The difficulties of adjusting to the conditions of Palestine at the time and the need to compete with much cheaper Arab labor, combined with ideology, led to various experiments in mutual aid and in the creation of collective settlements. One result was the creation of a multi-purpose organization — the General Federation of Labor (the Histadrut). This is not simply a labor union, although the labor union consists of one of its departments. The Histadrut also provided health insurance, a labor exchange and it owned many business firms. Since 1923, each member of the Histadrut is automatically a shareholder in Hevrat Ovdim ('Workers Society'). Hevrat Ovdim owns the economic enterprises of labor (see chapter 4).

It was clear to the leaders of Ahduth Ha'Avoda that the party by itself did not possess the necessary resources to supply its members with both work and a system of welfare and social services, such as a sick fund, workers' kitchens, education, or schools for their children. The achievement of these objectives demanded considerable funds and the major source of funds was the national capital. The workers' leaders were sent to London to the Zionist executive office to lobby for receipt of more money. They were successful. In July-August 1920, the Zionist Congress resolved to create *Keren Hayesod* (the Foundation Fund) and to finance public investment. It also agreed to cooperate with the workers' organization, to support these organizations. It also undertook to participate in the creation of the Workers Bank. The proposal of the workers' leaders that private individuals would not be allowed to acquire land in Eretz Israel was not accepted.

Workers saw themselves as idealists, and as the salt of the earth, the spearhead of the nation — that will transform the turned-over pyramid of Jewish occupational structure. They strongly believed that their pioneering gave them the automatic right to receive money from the community in order to maintain and even to increase their standard of living. They also held that the collective must protect the egoist individual from bad individualistic inclinations and desires by creating institutions that would build a fence around wrong desires. As a result, the relation between individual workers and their political institutions was one of loyalty, but also of discipline and of clientele. There was a total congruence between personal ambitions and national objectives, individual fulfillment and the devotion of one's life to the good of the community — and a total submission of the individual to the community's goals, to which one had to be fully obedient or lose all social status. Social behavior rules had been established, in which conformism was advocated and anyone out of the consensus was to suffer — or to leave (as many indeed chose to do).

Everybody called for unity and consolidation of the power of the Yishuv. Everyone declared that without self-sacrifice of the individual, there is a danger both to the community and to the individual. Those who operated outside the general consensus were oppressed with a revolutionary zeal and fervor that included not only a political fight but also use of economic tools. The fight of the worker for Hebrew work forcing the Jewish farmer to pay higher wages was one of those. It resulted later in the denial of work, medical treatment, housing or trade union protection or even bank loans to those who were not part of the consensus and in some extreme cases, such as during the period known as 'the season,' in extradition of the dissidents to the hands of the British police. The National Workers Organization that was established by the Revisionist Party tried to protect its members, to find work for them, to ensure them loans and to supply them sport and cultural services. It was successful in doing that to some extent, often at a cost of fights with other workers. In the summer of 1932, there were several skirmishes resulting from Revisionists being taken on by employers who refused to use the Histadrut's labor exchange. A strike in a factory because of a demand to use only Histadrut's labor exchange was not honored by the Revisionists. The Histadrut refused to recognize the right of existence (and the right to work) of the Revisionists. In *Pessach* (Passover) 1933, a procession of the Betar youth movement was attacked violently by Histadrut members. The labor saw Betar as fascists and called for their eradication from any work (for details see for example, Anita Shapira, 1989, pp. 82-100).

Leaders were not always able to rise above small personal or party problems and to achieve fruitful work. These were people who had triumphed through many tests and over several decades of fighting for their ends. The leaders who remained from a much larger number through a Darwinistic natural selection process were only those who believed very much that they were right. Achieving the aims of Zionism as they perceived them was considered much more important than any private sacrifice. It was also deemed as justifying the use of unusual methods.

The debate on the role of the public sector after World War I

The Balfour Declaration in November 1917, and the creation of the British Mandate, elated the Zionists. Unfortunately, the masses of the Jews did not choose to immigrate to Eretz Israel. Many British proposed the creation of a colonial society, based on cheap Arab work. The Jews, for strong ideological reasons, chose to maintain an independent Jewish economy based on autonomous communities — not one integrated into the existing economy. This decision was not made haphazardly. Indeed, immediately after World War I, a major debate erupted among Zionist leaders over the development strategy of Eretz Israel. It started in the London Zionist Congress in 1920, and it continued for several years.

Judge Louis Brandeis of the United States advocated a free enterprise system as a basic means to colonize Eretz Israel. He proposed that the Zionist Organization encourage large-scale private investments and the immigration of potential investors into the country to achieve a rapid colonization. He also suggested that the Zionist Organization invest money only in profitable enterprises that were viable from an economic point of view, to avoid what he saw as corruption and demoralization. He believed that Jewish private capital would flow into the country only if there was a capitalist economic regime; and absorption of mass immigration would only be possible by developing urban centers. Brandeis interpreted the establishment of the British Mandate to mean the achievement of the Zionist movement's political objectives. Therefore, he felt all efforts should be directed to achieve the economic aims of building the Home Land. He believed in a decentralized Zionist movement, in which each Zionist federation in each country would undertake some specific tasks in Eretz Israel with the World Zionist Organization having a coordinating role.

On the other side stood the European leaders, headed by Chaim Weizmann. They argued that the American experience was not applicable to conditions in Eretz Israel, that the emphasis on private enterprise and profits was premature and that affluent Jews were not ready to come to Eretz Israel. Therefore, the Zionist Organization should subsidize those that were willing to immigrate and build communal settlements. Weizmann rejected the point of view that saw private investors as the most important engine for development. He believed in the need for subsidies to the agricultural settler. He also believed that without a strong agriculture basis there would not be any Jewish culture or even Jewish economics.

Most Zionist leaders coming from East Europe did not believe in urban build-up and opposed what they believed to be land speculation. They resisted strenuously any colonization scheme based on using the strengths the Diaspora Jews had: building up the National Home on the basis of small-scale manufacturing and commerce in urban centers. As Weizmann explained in a speech he made in Jerusalem in October 1924, when middle-class families from Poland came in the fourth Aliya and built private businesses in the cities with great diligence, industry and frugality:

It is essential to remember that we are not building our National Home on the model of Djika and Nalevki. [He was referring to two typical Ghetto districts of Warsaw.] The life of the ghetto we have always known to be merely a stage in our road; here we reached home and are building for eternity. (Weizmann, 1966, p. 301)

Weizmann also states in his memoirs:

I still believe that the backbone of our work is and always must be agricultural colonization. It is in the village that the real soil of a people — its language, its poetry, its literature, its traditions — springs up from the intimate contact between man and soils. The towns do no more than 'process' the fruits of the villages. (p. 278)

For Weizmann and his followers, the creation of a Jewish farmer, settling in a Jewish village, was a major and important mission, the success of which gave them deep and growing exultation. To achieve this goal, they needed the pioneers who were willing to become farmers. The Labor leaders of the second and the third Aliya were rough, indelicate, unrefined and uneducated. However, they were also tireless and stubborn. They persistently, single-mindedly and doggedly worked to transform themselves into farmers. They, like their ancestors for hundreds of years, had no experience of agricultural pursuits. They, however, had a strong will and were ready to skip meals, to suffer, to be sick with malaria, but to work diligently to achieve the dream of a new Jew in a different nation state. To achieve this dream they needed funds. Even if they were willing to skip meals, their cows had to be fed.

The left wing in Zionism aspired for economic equality and social justice. Many of its leaders believed that it was essential to nationalize all means of production and to establish a socialist economy. Many of them were against any partnership with any private capital as an independent factor in the process of building the Zionist dream even if this impeded or hindered economic development. Other socialist leaders were more pragmatic in their approach. They were willing to go in partnership with private capital. Some of them believed there was a need to have a capitalist class struggle, others believed they could nationalize the capital entity at a later date.

Others, mainly the Revisionists, later advocated political agitation to achieve a Jewish state, placing less emphasis on colonization efforts. Leaders like Jabotinsky believed that the large immigration required could be absorbed only in the cities, and that private capital would flow to the country only if it had a free enterprise system.

The debate among leaders was not about the Zionist objectives, but on the means to achieve these objectives. No one doubted the urgent necessity to increase the volume of economic activity in the country and the need to tap the high volume of economic resources to be put at the disposal of the Zionist Institutions. Further, the absence of Jewish sovereignty over Eretz Israel constrained the National Institutions' activities: these institutions did not have any legislative power nor could they have monetary policy. The National Institutions could work to establish the infrastructure and to help the economic development of Eretz Israel. It was also agreed that Jews should become a majority in Eretz Israel, that some Jews should settle the land, and that national capital was needed for land acquisition and reclamation. All believed the land should belong to the whole nation on national and social grounds. Profits on rent were seen as morally wrong. All were concerned that private ownership of the land might lead to a preference for Arab work. A very wide consensus also existed that the agricultural settlement was a central objective. The debate was on means: the degree of intervention, the methods of operation and whether the best way to achieve national development policy was a paternalistic and centralized apparatus or granting credit subsidies.

Several rules determined in the 1920 Zionist Congress in London became fundamentals that were accepted almost until the present day. These were, first, the belief that agricultural settlement was central for the economic colonization and development. Second, the conviction that only communal settlements could survive under the difficult conditions of Palestine, and therefore that these settlements should be accorded the highest priority. Third, the neglect of the industrial development and the urban infrastructure. Fourth, the assumption that trade and services were inferior professions that should be discouraged. Fifth, the creation of a paternalistic central management of the agricultural settlement, based on a covenant between the pioneer who aspires to settle but does not have the means and those who want to increase the settlement but also to manage it centrally. Therefore, a private individual should not be allowed to settle on the land without being a part of a collective group that can be directed, regulated and managed. Finally, leaders learn to dictate the budget size through the magnitude of the expenditures, creating deficits and achieving a *fait accompli* while avoiding the need to decide on priorities by taking loans.

Capital imports

Capital imports to Eretz Israel came from three sources: the national, public and private. The national capital imports included funds collected through contributions to different organs of the World Zionist Organization, such as *Keren Hayesod* and *Keren Kayemet* as well as funds to aid *Hadassa* hospitals or the settlement of German Jews. Public capital was defined as the funds of PJCA (the Palestine Jewish Colonization Association) and the AJJDC (the American Jewish Joint Distribution Committee), as well as funds collected to help political parties, mainly socialists and Mizrahi (today, the National Religious Party). The PJCA was established by Baron Rothschild, in 1924, to manage his colonization efforts, and was headed by Edmond's son James. When the State of Israel was established, the company transferred all its assets to the State of Israel and to *Keren Kayemet*. It also financed the Knesset building in Jerusalem. The AJJDC was a lay American Jewish organization, established in 1914, to help Jews all over the world.

Since the beginning of the first Aliyah until the establishment of the State of Israel, most capital imports consisted of private funds imported by private entrepreneurs. Private funds were the major engine for investment in construction (that consisted of a third of the total investment), in manufacturing, and in citrus orchards. Private individuals also bought most of the land — *Keren Kayemet* owned, by the end of 1937, only 30.5 per cent of all the land held by Jews.

As one might expect, there is a high correlation between Jewish immigration and investments of Jewish capital. Thus, during the period 1920-29, 106,000 Jewish immigrants came to the country (and the addition to the total population — Jews and non-Jews — was 282,000). New Jewish investments were 20 million Palestine pounds. In the period 1932-9, there were

Table 2.1 Jewish capital imports (millions of Palestinian pounds)

Period	Total	National	Public	Private	Private as % Total
1882-1922	19.4	2.8	5.1	11.5	59.3
1923-7	24.6	4.0	1.6	19.0	77.2
1918-29	44.0	7.8	4.2	32.0	73.0
1930-7	51.0	6.2	1.8	43.0	84.0
1938-9	13.3				

Source:　A. Cohen *Ebb and Flow in the Economy*, pp. 17, 21 (for 1882-1927); Ulitzur 1939, p. 246 (1918-37); 1938-9 *Statistical Handbook of Jewish Palestine*, (Jerusalem, 1947, p. 375).

238,000 Jewish immigrants, a population addition of 553,000 and new investments of Jewish capital worth 53 million Palestine pounds (Horowitz, 1948, pp. 13, 19, 24, 77). About half of the investment was in construction; 19 per cent in agriculture and orchards; 10 per cent in land; and 16 per cent in manufacturing (Table 2.1).

About 40 per cent of the public funds were directed at the acquisition of land and the creation of infrastructure for the agricultural settlement. The rest was investment in education, health, social work, security and general administration. Public funds were used to give land and means of production to those workers who did not have their own capital. The ability to control the allocation of these funds was of paramount importance to the Histadrut and the socialist leaders. Lacking any sources of capital of their own, it was essential for them to achieve hegemony in the Zionist organizations and control the use and allocation of their funds. Non-Socialist leaders saw the socialist pioneers as a major source of manpower for the settlement, ready and willing to settle wherever the need might arise. The result was a perceived synergy and mutual dependence between the Zionist leaders, who were interested in the settlement of the land, and the Histadrut with its needs for financial means for its economic organizations and support for its health institutions. Most of the public funds were allocated through the socialist political parties and the Histadrut.

During the period from 1917 until the fourth Aliyah Crisis in 1927, national capital was only 14 per cent of total Jewish capital imports. In the State of Israel on the other hand private capital investments were not more than 15 per cent of the total investment.

Economic growth

Before World War I, Eretz Israel was an extremely poor country, with 80 per cent of the national income stemming from primitive agriculture. Most inhabitants were nomads moving with their goats from one place to another. Jewish immigration and capital changed much of that, making the country part of the lower range of the middle-income countries. The economy also grew very fast in most years, although in some cases there were not enough resources for the absorption of immigrants. Such was the case, for example, in 1926, when the country suffered from a recession. Yet even between 1922 and 1928, according to Jewish Agency figures, production per capita rose by more than 50 per cent. Generally, immigration caused prosperity.

Between March 1919 and December 1947, the economy grew by 13.7 per cent per annum. It was also transformed from an extremely less developed country to a more modern economy. In 1923, the first electricity-generating power plant was installed. In 1927, the major electricity-generating power plant on the Jordan river was finished. Electricity consumption grew in leaps and bounds, from 11.6 million KWH in 1934 to 71.3 million KWH in 1937. The fifth Aliyah brought many skilled workers and capital; the small-scale manufacturing in Eretz Israel grew very fast and many more plants were erected. In 1945, 41.3 per cent of the product in the Jewish sector came from manufacturing (and 10.9 per cent from agriculture). In 1936, manufacturing comprised 26 per cent of total product. The large surge was mainly a result of the wartime demand, fueled through the Middle East Supply Center. In addition, during World War II, manufacturing was almost totally sheltered from foreign competition.

The legal tender was the Egyptian currency. At the end of 1927, a Palestine currency was introduced. This currency was 100 per cent covered by British sterling, invested in British securities by the Palestine Currency Board. The British authorities also built an infrastructure, in particular in the period 1920-24, during which the accumulated deficit in the government's budget was 6 per cent of GNP. The British built a modern port in Haifa (between 1929 and 1933), roads (they expanded the paved road network from 230 km paved by the Turks to 2,600 km in 1945), railroad and an oil pipeline from Iraq to the refineries built in Haifa. They also constructed a small airport near Haifa (1935) and an international airport in Lod (1937). Of course, the major objective of the British was the advancement of strategic goals of their empire. This meant an emphasis on law and order, on communication and transportation infrastructure and on encouragement of British exports. The British refused to intervene in the free market economy. They were reluctant to accept infant-industry arguments as a reason for protecting local manufacturers. Instead, they kept an open-door policy, under paragraph 18 of the Mandate, that made the development of local manufacturing more difficult. In general, the British Mandatory government saw its role as that of maintaining law and order and providing a minimum of social services. Except for post, telephone, and transportation, the Mandatory government refused to be a direct provider of services. After 1923, it also adhered to a 'sound financial management.' Between 1919 and 1939, government expenditure was 10 to 12 per cent of the net national product. Of this, 30 per cent was devoted to economic activities, 29 per cent to administration, 29 per cent to public safety, and 10-12 per cent to education and health. Government receipts came mainly from indirect taxes, mostly on imports. Income tax was introduced only in 1940. Since 1924, government expenditure has been consistently lower than its receipts.

One result of the Arab riots against Jews, in 1929, was the government's decision to check the absorption capacity of the country. The report, written by Sir John Hope Simpson, noted that 'nothing could be worse than the Jewish immigrants should feel that they have the right to be established in Palestine at the expense of others' (Simpson, 1930, p.50) .

Jewish leaders criticized the British government's policy, believing that the government should be much more active in achieving economic development. Indeed, the Jewish National Institutions did play an active role in fostering modernization and promoting growth. These institutions also spent on health double what the government did. The Zionist budget paid per Jewish capita 75 per cent of total costs until 1927. Since then, the share of the Zionist budget was reduced, reaching about a third of the total by the late 1930s. Many of the Jewish leaders' complaints concentrated on specific policy issues in which they felt the British government restrained the development of the Jewish sector.

One such area was that of immigration. The British based their immigration policy on what they defined as the economic absorptive capacity of the country. They issued certificates of immigration to several categories (such as capitalists, professionals, and people with prospective employment). Most of them were allocated by the Jewish Agency. The Jewish Agency demanded many more certificates than it received. Usually, the British government approved much less than half of the requests.

The Jews constantly argued that the absorptive capacity is an expanding concept, not a constant figure. Furthermore, the very Jewish immigration *increased* economic absorptive capacity. The British disagreed. They restricted the immigration by a political criterion, making sure Jews would not exceed one-third of the total population. Jews attempted to immigrate illegally. An Anglo-American Commission recommended, after World War II, allowing 100,000 survivors of the Holocaust to enter into Palestine. The British refused and transferred the Palestine problem to the UN — leading to the November 29, 1947, partition resolution.

Another area of severe disagreement was the monetary and fiscal policy. The British government did not have a central bank, and the Palestine Currency Board played a technical, inactive role. Fiscal policy, as already noted, was extremely conservative. The Jewish National Institutions, on the other hand, not only spent much on social services but took an active role in the promotion of economic development.

The transition to the state

The existence of an efficient and developed political system during the Yishuv period meant, on the one hand, that there was a foundation on which the bureaucratic apparatus and the political system of the state could build relatively fast. On the other hand, it also meant that many behavioral patterns which had developed during the Yishuv period were moved unchanged to the state.

The creation of the state also meant a sharp move from voluntary organizations based on consensus to a sovereign government with legitimate enforcing power. David Ben Gurion, the first Prime Minister, seems to have been reluctant to allow the many community organizations of the Yishuv period to sustain full power. These types of organizations would have perhaps maximized initiative, but could have also been a threat to the legitimate power of the government. In several extreme cases, when there were calls for negotiation, Ben Gurion refused, using the enforcement power of the government to change things. In the case of Altalena — a ship full of arms brought to Israel by the Irgun — the commanders of the Irgun demanded negotiations, but Ben Gurion preferred to use arms and government decisions. Ben Gurion also disbanded the separate headquarters of the special Commando units known as Palmach — to achieve one army.

Ben Gurion made strenuous attempts to expand the meaning of the transfer from a voluntary community (the Yishuv) and movement (Zionist movement) to a sovereign state. He attempted to disassociate the sovereign power of the state from the tradition of the Yishuv. One result was a very large number of coalition crises (six between 1949 and 1953, only seven between 1953 and 1977). He was successful in so far as military organizations were concerned: both dissident underground groups (Irgun Zvai Leumi and Lehi) decided on self-disbandment and created political parties. Prime Minister Ben Gurion failed to change the political culture. Political parties continued to be a source of employment and suppliers of services.

Ben Gurion was very consistent in his efforts to change the political culture of the Yishuv and to increase the power of the state. He insisted that the sovereignty of the state was complete and indivisible — and was unwilling to give any part of this sovereignty to any other organization, including the Zionist movement or the Histadrut. He therefore attempted to nationalize infrastructure services such as employment, education and health agencies — all of which had been operated by political parties or other voluntary organizations in the Yishuv period. He was successful in the first two, but not in health. Ben Gurion also attempted to depoliticize the civil service. Finally he believed that the voluntary zeal of the pre-state period was right for the time, but that the state apparatus could take care of all these roles that had been fulfilled in the past by voluntary and/or pioneering organizations. He coined the phrase 'from a class to a nation,' and preached for what he termed 'statehood' (*Mamlachtiyut*).

Ben Gurion also wanted to change the voting system from the proportional to a regional system (Yanai, 1982). In a speech in the Israeli Knesset in 1956, he claimed the proportional system educated the nation to become irresponsible, it was a cause of excessive disintegration, of instability and it disallowed the regular citizen to elect his representatives (Ben Gurion, 1959, p. 184). Ben Gurion did receive the assent of his party to the proposed changes. Later, however, the Party functionaries united in their opposition to this change. The proposed law to change the political voting system never reached the Knesset for consideration. A much later attempt at change did reach the Knesset but was quickly buried in a committee.

Israel did not alter its ideological beliefs nor did it move to become a free market economy. When Israel received large reparations from Germany, an economic expert proposed that the funds should be used to erect infrastructure that would allow the market to operate. The government decided this proposal was unrealistic, and used the funds to direct each and every project and firm in the economy. The means of government control are discussed in chapter 5. The conversion of the vision and voluntarism into a sovereign state apparatus and the absorption of hundreds of thousands of new immigrants were both carried out without causing revolutionary structural changes in the sectoral composition. Yet there was a diminution of the role of the private sector in the Israeli economy. The Histadrut sector was given special privileges for many years. The sectoral developments will be discussed in chapter 4. Here, a general narrative of the history during the state period is given as a general background.

The economic development of Israel can be divided into several sub-periods, according to economic situation. From a political economic perspective, the history of Israel can be summarized as follows.

1948-1954: from mass immigration to the forging of the major institutions

The state of Israel was declared on May 14, 1948, in the midst of battles and attempts of self-protection against Arab military attacks. Immediately thereafter, the fledgling state was attacked by its neighboring countries and had to defend itself against invaders. While fighting its war of independence, Israel also encouraged the Ingathering of the Exiles. Between May 1948 and the end of 1949 about 200,000 new immigrants arrived and until the end of 1951, Israeli Jewish population more than doubled and 687,000 immigrants came. Between 1948 and 1965, Israel absorbed 1.2 million immigrants, many of them lacking capital and education. Of these newcomers, 55 per cent came from Asia and Africa (see chapter 3). Many of them were refugees from Arab countries.

The new immigrants had to be housed, fed, taught the language, trained in new skills and employed. Later, the children of these new immigrants were to cause a major change in the structure of the political economy. Unlike the old timers, they were not raised to believe in the collective ideology. The predominant pioneering ideals were replaced by more adaptive individualism.

The provision of housing and employment as well as other services had to be organized in the aftermath of a major war and a current state of siege: all of Israel's neighbors were in a state of cold (and often actual) war against the state. Rapid population growth, mainly as a result of immigration, continued in the early 1950s with large numbers of newcomers arriving without capital or sophisticated education. By 1960 the Jewish population had reached 1.9 million compared with 650,000 on May 14, 1948.

The three dominant characteristics of the period, therefore, were high defense costs, build-up of mass immigration and erection of new institutions. The double burden — of fighting a war and losing civilian production because many adults were in the army on the one hand, and the cost of absorbing many new immigrants on the other hand — strained the economy to its limit. In addition, because of the state of war, all trade with neighboring countries stopped. Further, the oil supply from the pipeline between Mosul (Iraq) and Haifa (Israel) ceased. One result was that the large oil refineries had to be shut down. The state had to take all foreign currency assets from its citizens, issuing in return dollar-linked bonds, and to create and attempt to enforce a program of austerity. This program consisted of rationing all basic necessities — food, raw materials, clothing and later even furniture — as well as foreign currency. In addition, a large program of public investment was deemed essential to absorb the new immigrants — often in new agricultural settlements, and in providing the new immigrants (and many of the old timers) with housing. In addition, the state had to create its own institutions, setting up a civil service, creating a central bank, a national insurance institute and many other administrations. One of these was the office of the state controller, which was instrumental in making the government accountable before the public.

The Israeli political leadership may have not assessed correctly the enormous difficulties in achieving so many objectives simultaneously. It also attempted to construct a large scale military industry, to erect an administrative system, and to create an infrastructure — both physical and institutional. All of these caused many strains. In attempting to achieve so many goals in a very short period of time, it was inevitable that some major mistakes were made, and some economically unjustified enterprises were erected. Yet much was achieved, largely because of the spirit of elation which attended the creation of the Third Commonwealth of Israel.

The Labour political leadership believed in achieving what was called 'socialism in our time.' It certainly would not leave the regulation of the economy to uncertain market forces — nor could it, given the enormity of the tasks it attempted to achieve simultaneously. Yet, many Jewish investors, propelled and excited by the creation of a Jewish state after two thousand years, felt that their efforts to help were not always well received. They perceived the government as expecting them to get into a joint venture with Histadrut enterprises. This feeling persisted despite the enactment in 1950 of a Law for the Encouragement of Capital Investments (and the granting of even more favorable terms in the revised laws of 1955 and 1959). Foreign investments were only trickling to the country. Rightly or wrongly, foreign investors felt the government wanted them to be dependent on it and that it preferred the public and the Histadrut sector.

On March 1949, the government presented its program before the Knesset. It said it would nationalize all natural resources, the water and all services on which the defense of the country was dependent. It also said it would attempt to disperse the population. Based on this program, the government created several state-owned enterprises to exploit the natural resources in the Negev. It also acquired from their private owners both the Potash company and the electricity corporation. The government also established many other state-owned firms. Yet despite its official declarations, the government did not acquire the water company that belonged to the Histadrut, although the state financed the lion's share of the new water projects. The state also created several firms in partnership with the Jewish Agency and the Histadrut (such as the Israeli airline).

Most of the development budget was spent on agriculture and water development projects. In 1952-3, for example, agriculture and water consisted of 56 per cent of the development budget, compared to 11 per cent allocated to manufacturing industry. This budget was financed largely from a US ExIm bank loan and from the proceeds of Israel government bonds, floated in the USA since 1951. Tens of thousands of new immigrants were absorbed in many new agricultural settlements. These settlements were organized as Moshavim, on the basis of the same principles designed by the ideologists in 1921. The new immigrants were brought to the new Moshavim, and received a lot of aid and training. Their political affiliation and legal form of organization were both dictated to them by the central planners. As one example, 10 per cent of the new settlers were considered to belong to the religious political movement. The rest belonged to the Histadrut Moshavim (see chapter 5).

The very high level of public-sector activities caused a demand surplus of the public sector and a heated economy. The demand surplus of the public sector fuelled inflationary pressures and led also to increased imports above essential needs for defense and immigration reasons while the exports did not increase.

By the end of 1951, the fledgling state suffered from severe unemployment. In addition, many still lived in temporary housing. Further, despite a small amount of US grants, Jewish aid and various loans, the foreign exchange shortage was severe. The high level of public-sector activity caused strong inflationary pressures and the price controls did not reduce that inflation — it just caused the black market to flourish. In February 1952, after elections in which the right-wing General Zionists increased their power, the Labor government announced a 'New Economic Policy' (since that time, several 'new' economic policies have been proclaimed). Under this new economic policy, the government promised to cede its inflationary financing: it devalued the currency (in a series of steps) from IL0.36 to IL1.8 to the US dollar. This series of devaluations was one of the few in a long history of Israeli attempts to devalue its currency, to be successful. This was largely because the government was successful in reducing the excess purchasing power of the public. It curbed private credit and relinquished some of the price controls. As a result of these steps, the depressed inflation became overt: the consumer price index rose on the average, for 1952, by 56 per cent (and in 1953, by 28 per cent). In addition, unemployment increased, reaching 11.5 per cent in 1953, and public consumption went down. The government effectively abandoned its policy of mass immigration. Although immigration continued to be free, it was not actively encouraged until the existing immigrants could be absorbed.

The government also promised to reduce the size of the civil service, to make the income tax collection more efficient and to fight capital smuggling and the black market. These items have since become standard declarations in any announcement of a new economic policy. With time, politicians learned to make these declarations but not do anything about the implementation of these principles. The general public got accustomed to hear these promises but to expect little change.

1954-1965: rapid growth and strengthening

Partially as a result of the new economic policies and mainly due to massive investment made possible by the receipt of the equivalent of $850 million in reparations money from the Federal Republic of Germany, the Israeli economy enjoyed a period of a rapid growth. Population — largely as a result of renewed immigration — grew by 4 per cent per annum, the national product rose by 10 per cent per annum while unemployment dwindled to 3.5 per cent. These growth levels were accompanied by an acceleration of private consumption by 9 per cent per annum.

By the mid-1950s, it was clear that lack of land and water constrained the future growth of agriculture. The farmers were able by that time to supply all local demand in almost all foodstuffs. The agricultural rate of growth thus slowed down to 5 to 6 per cent per annum. Beginning in 1955, when Mr Pinhas Sapir became the Minister of Trade and Industry, manufacturing received a special inducement. The government encouraged investment and gave subsidized loans and grants to private investors. It also moved from the build-up of additional agriculturally based Moshavim, to the construction of 'development towns' in the Negev and Galilee. These towns needed a manufacturing base as a source of employment. Mr Sapir personally made a special effort to attract private investors to these towns, giving the investors all sorts of direct and disguised subsidies.

Exports, mainly industrial exports, also accelerated, as did local production that replaced imports. Some of the imports substitutions were costly to the economy, having been based mainly on the banning of competitive imports (and later on very high tariffs). Officially, the government initiated a widespread liberalization of raw materials and industrial imports. Yet import licenses were still needed, and habitually were refused for any consumer goods produced in Israel. Inflation was still higher than abroad, and because of balance-of-payments considerations, the rate of exchange had to be adjusted. The government did not want to devalue, largely because it was reluctant to give those individuals receiving private reparations from Germany large windfall gains. It chose to increase the effective rate of exchange by hiking import taxes and granting export subsidies. As one might expect, there were hundreds of different effective rates of exchange, resulting in many distortions to the price system and to resource allocations.

In July 1956, the Egyptian government announced the nationalization of the company operating the Suez Canal. In October 1956, Britain and France launched an attack on Egypt. Israel, helped by French supplies of military equipment, occupied the Sinai Peninsula and conquered the part of Palestine around Gaza that Egypt had occupied since the 1948-9 war. Under pressure from both the USSR and the USA, Israel evacuated these areas in 1957, and a United Nations Emergency

Force was established in Sinai.

In the period 1960-64, local economic activity was accelerated. GNP grew by 11 per cent per annum at 1966 prices. There was also a rapid rise of consumption and investment. Rapid increase in the means of payments and increasing demand pressures caused rising prices and higher costs of production — thus reducing the competitiveness of Israeli goods abroad. In 1955-9, exports grew by 19 per cent per annum; in 1960-4, by 14 per cent. The rising revenues caused a rapid rise of imports — 12 per cent as opposed to 8 per cent in 1955-9. In 1964, the current deficit in the balance of payments reached what was then an apex — $564 million, or 17.5 per cent of GDP.

In 1962, after the system of relative prices was almost totally distorted because of the existence of so many effective exchange rates, the Israeli pound was devalued by two-thirds, more imports were officially liberalized and export subsidies were eliminated. The change in the effective rate of exchange for exports was only 15 per cent. In addition, the government did not decrease the local demand. The recipients of personal reparations from Germany increased the value of this part of their wealth by 67 per cent. Those who borrowed funds linked to the dollar (mainly on mortgages) demonstrated, protested and pressured. The government gave in and changed the contracts retroactively — eliminating the linkage to the dollar. This was the beginning of a new era, in which the government borrowed by issuing COL (cost of living) linked bonds, but lent this money unlinked, thus giving the receivers of the loans, *ex-post facto*, unintended huge profits from inflation.

This was also a period of an accelerated rise in manufacturing, based on strong pressures and encouragement by Mr Sapir, the Trade and Industry Minister. Mr Sapir created state-owned enterprises that entered in joint venture with private individuals to erect new manufacturing firms. He also subsidized private entrepreneurs and coerced them to erect new plants on their own. In October 1957, a specialized Bank for Industrial Development was established. The government also created export companies for agricultural exports (Agrexco), several trading companies for different regions (West Africa, East Africa, Far East, Turkey, Latin America) or manufacturing branches (for example edible oil, textiles). Most of these firms lost funds and were not very successful.

In 1963, the major development work of building the National Water pipeline from the north to the Negev was finished. The construction and water firms did not have substitute employment — and left to find work in Latin America and Africa, incurring huge losses that were eventually covered by the Israeli taxpayers. In many joint ventures between private entrepreneurs and the government, it was found, in the words of the state controller, that 'the government in attempting to shift risks inherent in development plans to other investors . . . finds itself often carrying the risks and the financial burdens alone' (Israel State Controller, 1969, *Report on Audits of State Corporations*, p. 211).

In 1957, when Moshe Dayan became the Minister of Agriculture, he created the Production and Marketing Boards as a joint body of government and the growers. These boards encompassed all branches of agricultural production. These councils attempted to plan agricultural production, allocated production quotas and subsidies. Since 1959, when the Water Law was enacted, a government water commissioner was granted widespread authority, including the allocation of water quotas. Private farmers lost much of their autonomy. Even those owning the land and the means of production, for example some of the citrus growers, were legally barred from selling their products except to designated packaging houses.

In order to increase the health, welfare and educational levels of the population, the government had to organize services and mobilize finance. With few natural resources, it was realized that economic growth would in part be determined by educational development. This included the provision of literacy courses for many immigrants to teach them Hebrew, but also professional training.

On the social scene — the monolithic cultural dominance of the first decade was generally weakened and the consolidation power of the ideology significantly decreased. Equality became a social mythos, but in actual fact inequalities increased and feelings of deprivation intensified.

By the end of the 1950s, the government had built enough housing facilities to eliminate the need for all the temporary shacks of the mass immigration period. Special efforts were made to eliminate poverty housing enclaves. However, although the standard of living rose for all, the poor felt relatively poorer because inequality widened. The government created a National Insurance Institute and poured in funds to create better housing, schools, health and welfare. Yet the feeling of deprivation among Asian and African Jews intensified. On July 9, 1959, there were riots in a slum inhabited by North African Jews in Haifa (Vadi Salib) that shocked the government and the political establishment.

In May 1962, Mr Sapir called on rich Jews from Latin

America and the heads of the Israeli economy. They created jointly a new holding company, Clal — that was to be a means for Latin American Jewish investment in Israel. Clal is today a very large investment company, the majority of which is owned by Israeli financial institutions, mainly the Histadrut-owned Bank Hapoalim.

The dominant party also faced many internal power struggles. The Secretary General of the Histadrut, Pinhas Lavon, was concerned that the managers of the largest Histadrut enterprise Solel Boneh had become too powerful. In 1958 he partitioned the firm into three different corporations.

In the 1959 elections for the fourth Knesset, the General Zionists reduced their power to eight members of the Knesset only. Mapai enjoyed a great victory. Many began to feel that Mapai was unbeatable, and others attempted to merge all non-Socialist parties. Herut council decided to enter the Histadrut. In reality, by 1959, the seeds of destruction of Mapai had already started to grow. One was the major rift between Ben Gurion and his young Turks and the leaders of the Third Aliyah, resulting from attempts by Ben Gurion to get 'young Turks' as ministers, thus bypassing the old elite of the third Aliyah origin. Another was the after-effects of a major failure and foul play by Israel's intelligence officers in 1954. Lavon was accused of giving the order to Israeli agents in Egypt to cause sabotage aimed at creating tensions between Egypt and the United States. Prime Minister Moshe Sharett appointed a top secret inquiry committee to look into the affair. This committee did not come up with any clear vindication of Lavon, and he was forced to resign as a Minister of Defense.

The young leaders of Mapai demanded greater representation in the government. These leaders had organized themselves within the party since 1957 and developed a list of reforms they wanted to implement. The young leaders achieved a leadership position mainly because of excellence in military service or in civil service. They wanted more say in the political decision making, but avoided confrontation with the old political bosses. Instead, they called for 'a democratic reform.' Ben Gurion as a Prime Minister attempted to choose the national leaders, leaving many of the party leaders in secondary positions. Ben Gurion also tended to rely on his personal authority, and his foreign and defense policy initiatives were not always fully acceptable to other leaders. Golda Meir, then foreign minister, felt Shimon Peres, then Director General of the Defense Ministry, was initiating too many political contacts with France, circumventing her authority. This added another dimension to the tension between her, a major leader of the Third Aliyah group, and Ben Gurion.

In 1959, Ben Gurion added three young ministers and four of the old guard departed. Only three out of nine Mapai ministers in the government headed by Ben Gurion in November 1959 were old-timers. Lavon, in the meantime, created an alternative power base as a Secretary General of the Histadrut. In 1960 he received new information leading him to believe he could be acquitted and demanded that Ben Gurion declare him, Lavon, as not responsible for the 1954 foul play. Ben Gurion refused, but Lavon was able to get a partial acquittal through a government ministerial committee. Lavon also broke a long-cherished tradition by bringing his case for a discussion outside the closed rooms of his party caucus. There was also the accumulated resentment of several leaders against what they saw as Ben Gurion's dictatorial style of leadership. Ben Gurion was known as able to create confrontations and to use crises to get rid of alternative strong leaders. He also attempted to reduce the authority of the political party *vis à vis* the government. All these caused an accumulated resentment, if not hatred. He was seen as too strong and too uncompromising.

In 1961, Lavon was forced to resign as Secretary General of the Histadrut. Ben Gurion resigned from the government. The elections to the fifth Knesset took place earlier than planned — on August 15, 1961. Mapai lost six Knesset seats. The General Zionists merged with the Progressive Party to create the Liberal Party. Ben Gurion resigned again. Levi Leshkol became the Prime Minister.

By 1964, the import surplus had increased, and the reparations paid to the government from Germany ended. (Private individuals continued to receive restitution payments.) The government also faced strong pressures of huge wage hikes in the public sector. In 1964, Mapai agreed to create an alignment with left-wing parties. This meant that any change in the election method had been made impossible. In June 1965, Ben Gurion left his old party to create Rafi. Earlier, Herut decided to join the Histadrut. The Histadrut refused, and Herut created an alliance with the Liberals. As the Liberals were part of the Histadrut the leadership of the Histadrut did not then have to recognize a new entity. In addition, the Histadrut leadership was reluctant to postpone the elections, which would have allowed Rafi time to get organized — so Herut was accepted into the Histadrut. The Mapai party apparatus was recruited to stop Rafi and win the elections for the Histadrut in September 1965. The Alignment got only 58.0 per cent of the vote for the

Histadrut, whilst Rafi held 12 per cent. Mapam preserved its power (14.5 per cent) and Gahal got 15.2 per cent compared to 3.5 per cent the General Zionist alone received in 1959. Given the shock, Mapai machinery made greater efforts to win the elections to the Knesset. The government, having resolved on reduction of expenditures at the end of 1964, agreed to pay 30-40 per cent additional wages in the public sector before the elections. A concentrated attempt to win the election was aided by Minister Sapir.

This was a period of clashes in other parties, too. The sole leadership of Mr Begin in Herut was challenged by Mr Tamir, who was forced to leave. The Liberals also had their share of skirmishes among various leaders. These rivalries were not based on ideological hair splitting as in the past, but on the straight quest for power. The major one was the uninterrupted Diadochim battle within the dominant party that weakened it considerably. A growing perception of the need to modify the political order, or at least to change the major players, led only to a tendency of young people to keep a distance from political careers.

1966-1972: growth between wars

Faced with the rapid rise in consumption, in investment and in import surplus, the government decided to cause a change in the economic structure to accelerate exports but to reduce government investments, increase indirect taxes to reduce demand and to have restrictive monetary policy. The recessionary policy was announced when demand started to be lowered anyway because large development projects were finished. Aggregate real demand was reduced, unemployment reached 12.5 per cent and most of the unemployed were of Asian and African origin. In 1966, GNP grew by only 1.0 per cent. Private consumption grew in 1966 by 0.6 per cent and was reduced in 1967 by 2 per cent. Gross investment was reduced by a third. Exports, however, did not grow in part because the reduction of real demand came without a parallel devaluation.

The recession caused many bankruptcies, including those of financial institutions. Starting in the last quarter of 1967, there were the beginnings of growth. This process was intensified as a result of the Six Days War. After the war, the government rapidly increased its defense consumption. In addition, the quick victory caused optimism and triggered larger immigration.

In May 1967, President Nasser of Egypt asked for withdrawal

of the United Nations Emergency Force in the Sinai and closed the Red Sea to Israeli shipping. This act resulted in major diplomatic efforts to get the large navigating nations to keep their promises for free navigation and intervene. After these efforts failed, Israel started the so called Six Days War. In the period of waiting before the Six Days War, it was decided to create a national unity government in which Herut participated by sending two ministers, thereby becoming legitimatized in the public's eyes.

The period between 1967 and 1972 was one of rapid growth, fuelled by large investments in a rapid expansion of the defense-related industries. The occupied territories were a source of low cost labor and the increased immigration was a cause of rising demand. The import surplus was covered by loans from the US government, and unilateral transfers of world Jewry contributions. In 1967, there was a 17 per cent devaluation and in 1971, an additional 20 per cent. Between 1967 and 1969, inflation went down so much that the COL index went up by only 2 per cent per annum on the average. Investments were 30 per cent of GNP and net taxes were 16 to 17 per cent of the GNP.

The enormity of economic tasks, carried out in a background of serious security problems, meant that many problems were neglected and inequalities persisted. These gave rise to resentments among the second, Israel born, generation of underprivileged immigrants, mainly from North Africa. This had social and political implications in the 1970s and the 1980s. The more the increase in the standard of living, the less citizens felt dependent on the government. Paradoxically, the less dependent citizens were, the more frustrated they became. More and more the regime had a despicable image, and the feeling of deprivation among the poor mounted. In 1971, a new group — black panthers — demonstrated against what they saw as deplorable inequalities. A special Prime Minister Committee on distressed children and youth was created. One consequence of its deliberations was a steep increase in the budget allocated to social services, largely on the basis of new laws instituted at that time. The rise was fuelled by social unrest and demands for equal opportunities by Israelis of Asian and African origin. The result has been a rapid increase in total transfers and subsidies (Table 2.2).

The motivating value of the ideology was reduced and the sense of cynicism grew. The melting pot policy — perceived as intended to erase all differences among Jews of different origins — was officially declared wrong and defunct. Politicians felt compelled to cater to voters of African and Asian origin. This

Table 2.2 Taxes and transfer payments to the public, 1968-1989 (% of GNP, current prices)

	Total transfers and direct subsidies	Public services	Taxes	Net tax burden
1968-72	14.0	17	38.0	24.0
1975-8	24.0	18	48.0	25.0
1979-83	22.0	20	49.0	25.0
1980-4	17.0	18	43.2	21.7
1985-9	15.4	17	45.2	28.4

Source:　Bank of Israel, *Annual Report*, various issues.

was another reason for the increase in social welfare expenditures in the 1970s. New social programs, and the reluctance to allow unemployment to rise, increased the size of civilian public services in the 1970s. In attempting to adjust to external shocks, the government raised taxes and reduced investments. In order to avoid further deterioration of the balance of payments, the currency was constantly devalued, but this only fuelled inflation. One of the effects of high government spending was to reduce growth both immediately and in future years because it limited the resources available to the business sector.

In 1970, prices were arrested by signing a package deal among government, employees and trade unions. From 1971, prices continued to rise and so did wages — fuelled by excess demand. The government was afraid to have another recession and prices rose by 15 per cent on the average in 1971-5.

Between 1968 and 1972, the government embarked on a privatization program: it sold forty-six state-owned enterprises, mostly small ones. More and more economists, trained in the Chicago school tradition in economics, pointed to the many distortions in the Israeli economy and called for use of market forces and unencumbered flow of resources in response to price signals, not government directions. The existing paternalistic economic structure was resented by many, but the defense needs and the imperative of integrating new immigrants to the mainstream of economic life were seen by the bureaucracy as important reasons to regulate and direct the economy, rather than leaving it to the impersonal vagaries of the market.

1973-1989: troubling questions

After Ariel Sharon retired from the army he was instrumental in the unification of the right-wing parties into the Likud. Only a few months later, the Egyptian and Syrian army started the Yom Kippur War. Israel was caught in total surprise, suffered heavy casualties and for the first time hundreds of Israelis were taken as prisoners of war. The final victory did not eradicate the shock caused by the surprise at the beginning. The public could not understand why the army was not readier for battle, nor could it grasp why the intelligence did not warn the army in advance. Many protest movements sprang up. Their pressure led to the resignation, in October 1974, of Prime Minister Golda Meir who was replaced by Yitzhak Rabin.

It was generally recognized that the Labor party led Israel to great achievements but there was also a growing feeling that it had been too long and too uninterruptedly in control and this had led it to be increasingly nonresponsive to public wishes. The public image of Labor was also tarnished by several cases of corruption. It was hamstrung by domineering leaders that, as the public saw it, did not prevent the surprise of the Yom Kippur War. It was widely felt that the party was crippling the country and that a major change was needed. Many of the young generation resented the central control and the strong political directions of all walks of life. They were affluent, and thus less dependent on the government in their daily affairs. Unlike their parents, who were brought up in the absolutionist regime of Russia, most of the young looked to the United States as a symbol of freedom, liberty and mainly economic efficiency. They wanted to make their own decisions and be responsible for their own individual destiny. For them, any institution not compatible with a free market approach was wrong. This included also ideas entrenched in Israel such as lifetime employment or business-government cooperation, to be advocated later in the United States as the major reason for the Japanese economic miracle. Disillusioned Labor supporters defected to a new party — the Democratic Movement for Change. The emergence of this new party made it easier to defect from Labor. The Democratic Movement for Change hoped to get a large enough number of votes so that no large party would be able to create a government without this bloc.

On December 17, 1976, a government ceremony to celebrate the arrival of the first new F-15 fighter planes was said by religious parties to cause participants to violate the Sabbath by returning home after it had begun. This incident resulted in a parliamentary proposal for a vote of no confidence in the government and Prime Minister Rabin decided to resign, thus initiating an earlier than scheduled general election. In the meantime Rabin headed a caretaker government. In March 1977, it was disclosed that Rabin's wife, contrary to Israel foreign exchange regulations, kept a bank account in Washington, DC. Rabin stepped down and Shimon Peres led the Labor alignment to the elections.

The 1977 elections were the first since 1935 in which a Labor party ceased to be the dominant party. The Likud created the first government it headed in the history of Israel. Minister of Finance Ehrlich attempted a liberalization in the holding of foreign exchange. The government also announced a major effort for selling state-owned enterprises, but sold very little. The Prime Minister was busy mainly in foreign affairs issues and in negotiating the peace treaty with Egypt. He had very little patience for or comprehension of economic issues. So much so, it was said, that when he signed the Camp David Accord and agreed to leave the air bases Israel had built in the Sinai and to build others in the Negev at a cost of billions of dollars, he proudly explained to Jimmy Carter, the United States' President, that Israel would not ask for a grant to finance the additional costs, but would prefer a loan that it would repay. During the period of that government and the next — elected in 1981, and again headed by Mr Begin — there were frequent changes in the post of the Finance Minister. Ehrlich was replaced by Horowitz (1979-80). Then came Aridor (1981-3), followed by Cohen Orgad (1983-4). In June 1982, the Israel Defense Forces invaded Lebanon, starting the most controversial war in the history of Israel. The war, of course, increased defense spending. In most of that period, public expenditure grew, inflation zoomed and private consumption grew, too. This situation was made possible by tripling foreign debt. Before the Likud came to power Israel's gross foreign debt was $11.5 billion. By the end of 1985, it had reached $30.5 billion. The net foreign debt (after deducting assets abroad) was $7.6 billion in 1976 and $20 billion by the end of 1983.

In January 1983, prices at the Tel Aviv stock exchange plummeted. In October 1983, it turned out that the banks, who up to that time artificially raised the prices of their shares in order to compete with COL linked Government Bonds, could not continue that manipulation, facing massive sales by a public anticipating devaluation and moving into foreign currency. The trade in bank shares was stopped. In October 1983, the government, headed by Mr Shamir (Mr Begin resigned in the meantime), announced a devaluation but also transformed the bank shares effectively to government bonds, a decision that had cost the taxpayers more than $8 billion. In 1984, there were new elections.

In the first twenty-five years of its existence, Israel's economy grew in leaps and bounds. In the 1950s, the rate of growth of the economy was 11.1 per cent per annum. In the 1960s, it was 9 per cent. During those years the economy was transformed. In 1950, agriculture provided 11.4 per cent of the national product; in 1984, its share had declined to 4 per cent. The share of industry in GNP changed little but its composition altered dramatically with the creation of new sectors and the modernization of others. The growth of the service sector, from a 36.1 per cent share in 1950 to 45.9 per cent in 1984, was in part the result of large-scale government activity in the economy. In part, this was a result of the continuous inflation, which triggered greater employment in the financial sector. Between 1965 and 1972, the annual rate of growth was 8.7 per cent on the average. Since 1973, and throughout the 1980s, the growth stopped. In 1982, for the first time since 1953, growth was virtually zero; and from 1983 to 1988, the annual average increase was only 3.1 per cent or 1.4 per cent per capita. One possible reason for the arrest of growth was the steep rise in defense expenditure. The increasing share of defense in the national expenditure is thought by many economists to have been at the expense of investment and thus growth. Another was the massive increase of energy costs and the world recession (see Table 2.3). A third possibility is that the structure of the economy needed to be adapted to a changing reality. The growth stopped because weak governments were unable or unwilling to take the necessary bold steps needed. Instead, the government succumbed to strong lobbying by defense interests and the social lobby and followed populist policies. Finally, it is possible that Israel exhausted the growth possibilities inherent in import substitution and export based on natural resources, while it was not ready yet to achieve growth based on new products based on emerging technologies. This possibility is discussed in chapter 7.

The steep decline in the rate of growth came about in parallel to an accelerated accumulation of both foreign and domestic debts and rampant inflation. Increased foreign debt allowed in the short run a constant rise in the level of private consumption per capita. The public sector also grew and its share rose from 20 to 30 per cent of the labor force. The size of the public sector deficit to GDP grew and peaked at 17 per cent. The rising public and private consumption in the face of stagnant output led to a

Table 2.3 Changes in external conditions facing the Israeli economy 1960-1988[a] (% of GNP)

	Import of oil (1)	Total defense expenditure (2)	Defense expenditure less US grants[b] (3)	Oil and defense (4) = (1)+(3)	World trade average annual rate of change (constant prices) (5)
1960-6	1.7	10.0	9.0	10.7	10.0
1968-72	1.6	22.0	21.0	22.6	10.3
1974-8	5.8	29.0	18.0	23.8	4.5
1979-80	10.3	22.0	17.0	27.3	4.0
1981-3	7.9	23.0	16.0	23.9	0.0
1984-5	6.3	24.0	10.0	16.3	6.0
1986-8	3.1	17.4	12.1	15.2	6.8
1989	2.9	14.0	10.3	13.2	7.6

Source: Bank of Israel, Annual Report, various issues.
Notes: [a]Turning points with regards to oil prices and defense (1967, 1973, 1979) have been excluded, so as to focus on 'before' and 'after' picture.
[b]Total grants plus the grant equivalent

reduction in investment, to growing foreign debt and to recurring difficulties in the balance of payments and later — to a serious liquidity crisis. All these led also to a step-wise acceleration of inflation. Since most financial instruments in Israel have been linked, each price hike due to an external shock or to a deliberate government action (such as devaluation) simply translated into a higher inflation plateau. In 1984 and the first half of 1985, inflation rose to a monthly rate of 10 to 25 per cent and Israel was losing its foreign exchange reserves very rapidly. Pressures mounted for a major policy change that would steer the economy in a different direction, change its structure and move it back to a growth path.

At such times as 1975-7 and 1979-80, the government adopted contractional economic policies and, from 1978 to 1985, hyper-inflation made planning and investment extremely difficult if not impossible. After a decade of rampant inflation it was extremely difficult to manage any firm and know whether one made or lost money. This was reflected in very volatile investment levels: gross fixed investment in real terms rose by 13.7 per cent in 1979 and fell by 16.3 per cent in 1980. It increased by 10.3 per cent in 1983, but fell in 1984 by 7.6 per cent and in 1985 by 13.4 per cent.

Increasing government deficits caused high levels of inflation, which were not felt at the beginning as having a high cost because of a widespread indexation. Inflation costs began to be widely felt when its rates zoomed to 10 and 20 per cent a month, so that COL indexing was totally inadequate as a shield. Inflation also increased uncertainty, stimulated rapid growth of the financial sector — to cater to the growing demands of hedging — and shifted attention from production and marketing efficiency to financial transactions. If 1976 was 100, Israel's cost of living index rose by the end of 1980 to 1,215. From 1980 to the end of 1984, a new index (1980 = 100) reached 10,755 (all figures are December as against December of the previous year). The economy increasingly became involved in switching assets rather than their production; the increase in the financial sector of the economy alone may have cost up to 3 to 4 per cent of GNP in the early 1980s. Hyper-inflation also had serious consequences for industrial planning, costing, organization and profitability, and therefore for output and exports. Seven years of triple-digit inflation distorted financial statements. One result was negligible productivity growth (Table 2.4).

After the general elections in 1984, it was clear that neither of the two major blocs could create a government. In September 1984, a national unity government was created, composed of a wide coalition of the major parties from left to right. The new government made two attempts to patch over the difficult economic problems by negotiating a 'package deal' among labor unions, employers and government. Only in June 1985, faced with a growing magnitude of foreign currency outflow and loss of control over the inflationary process, the Prime Minister and the Minister of Finance jointly nominated a professional team of economists, headed by the Director General of the Ministry of Finance, to design a new economic program. The team was given three weeks for its deliberations, and its program was approved by the government in July 1985.

The program relied on a wide national consensus to initiate a fall in public and private consumption in order to halt the accelerating spiral of price rises, devaluations and wage adjustments, bringing inflation from a 25 per cent a month level to a target of virtually nil. To achieve such an ambitious goal, the plan had to be drastic and comprehensive and achieve a major impact on public expectations. The program announced several simultaneous steps: the budget deficit was cut by $1.5 billion (7.5 per cent of GDP). The Israeli shekel was devalued by 20 per cent and export subsidies as well as import duties were reduced. The Cost of Living Adjustment (COLA) agreement was temporarily suspended and all shekel-denominated aggregates were frozen. These included price control, wage freeze, rate of exchange pegging and credit restrictions. Finally, the indexed or dollar-linked instruments remained, but their liquidity was drastically reduced. The US government granted a special aid for the achievement of the program.

Two areas of obvious success of the 1985 program were in arresting inflation and reducing the public sector's deficit. Inflation was reduced from 118 per cent in the six months to August 1985 to 10 per cent in the following half year, 19.6 per cent in the calendar year 1986, 16.1 per cent in 1987, and 16.4 per cent in 1988 and 20.2 per cent in 1989. The public-sector budgetary deficit (and therefore infusion) measured by the excess of local spending over revenues dropped from over 7 per cent of GDP in the first half of 1985, to zero in the second half. In 1986 and 1987, the budget showed surplus, and therefore negative infusion. The rapid and decisive action was very successful, and several factors contributed to the success: US government's aid eased the pressures on the balance of payments front and allowed a foreign exchange freeze. Also helpful were the exchange rate erosion of the dollar compared to other currencies and the wage erosion as well as the reduction in oil prices. The major impact of the plan was achieved by the ability

Table 2.4 Products, inputs of labor and capital and productivity: business sector[a]

	1961-72	1973-9	Average annual rate of growth 1980-5	1986-7	1988-9	1988	1989
Product	9.1	3.9	2.4	5.6	0.8	0.0	1.6
Labor input	3.6	1.1	3.0	0.9	3.8	0.3	1.4
Capital stock-gross	8.7	6.3	3.6	2.4	2.7	3.0	2.4
Labor productivity	5.3	2.8	1.3	2.5	-0.1	-0.3	0.2
Total factor prod.	3.7	1.1	0.5	2.7	0.7	-1.2	-0.1
Unemployment (% of labor force)	5.5[b]	3.5	4.1	5.5	7.6	6.4	8.9

Sources: Bank of Israel, *Annual Report*, 1989, p. 20.
Central Bureau of Statistics, *Statistical Abstract of Israel.*

Notes: [a]Total Factor Productivity has been calculated by assigning weights of 0.68 to labor and 0.32 to capital.
[b]1966-72.

to maintain fiscal restraint. Instead of being an injector of funds into the economy, the public sector drew funds out of the economy at a rapid rate.

Although successful in combatting inflation, attempts to reduce inflation to a one-digit level failed. Further, the new program did not bring about any of the major structural changes that most economists felt were of paramount importance. There were very few changes in the heavy reliance of most economic, social and cultural institutions on the government and no serious dent in the degree of openness of the capital market. In fact, it is often alleged that one reason the Labor Alignment joined the second national unity government, in 1988, was largely to allow the major economic institutions dependent on it — Koor Industries, the Sick Fund, the Kibbutzim and the Moshavim —to be able to get a large influx of funds from the government again. Nor did the new program increase competition or reduce government's intervention. The Bank of Israel's monetary policy made interest rates in real terms extremely high, even exorbitant. The expensive credit caused severe difficulties to many business firms, who got used in the past to cheap credit and did not have enough equity. Many of them could not survive. In addition, the freezing of the rate of exchange allowed rapid price stabilization, but became an obstacle to exports.

By 1989, it became clear that at least some portions of the program assumed a nonexistent market competition and did not take into account the degree of monopolization and cartelization of the Israeli economy. A sharp reduction in the profitability of the business sector led to a recession, in 1989, that was totally unpredicted by the macroeconomists. By the end of 1988, the government decided to devalue the shekel by 5 per cent and devalued by another 8 per cent at the beginning of January 1989. The best way to move onto a sustainable growth path was not yet found, and the Israeli economy, in 1989, was in a deep recession coupled with a relatively high rate of unemployment. In retrospect it is recognized the recession reflects the cumulated effects of eroded profitability since 1985 In 1989, the public sector deficit was 6 per cent of GDP, up from 2 per cent in 1988, and surpluses in the three previous years.

In December 1987, civil disobedience against Israeli rule of the occupied territories intensified, and stone throwing and other violence spread with increasing severity. The many live television reports of riots, tire burnings and stone throwing by small children helped drive a wedge between Israel and her friends, and among Israelis themselves. The *Intifadah* (uprising) has succeeded in gaining the sympathies of an ever-wider circle of people to the Palestinian problem. At the end of July 1988, King Hussein abrogated Jordan's financial, administrative and political support from the West Bank, declaring he was no longer prepared to represent the Palestinians. In November 1988, the PLO declared an independent Palestine. Israel proposed elections for 'true representatives' of the Palestinians, not willing to negotiate with the PLO.

Some structural problems

The ability of the Israeli economy to achieve more flexibility in wages structure, to infuse competition into goods and services markets, and to reduce the size and mainly the scope of the government are still unknown. It certainly depends more on political factors than on economic variables.

One structural problem is the size of the non-tradeable sector. Business activities in any country can be divided into those which are traded and those which are not traded internationally. In Israel until recently, the size of the non-tradeable sector has been growing (Table 2.5).

The proportion of the non-tradeable sector out of total GDP grew from 31 per cent in 1955 to 35 per cent in 1981 and went down to 32.6 per cent in 1985, largely because of a drop in construction activities and grew again to 34.2 per cent in 1988. As can be seen from Table 2.5, the public services have risen, in particular since the mid-1970s. The size of public services has grown even more as a percentage of civilians employed: from 23 per cent in 1972 to 29 per cent in 1979 and 30 per cent since 1985. Indeed, much of the growth in employment in Israel went into non-traded sectors. During the period 1975-84, only 1 out of 7 additional employees was employed by industry. Six went to services — half of them to the public sector. The number of employed persons per 100 residents in services increased from 18.9 in 1974 to 21.1 in mid-1985. In public and community services alone, the growth was from 8.3 in 1974 to 9.4 in mid-1985; since then the growth has been arrested (Table 2.6). In 1989, according to the Bank of Israel, only 26.6 per cent of those employed worked in tradeable branches; 73.4 per cent were in non-tradeable branches.

One reason for increased services was a rise in national expenditure on education (from 6.0 per cent of GNP in 1962-3 to 8.4 per cent in 1981-2 and 8.5 per cent in 1984-5) and on health (from 5.5 per cent in 1962-3 to 7.5 per cent in 1979-80 to 7.1 per cent in 1981-2 and 7.4 per cent in 1984-5). Another

Table 2.5 The share of tradeables, non-tradeables, and semi-tradeables in GDP, employment and capital

	1 Trade-ables[a]	2 Non-trade-ables[b]	(of which public services)[c]	3 Semi-trade-ables[d]
A GDP				
1955	43.0	31.0	22.0	26.0
1960	45.0	31.0	18.0	24.0
1972	42.0	33.0	18.0	24.0
1981	40.0	35.0	21.0	25.0
1985	38.2	40.0	30.5	21.8
1986	39.2	38.3	29.2	22.5
1987	39.1	38.3	29.2	22.6
1988	37.3	39.5	30.2	23.2
1989	36.5	40.0	30.7	23.5
B Civilian employment				
1955	45.0	32.0	21.0	23.0
1960	46.0	34.0	23.0	21.0
1972	40.0	35.0	23.0	25.0
1981	40.0	38.0	28.0	22.0
1985	35.2	36.1	30.0	28.7
1986	35.7	35.1	29.7	29.2
1987	35.7	34.6	28.8	29.7
1988	33.9	35.1	29.0	31.0
1989	32.5	35.8	29.9	31.7
C Non-residential capital				
1960	72.0	21.0	10.0	7.0
1972	69.0	24.0	15.0	7.0
1981	66.0	25.0	19.0	9.0
1985	58.0	34.0	23.0	8.0
1986	58.6	33.4	23.4	8.0
1987	58.2	33.8	23.8	8.0
1988	57.9	34.2	24.2	7.9
1989	57.7	34.6	24.6	7.7

Sources: For 1955, 1981, Ruth Klinov-Malul, 'Israel's Changing Industrial Structure: Years of Growth and Years of Slowdown', Jerusalem, Falk Institute, December 1984, Tables 17-6, 17-7. For 1960, 1972, 1985: Bank of Israel, Report 1985, 1985, p.133. For 1986-1989, Bank of Israel, Annual Report, various issues; CBS Statistical Abstract, 1989.

Notes: [a]Agriculture, manufacturing, transportation and communications. [b]Public services and construction (including water and electricity). [c]Public services are characterized by the nature of the service, not by ownership. They include the administrative services of the government, national institutions, and local authorities; educational, research and scientific services; health services, religious, political and trade-union services. The defense sector is included only in part: in GDP accounts, the value added by the defense ministry is included in public services, and military expenditure on local purchases – under the appropriate business-sector industries. [d]Business and financial services, commerce (including tourism) and personal services.

Table 26 Number of service workers per 100 inhabitants, 1974-85

Services	1974	1984	Jan.-June 1985	1985	1986	1987	1988	1989
Business services:								
Commerce, restaurants and hotels	3.9	4.0	3.9	4.0	4.1	4.4	4.6	4.6
Transport, storage and communication	2.5	2.1	2.1	2.0	2.0	2.1	2.1	2.0
Finance and business services	2.1	3.1	3.1	3.1	3.1	3.0	3.3	3.2
Personal and other services	2.1	2.0	2.2	2.1	2.0	2.0	2.2	2.4
Total business services	10.6	11.2	11.3	11.2	11.2	11.5	12.2	12.2
Public and communal services	8.3	9.5	9.8	9.5	9.4	9.2	9.4	9.4
Total services	18.9	20.7	21.1	20.7	20.6	20.7	21.6	21.6

Sources: CBS, *Monthly Bulletin of Statistics*, Sept. 1985, March 1989.
            CBS, *Statistical Abstract of Israel*, 1989.

Table 2.7 Distribution of employed persons by economic branches from 1972-87: international comparison (%)

Country	Total	Agriculture, hunting, forestry, and fishing						Manufacturing mining, and quarrying						Others					
		1972	1975	1978	1981	1984	1987	1972	1975	1978	1981	1984	1987	1972	1975	1978	1981	1984	1987
Israel	100%	7.97	6.44	6.09	6.00	5.31	5.13	23.72	24.67	23.50	23.25	22.94	23.40	68.31	68.89	70.41	70.75	71.75	71.47
Canada	100%	6.75	6.07	5.75	5.42	5.33	4.88	22.54	21.65	21.19	21.19	19.55	18.62	70.71	72.28	73.06	73.39	75.12	76.50
UK	100%	2.95	2.71	2.72	2.62	2.56	2.37	34.50	32.33	31.13	27.59	24.44	22.43	62.55	64.96	66.15	69.79	73.00	75.20
Japan	100%	14.73	12.66	11.70	9.98	8.88	8.27	27.29	26.08	24.80	25.00	25.03	24.24	57.98	61.26	63.50	65.02	66.09	67.49
Italy	100%	n/a	n/a	15.18	13.18	11.66	10.34	n/a	n/a	27.62	26.80	24.45	23.19	n/a	n/a	57.20	60.02	63.89	66.47
West Germany	100%	7.78	7.35	6.10	5.50	5.54	5.22	38.07	37.29	36.14	34.97	33.22	33.16	54.15	55.36	57.76	59.53	61.24	61.62
France	100%	12.31	10.16	9.06	8.32	7.64	7.00	29.19	28.76	26.87	25.36	24.05	22.27	58.50	61.08	64.07	66.32	68.31	70.73
USA	100%	4.38	4.08	3.70	3.51	3.30	3.02	25.01	23.54	23.57	22.84	20.91	19.35	70.61	72.38	72.73	73.65	75.79	77.63

Source: Compiled from International Labour Office (1982, 1988), Year Book of Labour Statistics. Geneva: ILO.

Table 2.8 Public-sector share in GDP and employment, 1983 (in current prices)

	As % of:	
	GDP	*Employment*
Sweden	21.3	35.2
France	12.9	22.8
Germany	11.7	18.3
Japan	8.7	9.1
Belgium	14.5	23.5
Israel	22.1	29.3

Sources: OECD. Statistical Abstract of Israel, 1983, Manpower Planning Authority.

reason was that the public sector has become an employer of last resort, employing about 30 per cent of civilian employees. A third was, as already noted, increased social welfare and defense costs. All in all, total public expenditures in current prices were 72.8 per cent of GNP in 1980-1984, reaching a high of 73.3 per cent of GNP in 1984. Although this figure was reduced to 71.2 per cent in 1985, 65.5 per cent in 1986, 62.7 per cent in 1987 and 62.8 per cent in 1988 — it was still quite high.

Increasing share of services in the economy is a common phenomenon in the Western world (Table 2.7), but the share of services in Israel is markedly higher than in other countries with a similar level of per capita national income. The over-concentration in services has been explained by Ofer (1967) by the effects of import surplus. The share of the public sector in GDP and in employment in Israel is about the same as in Sweden (Table 2.8).

The large and growing public sector has been protected during economic crises. It has proved extremely difficult to reduce the level of certain public services and virtually impossible to fire civil servants even during recession as in 1966-7 or in 1985 and 1989. Since 1985, the expenditures did go down, but mainly by reducing the purchases of the public sector — for example for defense. There was also a sharp reduction in the real wages paid by the public sector but also a sharp increase in government revenues — from 48.3 per cent of GNP in 1984 to 61.4 per cent in 1986, (and 51.8 per cent in 1987). The government also reduced its budget by decreasing its investment in infrastructure, for example roads. The burden of economic adjustment fell mainly on the business sector. Even in that sector, large firms assumed in the past that the government would have to rescue them if they ran into difficulties, and consequently had little incentive to become more efficient. While part of the business sector made at least some efforts to adjust itself to a new policy of reduced subsidies and less public sector demand for goods — large quasi-public bodies such as the sick funds, the bus cooperatives, Solel Boneh, Zim, and El Al, as well as the kibbutzim and moshavim behaved as if they assumed the government would be forced to bail them out. They did not adjust to the new environment created in 1985. Many of them still rely heavily on government-subsidized funds to rescue them.

Conclusions

This chapter gave a bird's-eye view of the political economy of Israel. It was shown that Israel is unique among immigration countries in that it was able to tap a flow of public capital imports. It is also unique in that the generation of those establishing the state believed in the power of human beings to enforce their will on reality and to mold it to their ideology. Third, the Founding Fathers did not believe in economic laws, nor were they willing to rely on unfettered market forces to bring about economic growth or socially desirable income distribution. They thus attempted to mold a strong political power, that was combined with the lure of ideology, to control the allocation of public funds and to develop a political economy based on ideas of a cooperative community. In the relatively small Yishuv community, the system was possible because of voluntary compliance. In Israel, this meant a steady increase in the scale and scope of government's intervention in the economy.

One result is that Israel has a high import surplus. It also has a high (and growing) service sector, a large defense sector and, partially because of that, a low participation rate in the civilian work force. The combination of these factors makes it extremely difficult to increase civilian exports to a level of economic independence. One condition that would help in achieving such a task is a reduction of the public-sector size to free resources for the business sector. Another is an increase in the rate of participation in the labor force. Most changes called for by economists mean that a major transformation of economic institutions is a prerequisite. The economic woes of Israel are a result of its political problems and institutional structures, much more than economic variables. In the past, growth of product was entwined with that of population.

3 The human resources

Introduction

The size, quality, composition, and morale of the population is a key element in the ability of Israel to achieve its goals. Moreover, the Ingathering of the Exiles has been one of the major *raisons d'être* of the existence of Israel. Free immigration was one of the main political aims of the Zionist movement in its attempt to get the majority of the Jews to Eretz Israel. Population characteristics also explain voting behavior. Finally and most significantly, human capital is of utmost importance in achieving economic growth. The long-term competitive advantage of Israeli firms is largely a function of their ability to exploit unique human capital capabilities.

In this chapter we shall discuss the important trends related to the size and the composition of the population. We shall also look at labor as a factor of production and describe its major characteristics in Israel. Institutional arrangements in the labor market impinge on the efficiency of that market and on the ability to adjust labor conditions to large external shocks. Israel is unique in the sense that it had for a very long time a system of wage indexation. We shall survey these institutional arrangements.

Population and its growth

The Jewish population of Israel and Eretz Israel before it has been characterized by a rapid growth rate. During the period 1919-47, the Jewish population grew by 8.3 per cent per annum. The total population of Palestine during that period grew by 3.8 per cent annually. The Jewish population in Eretz Israel thus grew ten fold from 65,000 to 630,000. The main reason for the growth in the size of the Jewish population was the migration balance. Another variable affecting growth has been the natural increase. The economic impact of population growth is a function not only of the absolute numbers but also of the age composition of the population, its level of education, and its possession of skills.

During the Yishuv period, the rate of natural increase among Moslems accelerated: a very high birth rate, about 50 per 1,000, was combined with a decreasing death rate, reaching about 20 per 1,000. By 1941, the natural increase of the Moslem population was 28 per 1,000 (Halevi and Malul, p. 16). In contrast, the Jewish rate of natural increase was about 20 per 1,000 — high by international standards but low relative to Moslem ones. Seventy two per cent of the population growth among Jews in the period 1919-48 was a result of immigration (Sicron, p. 3). Sicron estimated the total Jewish immigration, from 1919 to May 1948, to be 487,000 and the emigration at 60,000. Non-Jewish population doubled from 583,000, in March 1919, to 1,269,000 in December 1947 (Table 3.1).

By the end of the War of Independence there were two important demographic changes. First, most Arabs left the parts of Eretz Israel that became the State of Israel. Some of them moved to Lebanon, others were in the Gaza Strip — under Egyptian ruling, and the West Bank — conquered by Transjordan. On December 1, 1948, the latter annexed the territories it had conquered in the war against Israel. It also changed its name, on April 26,1949, to the Hashemite Kingdom of Jordan. Refugees were kept in separate camps, aided by UNRWA (United Nations Relief and Work Agency), but were denied the right to be absorbed into the economy. (Jordan did offer Jordanian citizenship to the 400,000 refugees under its control.) Such a denial by their own brothers was designed to continue the state of belligerency. Second, Israel held wide-open gates for Jewish immigration, much of which came from the Arab countries. Israel doubled its population in the first four years of its existence. The rich and healthy, however, were often reluctant to come. Thus, many North African intellectuals or upper-class Jews immigrated to France.

Outside the Arab countries, most of the Jews did not choose to avail themselves of the opportunity to immigrate. In 1939, the Jewish population in Eretz Israel was comprised of 2.8 per cent of the world Jewish population. By the time the state was proclaimed on May 15, 1948, this ratio doubled to 5.7 per cent. This was to a large extent a result of the Holocaust, in which six million Jews lost their lives in gas chambers or other ways. The world Jewish population dwindled, between 1939 and 1948, from sixteen to eleven million. By the end of 1987, Israeli Jews

Table 3.1 Population: selected years, 1919-1948[a]

	Thousands			%			Jews in Israel
	Total	Jews	Non-Jews	Total	Jews	Non-Jews	
1882	600	24			4.0		0.3
1919 (March)	648	65	583	100.0	10.0	90.0	
1922 (October)	752	84	668	100.0	11.2	88.8	1.1
1931 (November)	1,033	174	859	100.0	16.9	83.1	
1939 (December)	1,506	450	1,056	100.0	29.9	70.1	2.8
1947 (December)[b]	1,899	630	1,269	100.0	33.2	66.8	
1948 (May)	–	650	–	–	–	–	5.7

Sources: Nadav Halevi and Ruth Klinov-Malul, *The Economic Development of Israel*, New York, Praeger, 1968, p. 15; various volumes of American Jewish Yearbook.

Notes: [a]Census results for 1922 and 1931; the figures for other years are estimates. [b]Excluding Bedouins, estimated at 67,000 in December, 1944.

Table 3.2 The population, by religion (at end of year)

Year	Total	Jews	Moslems	Christians	Druze and others
1948 Nov. 8[a]	872.7	716.7		156.0	
1948	758.7				
1949	1,173.9	1,013.9	111.5	34.0	14.5
1950	1,370.1	1,203.0	116.1	36.0	15.0
1954	1,717.8	1,526.0	131.8	42.0	18.0
1958	2,031.7	1,810.2	152.8	47.3	21.4
1965	2,598.4	2,299.1	212.4	57.1	29.8
1970	3,022.1	2,582.0	328.6	75.5	35.9
1972[a]	3,225.0	2,752.7	360.7	73.8	37.8
1975	3,493.2	2,959.4	411.4	80.2	42.2
1980	3,921.7	3,282.7	498.3	89.9	50.7
1983[a]	4,118.6	3,412.5	542.2	95.9	68.0
1984	4,119.7	3,471.7	559.7	98.2	70.0
1985	4,266.2	3,517.2	577.6	99.4	72.0
1986	4,331.3	3,561.4	595.0	100.9	74.0
1987	4,406.5	3,612.9	614.5	103.0	76.1
1988	4,476.8	3,659.0	634.6	105.0	78.0
1989	4,559.6	3,717.1			

Source: Statistical Abstract of Israel.
Note: [a]Census year.

consisted of 28 per cent of the world Jewish population. All told, most Jews did not immigrate to Israel: some of them, mainly from the USSR, were not allowed to leave (and later, when many of them could, the majority chose to go the United States). Most of them chose to remain in their countries of inheritance — mainly in the United States and in Western Europe. Those who did immigrate came mainly from Arab countries or other countries where Jews were persecuted.

By the end of 1988, 81.7 per cent of Israel's population of 4,476,800 were Jews, 14.2 per cent Moslems, 2.4 per cent Christians and 1.7 per cent Druze and others (Table 3.2). In addition, Israel controlled 837,700 Arabs in Judea and Samaria and 545,000 in Gaza Strip. The Jewish population has rapidly multiplied because since May 15, 1948, Jewish immigration has increased in leaps and bounds. By November 8, 1948, when the first population census was taken, the Jewish population reached 716,700 compared to less than 650,000 in May 1948. By the end of 1951, the total number of immigrants was more than double the size of the original population. Such an increase had taxed the absorption capacity of the country. New immigrants were put into tent-houses and were employed in public employment such as planting trees along the main highways.

In 1952, faced with enormous absorption difficulties, the government was forced to reduce temporarily the influx of new immigrants. Between 1952 and 1954, Israel accepted 54,000 immigrants — a mere 3 per cent population increase. Some immigrants (and others) chose to emigrate. Thus, from 1948 to 1954, emigration was 60,000. Between 1948 and 1987, Israel received 1,767,400 immigrants.

When Israel was proclaimed as a state, its population consisted of 649,600 Jews and 156,000 non-Jews. By the end of 1987, the natural increase added 1,583,000 Jews and 558,800 non-Jews. The migration balance (immigration less emigration) added 1,403,500 Jews (from a total of 1,767,400 immigrants). The migration balance added to the non-Jewish population only 9,900 out of 30,800 immigrants. Thus, the percentage of the immigration balance out of the total population growth was 47.0 per cent for Jews, 1.7 per cent for non-Jews.

In the more developed countries, the life expectancy is higher, while the gross reproduction rate is relatively low. As a result, the country has relatively more persons of 65 years of age and above. The opposite is true in the less developed countries. Thus, life expectancy at birth, in 1986, was 77 in most developed market economies (78 in Australia) but only 41 in Sierra Leone, 42 in Guinea, 44 in Niger, and 45 in Chad. Israel's life expectancy at birth was 75, compared to 61 in Egypt and 64 in Jordan.

Immigration and emigration

Israel is a country of immigrants, who came to it from more than a hundred countries. It is also a country to which the majority of European and US Jews preferred not to come.

Immigration to Israel, and to Eretz Israel before, has been a result of strong 'pulls' — ideological passion, religious vision and Zionist zeal as well as the government's policy toward immigration on the one hand and 'push' factors, those that make the country of inheritance unattractive, on the other hand. A third factor is the available alternatives. Thus, the more difficult it was for East European Jews to emigrate to the United States, the more attractive Eretz Israel became. Jews came to Israel in several waves. Most of these waves were the result of 'push' factors. The fourth wave of Aliyah came largely from Poland because a general boycott was declared against Jewish business but also because the Johnson-Lodge Immigration Act of 1924 limited access to the United States.

Immigration is also affected by the policy of the government in the immigration country. The Turks opposed immigration but were not very effective in stopping it. The British at first did not intervene, but as early as in 1920, they tried to limit immigration to what they believed was the economic absorptive capacity of the country. Certificates for immigration were given only to persons with independent means or to those whose employment prospects and maintenance were guaranteed by the World Zionist Organization. Since most certificates were issued to the World Zionist Executive, this organization had a great power of discretion in choosing the immigrants. These were chosen by the political parties, and certificates were allocated among parties according to their political power. Israel, enacting the unique Law of the Return, opened its door to new immigrants — and subsidized their travel and absorption costs.

By the nature of things, not all immigrants were able to find new roots in the new country. There are different estimates of emigration — it is generally estimated to be around 12 to 15 per cent of the immigrants. Those leaving Israel are generally scorned, termed by then Prime Minister Rabin as the 'fallen or the weaklings.' Many emigrants were ashamed to admit they were leaving. Later, those who were able to reach prominence in another country gained prestige in Israel, too. Because people do not announce publicly their intention to leave, statistics on the size of emigration are obviously less reliable than those of immigration. The Israeli Central Bureau of Statistics estimates emigration by the number of residents who left the country and did not come back within twelve months less residents returning after being away for more than a year. In the second half of the 1980s, the immigration balance has become negative. That is, more people emigrated than those immigrating. This balance was changed in 1989, as a result of a wave of immigrants from the USSR.

Each new wave of immigration found that the older immigrants had become 'established.' Often, new immigrants envied the 'old timers.' They reached a status of 'old timers' when even newer immigrants came. Each group of newcomers alleviates the status of the one arriving just before it and reduces its deprivation, at least in relative terms.

In 1882, there were 24,000 Jews in Eretz Israel (0.32 per cent of the world's Jews). They were concentrated mainly in the four holy cities — Jerusalem, Hebron, Tiberias, and Safed. A portion of the Jewish community in Eretz Israel, largely those that were descendants of the Jews that had been exiled from Spain at the end of the 15th century, were mainly traders and money changers. Others, mostly new immigrants and their offspring from European countries, spent all their time in religious learning and prayers. They were sustained by money contributions collected in Jewish communities in the Diaspora and distributed among the Jews in Eretz Israel, giving priority to religious dignitaries. The first wave of immigration brought 20,000 to 30,000 Jews. The second — another 35,000 to 40,000 (Table 3.3). By 1914, there were about 85,000 Jews in Eretz Israel. The number declined to 56,000 during World War I and reached 65,000 in March 1919. By that date, Jews were 10 per cent of the total population.

In terms of impact on the future structure of the country, the first waves of settlers had everlasting importance. They were poor in agricultural skills, had little funds, but were strongly ideologically indoctrinated. They were all relatively educated, but also totally unprepared for the difficult conditions of a barren wasteland. The early beginning was rescued from failure by the aid injected by Baron Edmond de Rothschild (see chapter 2). This immigration influx was also part of a much larger one. The first three Aliyah waves consisted of less than 100,000 persons — compared with three million Jews who left Eastern Europe between 1881 and 1914.

After the assassination of the Czar Alexander II, there started a wave of pogroms (riots against Jews) in Russia. These, combined with social and national tension in conjunction with the strong nationalistic movements of the time in Eastern Europe, caused a wave of Jewish emigration from Russia, Poland and Romania, mainly to the United States and to Western Europe. A small minority of these persons went to Palestine, motivated by a strong ideological desire to rebuild Israel on the basis of agricultural settlements. Indeed, the Zionist movement started partially as a result of the Russian pogroms, partly because of increasing secularization among Jews and a belief that the only way to solve 'the Jewish problem' was for the Jews to have their own state. The new movement believed Jews should create their own homeland in the ancient land of their ancestors.

The second and third Aliyah comers were those to become the leaders of modern Israel. The second Aliyah (1904-14) was largely a result of the unsuccessful 1905 revolution in Russia (but about 2,000 came from Yemen and a few thousands from Romania). The new settlers were undaunted by reports of

Table 3.3 Immigrants and potential immigrants, 1882–1987 (thousands)

Period of immigration	Total	Asia	Africa	Europe	America and Oceania	Not known	Asia Africa % of total	Europe America % of total
1882–1903	20–30							
1904–14	35–40							
1919–23	35,183	1,181	230	27,872	678		10.4	89.6
1924–31	81,613	9,182	621	66,917	2,241		12.4	87.6
1932–8	197,235	16,272	1,212	171,173	4,589		9.0	91.0
1939–45	81,808	13,116	1,072	62,968	108		18.4	81.6
1946–5/1948	56,467	1,144	906	48,451	138		4.0	96.0
1948–87	1,791,415	355,611	426,016	818,599	165,857	25,332	44.3	55.7
1948–51	686,739	237,352	93,951	326,786	5,140	23,510	49.9	50.1
1952–4	54,065	13,238	27,897	9,748	2,971	211	76.4	23.6
1955–7	164,936	8,801	103,846	48,616	3,632	41	68.3	31.7
1958–60	75,487	13,247	13,921	44,595	3,625	99	36.0	64.0
1961–4	228,046	19,525	115,876	77,537	14,841	267	59.4	40.6
1965–8	81,337	15,018	25,394	31,638	9,274	13	49.7	50.3
1969–71	116,484	19,700	12,065	50,558	33,891	270	27.3	72.7
1972–4	142,755	6,347	6,821	102,763	26,775	49	9.2	90.8
1975–9	124,827	11,793	6,029	77,167	29,293	545	14.3	85.7
1980–4	83,637	6,912	15,711	35,508	25,230	276	27.1	72.9
1985	10,642	607	2,318	3,964	3,739	14	27.5	72.5
1986	9,505	1,183	982	3,675	3,634	31	22.9	77.1
1987	12,965	1,888	1,205	6,044	3,812	16	23.9	76.1
1988	13,034	1,700	1,334	6,012	3,969	19	23.3	76.7

Source: Statistical Abstract of Israel, 1989, p. 166.

difficult life in Eretz Israel. They came to create a new, socially just and economically equal society. To achieve this goal, they created political organizations that had an enduring impact on the political and economic structure of the country (see chapter 4).

They were all young, mostly single, innovative and idealistic. They developed new modes of organization — the kibbutz and the moshav. These zealous idealists were later (after 1919) joined by more ideologically oriented young socialists — this time having the experience of the Russian revolution. Based on what they learned in Russia, these newcomers (with second Aliyah leaders) developed the Histadrut (General Federation of Labor) and became a powerful political and economic organization.

The fourth Aliyah was very much different from the first three. It was mainly composed of middle-class families with independent means, not penniless young singles. Eighty-two thousand Jews came because conditions in Poland worsened and the United States restricted the inflow of immigrants. These new immigrants had more means, bought real estate mainly in the cities, and started small factories or shops. Twenty-three thousand of these immigrants left in 1926-7, when a severe recession hit. In 1927, emigration exceeded immigration.

The rise of Hitler was the major reason for the fifth Aliyah and influx of Jews from Germany and Central Europe. These Jews were highly educated, and started many new economic activities including the opening of a fledgling stock exchange in Tel Aviv. This wave brought with it many bankers and professionals. Unlike previous immigration waves, the fifth Aliyah consisted of more than 50 per cent of total Jewish immigration in that period.

Between 1919 and 1948, the number of the Jews rose ten fold and their proportion of the population — 10 per cent in 1919 — became about a third. By 1939, the Jews comprised 30 per cent of Palestine's population (Table 3.1). The economic development of the area also drew an influx of more Arabs (who could immigrate freely into the country), and natural increase caused that part of the population to grow steadily. All in all, the number of non-Jews in the population more than doubled between 1919 and 1948.

Arabs reacted violently to the increase of Jewish populations; Jewish communities were attacked in the 1920s and 1930s. There were demonstrations, strikes and political appeals. Since the 1930s, the British have been responsive to Arab resentment fed by economic difficulties and severely restricted Jewish immigration. In 1930, the British allowed only 1,800 new certificates.

Since 1934, any illegal Jewish immigrants — to the extent they could be determined — were deducted from the quota of certificates. In 1939, a new British White Paper limited Jewish immigration to 75,000 for the next five years. The objective of that quota was to ensure that Jews would not be more than a third of the total population.

After World War II, tens of thousands of desperate remnants of the Nazi Holocaust attempted to reach the shores of the promised 'National Home.' Many of them wandered in coffin boats that were prohibited from discharging their human cargo. Most illegal immigrants were intercepted by the British Navy. Fifty-six thousand of them were imprisoned in Cyprus, to be released only after the State of Israel was born.

The Jewish National Institutions attempted to help new immigrants to arrive and to be absorbed both socially and economically. The cry for free immigration was heard in dozens of demonstrations. The feeling that had people cared, the calamity of the Jews in Europe might have been avoidable made the anguish almost unbearable. In April 1944, a report of the British Labour Party National Executive Committee read in part:

> There is surely neither hope nor meaning in a Jewish National Home unless we are prepared to let the Jews, if they wish, enter this tiny land in such numbers as to become a majority. There was a strong case for this before the war, and there is an irresistible case for it now, after the unspeakable atrocities of the cold-blooded, calculated German-Nazi plans to kill the Jews of Europe . . . Let the Arabs be encouraged to move out as the Jews move in. Let them be compensated handsomely for their land, and their settlement elsewhere be carefully organized and generously financed. (quoted by Weizmann, 1966, p. 436)

When Labour came to power, however, it further restricted Jewish immigration. It is, therefore, not surprising that the first order enacted by the provisional government of Israel abolished the British restrictions on immigration and that the Declaration of Independence stated that the 'State of Israel is open to Jewish immigration and the Ingathering of Exiles.' The State also enacted the 1950 Law of the Return, inviting any Jew (except one fleeing criminal prosecution) to immigrate to Israel with practically no restrictions. Since then there have been many political skirmishes between the ultra-religious parties, who would like to assume that the word Jew refers only to those accepted by the *Halakha* or the ultra-Orthodox interpretation of

Jewish religious laws, and those who believe the word Jew should be interpreted more broadly. Notwithstanding this long and never resolved debate, the law allows Jews to come back to the country of their ancestors.

The effect of immigration balance on population growth has changed with time. Immediately after the state was proclaimed, it absorbed masses of Jews, mainly from Arab countries (Yemen, Morocco, Egypt, and Iraq). Once all the Jews left these countries the number of immigrants dwindled. The percentage of the immigration balance out of total sources of growth of the Jewish population was 68.9 for the period 1948-60; 45.0 per cent for 1961-71; 25.1 per cent in 1972-82; and 6.8 per cent for the period 1983-7 (17.0 per cent in 1983, 12.8 per cent in 1984, 5.7 per cent in 1987, and a negative balance in 1985, 1986 and 1988). Since the natural increase among non-Jews is much higher than that among Jews, the geometric mean of population growth for the non-Jewish population was double that of the Jewish one (3 per cent compared to 1.5 per cent per annum). During the period 1919-47, the Jewish population grew by 8.3 per cent per annum. The total population of Palestine during that period grew by 3.8 per cent annually. During the period 1948-87, both the Jewish and total populations grew by a geometric mean of 4.4 per cent per annum — non-Jews grew by 4.2 per cent per annum.

In the 1950s, Israel was clearly divided between 'the first' and the 'second' Israel. The first included the old timers in the cities, towns, kibbutzim and moshavim. The second — the new immigrants. The latter were brought into their places of dwelling by administrative fiat. They went through a double negative selection: first, the well-to-do and the educated (in particular those coming from North Africa) preferred not to emigrate to Israel. Second, those that did emigrate and could afford it or had some desirable skills preferred to get settled on their own and refused to settle wherever they were sent. The remaining anonymous crowd was 'allocated' among political parties for integration in proportion to the existing strengths of the parties. Each one of the parties attempted to adopt some ethnic group leaders. The party served as a conduit for transferring government aid. The immigrants were dependent on them — for work, housing and almost anything they needed in daily life. The new immigrants had little interest in ideology and political platforms. They became faithful voters for the party whose representatives ensured them work, food, clothing and housing. The system also made the new immigrants feel deprived. Later this feeling of deprivation was a major reason for a majority of the immigrants of Asian and African origin to vote for the Likud.

The great volume of immigration increased also the social diversity and widened the economic and social gap. Some of the new immigrants felt they were redeemed, and some even saw Ben Gurion as the Messiah. Most of the Israeli old timers' elite did not believe in the ability of the individual to decide on his/her own destiny and to find out what was good for them. They looked at the new immigrants as irresponsible and ungrateful children. They treated the new immigrants with forgiving paternalism since they considered them 'human dust' that has to be converted into a 'producing nation' (Ben Gurion, 1951). They attempted to eliminate any reference or identification with their old culture and the traditions from the hearts of the children of the new immigrants. This was done despite warnings issued by experts that the nation would be divided into two camps, one with a superiority and the other with an inferiority complex. In the eyes of the young generation, the governing party became a symbol of stupefaction, dullness of feelings and of insensitivity to their social status and cultural heritage. The new immigrants suffered also from multiple shock of a new environment, new culture and new institutions. The old timers did not attempt to adapt their institutions to the new immigrants' needs. For example, new immigrants were made members of moshavim without any appreciation of the ideological contents of the moshav. The government subsidized certain foods, including a bread it called 'uniform bread,' believing it could make all immigrants converge into the same taste.

Since 1981, immigration has trickled down to no more than 20,000 per annum. In 1989, it increased to 27,000. In the meantime, the children of the new immigrants (and the grandchildren of the old timers) have become adults. For them, the existence of the State was taken for granted and was not necessarily a source of exaltation. By December 31, 1987, Israeli-born Jews were 62.4 per cent of the total compared to 35.4 per cent in November 1948.

One major objective of the Zionist movement — that of creating a new Jewish nation by amalgamating the different segments of the Jews together — was thus not fully achieved. First, most Jews chose to remain in the Diaspora rather than moving to the newly created Jewish state. Many of them, because of strong ties to their brethren, felt they had to help Israeli Jews and contributed large amounts of money to the different welfare organizations, mainly through the United Jewish Appeal. However, they never even considered taking their accumulated wealth to Israel and certainly did not entertain the idea of settling there. The ideal of creating a Jewish state to all Jews remained the reason for the Law of the Return, but most have chosen not to return. Zionism turned out to mean only contribution to UJA and perhaps a preoccupation with debates on Israeli politics, but certainly only very few did immigrate to Israel, and many of those have gone back.

Jews and non-Jews

Non-Jews in Israel enjoy, of course, equal rights with the Jews. Yet, Israel was designed to become a Jewish state: one consideration in attempting to draw the proposed borders between the Jewish and Arab states that were to be established in the area of Eretz Israel west of the Jordan River was that of making one country a majority of Jews; the other, of Arabs. In 1947, non-Jews were 67 per cent of the population of all of Eretz Israel and 55 per cent in the areas that subsequently became Israel. By the end of 1949, the proportion in what was now Israel had fallen to a mere 14 per cent. This number was approximately 20 per cent of the previous Arab population in the territory defined by the 1949 armistice agreement. This had been a result, first, of a mass exodus of Arabs from the area during the War of Independence — most of them hoping the war would soon be over. This exodus was the beginning of the Arab refugee problem since the Arab states refused to settle their brethren from Palestine, even though 800,000 Jews from Arab countries were fully absorbed into the Israeli economy. The refugees concentrated in the Gaza Strip, under Egyptian rule, in the West Bank, annexed by Jordan, in Lebanon and in Syria. To some extent, this was also the result of the increased Jewish immigration. By 1951, the proportion of Jews had reached 89 per cent. Most Arabs concentrated in Galilee in the north and in the so called little triangle near the border with the West Bank.

The reduction in immigration and the much higher reproduction rates of the non-Jews in Israel reduced the proportion of Jews by the end of 1986 to 82.2 per cent (in 1986, birth rates per 1,000 population were 21.2 per cent for Jews, 33 per cent for Arabs. In 1972, the differences were even bigger, 55 per cent for Moslems and 23.9 for Jews). At that date 13.8 per cent of the population were Moslems, 2.3 per cent Christians, and 1.7 per cent Druze and others. The predominantly Palestinian populations of the West Bank and Gaza Strip, in 1967, numbered 586,000 and 381,000 respectively. By the end of 1987, these figures reached 860,000 and 564,100. Given the high rate of growth resulting from natural increase, if all these Arabs were added to the population of Israel there would be very little chance of maintaining a Jewish majority in Israel without a material increase in the rate of Jewish immigration. This problem is very much in the background of many discussions related to the future of the territories. The Judea and Samaria and Gaza Strip area populations became increasingly irritated by their being subjected to military rule. An uprising against Israel's occupation (Intifada) started in 1987, and it continued for many months, with the hope of forcing Israel to forfeit that land.

Yet, until the 1967 war, Palestinian Arabs residing in the West Bank and in Gaza never sought to establish their own national identity. Paradoxically, the demand for an independent Palestinian state came only after the 1967 war. The international climate, affected by petroleum politics and Third World hostility, sees Israel as a continual transgressor of international law. The United Nations, on November 10, 1975, even condemned Zionism 'as a form of racism and racial discrimination.' Yet it is an undeniable fact that no quest for an independent Palestinian state was documented before 1967. Until then, the PLO stand was the total denial of the right of Israel to exist, and insistence on the right of the Palestinians to return to Israel (see also chapter 6). It is extremely difficult to foresee whether Israel will succumb to pressures and change its posture on the question of negotiations with the PLO. Certainly, Israel is more and more sharply divided on this question.

As to the Israeli Arabs, they were promised full equality, but suffered from an identity crisis. They voted to the Israeli Knesset, enjoyed rapid modernization, high level of economic growth, great improvements in the methods of cultivation, irrigation, expanded network of roads and much better schooling. They did not build their own manufacturing industries, but were employed in Jewish factories. At the same time, the official equality was mingled with suspicion of the Arabs and ignorance of their problems. The Arabs did not find it easy to be loyal to a country fighting against many of their relatives. Their votes to the Knesset reflect the problem of their collective identity: until the sixth Knesset elections in 1965, the ruling party received more than 50 per cent of the Arab votes. By 1977, it received 27 per cent and more than 50 per cent were cast for the communist party. In 1981, the Arabs may have felt they could cause Labor to regain power. The Communists' share in Arab votes dropped for the first time since 1961, in both per cent and absolute terms, reaching 36 per cent. Arab votes to the Labor party jumped from 27 per cent in 1977, to 36 per cent in 1981.

The Israeli Arabs increased their standard of living and also their level of education. The number of Arab elementary schools grew from 45 in 1948-9 to 306 in 1978-9. In 1948-9, there was one Arab high school; in 1978-79, 90. In addition there are 43 junior high schools, 13 vocational high schools, 2 agricultural high schools and 2 teachers' colleges. Arabs also enjoy a full measure of civil liberties. Yet, Arabs feel discriminated against. In March 1976, the Communist Party organized an Arab general strike to protest against land expropriation. This 'Land Day' has been repeated; and sometimes the discontent has led to violence.

Ethnic origins and problems of integration

For many reasons, for example political behavior or social standing, an important criterion in demographic studies is ethnicity. The Jewish population is often divided by the country of origin or the country of origin of the father. It is generally believed that the important distinction is between those whose origin is in Europe or the United States and those coming from Asian and African countries. The first are generally referred to as Ashkenazim; the latter, as Sephardim. The ethnic distinction had its beginning in the Middle Ages. The original Sephardim actually came from Spain (and spoke Ladino). They also included communities such as Kurds, Yemenites and Magrabites (from Morocco) as well as Jews from Haleb (Syria). The word Ashkenazim refers to Jews who came from Germany. With time, the distinction received a meaning different from the original one — and is based, as already explained, on the country of origin and the father's country of origin. (For obvious reasons, the majority of the Israelis are Israeli born, and the per cent of Israeli born out of total population is increasing every year. This is one reason for using also father's place of birth.)

To be sure, there are many differences within the two groups, and the compression of ethnic differences into only two groups is somewhat misleading. Russian-born and German-born Jews are at least as different as Moroccan- and Iraqi-born Jews and the differences among them are greater than between those born in Bulgaria and Turkey. Some variables affecting these differences were the motivation to emigrate, Jewish orientation and identity, cultural traditions, social background, and the degree of cohesiveness. In some cases, whole communities, including the leaders, emigrated to Israel. In others, only part of the family arrived. Yet the distinction is common and sometimes helpful.

Table 3.4 Fertility rates, by religion and continent of birth

Mother's age	1988	1987	1986	1985	1980	1975	1970	1965	1960	1955
Total population										
General fertility rate	94.3	95.1	97.5	99.6	102.6	112.5	115.3	109.2	111.4	117.6
Up to 19	21.1	21.2	21.9	25.4	31.3	40.5	40.3	37.3	46.6	62.1
20-24	150.4	151.5	157.0	163.2	174.7	194.8	203.5	208.6	229.5	233.2
25-9	203.2	201.1	201.6	200.9	194.3	204.9	226.9	239.0	230.3	223.4
30-34	145.8	143.8	145.4	144.1	137.5	150.3	170.4	168.1	154.0	152.3
35-9	74.5	74.0	73.0	71.4	71.8	80.8	891.8	84.9	77.5	85.3
40-44	16.5	17.5	17.2	16.9	15.8	19.6	24.3	23.3	26.3	23.8
45-9	1.4	1.5	1.4	1.4	2.4	3.7	5.6	5.9	6.7	
Total fertility	3.06	3.05	3.09	3.12	3.13	3.47	3.80	3.83	3.85	3.93
Jews, total										
General fertility rate	84.2	85.9	89.1	91.1	92.3	98.7	99.5	94.5	96.6	105.3
Up to 19	12.9	13.5	15.0	17.7	22.8	31.2	29.3	31.3	38.8	53.9
20-24	127.5	131.2	137.7	145.0	156.3	175.0	184.5	192.2	209.1	216.7
25-9	192.5	190.8	192.6	191.8	181.5	187.5	205.7	217.1	210.0	206.4
30-34	138.0	136.3	138.9	137.3	127.0	129.0	146.3	144.6	133.9	136.7
35-9	69.3	69.0	68.0	35.7	60.8	62.8	73.3	67.5	63.3	74.2
40-44	13.8	14.0	13.0	12.3	10.5	12.6	16.0	16.0	19.3	19.8
45-9	0.9	0.9	1.1	0.8	0.6	1.0	1.7	3.3	3.7	4.5
Total fertility	2.77	2.78	2.83	2.85	2.80	3.00	3.28	3.36	3.39	3.56

Mother's continent of birth

Israel

General fertility rate	93.8	95.2	98.8	101.3	103.0	106.8	95.1	83.0	92.8	92.3
Up to 19	10.8	11.1	12.1	14.5	18.4	25.7	23.7	14.8	16.2	19.9
20-24	125.7	128.4	134.0	140.6	151.4	167.3	162.8	152.2	156.1	149.1
25-9	194.9	191.8	193.6	194.1	183.5	187.2	194.6	194.0	188.6	180.4
30-34	140.9	139.0	141.7	139.4	132.9	127.9	139.2	130.3	113.0	119.6
35-9	73.7	76.5	77.2	74.0	65.5	62.4	75.1	58.1	53.2	70.3
40-44	13.5	14.0	13.4	14.3	10.9	11.2	14.4	13.8	14.3	17.1
45-9	0.7	0.6	0.7	0.6	0.6	1.0	0.7	2.3	5.1	2.3
Total fertility	2.80	2.81	2.86	2.89	2.82	2.91	3.05	2.83	2.73	2.79

Asia-Africa

General fertility rate	66.9	70.4	75.9	76.5	81.5	101.6	124.7	137.6	151.8	173.1
Up to 19	32.2	37.1	47.9	51.3	44.4	47.6	49.6	61.0	69.5	89.3
20-24	152.3	163.7	177.7	177.6	183.4	202.1	223.5	234.4	260.0	289.9
25-9	196.6	198.1	200.2	190.7	184.0	197.4	222.6	245.8	254.0	276.8
30-34	140.6	139.7	145.5	138.8	129.7	140.3	166.1	183.5	196.9	216.7
35-9	72.5	70.5	72.1	69.8	64.0	74.0	91.3	102.8	120.5	140.9
40-44	16.0	15.5	14.7	12.9	12.2	17.5	25.7	33.2	46.3	50.2
45-9	0.9	1.1	1.6	1.2	0.8	1.9	4.4	8.7	11.9	15.8
Total fertility	3.06	3.13	3.30	3.21	3.09	3.40	3.92	4.35	4.79	5.40

Mother's age	1988	1987	1986	1985	1980	1975	1970	1965	1960	1955
					Jews, Europe-America					
General fertility rate	65.9	65.8	69.6	74.6	75.9	77.2	71.4	52.5	46.6	60.7
Up to 19	33.1	34.0	35.2	38.7	53.6	58.3	32.7	33.3	19.6	43.4
20-24	130.7	138.9	135.1	150.3	159.9	166.3	179.6	172.0	183.6	168.1
25-9	174.7	178.1	176.1	180.7	168.9	174.9	191.3	180.8	156.9	153.1
30-34	122.7	121.1	122.6	127.2	111.5	111.1	111.6	92.3	78.4	89.5
34-9	53.0	52.0	50.9	52.0	50.7	42.7	44.8	33.1	30.6	42.6
40-44	11.4	12.1	9.8	8.7	6.9	6.8	6.6	5.5	6.6	8.4
45-9	0.9	0.9	0.6	0.4	0.4	0.2	0.3	0.5	0.4	0.8
Total fertility	2.63	2.69	2.65	2.79	2.76	2.80	2.83	2.59	2.38	2.53
					Moslems					
General fertility rate	152.0	149.0	148.3	155.5	173.3	221.4	257.1	283.8	277.9	250.1
Up to 19	53.8	51.5	49.2	57.8	67.5	91.8	118.5	113.8	118.9	119.6
20-24	238.3	228.9	232.1	241.3	270.4	334.0	379.3	383.9	388.6	375.8
25-9	261.5	257.5	257.3	268.7	292.3	368.1	409.9	431.3	440.7	392.0
30-34	204.8	206.6	201.4	209.1	244.9	320.5	359.2	406.9	389.1	359.5
35-9	129.6	127.2	129.4	136.3	162.8	225.8	269.2	297.8	304.2	237.9
40-44	42.6	48.2	51.1	52.2	60.7	90.0	121.7	154.9	147.2	107.8
45-9	6.0	5.8	5.9	7.1	8.8	20.6	37.1	55.8	58.1	41.1
Total fertility	4.68	4.63	4.63	4.86	5.54	7.25	8.47	9.22	9.23	8.17

Source: Statistical Abstract of Israel, 1988, p. 121.

Of the 14.5 million Jews of the world, only 15 per cent are Sephardim but two-thirds of these live in Israel. In Israel, Sephardim make 55 per cent of the Jewish population. Asian- and African-born (or children of those persons) are becoming the majority of Israeli voters, while the percentage of Israelis who are Ashkenazi has been shrinking.

The Ashkenazim group are often better educated and also have higher incomes, reflecting to some extent their earlier arrival in Israel. The two groups are also different in their reproduction rates, but this difference has been reduced over time. In 1969 the gross reproduction rates of Jewish mothers born in Asia or Africa was 2.04 compared to 1.32 for Jewish mothers of European or American origin. In 1980, this rate dropped for the first group to 1.47 and increased slightly for the second to 1.34. Still, these two groups are different in their age structure. The total fertility rate for all mothers in 1988 was 3.06, down from 3.93 for 1955-9. Among Jews the rate was 2.77, down from 3.56 in 1955-9. Among mothers born in Asia and Africa the rate was 3.06 compared to 5.40 in 1955-9 and 6.31 in 1951. Among Jewish mothers born in Europe and America, the rate was 2.63 (2.53 in 1955-9). For Moslems the rate was 4.68 (8.17 in 1955-9) (Table 3.4). One major change was a sharp reduction in fertility rates of mothers of Asian and African origin at an age group of 40-49. The major explanatory variable to differences in fertility is the level of education of the mother. As more immigrants had higher levels of education then the differential in total fertility tended to narrow down.

Since the large influx of new immigrants was that of Jews coming from Moslem countries, there has been a major change in the composition of the Jewish population by origin, creating a demographic transformation with far-reaching consequences. The majority of the Jewish population in Israel when the state was proclaimed was of European, largely Eastern European, origin. In November 1948, out of 716,700 Jews in Israel, 253,700 were born in Israel (35.4 per cent). Out of those born abroad only 15.1 per cent were born in Asia or Africa. The majority of the new immigrants, on the other hand, are Jews of Asian and African origin. In May 1961, out of 1,932,400 Jews in Israel 42.3 per cent of Jews were born in Asia or Africa or were born in Israel to a father born in Asia or Africa. By May 1972 47.4 per cent of all Israeli Jews were Sephardim Jews and by December 31, 1987 the percentage had tapered down to 42.6 per cent. Among those not born in Israel to a father born in Israel, Jews of Asian and African origin were 53.36 per cent of the total. Israel was thus transformed from a country with a majority of

Eastern European Jews to one in which the dominant numbers are of Asian and African origin.

The changing demographic composition can be shown also by the figures on immigrants by period of immigration and last continent of residence. Between 1919 and May 14, 1948, there were 482,857 immigrants. Of these 44,936 (9.3 per cent) came from Asia or Africa, 377,381 (78.2 per cent) from Europe, 7,754 (1.6 per cent) from America and Oceania while for 52,786 (10.9 per cent) the last continent of residence is unknown.

In contrast, out of 686,739 new immigrants arriving between May 15, 1948, and the end of 1951: 331,303 (48.2 per cent) came from Asia or Africa; 326,786 (47.6 per cent) from Europe; and 5,140 (0.74 per cent) from America and Oceania. For 23,510 (3.4 per cent) there is no information. When the unknown are not counted, Asia and Africa contributed 10.4 per cent of the immigrants until 1948; 49.9 per cent from 1948 to 1951; and 44.4 per cent from May 15, 1948 to the end of 1986. Europe and America, 89.6 per cent until the declaration of the state; 50.1 per cent in the period May 15, 1948 to 1951, and 55.6 per cent from 1948 to 1986. In 1987 and 1988, Europe and the US contributed more than 76 per cent of the total.

By the end of 1988, Jews of European and American origin were 1,331,200; 794,000 were of African origin (mostly from Morocco, Tangiers, Algeria, Tunisia, Libya, Egypt, and Sudan) and about 747,500 Jews were of Asian origin (mainly from Iraq, Iran, Yemen). Another 786,300 were Israeli-born to a father born in Israel. By the nature of things, this last category was composed mainly of the young: 80 per cent of those born in Israel with fathers born in Israel were 19 or less. One result has been that the per cent of Jews of European and American origin out of the total is decreasing: it was 52.1 per cent in 1961, 40.0 per cent in 1983, and 36.4 per cent by the end of 1988.

In the first decade of the state, many believed in a policy of 'melting pot' that should abolish any difference between Jews of different ethnic origin and any reference to ethnic origin (see Ben Gurion in Divrei Ha'Knesset, 1952, p. 1,102). In the 1970s, it was clear that the melting pot policy failed. The young generation among the oriental Jews saw this policy as an Ashkenazi trick to assimilate the oriental Jews. In 1976, the minister of education and culture confessed that the melting pot idea was wrong.

The feelings of deprivation, especially among the poor oriental Jews in the poor neighborhoods have increased. Demonstrations in 1971 caused public opinion to focus again on the question of inequality and led to the creation of a special committee of the Prime Minister on poor children. One result was an increase in the government social services supply and a rise in social legislation.

The government's social welfare policies were strongly influenced by the desire to achieve rapid integration and the objective of closing gaps among Jews of different ethnic origins. The forging of one nation and the early belief in Israel as a melting pot is turning out to be much less successful than originally hoped for. The majority of Sephardim have extremely strong roots to their past. They are certainly not willing to sacrifice their traditions in order to be assimilated into the culture of Eastern European Judaism, a culture they find quite antagonizing.

Religious and secular Jews

Another consequence of the changing composition of the population has been an increased importance of the ultra-Orthodox parties in the political life of Israel. Traditionally, most ultra-Orthodox Jews were anti-Zionist. They felt a good pious Jew should wait for the Messiah, not try to force God's will by creating a new state. Many of the extremely Orthodox Jews have been concentrated in certain holy cities, notably Jerusalem. They opposed the basic premises of the Zionist aspirations and did not participate in the political life of the Yishuv. Some of these ultra-Orthodox voted for Agudat Israel — a party of ultra-Orthodox Jews established in Eastern Europe in 1912. Agudat Israel developed many philanthropic organizations as well as its own school system. The labor wing of that party (Poalei Agudat Israel) was founded, in 1924, in Poland. At that time, its major aim was to protect Orthodox Jews in industry. Those more extreme — *Neturei Karta* ('The Guardians of the Walls') — denied the possibility of any recognition of secular Zionists. Even today, they refuse to recognize the State of Israel or to vote for the political institutions of the secular state. On the other side of the Orthodox camp were the National Religious Party followers, who combined their religious beliefs with Zionist zeal. The representatives of that party have been traditionally allies to the Labor Party, and generally agreed to create a coalition with it in return for a strong influence on the affairs of the religious establishment. This tradition started from the Yishuv period. The major source of power of the National Religious Party (called at that period 'Mizrahi') was the Chief Rabbinates and the local religious councils. As a part of agreements with the Mizrahi (and its sister party Hapoel Hamizrahi), contracts on land lease from *Keren Kayemet* required the observance of the Sabbath and the rules of Shmita (no work on the seventh year). These rules were not always upheld.

In addition, the laws of personal status, mainly marriage and divorce, were vested in the hands of the Rabbinical courts (established in 1922) and for other religions, in their religious courts. One cannot marry or divorce in Israel without being a member of a religious community — no civil marriages exist. The law does not require religious burial. Theoretically, therefore, one could initiate a secular cemetery. A license to operate a mortuary depends only on an agreement with the National Insurance Institute (that pays for the burial costs). In practice, most burials outside the kibbutzim are done by religious organizations. While on matters of marriage and divorce of Israeli Jews the Rabbinical courts have exclusive jurisdiction, they have concurrent jurisdiction with the district courts with the consent of the parties on all other matters of personal status. (Other religious courts have the jurisdiction over marriages and divorce for their own religions.)

There were also agreements restraining public transportation, shopping and the opening of entertainment facilities on the Sabbath. In addition, the Rabbinates had the power to grant Kashrut certificates. To many religious Jews these arrangements also meant good jobs in the religious establishment. The Israeli government has financed Rabbinical jobs as well as other jobs related to religious needs and creeds.

The aftermath of the 1967 war elated many religious Jews. The prospects of returning to the ancient land of their forefathers in Judea and Samaria have gradually made them more extreme and intransigent in their political views. They have been adamantly against any withdrawal from these territories and thus have become closer in their views to that of the political right. As a result, the followers of the National Religious Party became less willing to join a Labor coalition.

Many of the ultra-Orthodox Jews have learned that by voting in the election they can receive political power and therefore also economic goods. In the first years of the state, Agudat Israel participated in the government. Later, it decided to participate only in the Knesset. It was able to control the very powerful finance commission of the Knesset. More of the anti-Zionist Rabbis told their constituents to vote in the elections. Because of their feelings of deprivation many oriental Jews voted for a newly created Orthodox party that has become, since 1984, a very crucial balance of power in allowing the large parties to create a coalition. This party, Shas, grew very fast and became a major power in the religious camp. Its leaders are reputed to be more willing to allow territorial compromises than the National Religious Party leaders. Other religious parties are Tami, a breakaway from the NRP, and *Degel Hatora*, who broke away from Agudat Israel in 1988. Morasha (heritage) merged with the NRP.

Since 1928, no Israeli government (or National Institution) has been possible without a religious party. The result of the 1988 elections points to an important paradox in Israeli life: that major problems of the country will be decided by anti-Zionists, or at least non-Zionists. Moreover, for an ultra-Orthodox Jew, secular laws are not binding, certainly not when they are in conflict with divine law.

Quality of immigrants and of population

The Jewish immigrants to Palestine in the Yishuv period were on the whole of very high quality. This can be partially measured by such attributes as age and education. Thus, half of the immigrants were between 15 and 29 and less than 16 per cent were over 44. They were ready to participate in the labor force. In the second and third Aliyah periods, there were many young persons at labor participation age, and very few young and old persons to support. Their level of education was also very high, with more than 93 per cent of males aged 7 and up literate, with an educational level that was among the highest in the world. According to Richard Easterlin (1961, p. 71) almost 10 per cent of the Jewish males in Palestine had completed higher education, and that ratio was higher than that of the United States in 1950 and more than twice as high as in any other country for which Easterlin found data. In addition, most of the new immigrants came with skills acquired abroad (only 13 per cent were unskilled laborers), and their health level, as manifested in the life expectancy, was very high. Perhaps more important, these immigrants were idealists, ready for self-sacrifice, highly dedicated with a high level of stubborn optimism. These traits were also aided by a large inflow of capital — both in the form of transfer by immigrants and in the form of Jewish national capital-contributions to different financial instruments of the Zionist organization. All this created a very fertile ground for a steady economic growth. In 1948, the educational level of the Jewish population in Israel was among the highest in the world

Table 3.5 Immigrants and potential immigrants, by period of immigration and age

Age	Period of immigration								
	1948-1951[a]	1952-1960	1961-1964	1965-1971	1972-1979	1980-1984	1985-1986	1987	1988
	Absolute numbers								
Total	682,361	294,488	228,036	197,821	267,582	83,637	20,147	12,965	13,034
0-14	192,532	105,037	77,896	48,240	57,490	18,512	4,233	2,530	2,617
15-19	65,747	26,094	24,018	23,615	26,234	8,657	1,722	1,063	1,108
20-24	68,958	23,618	15,700	25,475	31,742	12,295	3,060	1,777	1,691
25-34	113,760	36,677	25,369	25,774	44,561	16,267	4,340	2,758	2,752
35-44	96,143	39,374	28,260	21,059	29,225	6,981	2,046	1,454	1,599
45-64	115,118	51,361	44,198	37,302	49,714	12,037	2,619	1,872	1,814
65+	29,024	12,192	12,416	15,590	28,074	8,516	2,127	1,511	1,453
Not known	1,079	136	179	766	542	372	–		–
	Percentages								
Total	100.0	100.0	100.0	100.0	100.0	100.0	100.0	100.0	100.0
0-14	28.2	35.7	34.2	24.4	21.5	22.1	21.0	19.5	20.1
15-19	9.6	8.9	10.5	11.9	9.8	10.4	8.5	8.2	8.5
20-24	10.1	8.0	6.9	12.9	11.9	14.7	15.2	13.7	13.0
25-34	16.7	12.5	11.1	13.0	16.7	19.4	21.5	21.3	21.1
35-44	14.1	13.4	12.4	10.6	10.9	8.3	10.2	11.2	12.3
45-64	16.9	17.4	19.4	18.8	18.6	14.4	13.0	14.4	13.9
65+	4.3	4.1	5.4	7.9	10.5	10.2	10.6	11.7	11.2

Source: Statistical Abstract of Israel, 1989, p. 173.
Note: [a] Excl. 4,386 immigrants and settling tourists in 1948, 1949 and 1950 whose sex and age are not known.

as measured by completion of both secondary and higher education.

The mass immigration reaching Israel was mainly 'rescue immigration': displaced persons from concentration camps or Jews arriving from countries from which it was not certain they could leave later, be it Egypt and Hungary in 1956, or Morocco in an earlier period. During the mass immigration, there were more children and old persons. Among those immigrating between May 15, 1948 and 1951, 28.2 per cent were in the 0-14 age group. In the period 1952-60, 35.7 per cent of immigrants were in this age group. Since 1972, more than 10 per cent of the immigrants have been at an age of 65 and above.

Only 36.4 per cent of the immigrants in the first three years of the state were in the age groups 15-39, 21.1 per cent were over 45 (Table 3.5). The level of education of the immigrants was also lower than that of the Yishuv period.

In the first year of the state, the share of working age population (15-64) went down from 67 per cent in 1950, to 61.7 per cent in 1955 — as a direct result of the age composition of the new immigration. In later years, the share of children at the age group 0-14 declined (from 36 per cent in the 1950s, to 31 per cent in 1980) but a sharp increase in the rate of elderly — from 3.4 per cent in 1950, to the range of 10 per cent in the 1980s — meant that the share of the 15-64 age group remained stable. Between 1950 and 1980, the number of elderly (65 and over) grew eight-fold, while the number of those of labor force age more than doubled.

Among immigrants aged 15 and over, 42.7 per cent of those immigrating in the period 1970-74 were 45 and over. For the period 1975-9, the per cent was 40.5; and for 1980-83, 30.2 per cent. Many of these immigrants had less education, and the per cent of children aged up to 14 and aged persons was much higher than in the Yishuv period. One result has been that the overall educational level of Jews declined drastically in the 1950s.

Every Israeli child must study in kindergarten at the age of 5 and in elementary school from age 6 until age 14. The number of pupils in these schools grew by 896 per cent between 1948-89 and 1981-2. Until 1979, high-school education was not mandatory, and the tuition fee was based on a progressive system, from which low income families were exempted. Others paid in proportion to revenue per capita in the family, while the more well-to-do paid full tuition fees. About 78 per cent of those aged 14-17 received high-school educations.

In 1979, the system was changed. Compulsory studies were extended to age 16, and the high-school education until age 18 has become free. It is financed by an additional 0.4 per cent levy on national insurance payments. Here again, there was a sharp rise in the numbers. In 1987-8, there were 112,571 pupils in Jewish intermediate schools and 24,021 in Arab intermediate schools. There were also 198,670 Jewish pupils and 37,488 Arab pupils in high schools. More relevant, among Jewish pupils, the rates (per 1,000) of students in secondary education among this age group were 894 for age 14; 900 for age 15, 863 for age 16 and 807 for age 17.

The number of students in colleges and universities was 1,635 in 1948-9. In 1987-8, there were 64,190 — an increase of about 4,000 per cent. National expenditure in education in the 1980s was around 8.5 of GNP, of which about 20 per cent was for higher education. A special effort has been made to get the best possible education to new immigrants, to Sephardim, to the poor and to Arabs. In 1984-5, 22.5 per cent of university students were born (or their fathers were born) in Asia or Africa, and 6.7 per cent were non-Jews. This was a sharp rise from 1969-70, when the Asian-Africans were 13.5 per cent of students, and non-Jews — 1.5 per cent.

Because of high investments in education, the educational level has increased constantly since the 1960s. In 1970-74, 25.8 per cent of immigrants aged 15 and over, had less than 9 years of schooling; 40.6 per cent had high-school education; and 33.6 per cent had university education. In the period 1975-9, 40.6 per cent had 13 years of schooling or more; and in 1980-83, 47.6 per cent. Further, in 1961, 15 per cent of those born in Israel aged 14 or more had more than 13 years of education. The same was true for those born in Europe and America, but only 3 per cent of Jews born in Asia and Africa. When those born in Israel are analyzed according to where the father was born, the per cent of those with 13 and more years of schooling were in 1961: 13 per cent for Israeli-born; 19.7 per cent for Europe-American-born; and only 4.5 per cent for Asian-African-born. In contrast, 15 years later, in 1978, those having 13 or more years of schooling were: 25.9 per cent of those born in Europe or America; 23.6 per cent of Israeli-born, and 8.4 per cent of those born in Asia and Africa. For the Israeli-born, of those whose father was born in Europe or America, 39.4 per cent had 13 or more years of schooling; in Israel — 23.1 per cent, and in Asia or Africa, 9.2 per cent. Among non-Jews, 1.3 per cent had 13 or more years of schooling.

Israel spends increasing amounts of funds on education (8.5 per cent of GNP in 1986-7, compared to 6 per cent of GNP in 1962-3; 7.6 per cent in 1965-6, 8.4 per cent in 1975-6 and 8.2

per cent in 1980-81). All Arab and Jewish populations experienced a rapid rise in the level of schooling — and this increase is intricately linked to narrowing gaps in income and rising standard of living.

A 1984 survey of post-secondary and university graduates counted 205,700 Israeli graduates; 130,400 with undergraduate degree; 64,500 with second; and 10,800 with a third degree. Out of those, 14.6 per cent had Asian and African origin; 79 per cent had Europe and American origin; and 6.4 per cent were Israeli-born with their father born in Israel. Since 1984, about 12,000 students graduate from Israeli universities each year. Today, the Israeli labor force is well educated. Fifteen per cent of all employees had 16 or more years of schooling; 17.5 per cent, 13 to 15 years; 33.5 per cent, 11 to 12 years. Only 4.3 per cent had 4 or less years of schooling; 15.9 per cent, between 5 and 8; and 13.5 per cent, between 9 and 10 years of schooling. The median years of schooling moved up from 8.0 in 1961 (8.4 for Jewish population) to 11.4 in 1987 (11.7 for Jewish population).

Another indication of the quality of labor is that on a per capita basis, sales of books and other publications in Israel is one of the highest in the world.

Population dispersal

A major policy objective of all Israeli governments has been to disperse the population — mainly to the Negev in the south and to the Galilee in the north. There were at least four reasons for this policy. First, ideological: the Zionist movement believed strongly that the occupational structure of the Jews in the Diaspora should be changed and that Jews should be mainly farmers. Hence, living in the city was less desirable. Second, general economic reasoning: concentration of the population in the large cities causes all kinds of side effects — including pollution, high and disturbing noise levels, transportation problems and so on. These negative externalities create high costs that are not borne by the individual city dweller. Third, political: in 1920, when the British and the French decided on the border between Palestine and Lebanon. The existence of some villages such as Tel Hai is said to have caused them to include more area within the border of Palestine, moving the border further north in what had become known as 'the finger.' Since then, it was believed that the map of Jewish villages would be of extreme importance in any future decision on the borders of the country. Specifically, leaving areas uninhabited was considered dangerous

Table 3.6 Population density per land sq. km, by district and sub-district

District and Sub-district	31 Dec. 1988	31 Dec. 1987	31 Dec. 1986	31 Dec. 1985	31 Dec. 1985	4 June 1983	20 May 1972	22 May 1961	8 Nov. 1948
Grand total	205.1[b]	202.1[b]	199.0[b]	196.3[b]	193.6[b]	186.7[b]	154.8[a]	107.6	43.1
Jerusalem district	867.9	849.4	826.5	807.4	789.5	754.2	554.0	344.5	159.5
Northern district	165.9	162.7	159.7	157.0	153.6	145.7	142.3	101.4	44.2
Zefat Sub-district	103.1	102.7	102.7	102.1	101.1	96.6	84.4	67.9	16.4
Kinnert Sub-district	135.5	133.4	131.4	129.4	126.5	120.2	95.2	83.1	38.2
Yizreel Sub-district	219.6	215.7	212.0	208.6	204.2	194.2	145.1	100.4	50.3
Akko Sub-district	341.4	333.3	325.4	319.0	311.9	295.2	206.6	136.8	59.6
Golan Sub-district	20.6	20.3	19.7	19.1	18.2	16.8			
Haifa District	708.5	703.2	698.0	694.0	689.2	673.7	566.5	433.6	209.2
Haifa Sub-district	1,483.9	1,479.3	1,472.7	1,470.0	1,466.6	1,477.2	1,260.5	976.0	452.4
Hadera Sub-district	324.2	318.6	314.1	309.5	303.8	290.3	222.6	164.8	88.6
Central District	764.4	747.1	730.8	715.9	701.8	668.8	466.7	327.8	100.4
Sharon Sub-district	624.0	607.9	596.4	585.4	573.0	547.1	412.3	294.7	108.2
Petah Tiqva Sub-district	1,215.2	1,186.5	1,156.0	1,128.9	1,103.6	1,047.5	714.0	480.6	175.6
Ramala Sub-district	370.7	365.9	363.2	362.0	359.1	351.5	286.0	218.9	14.4
Rehovot Sub-district	910.9	890.0	867.4	845.1	828.2	782.3	484.0	334.6	109.8
Tel Aviv District	6,071.9	6,042.5	5,993.2	5,972.3	5,966.2	5,883.8	5,336.7	4,113.5	1,834.0
Southern District	37.8	37.3	36.7	36.2	35.6	33.9	25.1	12.3	1.5
Ashquelon Sub-district	173.9	171.8	169.9	168.2	166.1	160.2	120.3	60.3	5.8
Beer Sheva Sub-district	24.3	23.9	23.5	23.1	22.6	21.4	15.7	7.6	1.1

Source: CBS Statistical Abstract of Israel, 1989, p. 41.
Notes: [a] Excl. Israelis in the Golan and Gaza Area. [b] Excl. Israelis in Judea, Samaria and Gaza Area.

in terms of any future decision on the borders of the state. Last and maybe most important was the problem of defense. In its narrowest band, the width of Israel within its armistice borders is no more than 10 km. A major problem for the army was always how to defend Israel against being cut in the middle. Concentration of the population in the cities and mainly in the narrow band along the coast line also made it subject to a threat of missile attack. Despite strenuous efforts and strong attempts by several governments to achieve a more balanced distribution of the population, Israel has failed to achieve this goal.

The Zionist ideology called for a transformation of the nation to a people of farmers. For several decades, since 1915, strong preferences were given to communal villages, believing the backbone of Zionist work and the road for redemption must be agricultural colonization. Yet the majority of the Jewish population in the Yishuv and in Israel always lived in cities. When the British mandate authorities carried out the first census on October 23, 1922, they found 83,800 Jews in Palestine, and fully 68,622 of these Jews (81.9 per cent) lived in cities, half of them in Jerusalem. The first census carried out by the central bureau of statistics of Israel (November 8, 1948) showed that 80.4 per cent of the population lived in cities. Jerusalem lost by then the seniority status: 12 per cent of the Jews lived within its border. The biggest city was Tel Aviv, with a full 43 per cent of the population concentrated within it.

The population density per land square kilometer was on average 43.1. In the Tel Aviv district, it was 1,834 compared to 1.5 in the southern district and 1.1 in the Beer Sheva sub-district. By the end of 1988, the population density was 205.1 on average (excluding Israelis in the Judea, Samaria, and Gaza areas). The Tel Aviv district was still very highly populated, with a population density of 6,071.9; and the south had a population density of 37.8; with 24.3 for the Beer Sheva sub-district (Table 3.6).

The Israelis also continue to live in urban localities. By December 31, 1987, 89.6 per cent of the total population (and 89.8 per cent of the Jewish population) lived in urban localities. Only 10.4 per cent (10.2 per cent of the Jews) lived in rural communities. Four per cent of the Jews lived in moshavim: 0.3 per cent in communal moshavim; 3.5 per cent in kibbutzim and the rest lived in various other rural communities.

Another way of looking at the population distribution is by noting the percentage of Jews living in different parts of the country. In November 1948, 43.2 per cent of the Jews lived in the Tel Aviv district and 15.2 per cent more in the adjoining

Table 3.7 Locations and population, by district, sub-district, population group and religion (%)

District and sub-district	Population							
	31 Dec. 1988	31 Dec. 1987	31 Dec. 1986	31 Dec. 1985	4 June 1983	20 May 1972	22 May 1961	8 Nov. 1948
				Total population %				
Grand total	100.0	100.0	100.0	100.0	100.0	100.0	100.0	100.0
Jerusalem District	12.2	12.0	11.9	11.8	11.7	11.0	8.8	10.2
Northern District	16.7	16.6	16.6	16.5	16.2	15.0	15.5	16.8
Zafat Sub-district	1.5	1.6	1.7	1.7	1.6	1.8	2.1	1.2
Kinneret Sub-district	1.6	1.6	1.6	1.6	1.5	1.6	2.0	2.3
Yizreel Sub-district	5.9	5.9	5.8	5.8	5.8	5.5	5.5	6.9
Akko Sub-district	7.1	7.0	7.0	6.9	6.8	6.1	5.9	6.4
Golan Sub-district	0.5	0.5	0.5	0.5	0.5	–	–	–
Haifa District	13.5	13.7	13.9	14.0	14.2	15.4	17.0	20.5
Haifa Sub-district	9.4	9.6	9.7	9.9	10.1	11.3	12.7	14.7
Hadera Sub-district	4.1	4.1	4.1	4.1	4.1	4.0	4.3	5.8
Central District	21.2	21.0	20.8	20.8	20.6	18.4	18.7	14.3
Sharon Sub-district	4.9	4.8	4.8	4.7	4.7	4.6	4.7	4.3
Petah Tiqva Sub-district	7.7	7.6	7.5	7.5	7.4	6.4	6.3	5.7
Ramla Sub-district	2.6	2.6	2.6	2.7	2.7	2.8	3.1	0.5
Rehovot Sub-district	6.1	6.0	5.9	5.9	5.8	4.6	4.6	3.8
Tel Aviv District	23.1	23.5	23.8	24.1	24.8	28.8	32.0	35.7
Southern District	11.9	12.0	12.0	11.9	11.8	11.3	8.0	2.5
Ashquelon Sub-district	4.9	5.0	5.0	5.0	5.0	4.9	3.5	0.8
Be'er Sheva Sub-district	7.0	7.0	6.9	6.9	6.8	6.4	4.5	1.7
Judea, Samaria and Gaza Area	1.5	1.2	1.1	0.9	0.6	0.1	–	–
Judea and Samaria	1.4	1.2	1.0	0.9	0.6	0.0	–	–
Gaza Area	0.1	0.0	0.0	0.0	0.0	0.0	–	–

	Jews							
Total	100.0	100.0	100.0	100.0	100.0	100.0	100.0	100.0
Jerusalem District	10.9	10.8	10.7	10.5	10.4	9.7	9.7	12.0
Northern District	9.8	9.9	9.9	10.0	9.8	9.5	10.0	7.6
Zefat Sub-district	1.7	1.7	1.8	1.8	1.8	2.0	2.2	1.3
Kinneret Sub-district	1.4	1.4	1.4	1.4	1.4	1.4	1.8	2.1
Yizreel Sub-district	3.4	3.4	3.5	3.5	3.4	3.4	3.4	3.4
Akko Sub-district	3.0	3.0	3.0	3.0	2.9	2.7	2.6	0.8
Golan Sub-district	0.3	0.3	0.3	0.3	0.2	–	–	–
Haifa District	13.0	13.1	13.3	13.5	13.9	15.2	16.7	21.1
Haifa Sub-district	10.3	10.4	10.6	10.7	11.1	12.3	13.3	16.6
Hadera Sub-district	2.7	2.7	2.7	2.7	2.7	2.9	3.4	4.5
Central District	23.8	23.6	23.4	23.2	22.8	19.9	19.7	15.2
Sharon Sub-district	4.7	4.6	4.6	4.6	4.5	4.3	4.4	3.8
Petah Tiqva Sub-district	9.0	8.9	8.8	8.7	8.5	7.2	6.8	6.6
Ramla Sub-district	2.7	2.7	2.8	2.8	2.9	3.0	3.3	0.2
Rehovot Sub-district	7.4	7.3	7.2	7.1	6.9	5.3	5.2	4.6
Tel Aviv District	27.8	28.1	28.3	28.5	29.5	33.5	35.9	43.2
Southern District	12.8	12.8	12.9	12.9	12.9	12.1	8.0	0.9
Ashquelon Sub-district	6.0	6.0	6.0	6.0	6.0	5.7	3.9	0.7
Be'er Sheva Sub-district	6.8	6.8	6.9	6.9	6.9	6.4	4.1	0.2
Judea, Samaria and Gaza Area	1.8	1.7	1.5	1.3	0.7	0.1	–	–
Judea and Samaria	1.7	1.6	1.4	1.3	0.7	0.0	–	–
Gaza Area	0.1	0.1	0.1	0.1	0.0	0.0	–	–

Source: Statistical Abstract of Israel, 1989, p. 44.

central district. By the end of 1987, the central part of the country was still home for more than half of the population. Many did move to the suburbs, so the Tel Aviv district included 28.1 per cent of the population while the central district included 23.6 per cent. The Haifa district declined from 21.1 per cent to 13.1 per cent. The percentage of Jews living in the northern district grew from 7.6 per cent in 1948 to 10.0 per cent on May 22, 1961, but by the end of 1987 it was 9.9. The major change was in the southern district, with 6.0 per cent of the Jews living in the Ashqulon sub-district — less than 90 kilometers from Tel Aviv and 6.8 per cent in the Be'er Sheva district. Both of these percentages had not changed since 1972. Jewish population in Judea and Samaria was 0.7 per cent of the total in 1983 and 1.7 per cent by the end of 1987.

Table 3.7 shows the population by district and sub-district. The table reflects the population dispersal policy's lack of success despite the relatively large amount of capital invested. The significant relative reduction in Tel Aviv was largely a result of increased population in greater Tel Aviv, or the central district. The relative population of the northern district has not changed since 1961, and that of Be'er Sheva sub-district — since 1972. Many of the agricultural settlements created in the north were not very successful and are still not independent. The development towns, despite huge spending, are still not very desirable places to live, being too small, too underdeveloped, with too few attractive employment sources. Only a handful of the development towns, such as Arad, are successful.

Israel seems to have made two basic mistakes in its population dispersal policies. First, too much was spent on subsidizing capital, while the idea was to get labor relocated. Second, too little was spent on infrastructure. Because capital was subsidized, factories would relocate to development regions. Many of them, however, did not continue beyond the period of tax exemptions. In any case, this subsidy did not necessarily attract professionals and skilled workers to the development towns. From a strict economic point of view, subsidies to manpower could have been more effective.

Unfortunately, very little investment was directed at the creation of highways, railroads or a telephone system. Israel is a tiny country. A good highway system might have encouraged people to relocate outside the central region without regard to employment. A rail line from a development town to a central city could have helped, too. Instead, Israel invested very large sums in creating a large number of relatively small towns, none of which can afford a good infrastructure of education or cultural institutions.

A study by Gabriel Lifschitz (1988) points out many differences among development towns. Some did not grow for a long time, others did. In some cases there was a negative flow of persons through the whole period (for example Hatzor or Or-Akiva). Only in one case (Eilat) did the researchers find a positive flow of persons throughout the period researched. In all development towns, except Eilat, the researchers found a negative internal migration balance for a long period. In most of them, it was the population with 13 and more years of education that left (a negative balance of internal migration). Young persons also left most of the development towns. The researchers also found high unemployment rates in 13 out of 23 towns in the northern and southern regions. In the development towns in the center, people can presumably find employment outside the town.

All in all, despite huge flows of funds, the dispersal of the population was not very successful. It was even less successful in attracting young academically educated persons to move to a development town, which is often economically nonviable. Some of these towns also have a high share of poverty, of crime and of delinquency. Many feel that some of these towns should be merged to create a critical mass. Perhaps a better infrastructure may help to bring these towns nearer to major urban centers.

Labor force

The Israeli Central Bureau of Statistics includes in its survey of civilian labor force all civilians aged fifteen or over who were either employed or unemployed in the period during which it carries out its annual labor force survey. Accordingly, all those fifteen years of age and over who were neither employed nor unemployed are not included in the civilian labor force. Not included in the civilian labor force are housewives, students who did not work even one hour during the week of the survey, persons living on pension, persons unable to work and persons serving in the army on compulsory military service. Those on active army reserve duty are included in the civilian labor force as part of those 'temporarily absent from work.'

Israel's civilian labor force is small compared to other countries, 34 per cent in national population, 50 per cent in working age population compared to 47 per cent and 61 per cent in the UK, 48 per cent and 64 per cent in the USA. This is explained partly because of the size of its armed services, and partly as a result of a large number of students and also because of the relatively low participation ratio of women in the work force: 32 per cent in 1974, and 38 per cent in 1984, compared to 38 per cent and 42 per cent in the UK, 38 per cent and 44 per cent in the USA. To be sure, the participation of females in the civilian labor force has been growing steadily: it was 26.5 per cent in 1955; 27.3 per cent in 1960; 29.3 per cent in 1970; 35.7 per cent in 1980, 38.2 per cent in 1985 and 40.0 per cent in 1988. Still, it is relatively low compared to Western developed countries. The increased participation of women is largely a result of the increase in women's educational levels. On the other hand, participation rates of Israelis aged 55 and over are higher than in Europe and in the United States. The labor force participation rate among men declined from 80.1 in 1955, to 63.2 in 1988. This was due primarily to delayed entry because of higher schooling. Thus, the rate of labor force participation of men at age 14–17 declined from 42.2 per cent in 1955, to 38.1 per cent in 1965, 27.3 per cent in 1970, 14.9 per cent in 1975, 12.6 per cent in 1980, and 11.7 per cent in 1987 (age cohort of 15–17).

Labor force participation is also a function of ethnic origin. The participation rate of men in the age group 14–17 is much lower among Israelis of European and American origin than those of Asian and African origins.

The relative number of professionals, scientists and academics has more than doubled since 1960; that of managers, administrators and clerks grew by 39 per cent, while the more sophisticated methods and technology employed in agriculture and manufacturing allowed a sharp reduction in the number of farmers and that of blue-collar workers. One indication of structural change is the deployment of engineers. In 1972, there were 9,825 engineers and 1,970 systems analysts and programmers. Only 1.2 per cent of employees in manufacturing were engineers. By 1983, the number of engineers more than doubled to 23,660, representing 3.0 per cent of employees in industry (by 1985, the ratio increased to 3.4 per cent). Fifty-seven per cent of these engineers were employed in the transportation, and electric and electronic branches. There were 7,685 systems analysts and programmers. The percentage of engineers in sophisticated industries rose from 3.6 per cent in 1970 to 6.9 per cent in 1982 and in traditional industries it increased from 0.5 per cent in 1970 to 1.3 per cent in 1982. The same story is true for technicians. The government civil service employed a relatively small number of engineers. According to the Civil Service Commissioner's report there were 1,694 persons receiving salaries as engineers, out of which 651 were in the Ministry of Agriculture and only 76 were in the Ministry of Industry and Trade.

A major source of demand for engineers has been the military. The introduction of more sophisticated weapons systems required a larger number of engineers and technicians for the operations and management of these systems. As one example, Israel's Air Force increased its engineers' establishment by 100 per cent between 1968 and 1974, estimating at the time an additional increase of more than 70 per cent by 1980. A source of worry for Israeli industrial planners is the ability of the country to produce enough engineers to foster a fast rate of economic growth. The number of immigrant engineers declined from 1,000 a year in the 1970s to about 500 at the beginning of the 1980s (but apparently has increased with the influx of Russian immigrants since 1989). The number of graduates in engineering is less than 1,500 per annum, and the proportion of graduates in engineering sciences out of total graduates receiving a degree from Israeli academic institutions fluctuated from 15.7 per cent in 1969-70 to 17.2 per cent in 1974-5, 13.2 per cent in 1984-5 and 13.4 per cent in 1986-7. To be sure, this reduction was not a result of fewer students in engineering, but of much faster increases in other fields of study. In fact, when 1969-70 = 100, students for first degrees in 1987 were 163.0; for second, 272.8; and for a third, 269.3. The number of graduates in engineering was 871 in 1969-70; 1,512 in 1974-5; 1,485 in 1984-5, and 1,623 in 1986-7.

Israel employs practical engineers as well as academics. The number of post-secondary graduate practical engineers and technicians reached 57,700 in 1984, out of which 80.4 per cent were employed. Only 49.4 per cent actually worked as technicians and practical engineers. Many practical engineers left the profession, and in many cases they acquired engineering degrees. According to the 1983 Census of Population and Housing, the total number of persons employed as engineering technicians and practical engineers was 39,305, of which 13,500 were in industry.

The percentage of technicians and practical engineers out of the total industrial labor force increased to 4.5 per cent in 1982 from 3.8 per cent in 1972. There was a decline in the ratio between engineers and technicians in industry from 2.5 in 1970, to 1.4 in 1982, which is predicted to level off to 1.2 in 1990.

A government forecast estimates the demand for technicians and practical engineers as 54,000 by 1990, of which 18,000 would be employed by industry (an increase of 4,000); and the

131

supply at 54,000. The number of graduates in this field in recent years was 2,500-3,000 per annum. It should be kept in mind that a considerable number of technicians are trained by the army.

Employment

Largely because of strong beliefs in the virtues of the welfare state, the per cent unemployed out of the total civilian labor force has always been very small in Israel. The Israeli government has always given a high priority to full employment. It was sensitive in particular to the problems of unemployment among Jews of Asian and African origins. It has also been committed to job security, being afraid that unemployment would cause emigration. The commitment to a full employment and to job security made workers' mobility very costly.

At the height of the recession in 1967, unemployment was 10.4 per cent, but in most years the percentage of unemployed has been between 3 and 6 per cent. Perhaps Israel has more disguised unemployment — that is, people that receive remuneration but whose employment is far from being necessary. While obviously it is almost impossible to have any reliable statistics of this type, clearly many of those employed in public services could have been dismissed without much loss of productivity. In the Histadrut sector, it took the managers several years before they started adjusting the size of the labor force to the opportunities for gainful employment. Solel Boneh, Israel's largest construction firm, continued to pay wages to its approximately 20,000 employees more than three years after the level of its actual orders and work went down more than 30 per cent. One result of the recession in 1988 and 1989 has been a rise in the unemployment rate: employment remained steady while the labor force rapidly increased. About half of this increase was a result of growth in the working age population, the rest was due to increased participation, mainly of females. In the second quarter of 1989, and the first quarter of 1990, the unemployment rate was 9.4 per cent, compared to 6.1 per cent in 1987, and 6.4 per cent in 1988.

Where are the Israelis employed? The distribution of employment by economic branch in Israel is abnormal for the level of development of the country: as shown by Gur Ofer, the employment structure resembles countries at a much higher level of economic development. Specifically, only 4.6 per cent of employed persons are employed in agriculture, forestry, and fishing. Because of increased productivity in this branch, the percentage has been going down: it was 10.4 per cent in 1968, 8.8 per cent in 1970, 6.5 per cent in 1975 and 6.4 per cent in 1980. Mining and manufacturing has been a source of employment for 23.7 per cent of the employed persons and this percentage has changed very little in the last 40 years. About 7 per cent are in construction, building and public works. This latter group has been dwindling as a result of the significant contraction of construction activities: as early as 1975, construction accounted for 11.6 per cent of the employed — much more than in other countries at the same development level (Table 3.8).

Most Israelis are employed in the service industries: in 1988, about 10 per cent are in finance and business services, (more than doubled from 4.9 per cent in 1968); 29.0 per cent are in public and community services, compared to 23.9 per cent in 1970; 13 per cent are in commerce, restaurants and hotels; 6.4 per cent in transport, storage and communications; while 6.5 per cent provide personal and other services.

One reason for the large increase in finance services may have been the much more frequent use of banking and other financial services as a result of rampant inflation. The major reason, however, for the ever increasing service sector seems to have been a result of the provisions of the welfare state. Health, education and other government services have been growing and were a source of an insatiable demand for more workers.

Labor institutions

Labor exchanges were organized during the Yishuv period by the Histadrut and the employers associations during the slump of 1930. The employers agreed at the time to recruit labor only through these exchanges. The exchanges were nationalized by the Employment Service Law, 1959, that placed the exchanges under the supervision of the Minister of Labor. The labor exchange is an important channel for finding work. However, skilled employees, professionals and managerial staff tend to avoid using this institution — and are allowed to do so. Blue-collar workers must be recruited through the labor exchange.

Almost all workers in Israel are unionized within the trade union department of the Histadrut (95 per cent, compared to 25 per cent in the United States). The Histadrut enters a collective bargaining negotiation with the employers' associations and the government on a national level, and these agreements may be made applicable to other Israeli firms by the Minister of Labor. Israeli labor legislation makes collective agreements binding, and

Table 3.8 Israeli employed persons, by economic branch

	1970	1975	1980	1983	1984	1985	1986	1987	1988	1989
Total										
Thousands	963.2	1,112.6	1,254.5	1,339.4	1,359.0	1,349.2	1,367.9	1,403.7	1,453.1	1,460.8
%	100.0	100.0	100.0	100.0	100.0	100.0	100.0	100.0	100.0	100.0
Agriculture, forestry and fishing	8.8	6.4	6.4	5.5	5.3	5.4	5.2	5.2	5.4	4.7
Industry (mining and manufacturing)	24.3	24.8	23.7	22.8	23.1	23.0	23.7	23.6	22.1	21.5
Electricity and water	1.2	1.0	1.0	1.0	0.9	0.9	0.9	1.0	0.9	0.9
Construction (building and public works)	8.3	8.1	6.4	6.5	5.9	5.4	4.5	4.9	5.1	4.9
Commerce, restaurants and hotels	13.0	12.3	11.7	12.8	12.6	12.5	13.1	13.9	14.3	14.5
Transport, storage and communication	7.5	7.3	6.9	6.5	6.6	6.4	6.4	6.6	6.1	6.4
Financing and business services	5.2	6.7	8.2	9.5	9.6	9.8	9.8	9.6	10.1	9.9
Public and community services	24.0	27.3	29.6	29.5	29.5	30.0	29.9	29.0	29.0	29.4
Personal and other services	7.7	6.1	6.2	5.8	6.4	6.6	6.5	6.4	6.7	7.3

Source: Statistical Abstract of Israel, 1989. Bank of Israel, *Annual Report*, 1988; 1989.
Note: Since 1985, the labor force includes only those of age cohort 15 and above (instead of 14, beforehand).

the Minister of Labor often also applies these agreements to the rest of the economy. Arbitration is done by labor tribunals.

Most working conditions are also centrally determined, and different labor unions attempt to receive equal treatment and whatever other unions were able to achieve. This makes wages in Israel very similar. It also made the unions and the employers continually search for innovative means of paying specific types of compensation to their workers. Once national negotiations are finished, employee committees and management at the firm and the plant level negotiate specific issues related to that particular firm or plant. They also negotiate the grading of individual workers — and this usually results in additional wage drift.

A unique part of the labor scene in Israel is the indexation of wages to the cost of living. The cost of living allowance (COLA) was first recommended by an inquiry commission, appointed in 1942, to look into wages problems. This committee recommended that allowance should be paid to all wage earners if the Consumer Price Index (CPI) prepared by the government exceeded a certain minimum threshold within three months. Since 1942, the COLA has been a key feature of the labor scene during the Yishuv period and in the state years. To be sure, certain details were changed. As an example, the interval between payments was set at one month in 1952; it was extended in 1957 to be six months. In the 1980s, it was set at three months again, and sometimes even monthly.

COLA is subject to a threshold clause of 5 per cent (3 per cent prior to 1975). Until 1975, COLA payments, subject to a ceiling, were tax exempt. Basically the COLA persisted as a means to adjust nominal wages when the CPI rises. To some, it was a means to reduce uncertainty and labor unrest. Others contended that the COLA is a cause of persistent cost inflation. Others objected to the uniformity of the COLA, preferring a system allowing different wage rises in different economic branches.

Economists tend to agree that the major problem with COLA is its impact on the rate of exchange. If prices are rising because of an increase in the money supply, one may argue that even without an automatic COLA, the demand for labor will increase and wages will rise in nominal terms. If, however, a change in the rate of exchange is introduced, aimed at making imports more expensive and reducing aggregate demand, the automatic mechanism of COLA means maintaining real wages constant. If total demand is to be reduced this means reduced profits and possible unemployment. It may also induce a cost inflation chain reaction. Since the mid-1960s, there were many negotiations

Table 3.9(a) Development of real wages, 1961-1987

Year	Old Israeli shekels (1979 prices) The whole economy	Business sector	Public sector	Indices The whole economy	Business sector	Public sector	Rate of change (%) The whole economy	Business sector	Public sector	Last year compared to all other years The whole economy	Business sector	Public sector
Calendar year (base: 1961 = 100)												
1961	931.27	891.75	1,023.97	100.0	100.0	100.0				115.0	141.4	67.6
1962	981.18	923.86	1,118.08	105.4	103.6	109.2	5.4	3.6	9.2	104.1	133.0	53.5
1963	1,028.02	983.60	1,137.43	110.4	110.3	111.1	4.8	6.5	1.7	94.8	118.8	50.9
1964	1,098.99	1,061.81	1,185.85	118.0	119.1	115.8	6.9	8.0	4.3	82.2	102.7	44.7
1965	1,203.57	1,158.12	1,304.85	129.2	129.9	127.4	9.5	9.1	10.0	66.4	85.8	31.5
1966	1,327.15	1,266.02	1,458.65	142.5	142.0	142.5	10.3	9.3	11.8	50.9	70.0	17.6
1967	1,308.71	1,249.53	1,426.29	140.5	140.1	139.3	-1.4	-1.3	-2.2	53.0	72.3	20.3
1968	1,324.07	1,282.16	1,412.88	142.2	143.8	138.0	1.2	2.6	-0.9	51.2	67.9	21.5
1969	1,351.64	1,325.95	1,408.68	145.1	148.7	137.6	2.1	3.4	-0.3	48.1	62.3	21.8
1970	1,382.00	1,361.80	1,431.31	148.4	152.7	139.8	2.2	2.7	1.6	44.9	58.0	19.9
1971	1,423.81	1,387.66	1,504.22	152.9	155.6	146.9	3.0	1.9	5.1	40.6	55.1	14.1
1972	1,433.03	1,419.58	1,471.86	153.9	159.2	143.7	0.6	2.3	-2.2	39.7	51.6	16.6
1973	1,521.22	1,489.68	1,591.67	163.3	167.1	155.4	6.2	4.9	8.1	31.6	44.5	7.8
1974	1,484.34	1,468.01	1,526.85	159.4	164.6	149.1	-2.4	-1.5	-4.1	34.9	46.6	12.4
1975	1,454.08	1,480.76	1,401.31	156.1	166.1	136.9	-2.0	0.9	-8.2	37.7	45.4	22.5
1976	1,473.82	1,543.27	1,340.69	158.3	173.1	130.9	1.4	4.2	-4.3	35.9	39.5	28.0
1977	1,630.05	1,657.47	1,567.27	175.0	185.9	153.1	10.6	7.4	16.9	22.8	29.9	9.5
1978	1,654.50	1,703.88	1,554.73	177.7	191.1	151.8	1.5	2.8	-0.8	21.0	26.3	10.4
1979	1,811.68	1,814.63	1,797.27	194.5	203.5	175.5	9.5	6.5	15.6	10.5	18.6	-4.5
1980	1,754.01	1,813.80	1,648.90	188.3	203.4	161.0	-3.2	-0.0	-8.3	14.2	18.7	4.1

1981	1,936.10	2,001.35	1,817.52	207.9	224.4	177.5	10.4	10.3	10.2	4.3	7.5	-5.6
1982	1,929.37	2,037.05	1,731.04	207.2	228.4	169.1	-0.3	1.8	-4.8	3.8	5.7	-0.9
1983	2,048.23	2,130.88	1,892.69	219.9	239.0	184.8	6.2	4.6	9.3	-2.2	1.0	-9.3
1984	2,040.96	2,107.61	1,917.90	219.2	236.3	187.3	-0.4	-1.1	1.3	-9.1	2.1	-10.5
1985	1,858.06	1,970.53	1,647.73	199.5	221.0	160.9	-9.0	-6.5	-14.1	7.8	9.2	4.1
1986	2,002.37	2,152.32	1,716.10	215.0	241.4	167.6	7.8	9.2	4.1	0.0	0.0	0.0
Budget years (Base: 1980/81 = 100)												
1977/78	1,622.76	1,657.47	1,559.89	90.7	89.7	92.4				24.8	30.7	12.4
1978/79	1,720.13	1,758.58	1,653.49	96.1	95.2	98.0	6.0	6.1	6.0	17.7	23.1	6.1
1979/80	1,775.17	1,799.02	1,732.85	99.2	97.4	102.7	3.2	2.3	4.8	14.0	20.4	1.2
1980/81	1,789.92	1,847.64	1,687.80	100.0	100.0	100.0	0.8	2.7	-2.6	13.1	17.2	3.9
1981/82	1,964.79	2,045.78	1,817.07	109.8	110.7	107.7	9.8	10.7	7.7	3.0	5.9	-3.5
1982/83	1,988.44	2,084.20	1,811.88	111.1	112.8	107.4	1.2	1.9	-0.3	1.8	3.9	-3.2
1983/84	1,973.37	2,064.40	1,801.47	110.2	111.7	106.7	-0.8	-1.0	-0.6	2.6	4.9	-2.6
1984/85	2,087.10	2,155.12	1,961.72	116.6	116.6	116.2	5.8	4.4	8.9	-3.0	0.5	-10.6
1985/86	1,815.54	1,946.73	1,569.30	101.4	105.4	93.0	-13.0	-9.7	-20.0	11.5	11.2	11.8
1986/87	2,024.50	2,165.60	1,754.00	113.1	117.2	103.9	11.5	11.2	11.8	0.0	0.0	0.0

Source: Wages: CBS Employer's Report to National Insurance; Prices: Cost of Living Index

Table 3.9(b): Annual rate of change of wages per salaried worker in the business sector, by wage components, 1976-1987 (each year compared to the previous year, by %)

Year	Cost of Living (COL) index	Changes of wages due to: Change of wages due to COL supplement as a % of the change of COL	COL supplement only	COL supplement and national wage agreements	Change in total wages as paid	total wages above COL supplement and national wage agreements	Real change in wages (% each year compared to the previous year) Change in After COL supplement	After COL supplement and national wage agreements	After all supplements
Calendar years									
1976	31.3	61.3	19.2	26.3	36.9	8.4	-9.1	-3.7	4.5
1977	34.6	68.5	23.7	30.5	44.5	10.7	-7.8	-2.9	7.7
1978	50.6	66.0	33.4	52.1	56.0	2.6	-11.5	0.9	2.8
1979	78.3	54.0	42.3	52.1	87.8	23.5	-19.1	-13.8	6.6
1980	131.0	71.5	93.6	110.2	132.8	10.8	-16.5	-9.8	-0.2
1981	116.8	82.4	96.2	119.5	139.6	9.2	-10.5	1.1	10.3
1982	120.4	71.2	85.7	101.0	123.3	11.1	-15.2	-8.5	1.8
1983	145.6	71.8	104.6	116.5	153.2	17.0	-15.4	-10.8	4.6
1984	373.8	71.7	268.1	333.8	376.5	9.8	-21.9	-9.2	-1.1
1985	304.6	56.9	173.3	196.3	268.8	24.5	-31.5	-24.5	-6.5
1986	48.2	74.9	36.1	38.9	66.4	19.8	-12.4	-10.2	9.2
1987	19.8	54.5	10.8	16.5	29.2	10.9	-7.6	-2.8	7.9

Budget years

1976/77	34.3	63.3	21.7	28.1	38.9	8.4	-9.3	-4.6	3.4
1977/78	38.0	70.8	26.9	37.8	45.7	5.7	-7.6	0.1	6.3
1978/79	52.1	59.7	31.1	45.5	63.0	12.0	-13.8	-3.9	6.1
1979/80	95.2	57.8	55.0	66.0	97.6	19.0	-19.7	-14.0	2.5
1980/81	133.6	74.9	100.0	122.9	142.9	9.0	-14.7	-5.8	2.6
1981/82	110.1	82.1	90.4	108.9	131.6	10.9	-9.6	-0.4	10.7
1982/83	127.0	72.3	91.8	106.1	133.4	13.2	-15.7	-9.5	1.9
1983/84	173.8	65.4	113.6	131.6	164.6	14.2	-19.4	-13.7	-1.0
1984/85	404.6	75.1	303.9	370.8	434.4	13.5	-19.2	-5.8	4.4
1985/86	231.3	55.2	127.7	142.3	197.4	22.7	-33.5	-28.2	-9.7
1986/87	30.2	75.8	22.9	26.2	45.7	15.5	-7.1	-4.8	11.2

Source: Histadrut Trade Union Research Department.
Note: The annual rates of change are calculated as arithmetic averages.

between the Manufacturers Association and the Histadrut aimed to keep COLA but mitigate some of these problems. The solution instituted was to pay COLA but only on a certain percentage of the CPI rise — and above a certain minimum. COLA was sometimes 80, sometimes 70, and sometimes 90 per cent of the CPI rise. In 1975, when the reform was instituted, COLA was on 70 per cent of the CPI rise with a threshold of 5 per cent and adjustments to be calculated at six-month intervals. In the early years of its operations, COLA was also paid only up to a certain ceiling, resulting in reduced wage differentials. On several occasions, the Histadrut, worried about unemployment, agreed to forgo COLA payment, but only on a temporary basis.

Table 3.9 shows the development of real wages (i.e., nominal wages adjusted to change in the cost of living). The second part of the table shows the per cent achieved by COLA, that stemming as a result of national wage agreements, and the rest of the changes. Real wage more than doubled in the 25 years between 1961-86, but COLA was not able to keep up with inflation.

In April 1987, the Knesset, mandated by social considerations, enacted a Minimum Wage Law. The minimum wage was linked to the average wages by an automatic adjustment to be made in April every two years, when collective bargaining agreements are signed. In between, the adjustment is made when COLA is paid. As a result of the law, the minimum wages increased by 49.8 per cent in 1987, by 32.2 per cent in 1988, and by 23.1 per cent in 1989. Wages in the business sector rose by 30.9 per cent, and 22.0 and 15.2 per cent respectively. Economists widely believe that a rise of minimum wages may contribute to unemployment.

Cost of labor

Absolute cost of labor is lower in Israel than in most of the developed countries. However, there is much less difference in the cost of top-level engineers or top managers in Israel versus the USA. Moreover, although Israel's cost of labor is competitive, its product per employee is 60 per cent of that in OECD countries. The average annual increase in unit Israeli labor costs between 1975-1984 was 5.6 per cent, only exceeded by the USA (5.7 per cent) and the UK (6 per cent). Only part of the cost of labor goes to the employee either as wages or fringe benefits. The remainder is deducted and goes to the government through direct and indirect taxes. There is a general belief in Israel that both fringe benefits and taxation are higher than in other countries.

Wages

Israel's wage structure reflects a commitment to the socialist egalitarian philosophy. Central to a socialist outlook is a belief that there is no need to link what each citizen contributes ('from each according to ability') with what each receives for working ('to each according to his needs'). This ideology has been distorted over time. Egalitarian beliefs were evident in the laws mandating universal military conscription; in the creation of a national insurance plan which provided flat rate pension and survivors' benefits; and in the inclusion in the wages paid to workers in some sectors of the economy of a 'family allowance' based on the number of dependants! With respect to compensation for work, the egalitarian ideology outside the kibbutz movement came to mean a commitment to three objectives: equal pay for equal work; only a limited differential between the lowest and highest paid worker; and use of the welfare and tax systems to maintain minimal differentials.

Despite the official ideology, however, there have always been pervasive economic pressures encouraging differentiation. Individual occupational groups claim that their services constitute unique contributions which entitle them to enhanced income payoffs. As early as the 1920s, a growing conflict between the very strict egalitarian ideology of the labor Zionists and the demands of skilled workers to a higher than nonskilled labor salary led the Histadrut to pay more to skilled workers without formally admitting it. Israel attempted to absorb into its economy large numbers of immigrants and also opted for a policy of rapid economic growth. The economy had increasing need for the technical and managerial skills necessary for building the state institutions and effecting rapid industrialization. Certain technical and managerial skills were very scarce, but ideological constraints prevented too large differences in income.

The result was the creation of many contradictions between the official ideology of equality and pressing economic needs. Any perception of an increase in inequality of income and wealth repeatedly caused public outcries and political debates. During a period of five years, two separate public commissions were established to examine developments in the distribution of income and to ensure that the government was maintaining equality. The first committee found that:

income differentiation in Israel is significantly lower than in other countries. The comparison of the net income distribution clearly shows that the influence of income tax further reduces the degree of inequality in Israel compared to other countries.

(Israel, Committee on Income Distribution
and Social Inequality, 1966, p. 3)

The second committee reported a further reduction in inequality among salaried urban Jewish families. It found 'inequality in 1970 was less than in 1963/4,' with 'an improvement in the relative position of the lower income brackets' (Israel, Committee on Income Distribution and Social Inequality, 1971, p. 4).

Despite these positive reports, doubts lingered. The committees drew their conclusions (in part) on the basis of income surveys that allegedly did not include many nontaxable sources of supplementary income. The reliability of the income surveys as a source of information on the income of salaried workers has been reduced during the 1960s since significant portions of the increases in salaries were in the form of benefits, many of which were not reported as income in the surveys. Others, too, questioned the reliability of the income surveys as a measure of inequality, noting scattered evidence of unreported supplemental payments (Roeter and Shamai, 1971).

Supplements to income

While the linkage mechanism was an obvious way to keep realistic the egalitarian ideology, there was still no room for rewarding occupational groups which, either because of special contribution, or scarcity of members, could command relatively higher pay in a free labor market. Over time, pressures for specialized pay treatment took the form of demands for 'supplements' to the pay packet for characteristics claimed to be unique to the occupational group.

In 1957, public-sector engineers started a battle for higher income. The engineers demanded 'selective supplements' from government and other employers, and simultaneously tried to convince the Histadrut that a supplementary payment for them would not affect other salaries. Based on the recommendations of a public commission appointed to investigate the status of the engineering profession, the engineers received three selective supplements: they were allowed payments for additional hours; the *Vetek*, or seniority supplement, was paid from the time the engineer graduated rather than from the date he started working at his job — up to a ceiling of 25 per cent of basic salary; and lastly, the engineers received a supplement of IL70-IL200 a month, according to rank, for the 'acquisition of professional literature.'

By 1961, supplementary payments of all kinds were granted to various groups of workers. The fourth government-appointed committee on public pay scales (Horowitz Committee) submitted its report in April 1963. The committee suggested yet another attempt to reach a uniform pay scale, based on evaluation of jobs across the whole public sector. All special allowances and different pay scales were abolished, unless they were granted for special and temporary conditions of work. The committee estimated that the job evaluation would result in a 3 per cent increase of average salaries. In fact, each group of workers demanded more points on the job evaluation scale each time another group was granted some points. The process of 'balancing upwards' (based on a 'linking' ideology) resulted in an increase of average salaries in the civil service by 38 per cent. (The increases were 'uniform' in the same pay scale and without any special supplements.) These large increases may have also been due to the approaching election. By 1975, 120 special supplements to income existed in the public sector. These special supplements are specific to individual occupations and, therefore, represent the (frequently successful) efforts of single occupational groups to claim differential treatment compared to other occupations in the same pay grade.

The realities of industrialization, with its significant differentiation of knowledge and skills needed in the labor force, run counter to the egalitarian ideology. This is clearly revealed, for example, in the conclusion that job evaluation should be the basis for ranking occupations and their income rewards in the public sector. The fundamental philosophy of job evaluation is that *differences* among occupations can be measured objectively, as a basis for assigning income rewards to each.

The mechanism of linking occupations, developed to insure that differentiation of income through the upward movement of individual occupations would occur only with difficulty, seems to have neutralized the effect of supplements with respect to the broad income distribution among civil service occupations.

In the business sector, in contrast, special supplements play a major role in differentiating the income among occupations, and mainly between top executives and others. These differences are realized through subrosa payments or other supplements, many of which do not appear in the pay slip, and are, therefore, less visible as a basis for individual comparisons by other groups of workers. Top executives among all occupations apparently receive the highest proportion of their income in the form of supplements. Other occupations also receive supplements that apparently have the effect of moving their gross income 'out of line' from what it might have been if supplements had constituted a smaller percentage of the total income.

Fringe benefits

In Israel, fringe benefits are a very important component of the cost of labor. Fringe benefits are that part of the compensation package that does not appear in the pay slip, but are part of the cost of employment to the employer. These include a whole list of legislated and customary items added to the salary. Among them are national insurance contributions (10.85 per cent of gross payments up to a prescribed limit), severance pay (8.3 per cent), provident fund contributions, clothing allowance, recreation allowance, transport between home and work, subsidized meals provided at work, car maintenance allowance, use of company cars, travel abroad, paid leave or vacation, sick leave, maternity leave, payments for training funds, free goods, gifts and the like, and many specific benefits that may include subsidies on products (for example all employees of the electricity company do not pay for the electricity they consume at home).

Fringe benefits as a percentage of gross salary in Israel rose from 15.6 per cent in 1960, to 29.5 per cent in 1977. The Israel Institute of Productivity estimated that fringe benefits ranged from 40 to 45 per cent in 1985. The statistical abstract for 1986 suggested a level of 25 to 36 per cent. Rates of fringe benefits also vary among the different categories of professionals and positions also reaching a level of fringe benefits.

The increased level of fringe benefits was partially a result of legal requirements (national insurance) but largely a result of free collective bargaining. This may mean that a conversion of fringe benefits to salaries is not what employees prefer. On the other hand, it is also possible that individuals do prefer to receive higher salaries (that will also be reflected in the pension payments), and the reported increase was based on employers' interests or misleading data.

All in all, the cost of labor to the employer is much higher than compensation perceived by employees, resulting in reduced motivation. However, comparison with other countries shows these costs to be competitive. Productivity in Israel grew much less than in other countries, reducing Israel's competitive position.

It seems obvious that organizations operating in the market economy — whether they are state or privately owned — are more responsive to labor market conditions than is the civil service. This labor market sensitivity takes the form of being more likely to increase total income in response to the labor market scarcity of a particular group of workers. The easiest and quickest response such a firm can make is to 'fatten' the supplements to basic salaries or the fringe benefits as a means for attracting and/or holding employees. This minimizes the visible differences among occupational groups in their base wage or salary, and, thus, minimizes individual comparisons, providing that the supplements can be kept reasonably concealed. Such secrecy is much more likely in the market sector than in the civil service sector of the economy.

All sectors of Israeli economy are affected by the socialist traditions that inspired the founding of the state and which persist to the present time. This tradition calls for linking of contributions and needs and minimum differentials of pay from the top to the bottom of the occupational structure. This is *ideology-as-goal*: when individual occupational groups seek special income treatment, they justify their claim on the basis of some distinctive feature of the group's work. Underlying such claims of uniqueness is an ideological conviction that inequality is legitimate. When that belief arises in an egalitarian society, it becomes an *ideology-as-rationalization* to justify departure from the egalitarian goal.

Ideology-as-goal and ideology-as-rationalization readily co-exist in Israel. Israel's image as a society guided by a dominant ideology seems less realistic than the image of a society having multiple ideologies affecting social action, where the ideologies may be incongruent, or even inconsistent (Dubin and Aharoni, 1981).

Human capital as a competitive advantage

Since the late 1970s, the world has been experiencing a technological revolution propelled by rapid scientific progress and an array of rapid, simultaneous and symbiotic advances in technologies including computers, robotics, biotechnology, lasers, telecommunication, electro-optics and new materials. These new technologies not only create new industries and new products, they transform traditional industries. The technological advances are also generating profound macroeconomic changes. In these new industries, competitive advantage is based much more on knowledge than on natural endowment. Less labor and capital is required to produce many manufactured goods. Venture capitalism has emerged as an engine of both change and growth, reflecting the increasing need to take risks in order to accelerate the pace of innovation required to remain competitive. Israel is poor in raw materials and quarries but rich in outstanding scientific manpower. Therefore, Israel has a high probability of reaping important advantages in the production of high-tech products based on local research and development. Some even argue that Israel's only opportunities for increased export lie in industrial fields where advanced technology is the basis of product offerings, and future success depends on businesses investing in rapidly growing high-tech markets. Transport costs for these products to and from foreign markets are less significant than for cement, for example. Since 1970, the government attempted to encourage so called 'noble horses' — leading edge knowledge-based firms that were expected to grow very rapidly. This belief has been reinforced by some significant successes of new knowledge-based firms.

Indeed, because Jews have always cherished the importance of education, the Israeli population is generally highly educated. In fact, one great advantage of Israel, in seeking for itself a place among nations, is its high quality of human capital. As one example, Israel boasts the highest ratio of medical doctors to total population; it has one doctor per 345 population, compared to about 500 in the USA or 18,500 in Morocco. Israel also has a very high ratio of technicians and engineers out of total population.

Conclusions

A key element of the Zionist dream has been to gather the exiled Jews in their ancient holy land. This objective was only partially achieved. The per cent of Jews in Israel grew from 0.31 in 1882, and 5.7 per cent in 1948, to 28 per cent by the end of 1987. Those who came (and remained) in Israel did it largely for ideological and religious reasons.

Israel has been successful in absorbing a very large number of immigrants. Within the first four years of its existence, Israel almost doubled its population and within a decade almost tripled it. To understand the magnitude of the task, the reader may want to ponder what had happened if the same tripling of population had happened in the reader's own country. Certainly, the probability of economic, social and political upheaval in a situation like that is quite high. This is more so if one remembers that those Jews who had comfortable lives in the developed countries did not leave and come en masse to Israel. The new immigrants were mainly the survivors of the Nazi Holocaust in Europe and more so the Asian and North African Jews, many of whom had been driven from the Moslem countries. This 'Ingathering of the Exiles' brought to Israel individuals from different backgrounds, cultures, and educational levels. The creation of a new fabric of an Israeli society from all this great diversity has been a costly, lengthy and not always successful task. Many of the North African Jews will never forget nor will they forgive the established Israelis for what they perceived as looking at them as second-rate citizens, attempting to force them to accept the culture of the East European Jews. Whether Israel has been able to integrate all these people into one nation is still debatable.

The Israeli government devoted significant resources to population dispersal. It built houses, erected factories, gave generous grants to those willing to invest in the so-called development regions, but was unable to reduce in any significant way the lure of living in the large cities and mainly in the coastal plains. In the 1960s, the government moved to build 'Development Cities.' It realized it would not be able to achieve population dispersal by building villages. Unfortunately there were too many development cities and the vast majority of them were not quite successful. In entering the 1990s, Israel faces a renewed challenge: to absorb an accelerating wave of immigrants from the USSR.

4 Economic structure and institutions

Introduction

In this chapter we shall survey the distinctive pluralistic composition of the Israeli economy and the unique structure it developed. A brief attempt is made to explain, based on the historical discussion of chapter 2, how this unique structure of institutions came into being and to analyze the changes introduced in the political economy of Israel once the Likud came to power. We shall start by looking at the public sector's share in the GNP and the means it uses to finance its operations. We shall move to discuss the many off-budget methods of intervention adopted by the Israeli government. Then we shall explain the structure of the unique Israeli institutions, show the evolution of the relative size of each sector, analyze the peculiar characteristics of each sector and the role of their managers. We shall point out some of the strengths and weaknesses of the institutional structure of Israel. We shall also point out the problems institutions face going into the 1990s. We shall explain the sectors, how big they are and what significance their operations have. We shall also show the impact of the many attempts in Israel to create cooperative institutions rather than to rely on unfettered market operations. The role of government in the different economic branches of the economy is discussed in the following chapter.

Some unique institutions

There are at least two variables in which the Israeli economy is very different from other economies. One is the depth of involvement of the government in the market economy. The second is its sectoral and economic structure and the degree of influence of political institutions on economic activities. Sectoral structure refers to the relative weight of the public, the private and the Histadrut sectors in the ownership and control of factors

x

148

of production. A phenomenon peculiar to Israel is that the public sector includes not only the government but also the National Institutions (the World Zionist Organization, the Jewish National Fund, and Keren Hayesod). There also exists a very large cooperative sector with other producing entities controlled by the Histadrut.

The share of the public sector in product, number of employees or total investment is one of the highest in the world, certainly in comparison to the United States or Japan but also in comparison to Europe. The truly unique Israeli characteristic, though, is not necessarily the very high volume of economic activity carried out directly by the government but mainly the degree of intervention of government bureaucracy and its involvement in the decisions of every single firm in the economy. This involvement is achieved by carrying out all sorts of economic activities that are not registered in the budget. It is also achieved by a complicated network of informal ties, contacts and influences.

One reason for this unique set of attributes is that all Israeli politico-economic institutions were forged in the period between the end of World War I and 1930. At that time, they were designed to create a new society, based on utopian visions. The forefathers of Israel abandoned the ghetto environment they scorned. They feverishly hoped to transfer themselves into new Jews: hardy, strong, courageous, and having deep roots to the land. They attempted to escape from what they perceived as the decadence of the big city and from what they termed the 'air occupations' (*luftgeschäften*) of their ancestors. By that term, they meant occupations not rooted in land or with manufacturing. They were not only revolutionaries but also dreamers, utopians and romantics. They yearned to create a new and just society, anchored in strong values of social justice and equality.

While these zealots were different in many ways, they all shared at least two basic beliefs. First, that cooperation, based on sentiments of brotherhood, could be made into the dominant mode for social relations. Second, that the needs of the country, of the movement, and of the community were the only criteria for judging the desirability of an operation. These persons did not live for themselves, but for the group, for the ideals, and for the future of the nation. Some of these persons created the kibbutz, based on the principle of total cooperation and communal activity. They believed in the saying: 'from each according to his ability; to each according to his needs.' The kibbutz founders believed they could abolish social classes by the abolition of both private property and hired labor. They also attempted to abolish power by rotating all leadership positions. They created the best educational system for their children but also moved the children from the basic family unit to the children house.

Kibbutz members do not own any private property and do not receive any salary or wages for their work. Actually, there are several kibbutz types, differing mainly by their political affiliations. Some also differ on an historically ideological debate between those who believed a kibbutz should be relatively small and those who held the banner of 'a large kibbutz.' At the time, Degania, the first kibbutz, created Degania B, a second kibbutz, to avoid having more than a few dozen members. Today, the largest kibbutz in Israel has more than two thousand inhabitants.

Other pioneers created the moshav, with less intensive communal life. The moshav, like the kibbutz, is located on nationally owned land, bans hired labor, and uses cooperative methods of marketing. In contrast to the kibbutz, each family is allocated at least a part of the land, where they work separately.

The major ideas of the moshav form of settlement were: self-employment, mutual guarantee and aid, private farms but cooperative and mutual marketing. The more efficient farmer may become more affluent. The first moshav, Nahalal, was established in 1921. In the moshav, each farmer owns the house and the land, but all are bound by a strict code of mutual aid and responsibility. By law, the municipal authority of the moshav and its communal agricultural association are identical. Each member of the moshav is responsible under mutual liability for all the debts, including those created by futile investments of the purchasing organization. In addition, a moshav member cannot sell his plot without an approval of all members. He usually will use the internal judicial system rather than the state one. A communal moshav has more communal property than a non-communal moshav, but less than in a kibbutz.

To make sure that the moshav remains an agricultural entity, the law requires that at least 80 per cent of the residents must be farmers. Moreover, only one son can continue as a member of the moshav. This regulation was originally designed to avoid having non-farmers residing in a moshav and to avoid partition of the land into too small plots. Because of this system some of the second-generation members were compelled to leave.

Both the individual kibbutz and the individual moshav are attached to a federation or movement. Each federation or movement is closely affiliated with a political party. Kibbutzim and moshavim consist of a tiny minority of the population, but enjoy an elite status. City dwellers also shared the basic strong belief in the supremacy of the country's needs over the wishes of any individual. Rural and urban dwellers alike struggled incessantly with despair and worked through hard and arduous times to achieve the national goals. The belief that objectives must be shared and that cooperation is important has survived in many ways in Israel, certainly insofar as the defense of the country is concerned (see chapter 6). Ideals still dictate certitudes about the future, and national needs are still accepted as much more important than individual wishes.

The pragmatism of the leaders of the founders' generation led them also to accept the idea of a pluralistic economy. Israel is a pluralistic society in several senses. First, ownership of economic units is sometimes held by the public sector, in other cases by labor or by cooperatives, and in still others by private individuals. The private sector is also very dispersed, not dominated by several large firms. Second, capitalist and socialist forms are intermingled in the Israeli economy.

Voluntary political system in the Yishuv period

The objectives of the Jewish institutions in Israel were far from identical to those of the British government. This fact meant that there was a great need among Jewish settlers to develop means of enforcement without enjoying the sanctions available to a government of a sovereign state. The Jewish Yishuv was able to achieve a far flung level of discipline and coherence by developing a political culture based largely on consensus as a basis for legitimacy. The consensus was achieved to some extent by having a high degree of political involvement: an individual was expected to belong to several associations, entities, organizations and political parties. These organized groups participated in carrying out many pseudo-government duties: education, security, immigration, welfare services. In addition, the political parties were carrying out more duties than common in other countries. The party gave its members not only ideological support but also health services and employment. It also organized cultural events, published books and newspapers, maintained kindergartens and school systems, initiated and built settlements, maintained welfare organizations and sports associations.

The legitimization was also achieved by inviting non-political organizations, based on economic interests (for example the manufacturers' associations), ethnic (for example Sephardim or Yemenites), or on a professional common denominator to participate in the political system. The organs of the Zionist organization encouraged this widespread participation (and since 1929, the expanded Jewish Agency invited participation of non-Zionists). After a consensus among those participants was reached, individuals (perceived as subservient to the organization), were expected to be disciplined and follow instructions of the national organizations. To be sure, in some extreme cases of crisis, legitimate consensus was not achieved. In all of these cases, one party left the National Institutes and the irrevocable differences of opinion caused the establishment of new organizations: the Revisionist party created, in 1935, a New Zionist Organization. It organized the *Irgun Zvai Leumi* militia, that left the *Hagana*; Yair Stern Pater left this *Irgun* and created *Lehi* (see chapter 6). These new organizations were stigmatized as being outside the consensus of the 'organized Yishuv' and their members were ostracized.

The politics of the Yishuv period were characterized by the enormous importance of ideas, beliefs and extreme ideological intensity and hair splitting, but also by the ability of the dominant party to achieve coherence around a wide consensus after a long process of debates, of convincing, and of compromises. The leadership was imbued with a strong belief in the need for building a new society in Eretz Israel. Partially because of that, legitimate differences of opinion among leaders about the way the Zionist movement should proceed turned into personal rivalries that caused a series of divisions and separations that were inflamed into blazing hatred. The pressures for conformism, for obedience and for putting the individual at the disposal of the community and the mission of building a new society were enormous — much stronger than any legal compulsion and coercion of a sovereign governmental system. At the same time, the need to reach coalition agreements necessitated a very wide consensus.

Conformism was also made possible because of the all-embracing network of the political party. The parties owned their own economic entities, developed their own newspapers and journals, nourished their own educational systems, ran their own banks, promoted their own sports associations, and even had their own army. This organization helped in achieving political control over almost every aspect of individual life. This system was transferred from the incipient Jewish commonwealth to the State of Israel. It influenced in a very significant way how the country organized its economy.

Individuals' subservience to the common good and to the community needs was based to a large extent on ideological belief and strong socialization. In addition, those who did not conform were faced with a loss of social esteem but also of place of work and source of income. The political economic system made individuals extremely dependent on the organization. The Histadrut organized and concentrated all of the economic, social and welfare activities of the workers. The executive body (*Va'ad Po'el*) of the Histadrut, composed of professional politicians, controlled all the economic units. Even the kibbutzim and moshavim (communal settlements) were put under the control of the *Va'ad Po'el* by creating a corporation called Nir that had a veto right on the activities of these communal settlements. As one example, an individual kibbutz was not allowed to sign contracts with the World Zionist Organization. The political party also organized the teachers, and made sure they would educate the children in the basic Zionist ideals as interpreted by the socialists.

As early as 1922, the tendency for central decisions was apparent. In 1920, the 'Work Regiment' was created, aspiring to build the land by the creation of a general commune of all Jewish workers. In 1921, one part of the Regiment created Ein Harod, the first 'large' kibbutz. This was in partnership with second Aliyah pioneers such as Shlomo Lavi, who preached for the 'Large Kibbutz,' and the first Jewish settlement in the newly acquired Valley of Jisreel. The two parties ran into intense skirmishes because of different ideological beliefs (such as whether a commune should be only in production or also in consumption). The Histadrut intervened, and dictated its solutions. One result of the rift was the division of Ein Harod into two different entities. Throughout these problems, decisions were enforced on the Work Regiment by the Histadrut central committee.

Another result of the voluntary aspect of all Jewish national organizations was a wide coalition of different parties that ran the national institutions. This coalition allocated among its members various resources including budget and managerial positions, but also 'certificates' that allowed immigration to Eretz Israel.

The industrial structure is also very specific to Israel. Generally, three stages in the development of economies are distinguished. In the very poor countries most of the labor force is employed in agriculture so that it can supply the required food and maintain subsistence. Productivity rises in agriculture and increased production cause the transfer of workers from agriculture to manufacturing industry. In the third and most developed stage the lion's share of employment is in services.

Table 4.1(a) The public-sector budget as a % of GNP, 1961-1989 (annual averages)

	1961-5	1966-70	1971-5	1976-80	1982-4	1985-9
Expenditures						
Domestic public consumption	15.9	21.6	25.0	25.7	28.0	30.0
Domestic public investment	4.6	4.3	4.8	4.0	3.1	2.4
Public consumption of imports	5.2	9.2	13.1	11.9	9.5	5.7
Interest in foreign currency	0.9	0.7	0.9	1.8	2.1	4.3
Total including subsidies and transfers	26.6	35.8	43.8	43.4	42.7	46.1
					72.8	62.7
Income						
Net taxes	23.6	22.2	21.3	17.8	17.2	24.0
Growth of money base	1.9	1.6	3.0	2.4	2.1	0.3
Increase in net internal debt	-3.6	0.6	5.4	4.4	7.0	-1.0
Increase in external debt	0.8	7.5	5.1	7.0	8.1	-1.4
Foreign grants	3.8	3.8	9.1	11.9	10.5	14.9
Growth of GNP (annual rates, %)	10.1	7.7	7.2	3.0	1.6	3.2

Source: Meridor, 1985, Bank of Israel, *Annual Report*, 1988, pp. 116, 117, 125; 1989, pp. 160, 162, 182.

Table 4.1(b) Mean growth rates, 1960-1989 (%)

	1960-5	1965-7	1967-72	1972-5	1975-7	1977-81	1981-4	1985-9
Business sector								
GDP	9.4	-0.2	13.9	3.5	2.8	3.8	2.5	1.3
Capital stock	10.6	7.3	7.8	8.6	5.7	4.1	3.8	2.8
Manhours	4.4	-5.8	7.4	-0.5	-0.1	2.0	1.1	1.7
Product wage	6.0	11.3	0.9	3.0	7.6	1.5	3.7	-1.4
Real rate of return[a]	14.3	9.6	21.6	19.5	16.3	16.3	17.0	10.9
Private consumption	9.7	2.1	8.1	5.4	4.0	5.8	5.2	-1.0
Public consumption	9.9	24.6	10.3	19.5	-11.1	3.8	0.2	-8.9
Investment	10.9	-19.3	24.5	1.8	-10.3	-1.7	2.7	-2.7
Exports	12.7	10.4	17.8	4.3	13.6	4.7	4.2	4.6
Imports	12.0	6.9	15.2	14.1	-3.8	4.2	4.8	-6.4
Import/export prices	-1.2	-1.3	0.0	3.3	-1.3	0.3	5.1	-2.3
Key macroeconomic targets								
Ratio of current account deficit to GDP (current prices)[a]	18.3	14.2	19.4	36.2	21.5	22.6	17.9	6.1
Unemployment rate[a]	3.6	10.4	2.8	3.2	4.1	5.3	5.1	8.9
Consumer prices	7.2	5.0	7.1	33.0	33.0	87.3	27.3	20.2

Sources: CBS, *Statistical Abstract*, various years.
Bank of Israel, *Annual Report*, 1988, pp. 14, 146.
Note: [a]End-of-period levels.

Table 4.2(a) Taxation and transfers as a % of GNP, 1961-1988

	1961-5	1966-70	1971-5	1976-80	1981-2	1980-84	1985-8
Taxes							
Direct taxes	14.3	16.5	21.2	24.7	25.7		
Income tax on wage earners	–	–	5.1	6.9	7.8		
National Insurance	2.8	3.5	5.2	6.7	7.4		
Taxes on domestic production	13.9	11.6	10.2	13.4	12.0		
VAT	–	–	–	3.8	5.6		
Taxes on civilian imports	6.8	5.6	9.3	8.6	7.8		
VAT	–	–	–	2.5	3.1		
Total taxes	35.1	33.6	40.8	46.6	45.5		
Compulsory loans	1.3	1.5	4.1	1.1	0.5		
Transfer payments							
To households and non-profit institutions	6.3	8.3	10.5	14.3	14.1	11.3	11.6
Subsidization of credit to households	–	–	1.6	2.1	0.9	4.5	1.5
Subsidization of domestic production	2.0	2.0	2.1	3.2	5.6		
Subsidization of credit to domestic production	–	–	–	4.1	2.9		
Direct support of exports	1.1	1.7	3.1	1.6	1.1		
Subsidization of credit to exports	–	–	–	1.5[a]	2.4		
Interest on internal debt	1.8	2.2	4.0	5.3	7.0		
Total excluding credit subsidization	11.2	14.2	19.7	24.4	27.8		
Total net taxation excluding credit subsidization	23.9	19.4	21.1	22.2	17.7		
Net taxes after deduction of implicit subsidization of credit	–	–	–	14.5	11.5		

Source: Berglas in Ben-Porath, 1986, p. 226.
Note: a The subsidization of credit for exports occurred in 1978-80, during which period it accounted for an annual average of 2.5 per cent of product.

Table 4.2(b) Tax burden, subsidies and transfer payments as a % of GNP, 1970-1989

	1970-74	1975-7	1978-80	1980-84	1985-8	1989
Total taxes and transfers from the public	41	45	46	43.2	46.5	41.1
Net taxes excluding credit subsidies	22	19	23	26.3	31.2	24.6
Credit subsidies	–	7	9	4.5	1.5	0.7
Net taxes				21.7	29.7	23.9
Direct taxes						
Total direct taxes	17	22	24	24.9	24.7	21.8
Income tax	12	16	17	16.0	16.5	14.2
Transfer payments to the public	10	14	14	11.3	11.6	13.4
Domestic production						
Net taxes on domestic production	8	2	3	4.2		11.0
Indirect taxes	10	13	14	11.0	13.7	13.6
Direct subsidies	2	3	3	4.4	2.5	1.9
Subsidization of credit to business	–	7	7	2.6	1.5	0.7
Foreign trade						
Net taxes on foreign trade	8	7	6	4.6	6.8	4.4

Source: Bank of Israel, *Annual Report*, 1980, p. 82; 1986, p. 104; 1988, p. 125; 1989, p. 182

This is a result both of the rise in the standard of living and the increase of business services in a modern economy. When different economies are arranged by their product per capita, Israel is anomalous. The share of services in the economy is much larger than one would expect based on the product per capita. Gur Ofer has demonstrated that the special composition of employment in Israel can be explained by the existence of a large and consistent import surplus (Ofer, 1967).

The size of the public sector

From a macroeconomic point of view, a major variable in understanding the Israeli economy is the size of the public sector as measured by its budget. For an economist, the budget is 'the framework within which all government activities are carried out' (Berglas, in Ben-Porath, 1986, p. 221). As a per cent of GNP, the budget grew from 36 per cent in 1955 to 39 per cent in 1960, from 44 per cent in 1965 to 63 per cent in 1970, and 80 per cent in 1975. In 1977, the budget was equal to 102 per cent of GNP! Since then, the ratio has gone down, but the budget is still more than 90 per cent of GNP. This can be ascribed both to the rapid rise in defense expenditures and to a much higher level of social costs. Thus, defense expenditure was 16 per cent of the budget in 1955, 25 per cent in 1960, 41 per cent in 1970, 29 per cent in 1980 and 29 per cent in 1988-9.

A third reason was the tendency in the past to finance the budget by levying compulsory loans instead of increased taxes. These loans have to be repaid. In the 1980s, interest and loan repayments consisted of a third or more of the total budget. Interest alone was 8 per cent of the budget in 1985, and 24 per cent in 1987. Domestic public consumption grew from 15.9 per cent of GNP in 1961-5 to 28.0 per cent in 1981-4, and to 32.1 per cent in 1985-8. Total public expenditures zoomed from 26.6 per cent in 1961-5 to 41.8 per cent in 1980-4, and 46.1 per cent in 1985-88. Government expenditures grew much faster than GDP (Table 4.1).

The government had to finance its increasing spending and that meant a rise in taxation. However, because of the high level of transfer payments, net taxes continuously declined. The government financed its operations by borrowing in foreign currency, selling the currency to Israeli residents in order to finance its expenditures and by borrowing locally. It has thus created a heavy debt service burden — both foreign and domestic.

Table 4.3 Tax revenues as a % of GNP

State	1965	1987
Sweden	35.6	56.7
Netherlands	35.5	48.0
Austria	34.6	42.3
Norway	33.2	48.3
Germany	31.6	37.6
Belgium	31.2	46.1
United Kingdom	30.8	37.5
Finland	30.1	35.9
Denmark	30.1	52.0
Israel	27.5	47.6
Italy	27.3	36.2
USA	26.5	30.0
Ireland	26.0	39.9
Canada	25.9	34.5
New Zealand	24.3	38.6
Australia	23.8	31.3
Switzerland	20.7	32.0
Portugal	18.6	31.4
Japan	18.1	30.2

Source: OECD, *Revenue Statistics of OECD Member Countries* in *1990 Statistical Abstract of United States*, p. 845.

Total taxes more than doubled in real terms between 1970 and 1980. Production in that decade grew by 65 per cent in constant price, while taxes as a per cent of product grew from 32.5 per cent in 1960, to 36.8 per cent in 1970, to a high of 48.0 per cent in 1986, back a little to 45.9 per cent in 1988, and 41.1 per cent in 1989 (Table 4.2). This steep increase in tax collection was used to increase transfer payments. Total transfer payments excluding implicit subsidies through credit were 12.2 per cent of GNP in 1960, 15.6 per cent in 1970 and 22.0 per cent in 1980. If implicit credit subsidies are included, total transfers to individuals, to domestic production and to exports (including interest on internal debts) in the beginning of the 1980s were about one-third of GNP, but 22.7 per cent in 1988. Taxpayers, however, care about gross taxes they pay. High taxes have increased the incentive for tax evasion and tax avoidance (for example by directing savings to tax-exempt channels or preferring leisure to additional work). The taxes:GNP ratio in Israel has reached world records (Table 4.3).

Important as the macroeconomic figures are, they reveal only

159

a small portion of the framework within which government activities are carried out. Much of what the government does is not revealed through the budget. First, the budget figures do not include the many activities carried out by units that are part of the public sector whose operations do not appear in the budget. Second, the government directs and regulates each and every large firm in the economy. It can decide on different prices for the factors of production or on different effective rates of exchange. Third, what is or is not budgeted has changed with time. Thus, implicit credit subsidies were not at one time shown in the budget. Later they were incorporated because of the insistence and pressures of the State Controller. The same story happened in many other cases, such as the equalization fund for oil (see chapter 5). Even today, some covert subsidies are still not budgeted.

The part of the economy directly managed by the government includes not only sectors such as education, defense, or police services. The government of Israel by the end of the 1980s was the owner of almost all the land, water, energy sources, radio and television, mines, defense industries and airline transportation.

Israel gives massive administrative protection to its local production. This fact, combined with the miniature size of Israel, meant that much of its production system was carried out under monopolistic or oligopolistic conditions. In addition, the nearest foreign markets have been closed, as they are in a state of war with Israel. Since it does not allow import competition, the government bureaucracy sees itself obligated to control prices. Consequently, almost every plant in Israel is administratively directed by a government that sees itself as the patron and custodian of both business and the national interest, but very rarely of consumers. The Histadrut, as we shall later see, sees its most important role as assuring employment. The fact that it represents workers did not deter its firms from joining cartel arrangements increasing consumers' costs. The government also decides what is an 'essential product' and what should be defined as a luxury product, levying very high tariffs and taxes on products it defines as luxurious. It also decides what the citizens will consume by subsidizing products it considers essential, by levying different taxes, and by banning the import of 'luxury products.' The government impact is only slightly the result of its size. Much more relevant is the arsenal of means of intervention and the ways by which they are used.

Means of intervention

The Israeli government intervenes in the market in many ways, and only a few of these result in an increased government budget. The government decides on the relative price of capital and labor — thus affecting business decisions regarding the mix of these two factors of production. Decisions on relative prices are often differentiated for different regions of the country. The government also decides in many cases what to produce. It requires licenses for the production of different goods, administratively banning imports and selectively encouraging goods by granting a subsidy, by loan guarantees or by allowing higher prices. Production is further influenced by the determination of the relative prices of the factors of production, sometimes through cross-subsidy to different factors of production and often by creating a myriad of effective rates of exchange. The government also protects import substitution firms from international competition.

The government allocates capital, land, water and, to a large extent, labor. It affects consumption by its income policy, using differential taxes, transfer payments, subsidies to selective products, tariffs and other levies. Sometimes it simply does not allow the supply of certain products (for example cable television was until recently illegal in Israel; it remains under heavy restrictions). Sometimes it uses its ability administratively to prevent a new competitor from emerging (as it did in gas distribution but also in many other fields). By requiring licenses, the government is able to create property rights stemming from artificial scarcity. Thus, a taxi license in Israel is traded for high prices.

The major means allowing the government to intervene in resource allocation, by far, is its total control of the capital market. No private firm may issue bonds or shares of stock without an approval of the Minister of Finance. Foreign exchange is controlled, and the government regulates and directs most of the flow of funds. This control enables many off-budget operations. Time and again, the government has announced a budget cut but in reality it simply moved from budget financing to granting of a right to get money for the same purpose from other government-controlled sources. The government also pays most of the budget of many non-profit organizations supplying education or health services. These institutions are sometimes counted as an integral part of the private sector even though the lion's share of their budget is paid by the government.

In the first decade of statehood, the government attempted

strong socialist methods as well as direct controls and allocations. Private ownership was not assumed to be an acceptable form of pioneering activity. Since the 1960s, the government has veered sharply away from direct control, but this has not meant a free market. The Israeli economy is still highly politicized, and it is almost impossible to be successful in a business without a favorable government attitude. The government today consults more with some business leaders, and has moved from a direct budgetary allocation to allocation by using its control of capital markets. Since the 1960s, it has been using discriminating rates of interest as its major means of aiding one firm or punishing another. Firms that undertook to operate in development regions, or to export, or to produce goods the government considered important, received both short- and long-term loans at a highly subsidized rate of interest. Because of the extremely high rate of inflation, most of these loans turned out to have a negative real rate of interest. Even short-term loans for working capital had a large dose of subsidy built into the very low interest rates. On the other hand, firms operating in the central part of the country and pursuing economic activities considered 'non-essential,' such as the wholesale or retail trade, paid generally confiscatory rates of interest: in the second half of 1985, the real rate of interest, net of inflation, was more than 20 per cent per annum. Such rates were paid on the so-called 'free funds.' In the grey market, the rates were generally higher. For those who received government preferences, interest rates were much lower. In addition, about 50 per cent of the country's towns receive some kind of tax break.

In addition to its absolute control of the capital market, the government possesses a variety of other tools. Most of the land in Israel is owned by *Keren Kayemet* (Jewish National Fund) or by the government directly. All of that land is administered by a government entity, the Israel Land Authority. Because of strong religious beliefs ('the land shall not be sold in perpetuity,' Leviticus, 25:23) the authority leases the land on a long-term (up to 99 years) basis. It can decide on the pricing of such land as well as on its availability. Water and electricity are also supplied by a monopoly firm (water by a jointly owned Histadrut and government firm named Mekorot, Hebrew for resources; electricity by a state-owned firm). In both cases, the firms are directed by the government to use a set of different prices for different users. Water for agriculture use is sold much below cost, and the price is equal for water in the rainy north and the desert south although water to the south is carried at a great expense in the 'national water pipeline.' Water is further subsidized by the electricity firm, charging its lowest rates to Mekorot. A somewhat higher rate is paid by manufacturers, while consumer households pay rates that are several times higher than the water company. Such a system of differentiated prices is also used for energy sources: fuel for household use costs much more than for manufacturing industry; and gasoline purchased for use in private cars cross-subsidizes oil used by industry. These cross-subsidies are achieved through an internal fund, receiving some of the household revenue to cover the manufacturing subsidized rates. This fund was also used to finance oil explorations and emergency inventories. The protests of the state controller made the size of the fund public.

Telephone is also a state-owned monopoly. So is the postal authority. There are also hundreds of SOEs, all of which are officially directed to give preference on their procurement to Israeli manufacturers located in so called 'development regions.'

The government has also a very large impact on the price of another factor of production — labor. First, it is itself a very large employer. Second, in many cases, wages were decided upon by a consensus decision of the employers, the Histadrut and the government. In several such agreements, the government consented not to raise taxes in exchange for a price and wages freeze. Of course, the use of labor was also influenced by the cost of capital. One result of the subsidized rates of interest on capital was a marked tendency to move to capital-intensive methods, and to the acquisition of equipment even for a few hours' use.

In 1990, there has been increasing talk about the need for a major structural change that would reduce the scope of the government's intervention, open the economy to import competition, deregulate most of the markets and privatize state-owned enterprises and social services. It is not easy to predict the extent to which these changes will be implemented rather than being left as a wish list.

Special relations with the Histadrut

Until 1980, the government also used funds to discriminate among sectors. All the funds accumulated by insurance firms and pension funds had to be invested in special bonds issued by the Finance Ministry. These bonds, incidentally, into 1990 carry a higher rate of interest, thus subsidizing the pension funds (most of which belong to the Histadrut). Moreover, from 1957 until 1980, the Histadrut funds were allowed to purchase 50 per cent of the bonds not from the government, but from financial institutions owned by the Histadrut.

The participation of the employees and the employers in the provident and the pension funds are the major source of private savings in Israel. In the Mandate period, there was no appropriate social legislation, and the Histadrut negotiated with the employers, in particular since the 1930s, to establish provident funds for the workers, based on equal contribution of the employee and the employer. After 1945, many of these funds were merged into larger entities, by economic branches (for example for construction workers in 1945, for salaried workers in agriculture in 1948). Because the capital market was extremely undeveloped, the managers of the funds encountered many difficulties in finding investments that would generate sufficient yield at a reasonable risk level.

In 1950, the Histadrut decided to act to coordinate the investment policies of the funds. For that purpose, it established a new firm, Gmul, with equity capital equally owned by Bank Hapoalim and the funds themselves. Since 1954, some of the members' contributions have been shifted to the newly created National Insurance Institution.

When these funds were recognized by the internal revenue authorities, the employer could show his contribution as a business expense and the employee could receive a tax credit. The profits of the provident funds have also been tax exempt. These exemptions were informal following the introduction of income tax in 1941, and were anchored in formal regulations in 1957.

Until 1957, the funds could invest their reserves as their managers saw fit. Between 1953 and 1957, 60.2 per cent of the investments of the pension funds affiliated to the Histadrut were invested in Hevrat Ovdim plants. So were 47.8 per cent of the provident funds. In 1957, the government decreed that to be recognized for tax purposes the funds must invest only in 'recognized investments.' On December 10, 1957, the government signed an agreement with the Histadrut, according to which the latter was to use its influence to assure that the funds would invest 65 per cent of their reserves in 'recognized investments.' The funds were to invest 60 per cent of these funds in government bonds and 40 per cent in the development of Hevrat Ovdim. In 1959, the proportion was changed to 50-50 between the government and Hevrat Ovdim. This proportion remained in effect until 1980.

In 1960, the Ministry of Finance signed a five-year contract with the Histadrut. The pension funds were to use 75 per cent of the reserves for 'recognized investments,' and these investments were to be 50 per cent in government bonds and 50 per cent in bonds issued by Gmul. The share of the reserves to be invested in recognized investments was raised to 80 per cent in 1963 (by changing the rules for tax exemption). Later, it was raised again to 92 per cent.

Moreover, all bonds issued in Israel are linked to some more stable anchor. Most loans are linked to the cost of living index (COL). Some are linked to the United States dollar. For several decades, the government allowed financial institutions to charge preferred customers (designated by government fiat) a nominal interest of 4 per cent as a 'linkage insurance.' If the COL index rose by more than 4 per cent, the lender did not pay that linkage differential. Rather, the government compensated the financial institution for the difference. Such a difference was in some years of rampant inflation equal to more than 400 per cent! The government gave linkage insurance also to the bonds issued by Hevrat Ovdim. In July 1968, some important changes were introduced. One was the inclusion, for the first time, of the Manufacturers' Association among the members of the exclusive club of those receiving linkage insurance.

The contract negotiated between the Histadrut and the government that was originally written for a five-year period was extended several times. It was not extended in 1980, when Yigal Horowitz was the finance minister. Horowitz also stopped the linkage differential insurance. Clearly, this arrangement and its discontinuation had a far-reaching impact on the structure of the Israeli economy.

The change in the bonds arrangements clearly affected the Histadrut enterprises in a significant way. In a coming recession, these enterprises — based on their ideology — were reluctant to reduce their work force or to reduce wages. Histadrut firms had great difficulty in making the necessary adjustments. As a result, several large Histadrut enterprises found themselves near bankruptcy. The first was Solel Boneh, which despite a 30 per cent reduction of construction activities continued to pay its workers a monthly paycheck even though they were really disguising unemployment. Then came Koor, the holding company owning 11 per cent of the Israeli manufacturing industry. One of the foreign banks to whom Koor owed money asked the courts to declare the firm bankrupt because it faced liquidity difficulties. Again, one reason was the continuation of losing activities. Another was an increased level of wages without regard to market conditions. In both cases, the government saw no other recourse except to help these firms, largely because of the potential repercussions of the collapse of such large firms.

The arrangement between the government and the Histadrut lasted more than twenty years. It was detailed in the state controller reports (for example number 21 for 1971, pp. 121-7; number 24, p. 43; number 25, pp. 47, 49, 53). Still, there was very little public debate about this topic, nor was it mentioned in academic research on Israel's economy and politics. A paper, 'Changing Domestic Policy 1977-81' by two prominent political scientists from the Hebrew University (Sharkansky and Radian, 1982), did not mention that the contract was not extended. Yet, Hevrat Ovdim not only received a substantial subsidy, but was able to direct billions of shekels to its enterprises, as a part of the so called 'financial plan' of Hevrat Ovdim. These funds were granted by Bank Hapoalim, not directly by the pension funds. The bank also demanded and received a floating lien on all assets of the Histadrut enterprises, making it extremely hard for them to work with another bank. The bank also received nice commissions and was able to grow fast. Hevrat Ovdim, in turn, could use the funds to continue and maintain unprofitable enterprises. Obviously, the easier access to funds gave the Histadrut an important competitive advantage. It also allowed the Histadrut firms to tolerate relatively high levels of featherbedding and inefficiencies.

Given the arsenal of tools the government has in its possession, and the fact that the Israeli economy is extremely politicized, it is clearly impossible to understand the way the Israeli economy operates only on the basis of macroeconomic models assuming free competition. It is worthwhile to go back to a short analysis of the forces which make up the Israeli political economy.

The service class in a *Proportzdemokratie*

In earlier chapters, it was shown that the majority of Israel's leaders came from Russia, and their world view was influenced by the regime there and the hopes for a socialist revolution. The leaders of the second and the third Aliyah aspired for a dual ideal: the creation of a Jewish state that would also be socialist and egalitarian. They believed in their destiny as the leaders of the new revolution, and used their political organizations to achieve both economic and political aims as based on their ideological proclivities. Some of the old timers of Sephardic origin fought against the new system (Horowitz and Lissak, 1978, pp. 53-4). However, they were not equipped for a political battle and their opposition was not very effective. The so called 'civilian' (*ezrahi*) or bourgeois sector was not very interested in politics, and was also accepting the halo of the pioneer. Mapai achieved a dominant position, with which it gained control.

Having control of the state organs, Ben Gurion believed he could use the power of the state to enforce a way of achieving goals. He considered, accordingly, that many institutions, previously controlled by the Histadrut or by political parties, should be transferred to state control under Mapai hegemony. The second echelon of leaders disagreed, and sometimes won their cases. All did not believe in a market solution or in the regulation of the economic activities by the invisible hand. They believed instead in centralization of control, and in the invisible hand of the political party.

The State of Israel inherited a well-developed bureaucracy from the National Institutions. The civil servants were recruited from this source or by political recommendations. Most senior civil servants were loyal to the political bosses. Some of them were university graduates in Israel, who were educated in their youth by the ideals of the Labor and believed in the need for pioneering and the priorities to be granted to the pioneers. They were not interested in self-employed careers, only in good salaries. They created a bureaucracy based on overcentralization, antiquated management systems and administrative procedures, that made every citizen dependent on a bloated bureaucracy, granting licenses at its discretion. In the first years of the state, it was deemed necessary to ration food, clothing and furniture.

It is hardly surprising that the middle class felt discriminated against. Their feeling of deprivation had an impact in the November 1950 municipal elections, and in the 1951 national elections. In the latter, the General Zionists' Knesset members increased from 7 to 20. Mapai functionaries learned a lesson. The system of rationing of food and clothing was abolished; and the government established a special state-owned 'bank for artisans' to help small self-employed firms or individuals. Little by little, Mapai leaders compromised on the creation of a pluralistic economy, in which all sectors could survive but under the government's close guidance. Political and personal contacts among the old boy network became increasingly important, and the rules of joining the exclusive club of those receiving government largesse irrespective of sector, enormously important.

By the end of 1952, Israel could have decided on a different kind of a political economy. On September 10, 1952, the Israeli government signed the reparations agreement with the Federal Republic of Germany. This gave the Israeli economy about $850 million for the financing of imports. A naive expert, Mr Trone, was asked to prepare a plan for the use of the reparations funds. He proposed to invest these funds in building an infrastructure of roads, telephones, electricity and water as well as manpower training to allow the economy to flourish without detailed government directions. His basic assumption, records a Bank of Israel piece of research, 'was that the production system in Israel will be based in the long run on private initiative and investment' (p. 81). He was told this was unrealistic under the special circumstances of Israel 'since conditions were changing fast. The manufacturing industry needed government aid for its fast expansion and this fact was incompatible with the basic premise of Trone's plan' (ibid., p. 82). Instead, the agreement determined that all goods and services under it would be executed only by the government of Israel. The government established a special state-owned enterprise for this task. The acquisitions were to create heavy industry and a higher value added by backward integration of industry (ibid., p. 78). The chief executive officer of Solel Boneh, the largest Histadrut enterprise, was made the manager of the new SOE. The State Controller, in his fourth annual report (p. 96) found that the corporation decided on the policies on acquisition, without any governmental guidance or plan. About 16 per cent of all the funds were used to acquire ships for Zim shipping line and 43 per cent was used to acquire machinery for manufacturing. Only $6 million was invested in the development of telephone infrastructure. Because of the priority given to heavy industry, the Histadrut enterprises received quite large sums for such firms as their steel plant and chemical factories. Hillel Dan, Solel Boneh's CEO, was of the opinion that private industry was unable to execute the needed plans for the industrialization of the country. Mr Dan also stressed that 'We shall decide — not the experts.' Mr Avineri, a journalist who wrote several books on leaders of the Israeli economy, claims that Mr Dan wanted the government to give Solel Boneh the railways, the right to construct highways, and a monopoly in the development of several basic industries (Avineri, 1977, pp. 124-5).

For the civil servants, the deep governmental involvement was a sure means of increasing their power. In addition, the senior civil servants could look forward to compensation for their services by becoming directors (and later managers) in state-owned enterprises, or in other large firms. This gave them a strong incentive to avoid any open dispute or conflict of interests with politicians or with important industrialists or powerful bankers. Many firms were managed by political party nominees.

Many leaders had a Spartan point of view believing in the superiority of community life. They saw profits as theft. Ideological beliefs and political pressure reduced the freedom of the individual. The belief in the rotation of managers was one manifestation of the lack of appreciation for management as a profession. Managers were recruited because of political loyalty more than because of skills. In the mid-1950s, it took much effort to convince the conservative academic leaders of the Hebrew University to agree to offer a course of studies leading to an academic degree in Business Administration.

The system was accepted not only by those first to gain, such as the politicians or the civil servants. Many private individuals supported the system first because they believed in the need for pioneering and later because it allowed them to gain in terms of their wealth or their standard of living. Moreover, the elections system did not give the individual much opportunity to influence the political system. For example, a farmer found he was represented by people nominated for their role. As long as the government paid for costly mistakes, very few rebelled. Some simply left, emigrating to other countries, others accepted the system. Many circumvented it by evading taxes, or selling their produce privately (and therefore illegally). Taxpayers could do very little to change the system. They often looked for ways to be part of those enjoying it. Israel has developed as a pluralistic system, in which many in all sectors enjoyed government's largesse and an increasing standard of living. Those that were unwilling to conform were often literally ostracized. Many laws were enacted that were generally ignored.

In many cases, the bureaucracy turned a blind eye to these breaches of the law, at the same time using this disregard of the law to punish certain individuals. The income tax authorities in Israel consistently refused to issue any tax rulings, thus increasing the uncertainty of taxpayers but also making informal connections very valuable. Most laws allow exemptions of specific transactions at the discretion of the civil service, that like to control and license. An Israeli farmer who insisted on growing flowers and exporting them on his own, not through the Flowers Council, had to appeal five times to the High Court of Justice to avoid paternalistic government control (and aid).

The severe economic crisis in 1988, in which many business firms — and most large Histadrut firms — faced bankruptcy forced a critical reexamination of the interdependency of business firms and government bureacracy. Faced with heavy accumulated losses in many of its firms, Hevrat Ovdim replaced most top managers, attempted to bring about some changes in management methods, implemented more decentralization and strengthened the overseeing power of its boards of directors. In the state sector, a socialist minister of finance has pushed for privatization of more state-owned enterprises against the opposition of Liberal ministers.

The sectorial distribution

The Israeli economy is composed of three sectors: the public, the Histadrut and the private sector. The public sector includes all economic units owned by the state of Israel. Because of the heritage of the Yishuv period, the public sector is defined also to include the institutions owned or controlled by the Jewish Agency — and therefore owned by the Jewish people of the world. For some purposes, it makes sense also to include in this sector many of the non-profit organizations offering such services as health or education. These institutions generally receive the lion's share of the resources they spend from the government.

The Histadrut sector includes all the institutions and enterprises owned by the organized Labor in Israel either through Hevrat Ovdim or through cooperative entities. The rest of the economy is in private hands. Most of the large enterprises are not part of the private sector: this sector is composed of many small or medium-sized firms, more often than not controlled and managed by one or more family owners.

Before we discuss the relative size and share of the different sectors, some elaboration of their composition and the differences in their behavior might be in order. The public sector includes those units which are an integral part of the government — not only the government ministries but also ancillary units of different ministries, such as the Government Printing Office or the rehabilitation and maintenance plants and the Merkava tank production line of the Israeli Defense Forces (IDF) or the Israel Military Industries. It also includes several dozen economic or non-profit-making statutory authorities that were established by a special enabling law. Examples are the Bank of Israel, the National Insurance Institution or the Port Authority. The latter institution manages all the ports of Israel. Because of its activities it had surplus funds and was asked to acquire the Israel railway. Other institutions are the various Councils for Production and Marketing that control, in collaboration with the representatives of the organized farmers, the resource allocation in the various branches of agricultural production. The number of all these entities is quite large and there is no point in listing them all.

Finally, the government sector includes approximately two hundred state-owned enterprises, each legally defined as a corporation but in which voting shares are owned by government bodies or by the state. Some of these enterprises are very small and carry out peripheral activities, such as advanced education for engineers or a firm managing a theatre building. Others are giant (in Israeli scale) enterprises, controlling important national resources or fields of activities. Examples are the Bank for Industrial Development; the oil refineries, the Bezek (telephone and telecommunications) company, Israel Chemicals, or the electricity company. Through one or another of these institutions the government holds a monopoly position in several important fields including electricity, international air transportation, and the production and marketing of potash, bromine, and phosphates.

Since the mid-1970s, the government has been declaring its serious intention to privatize many of these activities, but in actual fact had done very little toward achieving this goal until 1988, when several state-owned enterprises were sold. The government is also the sole importer of many raw materials, including, for example, dry fodder and several food items such as meat. The government is also a major industrial producer, mainly producing for military needs but also processing chemicals. Its wholly-owned production facilities are sometimes state-owned corporations, for example Israel Aviation Industries or Beit Shemesh Engines. Sometimes they are ancillary units directly responsible to the director general of the ministry of defense, and sometimes these units report to the IDF general staff as in the case of the Merkava tank project.

The pseudo-government institution of the Yishuv period was the Jewish Agency, created in 1929 to allow also non Zionists to participate in helping the building of a new nation in Eretz Israel. Even before the Jewish Agency was formed, the World Zionist Organization created some so-called National Institutions. The two most important ones were *Keren Kayemet* — mainly for acquisition of land and afforestation, and *Keren Hayesod* — for the creation of infrastructure in the country. The debate on the role of *Keren Hayesod* before it was created in 1920 divided the Zionist organization and reflected many of the problems regarding the best means of creating a new and modern economic order in Eretz Israel. It was described in detail in chapter 2.

In theory, the Jewish Agency and the national institutions could have been dismantled in 1948, when the administrative machinery of the state came to replace any Yishuv period organizations. Old organizations, however, never die. They just change tasks. *Keren Kayemet* was obviously not needed any more for the purchase of land. The Israel Land Authority manages all land belonging to the nation, including that acquired by *Keren Kayemet*. This authority now controls about 93 per cent of the land in Israel. *Keren Kayemet* continued, mainly in land reclamation and in planting forests. *Keren Hayesod* also continues, and has been raising money among Jews in the Diaspora to be used by the Jewish Agency. These funds have been used partly to encourage immigration to Israel and partly to educate new immigrants in maintenance of farms. Even today, one cannot simply become a farmer in Israel. One must join a political entity, and then create a moshav or kibbutz. To do that, one must receive the blessing of the leading establishment of these movements. The Jewish Agency (and the other National Institutions) also remains to supply employment to those the party wants to help, to get important positions for party leaders — and to finance political activities. In theory, the Jewish Agency is a representative of all Jews — inside and outside Israel. The State of Israel and the World Zionist Organization entered into a covenant in 1952 in which the roles of the two bodies were defined.

The Agency and the National Institutions own (although apparently not always control) many important economic institutions. First and foremost, the Jewish Agency owns the majority of the voting shares of one of the largest Israeli banks — Bank Leumi. This bank is a descendant of the *Otzar Hityashvut Hayehudim* initiated by Herzl in 1899. It was also responsible for the issue of the Israeli money notes and for other central bank functions before the Bank of Israel came into being in 1954. The bank, as do other banks in Israel, operates not only as a retail banker but also as a merchant bank, as a dealer in securities, and in many other financial activities. It owns a large number of subsidiaries that are specialized banks (for example for mortgage) both in Israel and abroad. The Jewish Agency also owns furniture factories, houses rented to new immigrants, a Congress building, a citrus packaging firm (in partnership with the Histadrut) and many other smaller firms. The Jewish Agency is also a partner with the government and the Histadrut in the major transportation firms — Zim shipping lines and ElAl Israel airlines. All in all, the Jewish Agency is a very important source of desirable jobs, trips abroad, funds, and possibilities for political patronage. In the 1980s, the Agency announced its intention to sell some of its economic assets but, not unlike the Israeli government, found it difficult to implement this policy.

The Jewish Agency is the major means by which Jews abroad

donate money to Israeli organizations. When a Jew outside Israel is asked to give to Israel, it usually means giving to a United Jewish Appeal organization (or its equivalent in other countries), in which a certain per cent of the funds donated, after allocating funds for local Jewish institutions, is channelled to the Jewish Agency as well as to some other institutions such as Hadassah (for medical care). Because of this fact, the position of the Jewish Agency's treasurer and that of the chairman are of utmost importance.

The sector that is a unique Israeli creation, without any parallel outside Israel, is the Histadrut sector. Literally, this word means 'the Federation'. It comes from the full name: the general federation of labor. It was established in December 1920, to unite the power of the different labor socialist political parties in Eretz Israel. It was an organization created by idealists who wanted to build a new society in the old land of their forefathers. Their leaders were very pragmatic and shrewd politicians. They realized the enormous difficulties faced by the workers trying to settle in the barren land. They also knew that a majority of them despaired and left or were dead as a result of famine and sicknesses. They felt compelled to organize communities and multiply aid. They also believed that they had to control the economic institutions by controlling the political machinery. They thus decided to make each and every institution, and of course each and every individual, subservient to what were seen as the community needs. The Histadrut is not just a trade union: the trade unions are one department of the Histadrut. It is also an organization taking care of foreign relations, welfare, health, mutual aid, old age institutions as well as many economic institutions. In the economic side, the Histadrut includes some large holding companies it controls directly, such as Solel Boneh — the largest construction firm in Israel, Koor with more than a hundred manufacturing plants, and Bank Hapoalim (the Workers Bank) — the largest Bank in Israel. In addition to these units (known as 'the institutional economy'), the Histadrut has a veto power in all kibbutzim and moshavim, in hundreds of cooperatives in manufacturing, transportation and retailing ('the owned economy') and in several large firms in which it owns less than majority shares, such as the Mekorot water company and Zim shipping lines. The cooperative organizations also own such firms as Tnuva — which dominates the marketing of fresh agricultural products (fruits, vegetables, eggs, poultry, fish) and Hamashbir — a major importer.

The Histadrut is to a large extent self contained. It is sometimes accused of being 'a state within the state.' For historical reasons related to the Yishuv period, Hamashbir is a monopolist supplier to much of the communal settlement; Tnuva, on the other hand, is a monopsonist buyer from them. Many of the Israelis are members of the Histadrut, very often not for ideological reasons but for very pragmatic ones: 80 per cent of the population receive first rate medical services from the Histadrut's Sick Fund. In 1988, the number of Histadrut members was 1.6 million (Table 4.4). All Histadrut members elect the Histadrut *veida* (convention). Like other elections in Israel, these elections are based on a proportional method, and political parties' nominees are elected. The Labor party has always enjoyed a comfortable majority in the Histadrut. In the November 1989 elections, it received 55.5 per cent of the votes; the left-wing Mapam got 8.9 per cent, Ratz received 4.3 per cent; the Arab list, 4.17 per cent; and the Likud, 27.4 per cent. The convention elects the general council (*Vaad Hopoel*), and it elects the Executive Bureau (literally, the central committee: *Vaada Merakezet*). The 43 members of this committee are responsible for the implementation of the Histadrut policies in its many facets: trade unions, Arab members, finance, international relations, vocational training, mutual security, culture and education, Diaspora communities, youth and sports, consumers' authority, industrial democracy, higher education and religious affairs. The committee supervises the 72 local labor councils. The chairperson of the committee is the general secretary of the Histadrut, who is elected by the Executive Bureau. The general secretary is also *ex officio* the chairperson of Hevrat Ovdim. In the first decade of the state's existence, many new enterprises were created jointly by the state, the National Institutions and the Histadrut.

Table 4.4 Number of Histadrut members since its establishment

End of year	Number of members	Average rate of growth in the decade (%)
1920	4,433	
1930	28,453	54.2
1940	111,579	29.3
1950	352,030	21.5
1960	724,704	10.6
1970	1,078,890	4.9
1980	1,500,000	3.9
1988	1,600,000	

Source: Histadrut.

Size of the different sectors

During the Yishuv period, the Histadrut sector comprised mainly the various moshav and kibbutz settlements, the large construction firm Solel Boneh and Bank Hapoalim. The private sector, known in Hebrew as the 'civilian' (*ezrahi*) sector, included urban establishments and private rural settlements (Moshavot). In addition, there were the national-religious settlements. The Revisionist party members, in contrast, did not develop their own economic institutions. The party did own its own sick fund, sports clubs and youth movements. It also managed its own labor-exchange institution. In 1934, Jabotinsky and Ben Gurion agreed to allow Revisionists to use the Histadrut labor exchange. This agreement was not ratified by the Histadrut organs.

The private sector is largely composed of small firms. In 1984 95.2 per cent of all Israeli manufacturing plants were private, but only 53 per cent of the 100 largest industrial firms in Israel were private. In contrast, the government owned 0.4 per cent of all plants but 12 per cent of the largest 100; the Histadrut, 4.4 per cent and 35 per cent respectively. The private sector may be further broken down to family-owned firms, managed by their family owners, and firms managed by professional managers. Most private firms are family-owned, with the exception of the Clal group (shown as private, although 40 per cent are owned by Bank Hapoalim), Discount Investment Company and Elron.

Dun and Bradstreet published every year a list of the largest industrial firms in Israel. The classification of Dun's does not include some of the largest defense establishments. In addition, it is one step below the concern level. If these are combined, then out of the 175 largest industrial firms for which Dun and Bradstreet published figures, 29 belong to Koor, 6 are subsidiaries of Israel Chemicals, 9 belong at least partially to Clal Industries and 12 include participation of Discount Investment Group. Table 4.5 shows the breakdown by sectors when each of the above is counted as one firm. Note that out of these firms the private sector accounted for 41 per cent of sales, 46 per cent of employment, but only 39 per cent of exports; the kibbutzim accounted for 8 per cent of sales, 4 per cent of employment and 6 per cent of exports. The government manufacturing sector accounted for 22 per cent of sales, but 33 per cent of exports. The Histadrut share in sales and employment was 29 per cent, but only 22 per cent in exports.

Table 4.5 Sectorial breakdown of Israel's largest industrial firms

	Number of companies		Sales		Employment		Exports		Export out of sales	
	1981	1985	1981	1985	1981	1985	1981	1985	1981	1985
($ millions)										
Total D&B's 100	118	123	6,272	8,693	134,212	139,219	2,472	3,426	–	–
(%)										
Total D&B's 100	100	100	100	100	100	100	100	100	39	39
Private, family owned	59	54	30	25	33	29	22	20	30	32
Foreign owned	2	4	2	3	1	3	4	6	76	72
Private concerns	3	3	13	13	13	14	9	13	28	39
Kibbutzim	26	28	7	8	4	4	6	6	30	29
Histadrut	5	7	25	29	27	29	22	22	34	29
Government	5	4	23	22	22	21	37	33	63	61

Source: Dun and Bradstreet (1981, 1985) *Dun and Bradstreet 100: Israel's Leading Enterprises.*

Notes: (a)There is a big difference in export out of sales ratio between the kibbutz industry and their regional enterprises. In 1981, export/sales for kibbutz industry = 32% vs 14% in the latter. In 1985, export/sales for kibbutz industry = 31% vs 10% in the latter. (b)List of companies does not include IMI, Rafael. (c)Koor, Clal, ICL, Elron, Discount Investments, are represented as one company totaling the data of its subsidiaries which were included in the original list of Dun's 175.

Table 4.6 The share of the Histadrut sector in net national product by branches

Year	Agriculture	Manufacturing	Construction	Transportation	Trade, banking and services	Total
1953	55.1	18.0	32.3	33.1	8.0	17.9
1960	58.1	19.3	30.6	31.6	11.0	23.9
1965	72.6	20.4	28.6	28.9	12.0	22.2
1970	69.5	17.0	22.4	20.3	13.0	19.5
1975	69.8	19.3	25.0	16.1	15.4	29.1
1980	84.0	26.0	17.0	21.0	16.5	
1985	86.0	25.5	12.0	22.0	17.0	

Sources: 1953 figures, Barkai (1954); 1960-85 figures, Histadrut Economic and Social Planning Unit.

Table 4.7 The share of the Histadrut sector in exports (%)

Year	Industrial exports (excluding diamonds)	Agricultural exports
1960	21.9	62
1965	18.3	65
1970	18.0	67
1975	27.2	73
1980	22.0	76
1985	23.5	77

Source: See Table 4.5.

The labor sector organizations were the best organized, combining education, cultural, sports, economic and political organizations. It developed a unique federated structure. The system already had the kernels of the future political economy of Israel: a high degree of centralization; national capital aid to the labor sector with agrarian orientation; and total disregard for efficiency and profitability as criteria for operation.

According to the calculations of Hevrat Ovdim, the percentage of the Histadrut sector in the GNP reached 21 per cent in 1984. In 1988 the communal settlements generated 86 per cent of the value of the agriculture products. In manufacturing industries the workers' sector share in 1985 was 25.5 per cent and in industrial exports 25 per cent. This sector executed in that year 12 per cent of the construction output and controlled more than 30 per cent of all the bank branches in Israel, about 24 per cent of the life insurance portfolio of insurance firms in Israel and a very significant percentage of the wholesale and retail markets. The development of the share of the Histadrut sector is shown in Tables 4.6, 4.7 and 4.8.

The Histadrut also enjoys a dominant position in ground transportation. The different sectors of the workers economy include the communal settlements (mainly kibbutzim and moshavim). Kibbutzim own and operate more than 400 industrial plants comprising more than 6 per cent of Israeli industrial output and exports. The kibbutzim industries have a high market share of the plastics, metal and food industries. The kibbutzim also own and operate several dozen hotels. Table 4.8 shows the share of kibbutz industries in manufacturing outputs and exports. The dominance of kibbutz plastics and wood exports is seen very clearly. The kibbutzim are also significant exporters of food.

Table 4.8 The share of the Histadrut sector in employment

Year	Agriculture	Manufacturing	Construction	Trade, banking and services	Transportation	Public services[a]	Personal services[b]	Total
1954	–	–	–	–	–	–	–	28.5
1960	58.5	16.5	25.8	11.1	27.8	11.9	41.1	24.8
1965	70.2	15.5	23.1	11.0	26.1	12.2	34.5	24.1
1970	85.5	15.9	30.4	14.9	19.2	22.7	N.A.	22.7
1975	81.7	18.2	30.6	15.5	22.0	15.0	19.6	22.3
1980	75.0	21.0	27.1	17.6	22.6	N.A.	N.A.	N.A.
1985	77.0	18.6	12.0	19.0	23.0	N.A.	N.A.	N.A.

Source: See Table 4.5.
Notes: [a]Including water supply. [b]Including ownership of dwelling units.

Table 4.9 Output of kibbutz plants by branch, as a % of Israeli manufacturing output and exports (excluding diamonds) 1983-85 (dollars at current prices)

Branch	1983		1984		1985	
	as % of output	as % of export	as % of output	as % of export	as % of output	as % of export
Metal prod. and machinery	9.8	8.2	10.6	7.6	10.4	9.5
Basic metal	–	–	–	–	–	–
Printing and publishing	4.3	–	5.9	–	6.3	–
Electric and electronic equipment	3.5	1.3	3.1	1.5	2.7	1.4
Wood and its products	16.6	35.6	18.3	39.1	14.7	30.9
Plastic and rubber products	43.6	52.8	45.3	58.5	42.2	62.6
Textile, clothing and leather	2.3	0.6	2.2	1.2	2.2	1.7
Mining and quarrying	14.5	–	9.8	–	9.4	–
Food	5.5	19.3	6.9	20.5	5.1	22.4
Chemicals and fuel	2.6	0.9	2.0	0.7	2.3	0.9
Cardboard and its products	–	–	–	–	–	–
Non-metallic minerals	–	–	–	–	–	–
Transportation	–	–	–	–	–	–
Miscellaneous	17.1	3.4	20.3	4.6	18.9	5.5
Total (excl. diamonds)	7.0	5.9	7.4	6.4	6.5	6.7
Annual % rate of growth	1.2	1.3	9.0	29.8	(8.2)	12.7

Source: Kibbutz Industries, Report for 1985.

The workers' economy also includes the marketing arms of these entities: mainly Tnuva, Tnuva Export, Hamashbir Hamerkazi, the transportation cooperatives (which monopolize all bus transportation), as well as those in services, production and consumers' cooperatives. It also includes the so-called institutional economy of the Histadrut. The latter are holding companies owned by the Histadrut such as Koor Industries, Bank Hapoalim, Solel Boneh (the largest construction firm in Israel), Teus (a holding company of manufacturing plants in development regions), Shikun Ovdim (housing), Hassneh (insurance), as well as the Yachin group that manages and cultivates orchards and owns different packing houses and industries connected with citrus. The sector also includes other partnerships such as Zim shipping company, Haargaz, Mekorot water company, etc. The Histadrut also owns services: travel agencies, hotels as well as newspapers and publishing houses. It also has partial control of other firms in the economy, most importantly the holding company Clal, partially owned by the Bank Hapoalim (the Workers Bank).

In manufacturing industry, the Histadrut sector started to acquire plants in construction-related manufacturing during World War II. In 1942, the Histadrut manufacturing enterprises employed 3,700 persons, about 10 per cent of total employees in manufacturing. The Manufacturers Association complained at the time that the Histadrut received from the Jewish Agency more credit than it should have according to its share in manufacturing. The Manufacturers Association claimed that, between 1943 and 1945, the Histadrut received 66 per cent of the medium-term credit; 25 per cent of the credit granted by the fund to finance military orders; 45 per cent of the funds granted for expansion of manufacturing; and 55 per cent of the funds received against mortgaging rights (Beilin, 1987).

In the first years of the state's existence the number of workers in manufacturing grew by 15 per cent (while the total population increased by 60 per cent). The Histadrut sector absorbed 37 per cent of the addition of manpower to industry. The government sector also increased very fast. A study by Barkai (1954) found that the share of state-owned enterprises in the net product, in 1959, was 5.5 per cent. Barkai, however, did not include the military industry in his calculations.

Mapai leaders held most of the key social, cultural and economic positions in the government, the Histadrut and the National Institutions. Thus it was natural for these leaders to perceive all these institutions as if they belonged to the same sector. Mekorot water company received significant sums of money from the government without any guarantee of ownership rights to the state, and sometimes even without an orderly contract. The tiny and highly homogeneous Yishuv population swelled and tripled its size, accepting new immigrants with very little indoctrination for the communal life. Yet institutions did not change. The new immigrants became members of the Histadrut through the sick fund, or were brought into the moshavim in which they accepted the organizational structure, including the mutual guarantee of this institution, without any ideological training or willingness to accept this way of life.

Unlike the pre-state period, in which Solel Boneh acquired existing plants, in the first years of the state's existence this large Histadrut firm was very active in establishing new manufacturing firms. In 1949 it started a mortars plant as a joint venture with Finnish investors. It also built several other plants, in particular in basic metals. Many of these new plants were erected in new towns: an engine plant in Ramla, cigarettes in Lod, cement pipes in Ashkelon.

In quite a number of cases, the Ministry of Finance wanted Solel Boneh to be less active, and allow foreign investors to erect plants. Solel Boneh attempted to build a paper plant, but the then Minister of Finance, Eliezer Kaplan, had already signed an agreement with private investors. Solel Boneh finally erected a plant making paper sacks for cement. It also initiated a tire factory, competing neck and neck with a private group which built a similar plant. As a result, in a tiny Israeli market there were two tire plants, both of which were forced to export. They finally merged. In 1952, it also built the 'steel town.' By that year, the Histadrut owned 725 manufacturing plants that employed 10,700 employees. The four largest were for cement, casting, glass and cement pipes. They were much more capital-intensive than private firms.

The kibbutz industry also developed very fast, growing from small plants serving agriculture to other manufacturing plants. The kibbutz industry has grown much faster than other manufacturing sectors. Within the Histadrut sector different groups erected competing enterprises. Thus, two of the kibbutz federations established their own construction firms.

By the end of the first decade of the state's existence there were many calls for restructuring of Histadrut plants. Some of the leaders called for more cooperation with the government. The left wing, enjoying the right of opposition parties to be less pragmatic, opposed these moves in the name of 'violation of values and workers independence.' Of course, both those in the Histadrut who called for cooperation and those who believed in independence would have opposed any market operations and believed in centralized regulation.

By the end of the first decade, the employment in the Histadrut sector increased four fold. The left-wing leaders complained that Israel was turning into a capitalist nation. They pointed out that the means of production were not nationalized. The Histadrut general secretary reacted by pointing out that a part of the private sector is not capitalist, but consisted of cooperatives.

In point of fact, since the state was established, the shares of the Histadrut and public sectors have been rising both in products and in employment. When the state was born, most of the economy was privately-owned. The British government did operate the post, telephone and telegraph and the railroads, but very little more. The state also inherited some of the illegal military industry plants operated by the Haganah.

In the middle of the 1960s the public sector share in the product was 12 per cent, in 1980-1 it reached 24 per cent. The Histadrut sector acquired the first manufacturing plant it owned during World War II and when the state was born it owned less than 10 per cent of the industrial product. In the middle of the 1960s, according to the Hevrat Ovdim's calculations, its share rose to 18 per cent, and in 1980-1 it rose to 22 per cent. Only less than half of the business activities in the Israeli economy are in the hands of private enterprise in which business decisions are made by the owners of the firm. Private firms in Israel are relatively small in size and in most cases the managers of the firms are also the owners. Even in this sector, business decisions reflect the environment in which they operate and the influence of the government. The government influences firms both by protecting them from competition of foreign enterprises and by providing direct control. It also affects business profits through the use of differentiated rates of exchange, granting licenses, and by a very wide net of subsidies given off budget for land and money.

The private sector's share went down from 75 per cent of the product in the 1950s to less than half. Its share in the number of plants in the period 1964-81 was 96.4 per cent mainly because most private enterprises are much smaller than the public-sector ones. In 1965 the private sector employed only 72 per cent of manufacturing employees and created 64 per cent of industrial products. These firms are also much less capital-intensive than the public or Histadrut sector (Table 4.10).

Differences among sectors

One clear difference among the sectors is the way profits are used. The Histadrut firms do not distribute any profits to shareholders, but plough them back into new investment. The ploughing-back principle means that the economic enterprises are not required to subsidize the other parts of the Histadrut. This principle is also consistent with the natural inclinations of the managers to accumulate power and achieve as high autonomy as possible.

In setting up modern manufacturing industries, both the Histadrut and the government did it within a context of national goals, Zionist resettlement drive and socialist traditions. All that meant that profits were a constraint, since managers are ultimately responsible for the survival of the firm. Profit was never an objective. Within the different holding companies, losing plants were subsidized to avoid loss of employment or even a reduction of wages. Because of the large size of the sector and its diversified operations, it was able to achieve a large degree of risk spreading, thus reducing the risk (Table 4.10).

There were important differences in the degree of emphasis given to profits between managers and politicians. Managers of individual units aspired to have a *modus operandi* not at all different from the one encountered in a private firm. They were reluctant to keep for a long time losing, inefficient plants or to pay higher wages.

Until the 1970s, the managers in all three sectors were not business professionals. In the private sector, managers were the owners or their relatives; and nepotism is not necessarily the best means of recruiting managers. From the mid-1960s, ex-army generals were recruited to managerial positions. Since the army was professional, these were persons trained in administration but rarely in business. Most managers in the public and Histadrut sector were aware of the fact that to continue in their job they had to cater to certain interests. They did not have to be profitable, but had to make sure they maintained employment. Profitability was more a means to keep autonomy than a necessity.

Until the mid-1960s, managers were elected as representatives of the party. For many years, the Histadrut sector had two managers. One represented Ahdut Ha'avoda, one Hapoel Ha'zair (the two parties that merged into Mapai in 1930). Still, the role of managers made persons look for more autonomy and to see themselves responsible for profits. As early as 1921, when Ben Gurion proposed Hevrat Ovdim, the managers opposed

Table 4.10 Sectorial structure in manufacturing

	Number of employees				Capital stock per employed person[b]	Average product per employed person[c]		Average wage for employee[b]		Number of plants		
	1965	1971	1975	1987[a]	1982	1975	1985	1975	1985	1965-7	1971-2	1980-81
Private	72		67	69	669	17	18	8	12	97.2	97.5	96.4
Histadrut	16		18	18	1,146	21	29	10	18	2.2	2.3	3.3
Public	12		15	13	1,641	26	37	14	26	0.6	0.2	0.3
Total	100		100	100	925	19	23	9	16	100.0	100.0	100.0

Source: Bank of Israel, Annual Report, 1988, p. 204.
Notes: [a] All plants employing employees, for change in classification for 1987. [b] The only year for which detailed data on capital stock in manufacturing is available. [c] GNP at factor prices, only for plants employing five persons or more.

centralization and stressed autonomy. Managers of the Histadrut sector were attempting to achieve higher profits even by buying from Arabs or importing cheaper goods. The political leadership fought these attempts at economic thinking.

In 1927, during a deep recession, Solel Boneh was bankrupt because of too much concern for employment, too little concern about efficiency and a belief that the national importance of its action would ensure public help. This bankruptcy was a major shock to the Histadrut who turned to rely only on cooperatives. Some managers restarted Solel Boneh without approval and received official relegitimization only in 1935. The firm tried to hide its profits from the political leaderships. Time and again, opposition political parties' functionaries complained that Hevrat Ovdim did not control its plants and that the managers were too autonomous. The managers in turn tended to prefer profitability to ideological concerns. For many years they were allowed to do so because the leaders were under the trauma of the bankruptcy. By the end of World War II, and more so in the 1950s, the managers of Solel Boneh expanded their operations without ever consulting the political leaders.

In April 1958, the Histadrut decided to partition Solel Boneh into three separate firms, one for construction, one (Koor) for manufacturing, and the third for foreign operations and ports. This partition caused a major shake-up. Most top managers resigned; the foreign operations could not survive, largely because they lost the experienced skilled human capital of the home base. This firm was remerged with the construction company in 1963. Koor suffered losses partially because of its inefficient steel operations, partially because almost all of its plants were dependent on construction — a leading sufferer from the recession. Koor needed government aid. The government acquired preference shares in Koor and reorganization of the debt of the steel plants was undertaken. In this reorganization, the government agreed to write off much of the loans it had given to that plant.

The relationships between managers and politicians in both the public and the Histadrut sectors were full of tension. The Hevrat Ovdim council decided, in 1983, that each of its managers:

> must be not only an excellent professional, but also a partner to the vision of the labor movement, who gives personal example. Managers should be trained to be the forerunners of the socialist movement, to avoid social alienation and social gaps, to enhance the honor of the worker and the value

of work . . . the fact that 'Hevrat Ovdim' has social and national objectives in addition to economic objectives, such as egalitarian and cooperative point of view creates additional challenges to the management team.

Managers pointed out that trade-offs among objectives were never concretely defined. Yet the public has nourished a set of expectations about higher wages and better fringe benefits. The objectives were contradictory, even impossible — and all these caused frustration. The same type of problems were encountered by the SOEs.

In the middle of the 1960s, the founders' generation retired and new managers came, many of them ex-army generals. These managers attempted to make the SOEs and the Histadrut enterprises more profit oriented. These managers were able sometimes to close losing plants. However, their power to do so was often constrained by the need to get political approval. All large SOEs and Histadrut firms moved to a division-type organization and increased their investments. The Histadrut enterprises diversified from construction- and agriculture-related firms to chemical, electronics, rubber and plastics and machinery.

Until 1977, the confrontations and conflicts between the politicians in the government (mostly from second Aliyah) the Histadrut political leaders (mostly third Aliyah), and Histadrut managers and SOEs executives were all solved *in camera* 'within the family.' The high rate of growth of the enterprises allowed cross subsidies to the losing plants and neither the Histadrut nor the government received much of a return in the form of dividends on capital invested. In fact, Hevrat Ovdim's firms are not expected to pay dividends.

The objectives which SOEs (or Histadrut plants) actually fostered were compromises among expectations of various stakeholders. The managers were trying to enhance their autonomy largely by reducing their dependence on political and labor stakeholders for resources. It looked like the managers behaved as professional managers in a large investor-owned firm did. In fact, they could not manage only on the basis of economic efficiency, and therefore they could not afford to face a free and total market competition. Instead, they were attempting to concentrate in economic branches in which they could be monopolies. Managers, as already pointed out, could join cartels to raise prices against consumers' welfare even though they managed enterprises with social goals. Since they enjoyed a monopoly, or were sure the government would be willing to write off the loans or convert them into new ones, these managers were never faced with the cruel choice of having to fire workers, or reduce wages in order to maintain efficiency. Therefore, it was possible to pay lip service to the 'need for efficiency,' but continue to compromise for political reasons.

As discussed in chapter 2, the unique organization of the labor political and economic institutions allowed Mapai to be a dominant party for many years. However, the party had lost much of its ideological appeal in the eyes of a young generation which was much more influenced by the Chicago school of economics than by any remnant of ideology brought from Russia. For the third Aliyah, organizations of regional affairs through so-called Workers Councils, reminiscent of the Soviets, were natural. For the blue-collar labor today, most of what they get because the Histadrut exists (for example trade union protection) and all they receive today because the Histadrut demanded it in the past — say, legally required annual leave — is taken for granted. For them, the Work Council is a place for bureaucrats that exploit them. If they are employed by Koor or another Histadrut owned enterprise, they want better wages, improved work conditions and higher fringe benefits. For some decades, the Histadrut attempted to give the worker exactly that — and compelled the managers of the economic enterprises against their better judgement to raise wages, grant more attractive fringe benefits, and refrain from firing workers even when no work was available. To survive under these conditions, the economic enterprises of the Histadrut needed to achieve a monopoly position or to be able to get some type of subsidy. When these firms faced competition and when subsidies were not available, they ran into difficulties and were unable to adapt to changing economic circumstances.

The tendency to prefer the easy life of the monopolist was not a unique characteristic of the Histadrut sector. In fact, one reason it is sometimes difficult for an outsider to understand the working of the Israeli economy is that this tiny economy is far from being a free market economy, in which resources flow in response to price signals stemming from a competitive system. One reason the Israeli economy does not easily adjust to new realities is that it is far from facing competitive forces. Private sector firms in Israel are often protected from import competition and enjoy a monopoly position because the small size of the market makes it very difficult for a competitor to start. Thus Israel has only one producer of tires, one producer of paper, one producer of Passover Matzot, one producer of salt, or of instant coffee, of cement, hollow glass, glucose, electric bulbs, aluminium tubes, beer and matches — to name just a few products. In quite a few of these cases, the monopoly producer is also the sole importer of the goods. Private-sector firms may also be defense contractors or producers for telecommunications — facing a monopsonistic buyer. The political apparatus could not effectively monitor and discipline the managers. Product markets almost never played a disciplining role because the small size of the market and the protection from an import penetration meant most firms operated in a monopolistic environment.

There was very little need to spread financial risks because the risks were taken by the government and by Hevrat Ovdim. Both were reluctant to restructure firms or retrench. In general, as long as managers did not violate the politically imposed rules, they had a lot of autonomy. In the private sector, most firms were managed by a second and more often even a third generation of founders. In many cases, the third generation has been less interested in managing the firms, and an increasing number of firms have merged.

Thus, in terms of ability to unlock initiative and to face competition, many Israeli firms, irrespective of sector face a problem. Moreover, Israelis love to be organized. Each Israeli is a member of several associations and organizations based on almost any possible kind of kinship, from an association of immigrants from the United States (or from South Africa, or from Russia or even from Pinsk) to an association of garage owners or of auto mechanics. When one insurance company tried to reduce its costs of car repairs by offering the repair shops cheaper sources of spare parts supplies it was simply boycotted by the association of the shop owners. The association of pharmacies dictates the prices at which drugs are sold, claiming there is a health reason for not discounting drugs prices. This arrangement is enforced by the Ministry of Health (and by the law). The Ministry of Tourism issued regulations forbidding travel agents to give their clients any reduced price tickets. For many years, import licenses could be received only through such associations, so an average Israeli found it hard not to be organized and not to belong. Each one of these associations is a major lobbyist. It is also an important channel for receiving subsidies and a conduit for the transfer of government aid, but not less so a place for getting contacts, socialization, and employment for the 'active persons' — those working for some cause. A very large number of Israelis are 'active persons' in hundreds of such associations, organizations, or labor shop stewardship positions. The latter are paid by the employer for being full-time labor 'active persons.'

Firms who produce 50 per cent or more of the total Israeli production in their category must register as a monopoly. Other firms may organize themselves as a cartel — and may get a permit if such a cartel is deemed to be in the public interest. The public interest is very widely interpreted. It may include a reason such as that the cartel will export a part of its output even though this will be achieved by charging higher prices in the domestic market.

Many entities in the private sector get special considerations because they have some historical rights. Most gasoline retail stations are allocated to persons wounded in one or another of the wars of Israel. These licenses are sometimes openly, although not necessarily legally, traded, as are the licenses for taxicabs — that are also granted as a part of a rehabilitation program for disabled war veterans. Importers of many durable goods would be granted a monopoly position because they had agreed to maintain a level of spare parts inventory in Israel. The private sector was very adamant in demanding, and the government very generous in helping to erect, a whole list of barriers to entry for new firms to the industry. At least in some cases, these barriers are based on a law restricting entry to a certain profession. In other cases, the law prohibits a certain behavior, for example opening stores at late hours. Some of these barriers are, paradoxically, contained in the very law encouraging investment. Since one has to gain the status of 'an approved enterprise' in order to get subsidized loans or tax holidays, it is extremely difficult to compete against an entrenched producer who has received these rights if one is not 'approved.' Civil servants have been known to be reluctant to grant such an approved status when they felt 'there were enough suppliers' and the entrant would create 'excess capacity' if not waste. The idea that the new investor may be able to increase demand by reducing prices is generally not perceived as plausible by these civil servants. Nor do they believe that 'excess capacity' is another term for competition. One consequence of this situation has been that new entrants attempting to get an 'approved status' would habitually promise to export their production. To honor such a commitment they often did export — at a high cost to the economy.

All in all, Israel is a country in which more than a third of employed persons work for the government or similar institutions. It is also a country of a major Histadrut sector. In addition, a very large per cent of the private sector operates in a protective environment, achieved through a variety of administrative means, and in which an incumbent has entrenched rights. The above does not mean that there is no competition. In some small-scale services, competition is very fierce. In fact, from this point of view, the Israeli economy is really a dual economy, composed of the medium or large, well organized, firms and the thousands of small firms, many of which do not receive any government aid and do not always pay the full amount of taxes they should have paid by law.

The Likud regime

For reasons discussed in chapter 2, Labor was relegated to opposition in 1977, and the Likud (unity, in Hebrew), headed by Menachem Begin, created the government. In 1981, the election victory scored by Begin-led Likud returned this bloc of parties to power for the second time in a row. Both in 1984 and in 1988, the Likud created a unity government with Labor, and when Labor left the coalition, Likud created its own narrow coalition. Labor has been losing power in each consecutive election since 1977.

The Likud was in opposition for so long, and Mapai has been so dominant for more than forty years, that one would have expected many policy changes to have been implemented under the new government since 1977. Since the first finance minister was a leader of the Liberal party, it would be natural to expect many changes that could have affected the sectorial balance in Israel or that could introduce market forces and deregulation. It seems that at least some economic leaders of the Histadrut were sure such changes would enfold. In reality, there were more differences in the economic policies of the four ministers of finance in the first two periods of the Likud-led governments than between them and the Labor-led period. In particular, despite recommendations of a public commission, no new laws to create a national health service passed the Knesset. Most health services continue to be supplied by the sick fund of the Histadrut. Unquestionably, many became and remain Histadrut members mainly to avail themselves to these health services. The sick fund continued to receive a large percent of its budget from a government appropriation; and early attempts, after 1977, to change the health organization of Israel were not successful. The National Religious Party is said to have opposed changes in health care.

The major impact of Menachem Begin as a Prime Minister of Israel was in areas of foreign policy. The most important was the signing of the peace treaty with Egypt on March 26, 1979, after a tortuous process and despite opposition of more than a third of his own party's members of Knesset. A second important decision of Begin was the attack on the Iraqi nuclear energy reactor. A third was the invasion of Lebanon. The Lebanon war certainly caused intense strife, and many in Israel felt it was an uncalled-for war. Yet all these did not affect sectorial structure or the introduction of market forces.

A major policy pushed by the Likud, and mainly by Ariel Sharon personally in his capacity as the Minister of Agriculture, was the expansion of Jewish settlements in the occupied territories. Sharon was able to triple Jewish population in these areas in four years despite adverse court decisions, cabinet opposition and budget problems that stymied his work. Yet, controversies over the settlement policies were not only between Likud and Labor, but also inside each block. In the period 1967–77, the Labor-led government created or allowed to be created 76 new settlements (25 in the Golan Heights, 28 in the West Bank and 23 in Sinai and Gaza Strip). Labor refrained from settling within heavily populated Arab territories.

Two major domestic initiatives of the first Begin government were the extension of free tuition to all four years of high school financed by increasing the social security levies and Project Renewal, a major effort to eradicate slums. Both of these were to a large extent a continuation of policies initiated by Labor.

The government did announce its intention to implement a series of free market reforms and to cut subsidies. Minister of Finance Ehrlich allowed Israelis to hold foreign currency (but restrictions on these rights were introduced and further tightened in February 1980). He announced his intention to tax kibbutzim more heavily, claiming they escaped the tax burden imposed on others. A public commission he appointed, however, found the kibbutzim paid more rather than less tax than other economic enterprises in comparable income situations — and this issue was dead. A proposed tax amnesty that would appeal to some Likud voters was killed by the Prime Minister. Many announcements on the desirability and the intention to sell state-owned enterprises ended in increasing that sector. The only change was that the contract with the Histadrut on bonds allocations was not renewed in 1980.

Despite the ideology in the Liberal part of the Likud party it is very hard to show any significant shift in the economic regime in Israel. The liberalization of the foreign exchange, in October 1977, looked like the beginning of a major change. Yet, even in the first period of the Likud regime the role of government increased and expanded. There was a turn into a populist policy in terms of the economic objectives pursued. The objective of achieving economic independence was neglected. In the ten years between 1977 and 1987, the cost of living went up by 261,000 per cent.

Why was the Likud unable or unwilling to make policy changes that would affect the sectoral distribution of power? Why is it that the Likud did not make more changes that could have reduced the power of the Histadrut? Why didn't the Liberals introduce liberal environmental policies? One possibility for the lack of change despite pledges to do so may have been the preoccupation of the government with foreign policy and security issues. It is also possible that the Likud did not implement promised domestic political economic reforms because it was unable to do so. Entrenched bureaucracy supported the old ways, and strong interest groups opposed the changes. In addition, after twenty-nine years in opposition since the state was born and several decades more in the Yishuv period, the Likud had no real experience as the party at the helm. As a result, its platform was designed more as an attention catching device than as a serious set of ideas for implementation. Finally, it had little capacity to translate normative utterances to actual decisions on government policy. Another possible reason was that the power of the Histadrut, controlled by Labor, was still large enough to prevent any attempts to honor such electoral pledges as the nationalization of the health care system or privatizing government corporations. While this possibility is uttered by Israeli political scientists, it does not explain how Horowitz was able to curtail one major advantage of the Histadrut, nor does it explain why Mr Peres, a Labor minister of finance, began pushing privatization in 1988. A more plausible explanation is that the majority of the Likud believe in the social tenets promulgated by Labor. Herut today is more the representative of the low-income strata, and its leaders believe subsidies are important. The Liberals, who were supposed to represent free enterprise, simply do not have enough power within the Likud. Further, many of its constituents are addicted to government protection and subsidies — and do not have any real interest in the operations of an unfettered market economy. It is also plausible that Herut leaders believed they could gain control of the Histadrut by elections, and did not wish to weaken it, or reduce its political assets. If so, they were wrong. In the 1989 elections to the Histadrut, Labor received more than 50 per cent, even though Mapam decided to go separately. The Likud was unable to receive enough votes to block even decisions that must be carried by a two-thirds majority.

Whatever the reason, clearly only very few changes were

implemented. Those that were made were based on changes of nontransparent and little-known arrangements, such as the investments of the pension funds reserves. It is possible that the Histadrut lost power through other, lesser known, changes. More plausible is the idea that all power centers in Israel gain from the status quo and do not have any interest in change. Finally, 'left and right' in Israel differ mainly in their attitudes toward the Arabs and their beliefs on the borders. The right in Israel is certainly not liberal or a believer in a free enterprise economy.

Changes in ideology

At the beginning of the 1950s, the formal ideology of the labor movement leaders continued to oppose private property and called for *Hagshama* (fulfillment), pioneering, and sacrifice and the disciplining of the individual to achieve collective goals and the socialist vision. It also called for abolition or at least minimization of private property. The transfer from the voluntary institutions to the coercive power of the state was perceived as allowing 'Socialism in our time.' The private sector complained it was discriminated against, for example in the allocation of raw materials. The General Zionist party were carrying the flag of the ideological alternative to Mapai views in the economic arena. Their leaders professed liberal ideas and fought the increasing dependence on bureaucracy, against the high taxation and against the rising level of government intervention in the economy. Some of the leaders of Herut that came from the Revisionist party also believed in classical liberalism clung to by their original leader, Zeev Jabotinsky.

Tension emanated from very strong feelings and bitterness that precipitated from long history: the 1935 establishment of the New Zionist Organization; the belief that Arlozoroff was murdered by the Revisionists in 1933; the 'season' — a period between the end of 1944 and the beginning of 1945 of cooperation of the Jewish leaders of the Yishuv with the British Authorities against the dissidents at that time; and to a large extent the trauma of Ben Gurion's order to shoot with a cannon the ship *Altalena* on June 20, 1948. Hatred ran so deep that Ben Gurion was calling Begin 'the man sitting next to Mr Bader.'

The pure liberal ideology in the State of Israel has not been represented by any political party but only by the academic economists in the country. All of those were educated in the spirit of the Chicago school in economics and the strong belief in preferences of the market. Economists often spoke strongly against government intervention. Inasmuch as the power of the economists within the government administrative system has grown, there has been a somewhat greater inclination to promote the use of economic efficiency rules in government decisions. The increasing power of the Bureau of the Budget in the Ministry of Finance, much more than any political change, was the cause of a slow but continuous change to a liberalization of the import controls, to a reduction of the discrimination among different sectors and economic branches, and to the reduction and periodic abolition of subsidies. The opposition to subsidies for products and for textiles plants, or to grants to agricultural entities, or to the method of allocation of housing and land did not all stem from political parties' leaders but only from the pens of economists in the academic institutions of Israel and those in the Bureau of the Budget in the Ministry of Finance. These economists have advocated giving much more weight to economic efficiency considerations and therefore recommended a uniform and real rate of exchange. Economists, however, had very little political power. The different interest groups all insisted on their right to get a larger share of government aid, not for a change of the economic regime. Perhaps those that resisted the economic system of Israel simply decided to emigrate.

Yet the constant rise in the standard of living and the receipts of personal reparations money from Germany materially reduced the dependence of citizens on the political apparatus or the government system. The total dependence of the citizen on the government gradually changed into an interdependence among different sectors who affect each other and have a symbiotic relationship of give and take.

The 1970s also witnessed a deterioration of the value of ideology as a motivating factor. In the mythos on the Jewish Yishuv there is an enormous weight given to the ideology. Even then, there were many other factors, already discussed, that influenced the political and economic structure of Israel. The story of Israel is one of growing conflicts between the ideological demands and the wishes of the post-statehood generation. Israelis have become somewhat tired of working only for public objectives. Many decided it was time to take care of their own welfare. In the second generation, profits were not assumed to be only a result of immoral speculation or parasitism.

There was also a major change in the degree of transparency of operations. First, the state controller published annual reports. It was often said that the controller did not have teeth. However, the very publicity given was a deterring force against more wrongdoing. Civil servants refrained from acting when they were concerned about the state controller's publicity. Until the 1970s, both the Jewish Agency and the Histadrut rarely published their internal auditor's reports. The state controller always did. Second, Israel has always enjoyed free press. Many press persons took upon themselves to further investigate — and publicize reports in a much less elegant and understated language.

Since the second half of the 1980s, there has been an increasing recognition that resources are not insatiable and choices will have to be made. This recognition may finally lead to the formation of new institutions and a new mold for Israeli society. Yet by the end of the 1980s, Israel was a country in which the impact of the political system on the economy was still very large and decisive.

5 The role of the government in the different economic branches of the Israeli economy

Introduction

Most economists believe that the best method for resource allocation is to allow the market to reign freely. Government intervention in the market is justified only when the market fails. Market failure may result from the existence of public goods, externalities or economies of scale. It can then be impossible to get an equilibrium price, or the market price may not reflect all relevant social costs and benefits.

A public good is characterized by three features: an indivisibility of the production and the supply; the inability to prevent others from consuming the good once it is supplied; and the fact that the use of the good by one individual does not reduce the ability of another individual to consume it. Such a good can be supplied either by one type or another of a voluntary organization, or by a government. The government may finance the product through taxation. Governments may also regulate the supply of certain goods by the private sector, often because suppliers hold monopoly power. A market failure may also be a result of positive or negative externalities, that is when the operations of a firm affect other individuals or firms and the costs are not paid as a part of the operations. One example is air or water pollution.

All over the world, governments were expected to expand their role and supply more services. Governments now supply not only public goods such as defense, but also education, employment, welfare services and so on. This increased role may or may not result in a higher level of taxation to finance the government operations. Thus, education contributes not only to its receivers but to the society at large, causing positive externalities. For this reason, government may finance part of the cost of education. It can do so either directly through a budget or by granting a tax exemption. As another example, the government may enforce the cost of pollution on the producer

197

through law. The additional cost will equalize the social and private costs without any effect on the government budget. Of course, these different methods affect income and wealth distribution.

In general, an economist would condone government intervention either to correct market failure or to regulate the production of a public good. In reality, the government intervenes also because of ideological reasons or because of political pressures. In Israel, ideology has been very important in explaining government behavior. For example, the government intervenes more in agriculture than in retail trade. At the same time the political power of different economic branches has not been identical. Sectors possessing strong economic power developed organizations that lobbied the government and achieved much more help and therefore also much more government intervention than other sectors.

In the last chapter, the sectorial distribution of the economy was surveyed. In this chapter we shall survey the political intervention in different branches of the Israeli economy. We shall start with agriculture, then look at manufacturing firms, construction, transportation and communication, oil and energy, health, as well as banks. We shall finally analyze intervention in the capital market, government's major tool for achieving its objectives. We shall not deal with other economic branches such as retail and wholesale trade and restaurants — these are dominated by small firms in the private sector with very little government intervention. Tourism will be discussed in chapter 7.

Agriculture

Israeli agriculture has achieved world records in production of milk per cow and in yields and crops. It was able to develop new varieties of fruits and vegetables, to extend the shelf life of many products, to increase agricultural productivity and to save water by inventing drip irrigation, which delivers water to individual plants drop by drop to minimize evaporation losses; all of which increased productivity. It created organizations that enabled an extremely rapid dissemination of new technologies and techniques to all corners of the land. The new methods could originate in the extremely sophisticated agricultural experiments stations or on one individual farm.

Israeli farmers export as much as the limiting factors (mainly water) allow (26 per cent of their production), and supply 94 per cent of the needs of the local market. They also teach fifty-two countries of the Third World new methods developed in Israel to coax food from arid land and desert conditions.

Israel's exports of fresh food were largely based on high-quality produce, and imaginative promotion and introduction of new 'gourmet' or specialty products such as avocados and mangos. The market for specialty foods is unfortunately limited. Avocado, for example, captured an estimated 80 per cent of the European market with sales of $50 million in 1985. Because of the scarcity of water, it is unrealistic to expect significant growth in agricultural products.

Israeli agriculture has also grown very fast both in production and in productivity. Labor productivity in agriculture grew by 8.2 per cent per annum in 1960-65; 8.6 per cent in 1966-72, 8.0 per cent in 1977-9, 4.1 per cent in 1980-85; and 3.8 per cent in 1987-9. Agricultural production grew by 5.5 to 6.5 per cent until 1985. In 1986-8 has been only 0.6 per cent (Table 5.1). It decreased by 1 per cent in 1989. The percentage of employees in agriculture was 4.7 in 1989.

The reason for the small increase in 1986-88 was that 1988 was a difficult year. Agricultural output and producers' prices declined by 4.8 per cent. Agricultural exports dropped by 18.0 per cent. Many difficult natural conditions factored into the poor output of mostly citrus products, but also avocados, bananas, and wheat. For example, citrus export declined in 1988 by 21.5 per cent.

The cultivated area of Israel's agriculture grew from 1,650,000 dunams in 1949 to around 4.38 million dunams in 1987. The irrigated crop area increased from 300 thousand dunams in 1949 to 2,153,000 in 1987. The capital stock (quantity index with 1975-6 = 100) increased from 17.5 in 1949-50 to 113 in 1986-87. Agricultural production was 13 in 1948-9 when 1967-8 = 100 and 225 in 1986-8.

The value of agricultural production in the 648 kibbutzim, moshavim and communal moshavim represented by the Agricultural Center were, in the mid 1980s, 88 per cent of the total agricultural production, with the lowest share (62 per cent) in citrus production and the highest share of 95 per cent in the production of eggs, poultry, cotton, flowers, and cows' milk. In 1936, the workers settlement share among Jewish farming was 45 per cent. In milk production, the share of the workers settlement was 46.9 per cent in 1936, but 92 per cent by 1960.

Israeli agriculture is centrally planned and centrally regulated. The planning is achieved by high collaboration with the settlement movements. The planners decide in minute detail what should be produced and how much. They even designed the

Table 5.1 Gross domestic product at factor costs, 1970-1988

Year	Agriculture	Manufacturing	Transport and communication	Water and electricity	Construction	Commerce and services	Total business sector
			By economic branch at 1986 prices				
1970-73	6.3	30.8	13.7	3.6	17.4	28.2	100.0
1980-83	7.9	31.4	14.3	3.9	12.3	30.3	100.0
1985-8	7.9	31.8	15.0	4.0	9.0	32.3	100.0
1988-9	7.6	30.5	15.1	3.9	9.4	33.5	100.0
			Annual average % of change				
1960-88	5.5	6.8	6.7	6.3	3.4	5.6	5.8
1960-65	6.7	13.4	10.3	10.2	11.1	4.6	9.1
1966-72	6.4	10.3	10.8	9.1	7.9	9.0	9.2
1973-9	5.9	4.8	4.9	5.1	-1.7	4.8	3.9
1980-85	5.4	2.2	2.8	3.0	-1.8	3.1	2.4
1986-8	0.6	2.4	3.3	3.4	3.4	6.1	3.7
1989	3.0	-2.3	1.6	0.0	3.8	4.0	1.6
			Increase or decrease (-) from previous year				
1970	5.4	9.5	13.5	10.2	16.2	7.8	10.4
1971	10.3	10.5	14.7	9.9	12.9	12.5	12.0
1972	7.2	11.9	13.0	12.0	15.2	10.6	12.0
1973	-0.3	4.5	4.7	3.9	3.9	3.9	3.9
1974	10.1	5.1	4.3	4.2	0.4	3.6	4.0
1975	8.9	3.1	-1.6	4.9	3.3	0.3	2.1
1976	8.0	7.6	6.3	5.6	-11.7	4.7	3.2

Year							
1977	8.0	5.2	8.7	5.6	-13.9	3.2	2.5
1978	4.9	5.0	6.6	6.3	-0.2	11.7	6.5
1979	2.4	3.4	5.9	5.2	8.1	6.6	5.3
1980	5.2	-2.3	-3.9	-0.8	5.8	-1.6	-0.8
1981	10.0	2.3	5.5	5.9	0.8	7.2	4.7
1982	11.0	0.3	-0.2	3.4	-2.4	5.2	2.3
1983	3.6	4.0	7.9	3.0	-1.2	4.7	4.1
1984	-1.4	5.4	5.2	2.4	-7.1	-0.9	1.3
1985	4.7	3.9	2.7	4.1	-6.3	4.3	2.8
1986	0.8	4.8	1.9	4.4	-1.1	7.0	4.1
1987	8.2	5.5	8.3	5.6	8.6	7.3	7.0
1988	-7.2	-2.7	0.1	0.2	2.9	4.0	0.0
1989	3.0	-2.3	1.6	0.0	3.8	4.0	1.6

Source: Bank of Israel, *Annual Report*, 1988, p. 151.

individual houses in the moshav. Since 1957, when Moshe Dayan became the minister of agriculture (and the first such minister who was not a kibbutz member), all agricultural production has been carried out within a system of production and marketing boards, used to plan the production by allocating quotas. These boards also have monopoly power on marketing. A farmer is not allowed to sell his produce except through licensed marketers. They also allocate subsidies and have legal rights to enforce the quotas. Subsidies are channelled through regional purchasing organizations.

In the State of Israel, there are two central bodies responsible for agriculture: the settlement department of the Jewish Agency settles new immigrants and is responsible for bringing the new settlements to a condition of viable, orderly economic and social status. The Ministry of Agriculture is responsible for orderly agricultural planning. The two entities have not always agreed on priorities. However, in 1951-2, Levi Eshkol was both the minister of agriculture and the head of the settlement department. This made it possible to create a joint center for agricultural planning. With time, the ministry of agriculture attempted to push the economic-efficiency point of view in the agricultural planning. However, the strong political power of the agriculture lobby makes it very difficult to introduce any changes. Many leaders still refuse to accept profitability of operations as a criterion for their continuation. To them, agricultural settlement still has an absolute value on its own. It must be measured by its contribution to population dispersal, by the very settling of desolate parts of land or by security considerations, not by profitability.

The return to working on the land has been of great value to Zionist organizations. Working in agriculture, that is, being a farmer, was perceived as a major means in achieving the greatest of Zionist ideals — the return of the nation to its land and the redemption of the land of the forefathers. Because of this, agriculture received high priority by the Jewish Agency before the state was born and this priority was continued after the state was established. Agriculture was seen as a preferred means to achieve different ideological and social values, as well as several national objectives — from defense and security to the dispersal of the population in different parts of the country. The preference to agriculture led to sizeable investments with very little regard to economic considerations. In 1950, then minister Levi Eshkol presented the first development plan for agriculture in which it was suggested that farmers should account for 26 per cent of all employees in Israel. In 1953, a seven-year plan based agriculture on autarchic measures and assumed that Israel would produce all the olive oil and all the sugar needed for domestic consumption. It also assumed that Israeli farmers would produce all the fodder and animal feed required in the country and half of the wheat.

The buds of agriculture in Israel started at the time of the first Aliyah. At that time, Baron Rothschild invested a substantial amount of money in almonds and grapes (see chapter 2). Later, large sums of private Jewish capital were invested in citrus orchards and in land purchase. Despite these beginnings the official history of agriculture in Israel usually stresses mainly the communal settlement movements that created intensively cultivated mixed farms on national or public land. That is, the major emphasis is on agriculture built by the socialist movements, mainly by kibbutzim and moshavim.

Agricultural settlement and land acquisitions were the two major centers of operations of the National Institutions. Between 1918 and 1939, the National Institutions invested about 40 per cent of their total budget in these two fields of activities. There was a very wide consensus in Zionism that agriculture should be preferred: agriculture was seen as a quasi-source of life, a way to revitalize both mental and physical powers. Such a revitalization was deemed essential after generations of city living and detachment from the land.

After the second Aliyah, an alliance was formed between workers and the Zionist executive organizations. There was a perceived synergism between having uncultivated national land and pioneers that did not have any money, but wanted to settle on the land everywhere in this country. The cooperative worker groups were perceived as persons who would continue working despite enormous difficulties. The groups were a means to educate persons with very little understanding of agriculture. As a result, the Zionist executive financed the workers settlements, but rejected requests for help from private farmers or by private manufacturers. The village has always been perceived as more important than the city, and acts on behalf of the nation have always been more important than acts on behalf of oneself. Even the private manufacturers, in their memoranda to the Jewish Agency, agreed that agriculture had the most important role in building the new country. They were hoping manufacturing importance in economic development would *also* be recognized (Beilin, 1987).

While much of the agriculture was organized by the settlement organizations, the citrus orchards were planted and developed mainly by private capital. The area planted by citrus

Table 5.2(a) Localities and Jewish population, by type of locality and population group

Type of locality and population group	% of total population							Population[1] (Thousands)							
	22 May 1961	20 May 1972	4 June 1983	31 Dec 1985	31 Dec 1986	31 Dec 1987	31 Dec 1988	22 May 1961	20 May 1972	4 June 1983	31 Dec 1984	31 Dec 1985	31 Dec 1986	31 Nov 1987	31 Dec 1988
Rural localities	13.0	9.8	9.8	10.1	10.2	10.2	10.1	251.8	263.8	329.1	350.9	356.2	364.9	370.1	370.9
Moshavim	6.2	4.6	4.2	4.1	4.1	4.0	4.0	120.9	124.9	140.5	143.8	145.6	145.9	145.6	146.0
Collective Moshavim	0.2	0.2	0.3	0.3	0.3	0.3	0.3	4.0	5.5	9.0	10.1	10.5	10.8	10.9	11.1
Kibbuzim	4.0	3.3	3.4	3.5	3.5	3.5	3.4	77.0	89.5	114.8	121.8	124.3	125.7	126.0	124.9
Institutional localities	13.2	0.3	0.3	0.4	0.4	0.4	0.4	5.8	9.2	13.0	13.2	13.2	13.2	13.3	13.3
Other rural localities	2.1	1.2	1.4	1.6	1.8	1.8	1.1	40.6	33.3	46.0	56.2	56.6	63.3	68.4	69.3
Thereof: communal rural centers	—	—	0.2	0.4	0.4	0.5	0.5	0.7	2.8	7.8	10.5	12.7	14.8	18.6	21.1
Living outside localities	0.2	0.1	0.2	0.2	0.2	0.2	0.2	4.2	1.3	5.8	5.9	5.8	6.0	6.0	6.2

Source: Statistical Abstract of Israel, 1988, pp. 50-51; 1989, pp. 59-60.

Note: [1] Population in rural localities was 14,140 (17.0% of total Jewish population) in 1922; 87,100 (21.6% of total Jewish population in 1926; and 149,300 (25.4%) in 1948. Kibbuzim and Moshavim populations were 2,600 (3.1%), 27,580 (6.8%), and 68,600 (11.6%) respectively.

Table 5.2(b) Localities and Jewish population, by type of locality and population group

Type of locality and population group						Localities					
	1922	1936	1947	22 May 1961	20 May 1972	4 June 1983	31 Dec 1984	31 Dec 1985	31 Dec 1986	31 Dec 1987	31 Dec 1988
						Absolute numbers					
Rural localities	–	–	–	695	722	880	919	923	934	936	938
Moshavim	4	27	82	346	353	405	408	411	411	409	409
Communal Moshavim	–	–	11	20	33	43	46	47	47	47	47
Kibbuzim	19	47	140	228	233	267	268	268	269	268	270
Institutional localities	–	–	–	29	31	32	32	32	32	32	32
Other rural localities	–	–	–	68	72	133	165	165	175	180	180
Thereof: communal rural centers	–	–	–	11	19	24	24	24	24	24	24
Living outside localities	–	–	–	4	–	–	–	–	–	–	–

Sources: Statistical Abstract of Israel, 1988, p. 50-51; 1989, pp. 59-60. A. Gertz (ed.), 1947, Statistical Handbook of Jewish Palestine, 1947, p. 38.

orchards increased from 11,500 dunams at the end of 1925 to 17,000 dunams by the end of 1926; 24,000 dunams by the end of 1927; 31,000 dunams by the end of 1928; and 46,000 dunams by the end of 1929 (*Statistical Handbook of Jewish Palestine*, 1947). At the same time, the number of agricultural settlements organized by the socialist movements increased: from 12 in 1918, to 19 in 1921, and 25 in 1925. The number of collective settlements grew to 59 in 1932, 95 in 1937, 134 in 1939, and 179 in 1945. By 1941-2 there were 50,000 persons working on mixed farms, cultivating 534,089 dunams. Of all the cultivated agricultural land, 62.5 per cent was defined as national land, 24.2 per cent was owned by PJCA, 2.7 per cent was land belonging to other settlement organizations and only 10.6 per cent of the land was private. Today the majority of farming activities in Israel are still performed by 'workers' settlements' in three different communal types of organizations: the kibbutz, the moshav and the communal moshav. There is also some private farming not associated with the Histadrut.

By the end of 1947, the kibbutz members dwindled considerably. Most new additions to the rural population were new immigrants, who were not willing to live in a kibbutz. The major reservoir of the kibbutz was members of the Zionist youth movements in Eastern Europe. This reservoir vanished into ashes during the Holocaust. The only reservoir left were Israeli-born members of youth movements.

If the new immigrants had been given a free choice — they would probably not have chosen to be moshav members. However, the new immigrants were rarely asked. They were brought into new moshavim, for example in the mountainous corridor between the foothills west of Tel Aviv and Jerusalem, and were supplied with agricultural instructors to train them in modern agriculture methods. They were made members of the moshav and were also subject to its by-laws, which were designed for the pioneer generation of its founders with no ideological training for communal life. The result has been a large number of new immigrants' moshavim, many of which never reached economic independence. In the end of the 1980s, those moshavim are still organized in a different association than the 'old' pre-state period moshavim.

Moshava is a type of village like those in Russia before the revolution, in which each farmer owns the land and the factors of production. Table 5.2 shows the distribution of rural populations in Israel just before independence until the end of 1988. It shows a relative decrease in the weight of the kibbutz and a major increase in the moshav. It also shows the relative stagnation in the number of villages.

All workers' settlements are affiliated to the agricultural center of the Histadrut. The centralized organization of the agricultural settlements started, as already shown, in the 1920s. Nir was enforced on the kibbutzim and was granted a veto power. Since then (and even today), Israel is unique in the world in having its agricultural settlements under a political umbrella, strongly dominated by political movements. In fact, only farmers organized by a political party could (and still can) receive land and means of production. The allocation of the agricultural settlements is made by a committee deciding, on the basis of political considerations, which settlement movement would receive which 'land block.' An individual, or even a political group, would not be allocated any land or means of production. Only settlement movements could be allocated land and means of production, and those movements belong or are at least affiliated to political parties. The movements made sure that new immigrants, too, would be operating under the same type of an ideological system of cooperative marketing and mutual guarantees, made enforceable when the Moshavim Law was enacted.

To help the communal settlements, regional purchasing organizations were established. Originally, they were designed to reduce costs by concentrating the buying power of a whole region. The first of these organizations was established in the Jordan valley in 1938. Today, the purchasing organizations are the conduit through which all subsidies to farmers are channelled. They also receive the receipts from sales to the marketing organizations.

The ideological identity of the political party, the purchasing organization and the settlement movements helped in creating a very powerful and coherent lobbying power that crosses any one party line. This power resulted in a high level of governmental aid. The availability of government aid in turn diminished the efficient farmers' opposition to what they perceived as a waste of their money or an unjustified system.

Private farmers are organized in a similar fashion, having their own purchasing organization, centralized marketing body and forbidding the individual farmer to market the produce on his own. Many claim the farmers' representatives elected themselves, rather than being elected.

During the Mandate period, about four settlements a year were founded. In the first four years of the state's existence, about 70 settlements, mostly moshavim, were established each year, and in the six following years — about 20 per annum. At the end of 1948, there were in Israel 104 moshavim and

communal moshavim and 177 kibbutzim. By May 1961, there
were 366 moshavim and communal moshavim and 228 kibbutzim.
By the end of 1988, the number of moshavim and communal
moshavim reached 456. The number of kibbutzim was 270.

In the 1980s, the agricultural sector was facing a major crisis
as a result of inefficient planning, saturation of the absorption
capacity of the local market and difficulties in increasing its
exports. About 50 to 60 per cent of the moshavim members did
not work in agriculture. Further, 26 per cent of all units used
about 60 per cent of all water and land and produced 75 per cent
of all moshavim agricultural production. Clearly, in a pure
market economy, many of the less efficient producers would
have to leave. In the Israeli political economy system, the
inefficient are able to survive, being cross-subsidized by the
efficient producers and by the taxpayers. In the kibbutzim, there
has been a massive shift to manufacturing: about 60 per cent of
the value of the kibbutz movement production stems from
manufacturing. Such a change was more difficult to implement
under the moshav by-laws.

Kibbutz members are considered elite. Their numbers in the
central committees of the labor political parties or in the Knesset
and the government are very high in proportion to their
percentage share in the population. The farming lobby works for
the benefit of their constituents in various ways. Since 1920, the
budget allocation for private agriculture has been minimal.
Private agriculture allocations were generally the first candidates
for elimination under a budget cut (Lavski, 1980, p. 109).
Because of the ideological dominance of the settlement
movement, the government did not intervene in their affairs, but
did give them subsidies for capital, land and water. Israeli
settlements are politically oriented, and the Statistical Abstract
of Israel shows these political organizational affiliations (1988,
pp. 52-3).

Agricultural activity requires the use of four factors of
production: capital, labor, land, and water. In each of these
factors of production, political influence is extremely high. The
financing of the rural areas' development is supplied by the
government and the Jewish Agency. The initial capital was
granted through the Agricultural Center from *Keren Hayesod*
funds. Agricultural credit comes from the government-owned
and farm-movements-dominated Bank of Agriculture. The state
also financed the infrastructure, the housing, the purchase of
means of production, and later improvements. All of their
financing is highly subsidized. It is allocated through the
settlements' purchasing organization to the moshav or kibbutz,

not to any individual farmer. Settlements that faced difficulties in repaying the loans received conversion loans. Since many were brought in to the moshav without much training, they were not ready for the ideological responsibility. Dozens of new settlements were abandoned. Thousands left the moshav and did not pay their debt to the movement. While many settlements reached record production levels, others suffered from social and economic desolation. Efficient farmers could not buy the production (and water) rights of the inefficient ones — at least not legally. Several crises in individual moshavim were 'solved' by more conversion loans.

By 1985, many kibbutzim were tottering and dozens of moshavim collapsed. Real income in agriculture has gone down since 1987 (in 1988 by 14 per cent and in 1989 by 9.8 per cent). The reduced level of income made it difficult for farmers to pay their debt — or even to pay the interest on the swollen debt. The availability of very cheap credit in the past caused too many agricultural settlements to invest in not very profitable projects. All assumed the government would help if need be. In 1987, many moshavim faced a new crisis, in part because of past irresponsible investments and rising consumption but also because the real interest rate as a part of the economic policy in July 1985 reached a level of 29 per cent in real terms. The magnitude of the crisis this time was too large. Many of the efficient farmers called for more individual freedom, less cooperation, and a change in the moshav law. As they saw it, the communal values meant not only that the strong had to help and support the weak, but also that the efficient farmer had to pay for the losses caused by lazy ones.

Labor in agriculture joined the settlement units, during the Yishuv period, mainly because of ideological beliefs. In the state of Israel, the new immigrants were certainly not ideologically inclined. Still, most kibbutz populations live in this type of framework because of ideological beliefs. The kibbutz organizational structure has proven more resilient and more flexible in achieving transformation to manufacturing than the moshav.

Several new moshavim had been subject to the powerful control of members of one extended family. Since all accounts go through the moshav's association and since all subsidies have been channelled through the regional purchasing organizations, controlling the association grants a lot of power. As long as the association was managed by and for a few ideologically indoctrinated persons, the system worked. In many new moshavim, however, the system was abused. More efficient moshav members accepted the inequities of the system since it was generally assumed that debts would be consolidated, or paid for by the government or the Jewish Agency.

The number of those employed in agriculture reached an apex in 1961 — 127,600. Since then, it has been declining, reaching a low ebb in 1982 of 84,200. In 1985, the number was 89,400, of which 20,900 were kibbutz members, 26,300 self-employed and cooperative members (mainly moshavim members) and 36,200 wage earners. In 1987, agriculture employed 87,000; in 1988, 34,300 and in 1989, 81,800.

Virtually all the agricultural land is now owned by the state and leased on long-term leases to the farmers. In the Yishuv period, land acquisition had an enormous political and ideological importance. *Keren Kayemet* was responsible for the acquisition and all different parties agreed that land should be publicly owned and should not be sold. This idea stems from national but mainly moral beliefs, going back to the biblical dictate: 'The land shall not be sold in perpetuity, for the land is mine' (Leviticus, 25:23). It was also feared that private ownership would lead to preferences to Arab workers. The land lease price has always been much lower than the market price. Therefore, such a lease could include many restrictions.

From its establishment in 1902 to October 1920, *Keren Kayemet* acquired 24,940 dunams. By the end of 1937, it had acquired an additional 362,685 dunams. PJCA acquired about 470,000 dunams. Since 1960, all state, PJCA and *Keren Kayemet* lands are administered by the Israel Land Authority. This authority manages more than 90 per cent of all the land in Israel. The leasing costs are very low; no one has ever calculated the implicit subsidy thereby given to the land users.

The farmer has the right to use the land but leaves certain property rights in the hands of the community. The individual farmer cannot mortgage the land — and has to rely on the mutual guarantee of the moshav to get loans. This restriction reduces the ability of the farmers to specialize. In a free market system, the efficient farmers would have acquired the land (or the right for lease of land) from the less efficient farmer. In Israel, such a market is illegal. It is also illegal to sell water quotas.

Water is, of course, a major input for farming. It has become a major limiting factor for agricultural expansion, since Israel is an extremely arid country, and since aquifers are currently exploited beyond their recharge level (Table 5.3). Agricultural users consume about three-quarters of the water in Israel. The largest supplier of water in Israel is Mekorot, producing 58 per cent of all water, including the large national pipeline. This

Table 5.3 Water resources (millions of cubic meters)

	Sustainable yield	Exploitation	Annual deficit
Lake Kinneret and			
Upper Jordan	575	600	(25)
Coastal Aquifer	283	352	(69)
Yarkon Taninim			
Aquifer	330	385	(55)
Other sources	522	530	(8)
Total (annual)	1,710	1,867	(157)

Source: Israel's Ministry of Agriculture.

pipeline carries water from the Lake of Galilee to the arid Negev area.

All water in Israel is by law public property. The government regulates and directs the use of the water through a system of quotas. All water enterprises are planned by a state-owned body; and a water commissioner in the ministry of agriculture is responsible for all water management. The cost of producing water varies widely in the different parts of the country. The Water Law (1959) created a balancing fund to cross-subsidize the water prices across different areas of the country. In addition to the cross-subsidy, water is also subsidized through the budget, through calculation of the cost of the water on an historical-costs basis and by subsidizing the price of electricity charged in the production of water.

The relatively low price of water in Israel increased the demand for it to the point of endangering the aquifers. The state controller devoted a long report to the water situation, stating that the aquifer in the coastal plain 'was used in the last 20 years in a manner that endangers its future' (State Controller Annual Report, number 37, p. 543). The agricultural representatives keep pushing for more investments in water desalinization or the purification of sewage. Despite much talk on the obvious connection between the water price and the quantities used, the heavy subsidization of water continues. In 1982, the state controller found that the water price to farmers was less than the (subsidized) price paid for the electricity used for its production. In 1984, the water price was 5.85 US cents per cubic meter. In 1985, the price was raised to 9.47 cents and that brought the price back to previous levels (in 1980, the price was 9.49). In

1985, the cost of producing water was 29.7 cents on the average. This cost was of course much higher in some parts of the country. For ideological and political reasons, the price of water is equal in all of Israel.

Both ideology and politics combined to create a system in which such scarce factors of production as land or water cannot be traded in a free market to ensure efficiency. Water for agricultural use is allocated according to historically-based quotas, not on the existing use structure. The water quota to the kibbutzim is larger than their share in the total of agricultural employees. The kibbutzim also received more land than their share of employment. As a result, they have specialized in water-intensive products. When Moshe Dayan was Minister of Agriculture, he reduced water quotas to kibbutzim and increased them to moshavim. In his memoirs he argued that an average production unit in the kibbutz had 105 dunams and received 24,300 cubic meters of water and in the moshav it was 36.7 dunams with 10,600 cubic meters of water. He claimed he reduced the kibbutz water quota to 17,100 cubic meters and increased that of the moshav to 13,500 cubic meters (Dayan, 1976, p. 379).

During the 1970s, the kibbutzim had an image of arrogant and rich nobility. The 'new' moshavim (those starting after the state was created) developed their own leaders. One result was that only 49 per cent of moshav members of those moshavim affiliated to the Labor party voted for it as opposed to 90 per cent of the members of the kibbutz affiliated with the Labor party.

Thus, Israeli agriculture has a lobbying group with very significant political power. Such power cannot be explained by the number of farmers. It is much more a result of the ideological beliefs. As a result, factors of production used by farmers are heavily subsidized. New agricultural methods were developed by government-financed research facilities. The Israeli agriculture sector has been very eager to learn and change and has been very resourceful and resilient. It rapidly absorbed several major technological revolutions. It was able to increase the productivity level and to have a very fast rate of new product diffusion.

Because of the ideological stance, the pricing policy in agriculture is geared to the maintenance of farmers' income at a level equal to that of the urban dweller. This objective is achieved by producers' cartels, avoidance of surplus by the allocation of production quotas and absorption of surplus by destruction after paying a minimum price to the farmer. The planning center for agriculture accepts the institutional arrangements in allocating water and land and the organizational characteristics of the workers' settlement. Farmers do not receive production quotas directly, but through various organizations. Almost every farmer belongs to a moshav or a kibbutz. These units are members of regional procurement organizations — that has become a large bureaucracy serving its own interests and expanding its own (and badly managed) enterprises. Above those there are eleven 'settlement movements' — allocating factors of production and subsidies. Their representatives are directors of the monopoly production and marketing boards. All settlement organizations are subservient to the 'agricultural center' and Nir enjoys veto power in each kibbutz and moshav. Marketing is allowed only by 'licensed marketers.' Throughout the system, the individual farmer receives the remnant of the market price. The various organizations, each one of which enjoy monopoly power, deduct their expenditures from the revenue. Except for a communal sense of responsibility, their managers do not have any economic incentive to reduce their costs. In citrus products, the individual grower receives 15 per cent of the price paid by the final consumer. Some estimate the number of employees of all the agricultural organizations to be four times the number of the farmers. The political system in agriculture is dominated by those assigned to represent this sector, not by the government. The system is very far from even remotely resembling a free market allocation.

Manufacturing

The manufacturing industry in Eretz Israel started with a number of Arab-owned, very primitive, soap factories and a small number of machine shops. Baron Rothschild encouraged only those manufacturing plants that were needed by the farmers. He established the large wine cellars to absorb the grape production (the ownership of these cellars was transferred in 1906 to a farmers' cooperative). PJCA also established the Palestine Flour Mills. The Baron additionally invested in a cosmetic essence plant and in a bottles plant (both turned out to be unsuccessful).

Private Jewish entrepreneurs of Russian origin established an oil products plant in 1906. It later expanded to become, in 1925, the largest manufacturing plant in the country. In 1920, a cigarette factory was established, and in 1922 — a cement factory and a salt plant. A number of other entrepreneurs from Russia inquired about possibilities of erecting plants. Almost all were

213

rejected by the Zionist office in Eretz Israel either because it forecasted no local demand or too strong import competition. In 1920, a survey by a delegation sent by Poalei Zion, the Socialist party, found only ten manufacturing plants employing more than ten workers (among them a casting plant, the wine cellar and a German-owned pump manufacturer). It also reported that all the manufacturing plants together employed 5,000 Jews. A census of the Zionist Executive in 1922 found 1,850 manufacturing plants — all of them privately owned, in which 600,000 Egyptian liras had been invested and 4,750 workers produced revenues of 500,000 Egyptian liras. These were mainly small workshops in printing, tailoring, blacksmithing, and carpentry. A concession for the erection of an electricity plant was granted by the British government to Pinhas Ruthenberg. The first generating power plant started operations in Tel Aviv in July 1923. The main plant, in Naharayim, was finished only in 1931, largely because Ruthenberg had to face many difficulties in tapping the required funds. Moshe Novomeysky, a Russian Jewish engineer, spent large sums of his own money in scouting surveys to determine the best means to exploit the many mineral deposits of the Dead Sea. He was finally able to get a concession for these minerals from the British government and to produce potash and bromine.

A major push was given to manufacturing during the fourth Aliyah. Unlike its predecessors, this was an Aliyah of the middle class, with an individualistic point of view, strong need for achievement and highly influenced by the profit motive. These were also immigrants with a high level of education, some of which spent part of their time in Europe and part in Eretz Israel. The influx of new immigrants meant rising demand for consumer products, and many of the new immigrants came with capital — so they started import substituting manufacturing of sanitary products, textiles, biscuits, sausages, smoked meats, chocolates and other food items as well as silicate bricks, printing plants, furniture manufacturers, shoes, suitcases, horse harnesses and matches. Many of these pioneers did not possess sufficient funds for the working capital, and ran into difficulties. It was almost impossible at that time to get any bank credit, and the Jewish Agency, based on its ideological proclivities, refused to guarantee industrial loans. The British Mandate authorities clung to an 'open door' policy, based on paragraph 18 of the Mandate. The British believed that bringing immigrants to be employed in plants with a problematic economic vitality was a disastrous policy. The Jews attempted to convince the British to levy protective tariffs. The general policy of the British Mandate government was that an industry that cannot operate without protective tariffs of more than 15 per cent should not be established. In almost all cases, the government did not accept the argument that goods were imported at dumping prices. It saw itself as a protector of the consumers more than of the local manufacturers. However, the government did establish, as early as 1928, a standing committee for trade and industry that deliberated on the desirability of customs protection, generally allowing duties ranging from 20 to 33 per cent.

The high-quality human capital imports of the fifth Aliyah and the relatively large capital imports at that time caused a rapid growth of manufacturing industry. Between 1933 and 1937, an additional 600 manufacturing plants were established. In 1927, there were 6,000 employees in manufacturing. By 1937, the number had grown to 29,986.

Jewish diamond manufacturers in Antwerp were very apprehensive lest Belgium would be conquered by Germany. Some of them decided to erect modest diamond cutting plants in Eretz Israel. In 1939, diamond cutters in Palestine received for the first time an allocation of raw diamonds from the Syndicate. Later, when the major Antwerp diamond center was paralyzed during World War II, the Palestinian center was able to grow and gain significantly higher market share.

In 1939, the Twenty-second Zionist Congress resolved to call on the British government to change the customs method so as to aid the local manufacturing plants, and to protect local manufacturers against dumping-type import competition. The Zionist Congress also called for government procurement of locally made manufacturing goods, and for a reversal of the discrimination of Palestine as a country with an open-door policy. The Congress further called for a full exemption from customs duties for machinery and spare parts needed for agriculture and manufacturing and refund of customs paid on the imported portion of exported goods. Except for such declarations and demands from the British Mandate authorities, however, the Jewish Agency did not do much to aid manufacturing. The Association of the Owners of Manufacturing Plants, established partially as a countervailing power to the Histadrut in 1921, wrote many memoranda demanding national capital participation in at least pioneering plants such as the electricity company and the establishment of financial institutions to finance manufacturing. The Jewish Agency, however, felt its funds should be used mainly for land acquisition and the creation of agricultural settlements. A proposal by Dr Ruppin to create a bank for industry was rejected. The Manufacturers Association created such a bank on its own. Only 3.5 per cent of the 1939

Jewish Agency budget was used for aid to manufacturing. The Zionist leaders felt that all they had to do for manufacturing was to provide political support in attempting to change the tariff policy of the government.

Manufacturing suffered from a crisis due to the cessation of capital imports after 1935. It grew rapidly during World War II. Because of the difficulties in carrying out marine transportation, the British center in Cairo was ready to procure many products from the local manufacturing plants and to get them the raw materials so that they could supply the goods to the army. The increased military orders developed the industry and allowed it to move from consumers and construction products to other products. The index of industrial production zoomed from 100 in 1938 to 788 in 1945. Toward the end of World War II, the Histadrut construction firm began to acquire manufacturing plants. By 1947, about 10 per cent of manufacturing was Histadrut owned. All the rest was privately owned.

In the first few years of the State of Israel's existence, manufacturing suffered, with many others, from the acute shortage of foreign currency that did not allow a full utilization of plants' capacity. The manufacturers had high expectations from the government of Israel. First and foremost, they called for a change of the open-door policy of the Mandate period, hoping the government would stop 'unnecessary and excessive' imports. By the middle of the 1950s, it was clear that agriculture could not expand much more, faced with an acute shortage of water. In 1954, the government established an Investment Center, that turned in 1959 into an Investment Authority. It enacted a Law for Encouragement of Capital Investment in 1950, and added many more incentives and tax exemptions in the revised law of 1959. The money from the reparations was a major source for the acquisition of new machinery. The government drew up specific plans for the development of particular plants and helped those willing to erect these plants with subsidized loans and mainly by banning the imports of any product made in Israel. Production of basic consumer goods expanded to meet the needs of a rapidly growing population, resulting from large-scale immigration. The result was often inefficient production at extremely high costs. Profitability was possible only because of the absolute protection.

The government also erected manufacturing plants on its own. Direct ownership was used when the manufacturing involved military application or when it was based on Israel's natural resources, for example phosphates or potash. Indeed, some of the largest Israeli manufacturing enterprises are still state owned. This includes such firms as Israel Aviation Industry and Israel Chemicals as well as several military enterprises. The government also entered into joint ventures with private entrepreneurs that were willing to establish manufacturing plants in development towns. Mr Pinhas Sapir, at that time the Minister of Trade and Industry, was ready to aid and encourage any entrepreneur, not only the government or the Histadrut sectors, in various off-budget ways. Mr Sapir was extremely powerful, and Shimshoni (1982, p. 243) depicted him as 'Le Roi Soleil.' Mr Sapir promoted private industrial enterprises in development toward labor-intensive textiles. According to Mayshar (in Ben-Porath, 1986, p.113):

> Much of the promotion effort was conducted secretly to avoid public scrutiny. Toren (1979) estimated that in 1958–1965 the cumulative differential grant to these textile plants (over and above grants provided elsewhere) equalled 5 percent of the 1962-level GNP.

In Sapir's time, the system became one of interdependence: the government gave aid in exchange for development. The interdependence was limited to the small number of entrepreneurs who were known either to Mr Sapir personally or to his trusted civil servants. Since the 1970s, the intervention has been less specific than in Sapir's time.

On the basis of an average of 100, in 1978, industrial production grew from 15.7 in 1958, to 113.2 in 1983, and to about 132.7 in 1987. In 1988, industrial production decreased by 2.0 per cent; in 1989, a further 2.5 per cent decrease was recorded. The share of manufacturing employment in the total business sector's employment was about 30 per cent in 1965 and 32 per cent in 1988. In value added the share grew from 26 to 29 per cent. There was very little change in the weight of manufacturing in the business sector. Since 1975, the share of manufacturing in value added was 29–30 per cent. A major revolution, however, occurred in the composition of output. First, the manufacturing industry moved from predominantly supplying private consumers to one producing for exports (50 per cent of the uses in 1988, compared to 20 per cent in 1956). Defense demand increased the share of public consumption in uses from 7 per cent in 1965, to 19 per cent in 1975, and then decreased to 14 per cent in 1988 (Table 5.4). Second, there was a major transformation from traditional to high-tech, sophisticated capital-intensive products (Table 5.5).

217

Table 5.4 Industrial product by final destination,[a] selected years, 1958-89 (%)

	1958	1965	1975	1985	1988	1989
Private consumption	59	46	25	24	27.7	25.7
General government consumption	4	7	19	16	14.7	14.2
Gross domestic capital formation	22	27	19	12	13.1	12.9
Total domestic destinations	85	80	63	52	55.5	52.9
Exports	15	20	37	48	44.5	47.1
Total	100	100	100	100	100.0	100.0

Sources: 1958-85 Bregman, 1988-9, p. 16. 1989 Bank of Israel, *Annual Report*, 1989, p. 96.
Note: [a]This breakdown of industrial product (gross value added) takes account of the final destination of the intermediate outputs involved. For example, the value added of industrial inputs to exported agricultural products is here included in exports. The estimates are based on the input-output tables for 1958 and fiscal 1965-6, 1977-8, 1982-3 (Central Bureau of Statistics and Bank of Israel).

The significant rise in exports came mainly from high-tech firms (about 70 per cent of industrial exports excluding diamonds). An industry is considered 'high-tech' if the value added it produces is based primarily on the development efforts of engineers. In Israel, according to the Ministry of Industry and Commerce, these include precision and optical instrumentation, basic chemistry, pharmaceuticals, pesticides, and disinfectants, salt and mineral extractions, pumps and compressors, agricultural and industrial machinery, electric motors and transformers, electronic equipment, automobile parts as well as planes and their components. The high-tech firms were predominantly operating in the defense area (chapter 6). Since 1967, however, many such firms have been civilian-oriented. Thus, between 1976 and the end of 1985, there were 430 new start-up firms, 256 of which received funding from the office of the chief scientist in the Ministry of Trade and Industry. Others applied and were rejected or received funds from the United States-Israel Binational Industrial Research and Development Foundation (BIRD). The BIRD foundation was founded in 1977, by the governments of Israel and the United States. It is dedicated to financing projects for the development and commercialization of innovative non-defense products or processes. All funded projects must represent a joint team effort by a US and an Israeli company. Most applicant teams have complementary skills — often an Israeli firm's design and product development skills are combined with a US firm's market access and knowledge.

Table 5.5 Change in manufacturing structure excluding diamonds[a] 1965-88 (%)

Year	Human capital-intensive branches	Traditional branches	Total manufacturing
Human capital per employed person			
1965-6	20	14	17
1980-81	32	20	26
1985-6	36	23	28
Product distribution			
1965-6	35	65	100
1980-81	47	53	100
1986-8	48	52	100
Distribution of fixed capital			
1965-6	28	72	100
1980-81	40	60	100
1986-8	46	54	100
Distribution of labor input			
1965-6	31	69	100
1980-81	39	61	100
1986-8	40	60	100
Ratio of export in output[b]			
1965-6	18	19	19
1980-81	40	32	36
1986-8	46	33	40

Source: Bank of Israel, *Annual Report*, 1988.
Notes: [a]Classified by human capital per employee. Human capital-intensive branches are transportation vehicles, electricity and electrons, chemistry and oil, paper, printing and publishing, machinery and miscellaneous. [b]Excluding diamonds and exports to the occupied territories.

The fund's endowment of $110 million was contributed equally by the Israeli and US governments — $60 million in 1978 and $50 million in 1984. Grant contracts awarded have risen from $0.3 million in 1979 to $7.3 million in 1986. BIRD will give up to 45 per cent of total cost for projects over $150,000 and up to 50 per cent of cost on smaller projects. Limit for a single project is $1 million.

The Israeli government has viewed assistance in R&D as the primary means to support the emergence and growth of advanced-technology industries. In the 1950s and 1960s, funds were granted mainly for the development of military products and for agricultural research. Since 1968, private-sector R&D has been supported primarily through the offices of the chief scientists in the Ministries of Industry, Agriculture and Energy. The office of the chief scientist in the Ministry of Industry was established after the Katchalski-Katzir Committee Report recommended that R&D support of industry be channelled through a single industry-oriented office at a senior level. This, it was hoped, would accelerate the rate of creation and the probability of success of R&D based firms. Later, high-tech firms were given the option of selling tax-deductible bonds privately, taking government subsidy off budget. Several high-tech firms took advantage of this opportunity before the government decided to disallow it. Hi-tech companies also succeeded in issuing shares in US stock exchanges, thus raising considerable capital for financing their investments and growth.

The general principle governing assistance from the chief scientist's office is that government funds must be matched 50-50 by business contributions. Only research and development activities qualify for funding, but the R&D stage of projects is considered to include also the development of prototypes or pilot projects and market assessment. The main criteria for funding are that the project be truly innovative, technologically viable, and have good prospects for export. The chief scientist sometimes funds military R&D projects and product improvements, at a reduced level of 30 per cent of project cost. If a project succeeds, the chief scientist expects a royalty of 2 per cent of sales until the full inflation indexed cost of the grants is recovered. About four hundred project proposals are received annually from some three hundred companies.

Manufacturing in Israel is characterized by a high degree of central direction and by a network of personal relations that affects many decisions. Since the government can grant a manufacturing firm the status of an 'approved enterprise' another firm cannot compete unless it, too, is 'approved.' The need for approvals and the many licenses required made all industrialists dependent on the government. The government could not achieve its economic goals without the large manufacturers and the two were developing entwined interdependence. In many ways, the Israeli manufacturing scene is of a dual-economy type: on the one hand, thousands of small entrepreneurs operate with no government help (or intervention). On the other hand, a small number of large firms, responsible for a very high per cent of the manufacturing output, operate with many interlocking directorates and informal ties. The government aids these firms by encouraging investment, providing import protection, refusing to allow competing firms to enter the market and through a system of price controls that is effectively a cost-plus system. In the 1960s, most of the aid was based on improvisation and *ad hoc* decisions. With time, more of the encouragement methods and means were institutionalized into laws and regulations. Yet the discretion of the civil servants (and more so of the minister) is still very high.

A very large per cent of the official part of the encouragement was achieved by heavy subsidies to capital. Much of that subsidy came ex-post, because of high rates of inflation that reduced the effective interest rate to a negative figure (-2.5 per cent in 1970-72, and -16.6 per cent in the period 1973-8) (Mayshar, in Ben Porath, 1986, p. 114). This massive subsidization has caused a high level of investment, mainly in manufacturing but also in other businesses. Livtin and Meridor (1982) estimated, for the period 1975-9, that business investors in agriculture, manufacturing and hotels perceived about half of the investments as a free grant (and 27 per cent for the period 1970-74). *Ex post facto*, taking into account the much higher than anticipated inflation, the grants were even more substantial. Only since 1979 has the government linked a portion of its loans to manufacturing industry. In 1988, the Bank of Israel's report (p. 185) estimated the subsidy for investment resulting from grants and subsidized credit only as a per cent of total investments in manufacturing (such a total includes also 'non-approved' and subsidized interest). According to these figures, the subsidy was 5 per cent for 1965-9, 19 per cent for 1970-74, 31 per cent for 1975-9, 20 per cent for 1980-84 and 16 per cent for 1985-8.

One consequence of the massive subsidization of capital was an accumulation of unused manufacturing capacity. Much of the encouragement of industry was justified by the desire to create employment in developing regions. Yet capital subsidies made investments in development regions extremely capital-intensive, much more so than in other areas of the country. These developments had their consequences on productivity: production per man-hour grew by 6 per cent p.a. during the 1968-72 boom, but only by an average of 2 per cent in the 1980s. Total factor productivity slowed down more drastically, coming to a halt by the mid-1980s (Table 5.6). The poor productivity performance of manufacturing may be explained by a combination of several factors: increased uncertainty resulting from sharp swings in economic policy, and an accelerated inflation to three-digit annual rates. In addition, the subsidization of capital meant a high incentive for investment, carrying in turn excess capacity

Table 5.6 Indicators for the development of manufacturing (excluding diamonds, 1965-1989); quantitative rates of change, average per annum %

Period	Product	Labor work[a] (in days)	Gross capital[b] beg. of yr.	Product per labor unit[c]	Total productivity[d]	Export[e]
1950-59	9.7	6.7	15.9	2.8	0.0	25
1960-64	13.4	6.6	8.5	6.3	6.0	15
1965-7	-2.6	-6.4	4.0	4.0	1.3	12
1968-72	16.3	9.8	6.8	5.9	7.2	17
1973-9	3.9	0.3	7.5	3.6	1.9	11
1980-5	2.7	0.4	4.9	2.3	1.2	8
1986-7	4.3	1.0	3.9	3.2	2.0	8
1988	-3.1	-4.6	3.5	1.6	-1.3	4
1989	-2.0	-5.8	1.9	4.1	1.1	8

Sources: Bregman, 1989. Bank of Israel, *Annual Report*, 1988, p. 184.
Notes: [a]Man-hours. [b]Gross beginning-of-year stock. [c]Product per man-hour. [d]Product per unit of capital and labor (weighted by average weights for each sub-period: the average weight of labor over the entire period is 58 per cent; in the 1980s labor weight was 76%). [e]Excluding diamonds.

and lower productivity. A decisive effect on productivity growth was achieved by technological progress, related to R&D expenditures. This was estimated by Bregman (1989) to increase by 5.3 per cent p.a. both during the 1960-72 and 1973-85 periods.

Most of the private industrial plants were relatively small, and based on import substitution. Many of the industrial exports were made on the basis of marginal cost calculations, covering the full costs by charging much higher prices in the protected local market. The civil servants (and the ministers) tended to aid those they knew and the technologies with which they were familiar. New innovations and daring projects were looked at askance. As so often happens when tax exemption and subsidies are available, there were many cases of swindlers, imaginative manipulators and fly-by-night operators. One result was that civil servants felt all private-sector entrepreneurs (except those they knew intimately) could not be relied on. They became suspicious and weary of daring ideas in new fields. Up until the 1970s, most approved investments were in mature, import substitution plants, many of which degenerated later. However, the defense industry and a decision to aid R&D, and install a chief scientist, created the high-technology-skewed industry now present in Israel. A second consequence was that the ability to receive government aid has been much more important than the skill in managing a firm, the ability in achieving production efficiency or the knowledge of the ways to gain marketing effectiveness. The high level of government aid also meant that it was virtually impossible to start an industrial plant without government aid — such a plant would find it impossible to compete against those receiving subsidies.

The increasing recognition of the importance of the manufacturing industry has meant that the Manufacturing Association has become more politically powerful. The defense-related industries have also boomed since 1967, and 60 per cent of the output of the politically powerful kibbutzim now comes from manufacturing. The industrialization process of the kibbutz started in the late 1950s. From 1958 onward, virtually the total increment of the kibbutz labor force has been assigned to industry (Don, p. 372). All of these factors increased the political power of the manufacturing sector and its ability to receive government aid. In 1970, the manufacturing lobby was able to ensure the enactment of a specific Law for the Encouragement of Industry. The incentives granted to manufacturing were much higher than those received by hotels, for example. This was despite the fact that hotels generate foreign currency and the official policy was to increase export revenues. Value added in tourism has been about 80 per cent — as opposed to less than 20 per cent in diamond manufacturing. The small merchant, the workshop owner and the professionals granting essential services were those left without any governmental granted incentives, tax holiday or special subsidies. They were paying the high marginal market rate of interest and the full tax load.

To be sure, part of the aid to manufacturing was needed because of other government policies. Thus, since the rate of exchange was never left to the vagaries of the market, the government always felt it had to compensate the manufacturing exporters for the unrealistic rate of exchange. In 1985, for example, a committee charged with measuring all subsidies estimated the export subsidies to be equal to $485 million. Another possible estimate would be the import subsidy resulting from a low rate of exchange. By the same token, tax exemptions were necessary because taxes were very high. Without much of the government intervention — the subsidies were also redundant. Both, however, gave much political power to those having the discretion to grant subsidies or to levy different charges. They also gave high economic rents to those whom the government wanted to help.

Despite much lip service for 'liberalization of industry,' the government was never willing or able to really make Israeli industry face international competition (examples were given in chapter 4). More than twenty-five years after the government declared an 'exposure to international competition policy,' dozens of industrial firms continued to be profitable only because they were shielded from import competition.

In conclusion, since 1955, the manufacturing sector has no longer been a stepchild. The government made a special effort to accelerate the rate of growth of manufacturing. This was achieved by granting specific aid to each plant. As a result, close contacts with those having the authority to grant these concessions have been a most salient factor of production. Because of political and ideological reasons, the government chose not to encourage manufacturing by developing infrastructure services and by low taxation, but by specific intervention, regulation and control of each and every firm. A significant portion of the manufacturing, mainly science-based manufacturing, produces for the defense establishment — a sector in which resource allocation was made with less constraints than for other causes. In many cases, additional capacity was added for political reasons, in particular in the defense-related industry. In the Histadrut, much of the considerations were those of employment, not of efficiency. The larger manufacturing has become, the greater its political power has become, culminating, in 1970, with the enactment of the Law for Encouragement of Industry.

Construction

The state of Israel inherited from the Mandate government a very high density of inhabitants per residence and many slums. In addition, the influx of many immigrants increased the need for residential flats. About 110,000 persons found housing in flats left by the Arabs. Yet by December 1951, there were 256,506 persons living in temporary dwellings. Housing had thus become a major problem. The government created a state-owned enterprise ('Amidar') and made it responsible for the housing of new immigrants. At the end of 1949, the responsibility for housing was moved to a special branch of the Ministry of Labor, and later to a specialized Ministry of Housing that took the responsibility for the planning and execution of housing projects. In a typical fashion, the government did not implement a system of uniform subsidies, but built the houses on its own, or initiated the building. It sold housing in different conditions and different levels of subsidy to different groups, including army officers, civil servants, police persons, experts from abroad, ex-underground functionaries, widows of war veterans, as well as new immigrants. Some of the houses were built by construction firms owned by political parties for the members of the party. In quite a few cases, subsidized houses were granted in lieu of higher salaries. As one example, subsidized houses were sold by the army to officers who agreed to serve for a certain number of years.

Housing was a constant problem. After the new immigration, there was a period of social stresses because the poor felt they did not have sufficient housing opportunities. In the 1970s, the major housing problem was faced by young couples. In Israel it has always been almost impossible to find an apartment for rent at a reasonable cost. This was, at least to some extent, because a law designed to protect tenants froze rent at a level that made house ownership totally uneconomical (and those who owned houses for rent — much poorer). At the same time, the value of houses increased often more than inflation, and buying one's own house was seen as an inflation hedge.

While no free market apartments were available for rent, Amidar (and Amigur: a sister company owned by the Jewish Agency) owned and rented about 15 per cent of the flats in

Israel. These flats, however, were rented according to a complex set of criteria decided by a committee of civil servants, not even by the company. An Amidar tenant cannot rent the flat in an open market, nor can an ordinary citizen get such an apartment at a market rent. The majority of Amidar's tenants are Israeli Jews born in Asia and Africa. The rent has been based, since 1958, on social considerations and was determined by a ministers' committee. In 1980, the rent in Amidar was less than 2 per cent of a family income in the lowest two deciles of the population. The revenue was not even sufficient to pay for the regular maintenance of the houses. Amidar attempted to sell the flats to the tenants. However, since the average rent for a three-bedroom flat in March 1986 was $4.5 a month, or 0.6 per cent of the average wage, even the offering of the flats at 10 per cent of their market value was not a strong enough incentive for tenants to purchase the flats. The government found it politically difficult to raise the rent. It does not receive any return on its investment in these assets, estimated to have cost $2 billion.

In July 1973, the Israel Land Authority council ratified a decision of a ministerial committee on conditions of land allocation for self-building in development towns. In what has become a political pattern, the candidates had to be approved by a committee composed of civil servants. A young couple who wanted a mortgage had to purchase a flat approved by the Ministry that would not be larger than a certain size.

The government also controls the mortgages market as a part of its general control of the capital market. About 90 per cent of the liabilities of the mortgage banks are earmarked for uses decided by the government, on which the bank has no discretion. The banks administer these mortgages but do not decide on their allocation or their conditions. The public mortgages have always been subsidized. Until the 1980s, they were granted on a discretionary basis by civil servants. After the 1962 devaluation, the government was forced to change the contracts linking mortgages to the rate of exchange retroactively, and did not dare to link the mortgages again until July 1979.

Thus, the government influence in the construction market comes from its ability to allocate the land, the credit, and the right to many of the apartments. The government also owns a construction company and intervenes administratively, by virtue of the Planning and Building Law. This law was designed to ensure physical planning of the land. In the bureaucratic reality, it became a means of giving politically inspired largesse (for example by allowing building more on a certain land, or changing it from agriculture to residential use). It also makes the construction more expensive because cumbersome licensing arrangements take time. Further, the construction firms did not have enough of an incentive to use new methods and more modern technologies.

The idea that the government could give each new immigrant, or each young couple, a certain fixed amount of subsidized mortgage; or that Amidar could rent flats to whoever desires to live in them; and that government could subsidize the needy directly would not have occurred to the Ministry of Housing civil servants. Allowing the market to operate would have reduced the political dependence of the average citizen!

The construction sector has been an important factor in the economy because of the number of its employees, large investments and the impact on other sectors. In 1981, for example, investments in construction were 62 per cent of all investments and 13.5 per cent of GNP. In 1986, these investments were only 49 per cent of total investments and 9.6 per cent of GNP. From 1976 to 1986, the area of buildings begun went down by 40 per cent. The most significant decline was in the construction for residential dwellings. Construction of residential dwelling, in IS millions at 1986 prices increased at 30.1 per cent per annum on average in 1968-72 but decreased since then (average per annum: -2.9 per cent in 1973-9; -2.8 per cent in 1980-6; -5.9 in 1986). In 1987 there was a rise of 9.5 per cent; in 1988, 2.9 per cent; and in 1989, 3.8 per cent. In terms of area the change was even more pronounced: -5.8 per cent in 1973-9; -6.5 per cent in 1973-9, 6.5 per cent in 1980-6 (and a rise of 19.0 per cent in 1987 and 5.6 per cent in 1988, but a decline of -16.8 per cent in 1989). Many construction firms did not forecast the change — and suffered all sorts of difficulties. The largest construction firm — the Histadrut-owned Solel Boneh — found it even more difficult to adjust, having moral and political difficulties in firing workers or reducing their wages. Since 1984, the company has suffered heavy losses. In March 1986, the government decided to help by granting it $80 million new loans, and allowing the Histadrut to sell bank shares held by the pension funds to raise money for additional equity for the firm. In the political situation of 1986, the decision also meant that an equal amount had to be granted to other construction firms.

The government used to be a major builder. Up to 1975, it built almost half of the flats. Since then, its share declined to 13.8 per cent in 1987 (though it rose again in 1988, to 15.1 per cent and again in 1989, to 18.3 per cent) (Table 5.7). Government intervention is achieved today mainly by its control of the mortgage market. Directed mortgages are granted to those the government wants to aid. These loans are given for a longer period and at lower interest costs. Even so-called 'free mortgages' were regulated until 1989, mainly by fixing a ceiling of 50 per cent of the value of the flat.

In the construction area, the government changed significantly the means by which it intervened. It used to build on its own, and in the 1980s relied more on 'directed mortgages.' More important, it used to specify the size of the flat and its location for each individual case. It moved to a less bureaucratic method of objective criteria (known as 'points').

The level of investment in construction in Israel is quite unique. Summarizing the first decade of Israel's economy in 1960, Patinkin wondered 'how soon the backlog of demand for housing . . . will be met, with a corresponding release of resources for investment in other sectors' (p. 82). In 1986, Mayshar found it:

> rather incredible that long after the genuine backlog of the 1950s was met, the economy continued after 1973 to devote an internationally unparalleled 9.5 per cent of GNP annually to the expansion and upgrading of its stock of housing. [He added:] It is possible that the uncertainties created by inflation and the government control of capital markets are responsible both for the excessive demand for housing and for the anemic demand (only partly offset by subsidies) for private business investment.
> (Mayshar, in Ben-Porath, 1986, p. 117)

Table 5.7 Area of building begun by initiating sector (thousands of flats)

Year	% of public out of total	Public building	Private building	Total
Average 1970-5	46.5	26.2	30.2	56.4
Average 1976-8	27.1	8.4	22.5	31.0
Average 1979-86	31.5	8.9	19.3	28.2
1982	29.5	8.4	20.1	28.5
1983	27.9	7.3	18.9	26.2
1984	27.9	6.5	16.8	23.3
1985	24.9	5.2	15.7	20.9
1986	16.5	3.1	15.8	18.8
1987	13.8	3.0	18.7	21.5
1988	15.1	3.3	18.6	21.8
1989	18.3	3.6	15.7	19.3

Source: Bank of Israel, *Annual Report*, 1989, p. 67.

By the end of 1989, the weight of housing stock was 50 per cent of the total gross capital stock and 30 per cent of gross investment.

Energy

Israel did not have its own sources of fuel, except during 1967-79, when it produced oil in Sinai. Israel has always been extremely sensitive to the need to ensure energy supply on a long-term basis. It has also found it necessary to hold a relatively high emergency stock. After all, it was in a state of war with neighboring confronting states that were important suppliers of oil. It was also almost totally dependent on imported energy sources and the lines of oil supply were long and vulnerable to belligerency.

During the British Mandate, an oil pipeline was built from Mussol in Iraq to Haifa. The British also built a deep-water port in Haifa in 1933 and the oil refineries in 1938. Pressured by the oil producers, the large oil multinationals ceased their operations in Israel on April 10, 1949. Israel was forced to agree, after lengthy negotiations, to the conditions these companies imposed for the supply of energy. The ministry of finance established, in 1949, a Fuel Administration to represent the Israeli interests *vis-à-vis* the oil multinationals. In addition, the government initiated the creation of the Delek (fuel) company in 1951. This company received the government's right for refining 30 per cent of Israel's consumption. Despite the importance of energy, only 10 per cent of the shares were held by the state; the rest of the ownership was equally divided between the private and the Histadrut sector — 45 per cent each. Since 1977, the share of the government has been reduced to merely 1 per cent.

Between 1955 and 1958, the oil multinationals left Israel completely, largely because of the Arab economic blockade against Israel. The foreign multinationals sold their assets in Israel to Delek and to two additional companies created for that purpose — Paz and Sonol. These three firms acquired the unrefined oil, transported it and marketed it. Some of the transportation was done by state-owned enterprises. So was the inventory handling (technically, the three firms were part of the private sector; Paz became a state-owned enterprise in 1981, and was privatized in 1988). Refining was done in the two refineries in Haifa and Ashdod. The refineries were acquired by the government in 1958 and sold to the Israel Company in 1973.

Despite hundreds of millions of dollars spent on oil, gas and coal exploration very little was discovered. In 1952, a small oil field was discovered, with a production in an apex year (1965) of 202,000 barrels (8 per cent of consumption). In 1962, natural gas was discovered near Arad, and its energy was used for the manufacturing plants in the area. Lack of water meant it was impossible to create hydroelectric sources of energy. A dream of erecting a canal from the Mediterranean to the Dead Sea almost materialized under Begin's government. However, it was found to be much too costly, and the project was put on the back burner. In 1989, with the cost of oil doubling from $10 to $20 a barrel there was an additional interest in the project, but it was still considered uneconomical.

All energy for manufacturing comes from the (monopoly) electricity company. All generators are near the sea, to use the sea water for cooling. Up to 1989, the oil and energy sector was in effect a cartel. All energy sources were subject to price control according to the 1957 Law on Control of Goods and Services. Each of the three firms was in fact operating on the basis of government-induced allocation of market share. A firm that increased its market share had to compensate the others. The revenues of these firms were based on a cost-plus system.

In 1957, the Fuel Administration created a price equalization fund. The fund was used to cross-subsidize certain oil sources mainly through high prices on gasoline for private cars. The fund was managed off budget. The state controller questioned this practice and the fund was later shown in the government budget. It was changed to a department for the prices of fuel. The fund had also been used to subsidize the inputs of oil for electricity generation, to reduce the prices of natural gas and to fund oil explorations. It also financed the maintenance of emergency inventories.

As a result of these different arrangements, the government regulates each one of the stages of the oil supply: it decides on prices, it has the authority to fix the inventory levels, the sources of supply, the transportation means to Israel and within it, the refining plans and the prices of the various services. The government also made sure that no additional firm could enter the market in either oil or gas supply to the consumers. The government generally chose to levy high taxes on gasoline and cross-subsidize energy sources for electricity production, manufacturing and water supply.

On January 30, 1983, the energy and infrastructure minister appointed a committee of experts to examine the oil system in Israel. This committee recommended the liberalization of the system, allowing each oil firm and the refineries to import refined products. The oil firms felt the liberalization would strengthen the refineries. They fought against the changes. Only after a series of changes and compromises, was a partial liberalization introduced in 1988. The refineries were allowed to import oil, and a fourth energy firm received a license to sell oil, mainly wholesale. In August 1990, the court refused to recognize Paz as a 'protected tenant', thus allowing the first retail gas station to move to the fourth oil company as its supplier. Yet many believe a change in government means the reform will not continue.

Transportation and communications

Israel's geographic location has always made it an important link between different empires and between Asia and Africa. Until the end of the 19th century, the only transportation means were animals. In the 1890s, some roads allowing carriages to be driven were erected to allow transfer of pilgrims from Haifa to the holy places in the Galilee and from Jaffa to Jerusalem. Narrow-gauge railroads were erected from Jaffa to Jerusalem (1892) and from Haifa to Dar'a (1905).

The British Mandatory authorities gave priority for the development of infrastructure. It erected railroads at a standard gauge from Beirut to Kantara through Lod and Gaza. The railroad from Jaffa to Jerusalem was replaced to standard gauge. The British also constructed many highways. In 1948, the length of interurban roads was 1,622 km (of which 1,200 km were asphalt paved). By 1969, the length was 3,270 km. Since 1970, construction of roads has declined almost steadily. While in 1960 405 km of roads were constructed, and in 1965, 489 km, the length of roads constructed went down to totals such as 257.6 km in 1970, 207.9 km in 1974, 218.4 km in 1977, 312.8 km in 1980, but 141.1 in 1981, and 80.9 km in 1983.

Total non-urban road length was 3,239 km in 1970, 3,382 km in 1980, 3,910 km in 1985 and 3,995 km in 1988. At the same time the number of private cars zoomed from 23,980 on March 31, 1960, to 147,785 at the end of 1970, 409,510 at the end of 1980, and 735,450 by the end of 1988. Since 1975, the road areas have grown by 2.1 per cent per annum while the number of cards has grown at a rate of 6.3 per cent per annum, and the kilometers driven by 4.7 per cent per annum. Daily traffic volume swelled considerably, and the number of road accidents involving casualties increased from an average of 5,689 per annum in 1957-9 (320 per 100,000 population) to 10,577 in 1960-69, (422 per 100,000 population) 14,819 in 1970-79 (436 per 100,000 population). It declined somewhat to 13,111 in 1980-

231

84 (326 per 100,000 population) but rose to 14,955 in 1987 (342 per 100,000 population) and 15,497 in 1988.

About a fifth of the transportation, storage and communication branch output in Israel is in truck services, 19 per cent in buses and taxis, 3 per cent in railway services, 15 per cent in sea transport, 19 per cent in post services, 9 per cent air transport and airport services, and 14 per cent in communications. Except for trucks owned by private firms, all of these are either owned by the government (air transportation, ports) or regulated by it (truck services, taxis, buses). Bus transportation is supplied in the main by monopoly Histadrut-controlled cooperatives. Their rates, frequency of services and destinations are highly regulated. The gross tonnage of Israeli-owned ships increased drastically when the German reparations were used to acquire ships.

Telephones are a government monopoly, run since the mid-1980s as a state-owned enterprise, and woefully inadequate. The system is also based on queuing and priority to those deemed more important. Because of the inadequate telephone system, there is a priority list divided into seven groups for the installation of a phone. In the first priority group there are 13 categories, in the second 22, and so on. Thus, daily newspapers are no. 8 in the second priority. The first priority includes ministers, members of Knesset, Israel Defense forces, hospitals, fire brigades, etc. Foreign investors are number 11 in priority group D, much after bereaved parents (number 13 in priority B).

Banks

The first bank branch in Eretz Israel was opened in 1892 by Credit Lyonnais in Jaffa. Four years later, a German bank opened its branch in Jaffa. Anglo Palestine Bank (later Bank Leumi) was established in 1903 and for 18 years it was the only Jewish bank. In the 1920s, the banking system expanded considerably with the establishment of Bank Hapoalim (the workers' bank) in 1921, the central bank for cooperative institutions in 1922, Credit Bank and Bank Hamizrahi (owned by the Hamizrahi political party) in 1923. In addition, there were many credit cooperatives with 6,000 savings and loan associations.

Since the state was established, the banking system went through a continuous process of concentration and a sharp decrease in the number of banking institutions (Table 5.8). The credit cooperatives were the first to go and small banks disappeared or were acquired by the big three groups — Bank Leumi, Bank Hapoalim and the Discount Bank. Since the mid-1970s,

Table 5.8 Number of financial institutions, end of year

	1950	1954	1958	1961	1964	1968	1973	1974
Commercial banks	23	23	25	26	26	25	20	19
Credit corporations	85	95	52	27	23	26	13	11
Total	108	118	77	53	49	41	33	30

Source: Bank of Israel.
Note: By the end of 1989, the banking system comprised 30 ordinary banking corporations fully subject to the Bank of Israel's liquidity regulations, of which 2 were credit corporations and 19 were commercial banks, 2 were foreign banks, 2 investment banks and 5 specialized banks (e.g. for agriculture or construction). There were also 9 mortgage banks, 8 investment finance banks, 10 financial institutions, and 3 joint service companies (e.g. for automatic bank services). Of the 19 commercial banks, 4 belonged to the Bank Leumi group, 6 to the Bank Hapoalim group, 3 to the Discount Bank group, 2 to the United Mizrahi Bank group and 2 to the First International Bank group.

these three groups accounted for more than 90 per cent of all deposits or banking assets.

Until 1954, when the Bank of Israel was established, Bank Leumi served the nation by executing some of the duties of a central bank, including the issuance of currency. The Bank of Israel is now the Central Bank. It also controls the banks and its governor is also the economic advisor to the government. It generally has managed a very restrictive monetary policy aimed at reducing the demand for credit. Yet the large government deficit meant that the Bank of Israel was unable to neutralize fully the impact of the budget policy by its monetary policy restraints. The result was often extremely high real-interest rates, that reached an apex in mid-1985. The Bank of Israel also developed gradually a wide network of 'directed credit,' through which subsidized financing is granted for different purposes, the most important one being the financing of exports. The Bank of Israel is also responsible for foreign currency controls, a system that drastically limits the ability of an Israeli citizen to hold or trade with foreign currency. The bank also manages the foreign currency balances of Israel.

Israeli banks are extremely diversified, supplying a wide range of services in Israel and abroad. Most banks are both merchant banks and commercial banks. Banks work at both retail and wholesale levels. They also operate as brokers and dealers. Until 1956, the rate of growth of large, medium and small banks was about equal. Between 1956 and 1961, most of the credit cooperatives were merged into Bank Hapoalim. During the prosperity of the 1955-65 decade, many banks acquired insurance firms but also manufacturing and construction firms. By the same token, some large holding companies acquired a small bank. In the 1966 recession, several small banks got into trouble and were merged into larger and stronger banks. In 1971, Bank Leumi acquired control of the Union Bank and the Arab-Israel Bank. Barclays Bank International moved its branches to the management of the Discount Bank. In 1972 Bank Leumi acquired the troubled Bank Agudat Israel and in 1973 it bought Bank Kupt Am. Bank Hapoalim acquired Japhet Bank. By 1971, the market share of the three largest bank groups was 87 per cent and by the mid-1970s it reached 93 per cent. Informal pressures from the Bank of Israel have led since then to a much clearer demarcation between financial and other operations. The fastest growing of the three was Bank Hapoalim — partly because it managed the special funds granted to Hevrat Ovdim (see chapter 4), partly because of brilliant and aggressive management. Bank Leumi found itself unable to remain the leading bank and became second in rank in the 1980s. Discount Bank lost market share to the other two.

Faced with three large bank groups, the government decided to help in the creation of a fourth bank — the First International Bank — by merging two smaller banks. The profitability of an Israeli bank is very much a function of government's willingness to deposit government funds in it and to allow it to issue bonds. The new bank grew fast and acquired another small bank (Bank Poalei Aqudat Israel). It now also owns two mortgage banks and an investment finance bank.

The growing concentration of the banks came about because of the mergers of credit cooperatives into the banks, and the bankruptcy of several small banks during the recession, but also to a large extent because they issued bonds for the Ministry of Finance or through licenses granted by the ministry. The government severely limited banks' abilities to raise funds in the capital market and their discretion in the allocation of funds. The large banks were often preferred in getting more licenses to issue bonds. A license to operate a bank was not sufficient for smaller institutions without the authority — granted only by the finance ministry — to issue bonds. The criteria by which such authority was granted were never made public. In addition, the major buyers in that market — provident and pension funds — have always been highly regulated and had to invest only in 'recognized investments.' In addition, for many years the Othoman usury law limited the rate of interest a financial institution could charge. Most importantly, from 1962 financial institutions were able to grant non-linked loans and sell linked bonds to the public. This arrangement was possible because the government was willing to pay the linkage differential from its budget through a system known as 'linkage insurance' (see chapter 4). Such an insurance was available only if the financial institution was willing to comply with government's directives on the users of the credit. In other words, the government used the financial institutions as agents to grant loans for objectives it had defined, or to the collection of the loans. The government used the professional bureaucracy of the banks, paying them by the margin differences in interest rates. These financial institutions may have looked autonomous, but in fact they were totally dependent on the government's directives.

The State Controller took exception many times to the system in which the government used the banks and paid significant commissions for operations it could have done directly, saving a lot of money. At any rate, only a minimum amount of banks' funds were autonomously managed and allocated. Most of the banking operations consisted of managing government-directed funds.

The banks attempted to increase their equity. They felt it would be difficult to sell these shares in competition with government bonds that guaranteed a real rate of interest and indexation of both interest and principal. This was the beginning of the idea of regulating the shares that Bank Hapoalim started at the end of the 1960s and accelerated in the 1970s. Other banks also joined the regulation system: they used foreign subsidiaries to create artificial demand for their shares and made sure these shares would increase in market value daily. The only bank that consistently refused to regulate its shares was the First International Bank. Clearly, such a system could not operate for ever and the bubble burst in October 1983. The public, expecting devaluation, sold billions of shekels worth of bank shares and acquired foreign currency. The banks could not continue the 'regulation.' The stock exchange was closed and the government agreed to guarantee the bank shares at a cost to the taxpayer of more than $8 billion. For some time after this, the Bank of Israel attempted to ensure the banks higher profitability so that the public would be willing to continue holding the banks' shares. This was clearly found to be an impossible task. In 1988, most bank shares were redeemed. These shares held by the foreign subsidiaries of the banks caused a technical increase in Israel's foreign debt to the tune of $800 million. By 1989, the government had to decide how to sell off the shares it held and avoid becoming the owner of all Israeli Banks. The government attempted to negotiate an agreement with the major bank owners on equalization of the voting rights, to enhance the value of the shares held by the government. Partial agreements were finally reached and, in 1990, the government began an effort to sell these shares.

An inquiry commission, headed by Judge Beisky, found many illegal aspects in the behavior of the banks' managers. There were many vociferous demands to make sure the bankers would not only lose their jobs, as they did on the basis of the ruling of the Beisky commission, but also face trial. To these persons, this act was a test of basic norms such as personal responsibility and of one rule for the poor and the rich. The police, after their investigation, also recommended a criminal trial. In mid-November 1989, the Attorney General ruled there was no public interest in such a trial. He reasoned that the police investigation did not unearth any new evidence that was not before the Beisky commission, and that the bankers were already sanctioned by the commission (they were forced to leave the banking profession). He also ruled that the onus of a significant portion of the guilt was on the ministry of finance, the bank controller, the stock exchange and the securities and exchange commission, all of whom knew about the problem and did nothing to stop the 'regulation.' The proper norms, he said, were left in the books. Instead, different norms were used.

Since the new economic policy in 1985, the banking system has undergone major changes: an increase in the non-independence of banking operations, reaching an apex of 56 per cent of all profits, but going down to 49.8 per cent in 1989. There were also expanded activities in options, switch and futures and rising diversification of activities. Banks' profits were very low, partially because of increased bad debt reserves, partially because of reduced margins. Since 1985, the government and the Bank of Israel have also allowed the banks more discretion and have deregulated commissions. These policies should allow banks freer, rather than only institutional intermediary, operations.

Health

The national expenditures on health went up from 5.5 per cent of GNP in 1962-3 to 7.6 per cent in 1986-7. This is about the same level as in most developed countries, in which the level of salaries of the various medical professions is much higher than in Israel. In 1986-7, 53 per cent of these expenditures were financed by the government (52.2 per cent) and the local authorities (0.8 per cent). When all health expenditures are divided by operating sectors, sick funds account for 41.5 per cent; government, 21.9 per cent; local authorities, 0.9 per cent; other non-profit institutions 12.0 per cent; and others, 23.7 per cent. Ninety per cent of the population receives the health services from sick funds, and 80 per cent of those are members of the Histadrut sick fund that received 93 per cent of the government aid to all sick funds. In 1989, there was a major political strife on the allocation of these funds among the different entities. The Histadrut insisted on criteria that would take into account dispersal of the insured population. Other funds would have lost from such rules, and wanted a per capita allocation.

Israel has an extremely high ratio of medical doctors to population: one medical doctor per 340 persons in the population. Four medical schools produce additional doctors every year. In fact, the number of doctors increases by 6 per cent p.a. while the population increases at a third of that rate. Despite all that, many complain about loss of time in waiting in line and a large queue for less necessary operations. There is a severe scarcity of geriatric beds. For many years, there have been attempts to pass a National Health Insurance Law, but all these attempts failed. Most of the health services are still executed by the sick funds, the largest of which belongs to the Histadrut.

The Histadrut sick fund is very different from any other sick fund as well as from any other health insurance method in other countries. It is not only a middleman between medical service suppliers and those in need of such a service nor is it only a supplier. It believes in giving all the services — from the family doctor to the most expensive ones such as intensive care for heart patients — in its own institutions. These services are provided to both the insured persons and their families on the basis of payments in advance. Unlike the other sick funds in which the doctors see patients in their homes, the Histadrut built a large number of clinics and even its hospitalization services are also carried out partially in hospitals owned by it.

Since 1957, the Histadrut has collected from its members a uniform tax, part of which is used for the sick fund. In the 1960s, about 50 per cent of the uniform tax went to finance the sick fund. This proportion was increased as the government reduced its contribution. In 1975 the proportion was 55 per cent and in 1989, 71 per cent. One cannot be insured by the sick fund unless one is a Histadrut member. In addition, the National Insurance Institute collects the 'parallel tax' paid by employers for the sick fund. The cost of collection in the National

Insurance Institute is only a small fraction of that of the Histadrut's tax authority, but the latter is an important source of patronage for political reasons. In having the parallel tax, the Histadrut was able to initiate and implement a state enactment allowing an increased dependence on the Histadrut.

In 1948, about 35 per cent of the population was insured in the Histadrut's sick fund. By 1984, the percentage was 79, including 90 per cent of the new immigrants. The Histadrut owned 14.7 per cent of general hospital beds in 1948. In 1984 it owned 30 per cent. It employed 28,000 persons, of which 5,000 were medical doctors, 9,207 nurses and paramedics and 8,241 administrators. Part of the aid to the sick fund is in subsidizing the prices of beds in government hospitals. Arrangements regarding the use of such beds have been changing, and were always subject to negotiation.

Even when the Labor party was leading the government, the government accused the Histadrut sick funds of having an exaggerated construction inclination. Since 1949, different committees even inside Mapai have called for a national health system, and those political parties that did not have their own sick fund certainly pressured for the establishment of such a service. The Histadrut leaders vehemently and successfully opposed. The sick fund was considered a great magnet in convincing workers to join the Histadrut. By 1973, when the Histadrut already included 90 per cent of all workers, the government proposed a national health insurance to be executed through the sick funds. The General Zionist party proposed that a national sick fund should be established in addition to the existing one. Again, the Histadrut strongly opposed. Mapai also opposed a proposal that a person could continue to be a member of the Histadrut but choose another sick fund. The proposal never made it into a law. Another proposal was introduced by the Likud government in 1980 and never made it either.

The sick fund continues to be the major reason for persons to be members of the Histadrut and pay the uniform tax, which finances all the other Histadrut activities. A public commission chaired by a Supreme Court Judge recommended, in August 1990, an enactment of a national health act and a major reform in the health organization — including the separation of membership in sick funds from any criteria, including membership of the Histadrut. The Histadrut called this a destruction of health services. Thus, when a service was offered mainly by the Histadrut, the government could not find a way to offer it as a national service. Paradoxically, the right-wing opposition demanded to nationalize the health service, and Labor adamantly refused.

The capital market

The major instrument of government control in Israel is its absolute control of all sources of capital. All credit flows in the capital market are regulated by the government. The financial institutions are intermediaries between the savers, who supply the capital, and the government and business firms that need that capital. The capital suppliers save mainly through provident funds, life insurance firms, saving plans of the banks, funds for extension study, foreign currency deposits and direct acquisitions of securities by the public. All these are strictly controlled by the government. The government also controls most of the funds received from foreign sources. The government may also ban the use of any foreign credit (or make it more expensive by levying taxes). It affects the internal accumulation of funds in business firms by its impact on the profitability of the firms and the level of taxation. It can attract or deter foreign investors and it regulates the securities market. Most foreign currency arriving in Israel is channelled directly to the government. Through its almost absolute control of the capital market, the government is able to centrally control the economy.

In 1960, Patinkin concluded that 'the large degree to which government was responsible for the financing of the investment program was the inevitable consequence of the nature [that is, foreign sources] of funds that could be attained for this purpose.' He concluded that 'government's share of financing could have been drastically reduced only by a corresponding reduction of the investment program as a whole' (pp. 91-2). It can be argued that the premise and the conclusion were not the only possible ones even then. Since then, private savings have grown significantly, and government domination of the intermediation between private savers and investors has continued. This domination may have been a result of a deep-rooted mistrust of the market mechanism, or a thoroughly politicized society, dominated by a socialist party wishing to control all resource flow. The tight grip on domestic financial intermediation, the inefficiency of the capital market resulting from its political control, and the domination of foreign sources of funds by the government made allocation of investment resources less efficient and highly politicized.

The government's control of financial intermediaries has made it possible for the government to allocate investment funds.

As noted, the government subsidized investments in manufacturing, in agriculture and in hotel construction. The share of gross investments financed by public loans has been significant. In agriculture, it was between 75-93 per cent (and 130 per cent for 1979-82!). In manufacturing, it grew from 30-40 per cent in the 1950s and 1960s to 49 per cent in 1976-8 and to 71 per cent in 1979-82 (Mayshar, in Ben-Porath, 1986, p. 114). In the 1950s, these funds were allocated through the development budget. In the 1960s, the promotion of capital formation was achieved by directing subsidized loans to 'approved investments.' This new system enabled the government to avoid parliamentary appropriations approval. The privileges given to approved investments were ostensibly uniform. In reality, the civil service was left with considerable discretion. For example, some specific projects were granted conditions given in a development zone B, although the project was located in a non-development zone area (for example in Haifa Bay). Since 1985, there have been several attempts by the Bank of Israel to reduce government involvement in the capital market. Many plans were proposed but very few were actually implemented. The most important of these was a reduction of the need for institutions to deposit funds in the Ministry of Finance and the commercialization of the internal debt.

Some results

The detailed analysis of the different branches of the Israeli economy shows clearly the very high level of governmental intervention, achieved mainly through the absolute control of the capital market. This intervention is detailed to the standard of each plant, and causes a very high degree of dependency. The need to receive a license for almost any activity may have been a major curb, restraining private initiative and limiting responsibility. It may have also caused the recruitment of managers because they knew the ropes or because they were members of the party and could be relied on.

In a small economy like Israel's, the significant level of protection against imports allows the government a wide latitude in deciding who will become rich and who will remain poor. It can also manage the whole economy with very little regard to world prices.

Why is the government impact so large in Israel compared to other countries? One reason is the ideological heritage. Those who came to Eretz Israel at the turn of the century dreamt of building a just, equal, socialist society in the barren land to which they immigrated. With time, they mellowed. They were also forced to agree to many compromises to achieve a wider consensus. As a result, their leaders gave up the idea that Israel should be built only by public funds. Yet ideology has been very important, in particular as far as the treatment of services is considered.

In many cases, ideology was used as an excuse. The real reason for the intervention might have been the quest for power and the realization that political and economic power are very much interrelated. The pioneers of the third Aliyah were strongly influenced by the experience of the Bolshevik revolution. They learned the importance of using political power to achieve economic dominance, and the use of economic control of the means of production to achieve dependence and therefore control — leading to more political power.

In most periods, there was also a genuine need to develop the infrastructure and to subsidize immigration as well as defense. Both were seen as public goods, and their importance meant a very large role for government.

Further, the political system of Israel never allowed one political party to enjoy absolute majority. The proportional representative system encouraged splintering the political parties and the lists of candidates running for election. Israel has always been governed by coalitions, based on compromises. These compromises often meant that each member of the coalition demanded and received side-payments that increased both the budget and other methods of government's largesse.

The Israeli government is not a uniform body; it is composed of largely independent ministers, each representing certain strong interests. Despite its large influence and the availability of leverage points, the government is unable to agree on priorities. It suffers from a built-in structure that leads to budget deficits and bloated government debt (both foreign and domestic). Ministers can decide collectively to spend more than they 'earn' by collecting taxes or even borrowing. Every minister has an incentive to increase his own budget; and his responsibility for the negative effects of a larger budget, such as increased inflation, is very limited (inflation being perceived as the problem of the Ministry of Finance). As a result, there is a built-in bias in favor of overspending. Individual ministers fail to recognize the effect of their policies on furthering inflation and the serious balance-of-payments deficit. Although all agree on the wisdom of limiting the total government budget, there is no incentive to agree to a reduction of one's own departmental budget. Moreover, given the large influx of foreign capital,

Table 5.9 Total capital stock

	Gross capital stock (beginning of 1990) in NIS millions	Gross capital stock (beginning of 1990) (%)	Average rate of change (%) 1960-76	1976-80	1980-9	1988	1989	1990
1 Agriculture	14,222	4.76	4.5	4.5	1.5	0.3	0.1	-1.0
2 Water	6,076	2.03	4.9	2.6	1.9	0.7	-0.3	-0.1
3 Manufacturing	36,711	12.30	7.1	6.6	4.0	3.5	1.7	1.3
4 Construction equipment	1,656	0.55	7.3	3.4	-2.2	0.0	0.5	-1.7
5 Electricity	11,034	3.70	7.1	9.1	5.6	4.0	5.8	5.2
6 Transportation and telecommunications	43,046	14.42	12.0	3.0	2.3	3.5	3.3	1.0
of which:								
(a) transportation vehicles	18,927	6.34	-	-	-	-	-	-
(b) roads	11,631	3.90	-	-	-	-	-	-
(c) except transportation vehicles	24,119	8.08	10.5	4.2	3.1	4.4	4.4	4.4
7 Private services	13,938	4.67	11.9	5.7	5.0	3.7	3.3	2.4
8 Total business sectors (1-7)	126,684	42.44	8.3	4.8	3.1	3.0	2.4	1.3
9 Public services	41,547	13.92	13.1	6.4	3.5	4.0	4.0	3.8
10 Total economic branches (8+9)	168,231	56.36	9.1	5.1	3.2	3.2	2.8	1.8
(a) except transportation vehicles	149,304	50.02	8.4	5.7	3.5	3.3	2.9	2.5
11 Residential construction	130,235	43.63	8.9	5.8	4.2	3.1	2.9	3.0
12 Total	298,466	100.00	9.0	5.4	3.6	3.2	2.8	2.3

Source: Bank of Israel, *Annual Report*, 1988, pp. 151-2; 1989, pp. 89-90.

Israeli leaders did not feel they had to decide on priorities. Instead the various governments searched for additional sources of capital. They increased taxes but mainly took more loans or received additional grants.

Two additional major consequences of the intervention should be noted. First, most gross capital stock is invested in residential flats, much more than in other countries. Capital invested in residential construction was almost 43 per cent of total capital stock, up from 39 per cent as of January 1, 1981 (see Table 5.9 for details).

Second, Israel is a dual economy in at least three senses: first, as in all other dual economies, there is a modern economy with a high value added per employee and high wages simultaneously with a traditional sector, competing on the basis of low wages. Second, some firms think only domestically while others think in terms of the world market. Third, some firms are more politically motivated while others see profits as an overwhelming criterion for their operations.

Another duality is between the large exporters that look at the world as their market place, and the many firms that do not have an international outlook. Most Israeli firms are inner-directed, restricting their activities mainly to the domestic market, in which they are often protected. Only a few firms are truly international in their outlook, exporting a significant per cent of their output. For such firms, existing patterns of government assistance are irrelevant, because the time horizon is inconsistent with the required time horizon for effective business strategies, and bureaucratic costs are high. Government aid is also irrelevant to the hundreds of small firms motivated solely by profit considerations. This aid is crucial to firms mainly in the public and Histadrut sectors, driven more by the desire to create and maintain employment.

Conclusions

The Israeli political economy is patterned the same way in each and every economic branch: resource allocation to individuals by the government is made essential to be successful. Moreover, those who do not get concessions and exemptions, not mentioning licenses, cannot enter the market. In such a system, economic considerations of efficiency or optimal resource allocation has little significance (and a minimum meaning). To be successful in such a system, one has to be 'one of us' and able to put pressure on the government. Those firms (and economic sectors) with strong political backing would be able to be more successful. In this system, there has also been, at least until 1980, a clear priority granted to the labor economy, allowing it more funds and more monopolies. At the same time, those willing to help in achieving national aims were also heavily aided. In the beginning, this aid was just paying for services made for the defense of the state. Later, it also helped those willing to build manufacturing plants in development regions, or to export much of their production.

Ironically, those branches in which a high level of government intervention could easily be justified by market-failure arguments were not necessarily those to which funds were allocated. The level of investment in highways was so low as to enable Israel to achieve a world record in road accidents; moreover the telephone service is extremely backward.

The belief system of the bureaucracy is that they are omnipotent, and know best what is good for the citizen. The system is also based on a very large number of mutually agreed upon myths. Thus, as discussed in chapter 3, egalitarian ideology led to giving income in kind — through allowances or free telephone services (received also by the widows of chief justices!).

The expansion of the governmental activities was not based on a direct payment of citizens for the services. As a result, it entailed a very low political price and extremely high benefit. It also resulted in more dependence of citizens on their government and in a lack of connections between authority and responsibility, or between reward and punishment. There has also been a growing level of expectations of the citizens for expanded social services, higher level of economic growth, industrialization of development regions, more security and higher standard of living.

The institutional arrangements described above stemmed from the 1920s. One may or may not agree that these arrangements were necessary at the time. One may even speculate as to what would have been the fate of Israel today (or whether or not it had been established) if Brandeis had won in the debate with Weizmann. Many plausible economic reasons can be put forward for a high level of government intervention in order to absorb many immigrants in an extremely short period of time. It has become increasingly difficult to justify many of the institutions of the political economy when the collective ideology is less appealing to a majority of the population. Time and again, changes were promised or even announced, but very few were actually implemented. At least in some fields, defense considerations necessitated an extremely high level of government intervention.

6 The defense sector and the impact of security

Introduction

The relatively large share of GNP devoted to defense expenditure and the significant per cent of total industry represented by defense-related production and exports render the defense sector a crucial focal point for any analysis of Israel. Being limited by confidentiality restrictions, detailed analysis of this subject is not easy. Most figures related to the army are confidential, and accepted as such. By the nature of defense considerations, most strategic decisions in this area, including those on industrial structure, are made by very few persons. Those not belonging to the military elite cannot influence these decisions, and often do not know what these decisions were.

Yet it is extremely difficult to understand the Israeli economy or the society if one does not take into account the political environment in which Israel is embedded and in particular its perceptions about the need for defense. This chapter deals with the major impact of security and the problem of the defense burden. Then we discuss the role of the military-industrial complex. Third it surveys the civilian-military relations and the ways Israelis used to cope with their difficult situation.

Defense has been the most immediate issue since the beginning of the revival of Jewish settlement in Israel. The physical survival of its people has been the central concern of Israel since its inception. Israel has found itself surrounded by hostile neighbors who begrudge its very existence. Immediately after the United Nations decision on the creation of a Jewish state, the Arabs began fighting against the Jewish population. Once the fledgling state was proclaimed, several armies of all of its neighboring Arab countries invaded it and almost abolished it. Israelis have fought at least five wars since independence and have suffered in between wars from terrorist infiltration and border raids. Large-scale conflicts between Israel and Arab states occurred in 1948-9, 1956, 1967, 1973 and 1982. Some would also add the War of Attrition in 1970 and the Litani Operation. Even if these are not counted, Israel has not experienced a single decade without a war. In between these wars, Israel has been constantly barraged by numerous terrorist attacks of *fedayeen* (martyrs), attacks on its consulates, airline, sportspersons in the Olympic games, and a host of unceasing acts of aggression. Israel is one of the few states in the world in which the very legitimation of the state to exist is not automatically acceptable by everyone. It is also a country facing a permanent and declared threat of physical destruction. Each and every Israeli believes he or she faces a danger of being killed, not only in Israel, but in all countries; not only in a war but also because of a bomb, a terrorist attack or highjacking of an airplane.

Since the Jews returned to the land of their forefathers, they have learned the country was not empty as they thought. The conflict between Arabs and Jews caused a series of riots, in which both Jews and Arabs were killed. Some Jews believed the indigenous population was not a separate nation. Indeed, when the Jewish settlement in Eretz Israel started, very few were sedentary — most were nomads, moving through different parts of the Middle East. Many still believe there is no separate Palestinian nation. Other Jews were hoping that the fact that Jews brought prosperity to the area would force Arabs to agree to increased Jewish immigration. Ben Gurion discusses a meeting he had with Mussa Alami, in which, in response to arguments about the progress the Jews brought, Mr Alami responded: 'I would rather see the country poor and deserted for another hundred years until we Arabs would be able to build it on our own' (Ben Gurion, 1967, pp. 19-20). The conflict between the two nationalistic movements turned into a state of war between Israel and the Arab nations. Israelis perceive themselves as having to fight all the time, although in point of fact the number of days in which everyone was mobilized to war has not been very high. Still, for many, in particular the youth who are repeatedly called for reserve duty interrupting their normal life and civilian career, the price of belonging to Israeli society is not very low. This price is being paid not only (or even mainly) during the relatively short periods of active combat or even active reserve duty. It is paid by a constant state of readiness, anticipation of danger, exposure to artillery shelling or suicidal terrorist attacks, and by constant stress.

Since the country is very small, nearly everyone in the country knows someone who has lost a son in active duty. Practially every Israeli Jew — male and female — serves in the military: three years for males, two years for females. Israelis then serve in active reserve duty until the age of 54 for up to 40 days every year; but this number of days is habitually extended in the all-too-frequent emergencies. The Minister of Defense can lengthen it to whatever duration is needed for the security of the state. Females serve in reserve duty until they bear their first child. As a rule, Israelis start their careers later than their counterparts in other countries. Yet each accepts military conscription as a rite of passage for acceptance into society.

For the first time in the 1973 war and even more so in 1982, the majority of the generation that fought the Independence War, the 1956 Sinai campaign and the 1967 Six Days War was the generation of parents of soldiers in active duty. They realized that to be at war meant to raise children to become cannon fodder. They now have agonized through many sleepless nights, full of tension caused by a helpless waiting for news from their children. People have been on the knife's edge of their nerves. The ubiquitous tension and the seemingly unending atrocities make life in Israel extremely difficult.

Israel is also a country where listening to the news is a sacred ritual and a national obsession. The Israeli radio broadcasts news every hour, and the whole country stops to listen. This is just one manifestation of the strains and stress of a nation who feel, in the words of Moshe Dayan, that 'the only choice we have is to be armed, strong and resolute, else the sword will fall from our hands and the thread of our lives will be severed' (quoted in Teveth, 1972, p. 240).

History of the defense institutions

As in any other major part of Israel, it is difficult to understand the defense institutions without at least a short discourse on the Yishuv period.

The first body of self-defense in Israel was the clandestine and elitist *Hashomer* ('the guardian'). Its members believed themselves to be the early bud of renaissance of the new strong Hebrew man. Its members also believed in professional autonomy. The political leaders placed party loyalists in *Hashomer* to ensure its loyalty, and finally its dissolution.

The major military arm of the Yishuv became the *Haganah* ('Defense'). This was a militia force, formally under party authority, subordinated to a civilian decision-making process and clearly subject to a political decision-making process. Later, the authority over the Haganah was transferred to the Histadrut. To widen its legitimacy, the authority was further transferred to the national institutions, but only after Mapai achieved a leading and controlling position in these institutions. To the political leaders in the Yishuv period, the military appeared as a potential challenge. It therefore had to be controlled and constrained so that the party monopoly of power would be maintained. Political considerations were of utmost importance in appointments in the Haganah. Haganah commanders had to be loyal party members.

The same was true for the other militia organizations. The *Irgun Zvai Leumi* (Ezel) was distinctly revisionist. *Lohamei Herut Yisrael* (Lehi, the fighters for the freedom of Israel), whose leader Yair Stern left the *Irgun*, had strong polarized political influences of both right and left. Stern created his separate militia because Ezel decided to stop the struggle against the British during World War II. Stern opposed this decision, believing the fight should go on. The professional cadres of militia leaders in these organizations had strong ties with political leaders.

During World War II, *Palmach* (commando units) was created. These units were stationed in kibbutzim, working part-time to cover their maintenance costs. Many of the Palmach's commanders were left wing, later affiliated to the Mapam party. Mapam was a Marxist party, formed by a secession of a faction from within Mapai in 1944.

The burden of fighting against the Arabs in the period between the UN partition resolution in November 1947 and the proclamation of the State of Israel fell on the previously underground units of various military organizations. Haganah, Palmach, Ezel and Lehi were forged into the new army, termed Israel Defense Forces (IDF). Both Ezel and Lehi agreed on self-disbandment of their military units. Both transferred into political parties.

Perhaps the most enduring legacy of the invasion of the armies of the Arab League, the Jordanian Arab Legion and the Guerrilla Arab Liberation Army in 1948, was the refusal to create a Palestinian state, as the United Nations partition decision called for. King Abdulla of Transjordan flagrantly disregarded this resolution and annexed to his kingdom the territory his army had conquered during the war. The protracted and unresolved 'Palestine question' was not seen by members of the Arab League as one of the creation of another state between the Mediterranean and the River Jordan. Instead, it was perceived as a general pan-Arab problem. The Arab League was encouraged by the British and sponsored by Egypt and Iraq. It is composed today of twenty-one Arab states, as well as the Palestine

Liberation Organization. With the exception of Somalia, they all use Arabic as their official national language. In all except Lebanon, Islam is the official national religion. All except Egypt are officially at war with Israel (and all ceased diplomatic relations with Egypt, suspending its membership in the league in retaliation for signing the peace treaty with Israel). These nations could have solved the refugee problem a long time ago. The refugees, however, were cynically exploited for political gains by nations whose avowed goal has been the destruction of Israel.

There are several bones of contention between Israelis and Arabs. The most important, of course, is the right of Israel to exist. To those who may agree to give up the state of war and stop the bellicosity, there is still the question of the borders. The territorial depredations are on many fronts, the thorniest of which is that of Jerusalem — simply because Israelis refuse to see the city divided again, and Arabs declare their allegiance to the city. The Palestinian national covenant declared Palestine to be the homeland of the Arab Palestinian people and an indivisible part of the Arab homeland. It also declares the Palestinian people are an integral part of the Arab nation. The covenant declares the establishment of the State of Israel 'entirely illegal' and regards Zionism as an 'illegitimate movement,' 'organically associated with international imperialism and antagonistic to all action for liberation . . . racist and fanatic in its nature, aggressive, expansionist and colonial in its aims, and fascist in its methods.' It claims 'Israel is . . . placed strategically in the midst of the Arab homeland to combat the hopes of the Arab nation for liberation, unity and progress.' These brazen declarations and the many acts designed to eradicate Israel from the Middle East instill in Israel a sense of necessity of becoming strong and self-sufficient in weapons development. Many Israelis, despite their yearning for peace, find it hard to believe what they see as equivocated declarations from the Arab side, and are constantly concerned lest their security arrangement may be inept or ineffectual. They are concerned that even the truncated area of the original Palestine they now possess will be lost unless they protect it, afraid to rely on any piece of paper from which an adversary may disengage at the first opportune moment, and see no choice but to be armed and strong, irrespective of costs.

The ubiquity of defense

The continuous state of hostility affected all aspects of life in Israel, often in unquantifiable ways. The easiest to quantify is the very heavy burden of defense costs on the budget. The effects of defense are also indirect: billions of dollars have been spent on an activity which is essential but yields no economic return. Loans are taken but cannot be invested in something which will help to cover the cost of repayment. More difficult to put an exact figure on is the total costs of universal conscription, reserve duty, or the economic costs of losing at least three years of productive life, the impact on productivity of living in a continuous stage of siege, the effect on reduced economic growth of the large magnitude of investments of both physical and human capital on wars and military equipment and the impact of the Arab economic blockade against Israel.

There are also the positive externalities of defense: one is the use of female soldiers as teachers in development regions, another is the many who learned their skills during army service. A third is the range of military and semi-military industries set up which export high technology products as a result of military requirements.

In addition, the importance of defense has made the security establishment and the military industrial complex very influential. High-ranking army officers carry with them very high prestige. In fact, since they retire at a relatively early age (forty), the second career of these persons is of interest. Many of them have 'parachuted' to influential political positions. Five of the chiefs of staff (Moshe Dayan, Chaim Barlev, Raphael Eitan, Yitzhak Rabin and Yigael Yadin) and several Brigadier Generals (Aharon Yariv, Ariel Sharon, Meir Amit, Yuval Ne'eman and Ezer Weizmann) were ministers of government. Yigael Yadin, who was the Chief of Staff during the War of Independence, was offered a ministerial position by Ben Gurion and refused. He was considered a great asset when recruited by the newly created Democratic Movement to Change (DASH). Many more became managers of business firms. In fact, one externality of the defense burden has been the training of army officers who moved to a second career in the civilian sector. Unfortunately, army training does not always prepare a person for a business management job. Ex-army generals were not always very good in maintaining labor relations, or in looking for profitable ventures rather than grandiose projects. As a result of the trauma of the Yom Kippur War, army generals lost some of their prestige. In the 1980s, scores of ex-generals even attempted to find jobs as security experts in other countries.

Israelis are obsessed with security issues: these issues are of paramount concern, and very little debate exists on them. Rather, security considerations receive an overriding priority. A country that does not have money to build more highway intersections to reduce the very high incidence of life lost in road accidents may spend millions of dollars in getting one stranded soldier back to base. The unquestioned commitment to defense, the willingness to serve on reserve duty and be on call may be the one strand of ideology that has remained intact since the Yishuv period. It is also simply a part of life in Israel. The general consensus has always been that defense considerations are of supreme importance and that no funds should be spared if they can save a soldier's life. The army was thus able to get a lion's share of the country's resources, and that share has increased after each of the wars. Israel's prime ministers were primarily preoccupied with problems of security and of external relations. The predominance of security considerations has been evident in decisions taken on diverse matters — from location of highways to the emergency stock levels. Those privy to secret security matters have a greater ability to understand not only defense issues but also economic and political matters.

Israel does not have any strategic depth and is haunted even by the remote possibility of defeat in battle by the memory of the Holocaust. 'The Israelis' search for security is an obsession, a quest for an almost metaphysical security' (Perlmutter, 1989, p. 120). As a result, defense requisitions are hardly questioned. The Israeli army inherited the accumulated knowledge of the small underground units and also benefitted from the experience of many who served in the British army. During the War of Independence, the Arabs had a much superior firepower, and that fact cost the Israelis many lives. Since then, billions of dollars have been spent to equip the army with the most sophisticated weapons and other equipment, and to build Israel's own military R&D and production. As shown later in this chapter, the army also gave a big push to industrial development.

The leaders of the nation found themselves involved most of the time in urgent problems of foreign and security policies. Since the state was established, these have been major problems, and almost every month there has been a major foreign policy issue to be dealt with or an urgent security-related problem that has taken most of the time of the country leaders. Yitzhak Rabin, ex-prime minister, states in his memoirs that 'because of the critical survival nature of the security and foreign policy issues, the Prime Minister must put these problems in the apex of his priorities' (1979, vol. 2, p. 545, Hebrew). Questions of defense and security have always caused much effort and stress, leaving them little and in many cases no time to pay any attention to economic problems or economic considerations. Indeed, until mid-1985, Israeli prime ministers devoted almost all their time to problems of foreign and defense policies and were not interested at all in the economic policies issues. These were the exclusive domain of the finance ministers.

Sociologists in Israel agree that the conflict resulted in a perception of cooperation as necessary for survival, but also that it has become an outlet for aggression (see Peres, 1971, p. 1027). Moreover, some even argue that retaliatory actions against Arab states were taken to answer internal needs of population morale and to assure the population that attacks on Israel would not be tolerated with impunity (Aronson and Horowitz, 1971).

Defense has made significant demands not only on available financial resources, but also on human resources. First, as already mentioned, every Israeli serves in reserve duty. The opportunity cost of loss of civil production is not recorded. Second, a majority of Israeli scientific and engineering abilities have been directed toward the creation of a relatively large military-industrial complex. Third, the army in Israel is not a distant entity. It is composed of everyone and is therefore omnipresent. Danger is a way of life: every package received in the mail might be booby-trapped, every garbage can in any street corner might contain a bomb and any bus trip could unleash a disaster.

Indeed, because of the constant threat of war and the vulnerability of Israel's citizens and infrastructure to attacks by infiltrators, the influence of the military establishment is felt in all walks of life: from reserve duty to the layout of agricultural settlements and the location of roads or the construction costs. The Israeli Defense Forces (IDF) consist of a small nucleus of regular army, conscripts serving their three years (for female, two years) of national service, and a large reserve army. These reserves can be mobilized within 72 hours.

Defense considerations have also been entwined with those of egalitarian beliefs and social norms. A very important issue in Israel is the degree of equality in sharing the burden of defense. Time and again, the degree to which some serve more on reserve duty while others may not be called is raised. The only exemption from military service was granted to a few hundred students of Religious Studies (Yeshivot, a place of higher learning for Jewish religious studies). Several outstanding Rabbis convinced Ben Gurion of the importance of carrying out these studies in Yeshivot in light of the destruction of European Yeshivot in the Holocaust. Since then, the problem of this exemption is raised again and again. The number of exempt Yeshivot students has been rising from a few hundred to around

Table 6.1 The share of defense expenditure in the Israeli GNP, a multi-year average

	% of defense expenditure in the GNP	Direct defense imports	Indirect defense imports	Local defense expenditure
1950-55	7.1			
1956	13.4			
1955-61[a]	8.3	N/A	N/A	N/A
1962-6	10.1	3.9	1.2	6.2
1967	15.6			
1968-72	21.7	8.6	3.0	13.1
1973	32.7			
1973-5	32.8	16.0		16.8
1976-9	26.6	11.4		15.2
1974-80	27.8	12.4	4.2	
1981-5	23.2	8.1		14.3
1985-8	18.8	7.3		11.5
1989	14.0	2.9		10.5

Sources: 1955-84, Ariel Halperin, 1986, p. 27. 1973-9, Bank of Israel, *Annual Report*, 1979, p. 34. 1985, CBS Monthly Bulletin of Standards, May 1986. 1985-8 Calculated from Bank of Israel, *Annual Report*, 1988, p. 116; 1989, p. 173. See also Kochav, David and Yaakov Lifschitz, 1973.

Note: [a]Not including the 1956 Sinai Campaign.

16,000; and the general discontent with this exception has been growing. There is also an occasional grumbling about the length and the inequalities of reserve duties, mingled with a feeling of pride in being one who serves the country more! The exemption of females declaring religious reasons for not serving has not ever become a really inflammatory issue.

The defense burden

The constant threat of war with the Arabs forced Israel to spend a very large (and a growing) per cent of its resources to ensure its defense. A major characteristic of resource use in Israel is the very high and rapidly growing share of defense expenditures.

Apart from the war year of 1956, defense spending (as registered in the budget) took 8.3 per cent of GNP between 1955 and 1961. From 1962 to 1972, it took 16 per cent and between

1974 and 1980, 27.8 per cent. In 1981–5 there was a reduction to about 23.2 per cent, in 1985–8 to 18.8 per cent and to 14 per cent in 1989 (Table 6.1).

The economic defense burden as a per cent of GNP has been much higher than in other countries, as Table 6.2 demonstrates. Barkai (1981) shows that in 1976–7, Israel's absolute defense expenditures were higher than those of Sweden. As a share of GNP, Sweden spent 3.3 per cent, and Israel, more than 30 per cent (Table 6.2). Certainly, Israel stands at the top of the list of all developed countries when the economic capacity devoted to defense is measured by defense expenditures as a per cent of GNP, or per capita or by the number of individuals employed in national defense jobs. At the same time, the threat to Israel stems from its neighboring countries who have spent much more than Israel. In 1973, Iraq alone spent 66 per cent of the Israeli amount; Egypt, Syria and Jordan spent 25 per cent more than Israel. Since Israel may encounter more than one confronting state, she has to be able to fight on more than one front. In this sense, the ratio of defense expenditures to GNP in the confrontation states is of interest (Tables 6.2 and 6.3).

Certainly the defense burden is staggering. Yet, part of these costs have been covered by outside sources. Thus, since the mid-1970s US aid has covered a considerable share of the total defense budget (to a large extent imports of US equipment). A more accurate measure of the defense burden is therefore said to be the ratio of local defense expenditure to GNP. The earliest data available is for 1958 when it came to 6 per cent; in 1972 it came to 12.4 per cent; in 1979 14.5 per cent; and in 1984 14.3 per cent. In 1988, this ratio was 11 per cent and in 1989 10.5 per cent. As we shall see, however, there are many extra budgetary defense expenditures. In addition, these figures exclude military debt payments which have also increased substantially until the second half of the 1980s.

The defense burden is not a one-dimensional concept. Theoretically, it may be defined as the total resources precluded from other uses because they were diverted to defense. The total of these figures is shrouded in secrecy. Many items related to security are, understandably perhaps, among the most cherished secrets of the state. It is unclear, for example, where the budget of the internal security branch is included. In the British tradition of MI5, the existence of this branch was not officially acknowledged for quite some time and the name of its chief is not divulged even today. Moreover, different aspects of the defense burden are better measured by different criteria.

Table 6.2 Military expenditure of selected countries by manpower and financial resources, 1976-7[a]

Country	Manpower in the military (for each 1,000 inhabitants)	Military expenditure per capita (in 1976 $)	Military expenditure as % of the GNP
United Kingdom	5.91	195	4.90
USA	9.49	432	5.40
West Germany	8.00	251	3.45
Netherlands	8.00	224	3.45
Norway	9.67	230.50	3.15
France	10.26	258	3.85
Sweden	8.16	289	3.30
Israel	49.76	831	30.70

Source: Barkai, 1981.
Note: [a]Annual average.

Table 6.3 Defense expenditures as % of GNP in Israel and its neighboring countries, 1954-83

Country	1954	1963	1972	1979	1980	1982	1983
Egypt	6.1	10.0	18.1	11.5	7.4	7.2	7.4
Syria	4.2	9.6	15.8	24.7	17.3	13.7	14.9
Jordan	20.0	15.8	16.4	14.8	12.5	11.3	11.4
Average, three nations	6.4	10.3	17.4	15.7	–	–	–
Israel	6.3	10.8	20.8	21.0	24.0	23.0	17.3
Iraq	5.7	10.0	12.3	9.0	7.4	29.7	38.5

Sources: Israel: Bank of Israel. Other states: 1954-79, Eliezer Shefer, 'Israel's Defense Race', *Studies in Economics*, (*Iyunim Be'Kalkala*), 1981 (Hebrew). 1980-83, Ruth Leger Sivard, World Military and Social Expenditure.

Two long-term series of defense expenditures have been published. The Central Bureau of Statistics shows the non-civilian components of public consumption as defined in the national accounts and the Ministry of Finance publishes defense costs as defined in its budget series. The differences between the two have become smaller with time. The Bank of Israel shows the net defense burden, first by showing defense consumption as a percent of GNP plus unilateral transfers at an effective rate of exchange, then by deducting defense grants. It also shows domestic defense consumption and the weight of local consumption plus servicing of defense-related loans and defense imports paid for outside the US grants ('free currency'). Finally, the Bank of Israel measures the weight of wages in the defense sector out of total wages. These figures are available only for the recent years (Table 6.4).

Defense imports are subject to sharp swings, and have a strong impact on the balance of payments. Different indicators could give different feelings on the problem of the defense burden. All of the indicators, however, show the burden to be high, growing after each war and decreasing in the second half of the 1980s.

Since 1967, there has been an enormous change in the size of the army and of defense cost: from 1966 to 1978, the domestic defense expenditures grew five fold. Between 1978 and 1985 total defense spending in real terms rose by 19.8 per cent; local spending increased by 7 per cent. During this period the Lebanon war consumed considerable resources, and expenditure on local defense procurement fell sharply after 1983; the 1987 expenditures again increased by 5 per cent. The cut-back in local defense purchases contributed to recessions in 1988, particularly in the metal products and electronic industries.

The official figures on defense burden do not take into account many costs — some of which were already mentioned. Among the possibly quantifiable costs are the income forgone by conscripts during their years of service (official statistics include only the meager nominal pay received by conscripts and the cost of their maintenance). Berglas (1983) estimates these costs alone to be as high as 5 per cent of GNP.

Reserve duty unrecorded costs include the effect on productivity. Pension costs to former employees of the defense establishment are also excluded. These two were estimated by Berglas to be 1 to 2 per cent of GNP. To that he added 1 per cent of GNP as the indirect cost of loss of life and earning capacity and the cost of stock-piling of fuel and essential food. Other unrecorded costs include the requirement that every residential building must contain a shelter built to army specifications (and paid for by the buyer of the house). The army also holds sizeable tracts of very expensive land. Adding all these costs, Berglas came to more than additional 50 per cent to the reported local currency expenditures. He notes (p. 181):

Table 6.4 Indicators for Israel's defense expenditures, 1980-9, (% at current prices)

Year	Defense consumption[a] as a % of gross income from all sources[b]	Net total defense consumption[a] less defense grants	Domestic defense consumption[a,c]	Domestic defense expenditures; free currency and debt servicing[d]	Wages in defense sector as a % of total wages outlay
1980-84	19.9	19.2	14.3	18.2	10.4
1984	20.0	17.6	14.3	19.0	10.4
1985-8	16.4	12.6	11.5	15.4	9.4
1985	18.4	13.4	12.8	17.6	9.7
1986	13.9	9.7	11.1	15.3	9.2
1987	17.5	14.4	11.0	14.6	9.0
1988	15.6	12.9	11.0	14.0	9.6
1989	12.7	12.9	10.5	13.3	9.6

Source: Bank of Israel, *Annual Report*, 1988, p. 122; 1989, p. 173.
Notes: [a]Excluding soldiers in conscription service. [b] GNP + unilateral transfers by effective rate of exchange. [c]Gross domestic consumption less domestic sales. [d]Debt servicing includes both interest and principal paid for military loans of the US government.

These unreported elements have increased continuously. The period of conscription has been lengthened, as has the annual spell in the reserves, and the regular army has been enlarged. The increase in terrorist activity has promoted increased expenditures on counter-measures. Thus the major increase in local defense expenditures that followed the 1967 and 1973 wars certainly understates the actual increase.

Thus, the extremely high costs of defense in Israel are reflected not only in the official figures on defense consumption but also in the high and never measured alternative costs of the years spent by each young person in the army and the alternative costs of devoting such a large share of Israel's talents to the military needs. Moreover, direct defense imports are translated in terms of the undervalued official rate of exchange and until the late 1960s were exempt from import taxes. All the above does not count for the grief, the stress, or even the time taken by defense considerations. Despite the high level of all these costs, there has been very little public debate about them, or about the priority they represent. Moreover, it was generally accepted that Israel's defense needs are dictated by the size of military manpower and equipment in the Arab countries. The idea that an increased Israeli army may lead to increased Arab spending on defense was not ever publicly discussed as a real possibility.

Since 1973, there has been another significant increase in the size of the IDF, coupled with a fast transition to new-generation, more modern, sophisticated equipment. The equipment component in the military capital stock is estimated by Halperin (1986) to have grown by a real average rate of 8.5 per cent per annum, while in the same period, the real level of the defense budget did not change. This means an increase in the maintenance of equipment component — and presumably an increase in the need for military technicians and engineers.

Market prices of military equipment have been growing by leaps and bounds (Gansler, 1983). This process generates an increase in the R&D component, but at the same time reduces the ability to provide enough equipment, so that the ratio of R&D to unit price is rising.

While defense has been a burden, the disproportionately large defense sector is also a considerable source of domestic demand. Local defense purchases introduced stringent demands for quality, delivery, reliability, as well as large orders, cheap credit and know-how. One result has been the creation of a strong, well-managed and efficient military-industrial sector, which is the most modern sector of Israel's manufacturing industry. It also exports a growing per cent of its output, achieving economies of scale and having a good reputation. However, this type of export is political in nature and therefore suffers large swings. To many, arms sales are also immoral.

Further, a significant per cent of Israel's engineering talents (and knowledge-based commercial successes) is concentrated in large, defense-oriented firms, producing sophisticated defense-related equipment. In fact, the Authority For Development of Combat Means developed the first Israeli computer as well as solid fuel and rocket fuel as early as 1956.

In addition, the armed forces and the Ministry of Defense undertook activities beyond their direct military responsibilities, such as education, absorption of immigrants, and agricultural settlements. Moreover, the Israeli Army trained virtually all the computer programmers in the country, and many of the machinists, drivers and mechanics. The army, by training young people for all sorts of occupations, has been providing skills which are useful in civilian life. Because of the relatively large scale of the army, these training programs are an important source of certain skilled human capital.

The per cent of Israel's resources devoted to defense has been seen as a result of 'no choice'. The enormous burden of defense was noted and lamented, but rarely questioned, even after the peace treaty with Egypt in 1979. Note that a reduction of this burden to the proportion of the US defense expenditures during the Vietnam War — 8 or 9 per cent of GNP 'would have made it possible for Israel to free approximately $3.5 billion a year for productive purposes' (Sanbar, 1984, p. 3). This difference is equal to the total investment in the business sector.

To some extent, the higher defense consumption was also a result of increased pressure of the military establishment. Shocked by the suprise of the Yom Kippur War, the military wanted to make sure neither its intelligence nor its soldiers nor its equipment could be caught unprepared. No one wants to be accused of being the one causing a surprise or the loss of a war, particularly in a country believing a single disaster could spell total destruction. Those responsible for the degree of military readiness would certainly like to have more resources. This debate has been part and parcel of the Israeli society for a long time. In September 1952, when the then Chief of Staff felt the defense budget was inadequate, the Prime Minister and Minister of Defense David Ben Gurion wrote to him:

Briefly, this is my considered opinion:
1. The security of the State of Israel does not depend solely

on the army. It depends on the economic, financial, professional and moral capabilities of the whole nation.

2.   The defense forces should not be arranged based on the assumption that a war can erupt at any minute (although no one can guarantee the opposite). If the army will be ready for war all the time, the nation would not be ready for war when it will really erupt.

3.   It is impossible and even damaging to act without taking calculated risks. The state cannot afford the existing burden of the defense budget.

(Quoted by Arnon, 1981, p. 16)

Toward the early 1980s one can discern the beginning of a new trend: economists have begun to point out that the cost of defense may be too high and that security must be measured not only by increased military spending but also by taking into account economic strength and social cohesion. In 1980, a paper by Professor Haim Barkai of the economics department of the Hebrew University proposed a design to cost approach that would lead to a drastic cut in the defense budget as a means to reduce inflation. He proposed a reduction in domestic defense consumption to 12 to 13 per cent of GNP instead of the 15 to 16 per cent. This burden is still 3 or 4 times larger than the resource allocation in the NATO countries. By the mid-1980s, Dr Ariel Halperin of the Hebrew University pointed out another of the major costs of the defense budget: the allocation of the majority of scientific manpower to defense needs.

Defense needs have always competed against other major strategic aspirations in determining economic priorities. Throughout the forty-two years of its existence, Israel attempted to absorb as many immigrants as possible, narrow social gaps, and develop a strong economic base in an effort to allow economic independence. Yet, the secrecy surrounding defense issues is certainly important for national security reasons. At a time of war there is a national consensus that much information cannot be made public. One result of this confidentiality has been that it is not very easy to form an opinion about resource allocation in Israel. Since defense allocation decisions were rarely subject to any informed public debate despite their sometimes heavy impact on Israel's industry, the trade-offs, if any, between reduced dependence on weapons systems and increased economic and political dependence were not sufficiently considered. Thus, while the defense industry consists of a very large and growing segment of the economy, and its exports are estimated to be a significant per cent of total Israeli manufacturing exports, much of its operations are secret.

One has to be 'in' in order to have the relevant information, and having such information gives an important competitive advantage.

Civilian control of defense institutions

In chapter 2, we saw how Ben Gurion, in his attempt for 'statehood,' pushed for an abrupt change in behavior in many fronts, but mainly in anything connected with security. He did not hesitate to order the bombing of the ship *Altalena*. He also ordered the disbandment of the distinct command of the Palmach, the majority of whose officers leaned toward the left-wing Mapam. Ben Gurion was quick to make clear that the army is subservient to the government, that the state has a monopoly on use of power and that all underground pseudo-military units should finish their existence.

As a Prime Minister, Ben Gurion introduced bold reforms into this political system in the middle of the War of Independence (see chapter 2). He made the army subordinate to the Chief of Staff and the Chief of Staff subordinate to the government and to Ben Gurion himself as both Defense Minister and Prime Minister. Ben Gurion also made persistent efforts to make the army a national symbol, and an heir to the earlier pioneers. He also attempted to depoliticize the army and make appointments based on merit, so as to achieve efficiency, dedication and national responsibility. Yet after the War of Independence, most high-ranking officers leaning toward Mapam resigned, or were forced to leave. In other cases, promotions were delayed. Ben Gurion preferred officers who had served in the British army, and could be relied on to behave as loyal 'public servants.'

By the time of the War of Independence, IDF had emerged as the only legitimate military force. By that time, the shape of civilian control on the army was forged. Yigael Yadin, Israel's second Chief of Staff, organized the regular army and established the system of general conscription and that of reserve duty of one month a year, not unlike the Swiss method, making the slogan 'the whole nation is the army' a reality. He also referred to citizens as 'soldiers on 11 months leave.'

The creation of the new institutions had its own difficulties. Even during the War of Independence, in the summer of 1948, a group of high-ranking officers threatened to resign if Ben Gurion replaced Mapam-supporting commanders with commanders loyal to him.

Every Chief of Staff in Israel was chosen partly because of his political affiliation, except Haim Laskov, a professional soldier totally trusted by Ben Gurion to behave as a 'loyal public servant.' Mapai's functionaries attempted to ensure the loyalty of the high command through the appointment of party members. Mapai also established, in 1949, a clandestine servicemen's department that recruited military officers to party ranks. The leaders of the party refused to rely solely on national control. They attempted to create a dual control system — both to the party and the nation. Party control was achieved by appointments and through the servicemen's department. The party had an even greater control over the internal security services. These services, for example, were employed against Mapam's political leaders. Microphones were installed in the Mapam headquarter offices because Ben Gurion believed Mapam wanted to seize power by force (Peri, 1982).

The resignation of many combat proven officers after the War of Independence weakened the army, and the political leaders had to grudgingly consent to the mobilization of Mapam-affiliated generals.

In 1954, when Ben Gurion resigned and Sharett served as a Prime Minister, Lavon was the Defense Minister. At that time, the degree of subordination of the army to civil control became a major issue that caused much conflict. After the 1961 Knesset election, that took place under the shadow of the Lavon Affair (see chapter 2), the IDF general staff issued an explicit regulation banning political activities in the army. Service persons were directed to restrain from activity in political bodies, were not allowed to be speakers or take an active role in political meetings or conventions. Service persons were also not allowed to discuss in public any political question. The IDF has increasingly become a professional, apolitical army.

One means used to attract persons to the regular army was by giving them subsidized housing. More importantly, there had been conscious efforts to redefine the role of pioneers. In the Yishuv period, a pioneer (to be admired and serve as a role model) was one who cultivated the land and dried the marshes. In the early years of Israel, the young generation was offered a new vision of a pioneer — that of heroism in serving as a part of the regular army. Pioneers were also those serving the state civil service and those absorbing the immigrants, but mainly those who would serve their nation in making sure Israel would be a stronghold for Jews, that the terrible experience of the Holocaust, in which Jews went to their death as lambs to the slaughter, would never return.

Ben Gurion attempted to stress statehood as the epitome of realization of the Zionist movement. He fought against what he saw as the sectarian tendencies of others. In the institution of the army he was more successful. Indeed, once the original purge was carried out, ensuring total subordination of the military to civilian rule (and Ben Gurion's command), the army was becoming a professional body. It has also become a major source of mobility in Israeli society. Many were able to reach high-ranking position in the army or in other security services, using their newly acquired position as a springboard in civilian life. Ben Gurion used to talk about his dream of seeing a 'Chief of Staff of Yemenite origin.' At least one chief of staff was a Sephardic Jew.

One result of the dazzling victory in the Six Days War of 1967 was the glorification of the army, whose generals' prestige reached new heights. By that time, the army was perceived as the most efficient and innovative of bureaucratic machinery — and many felt it should carry on all kinds of civilian tasks, mainly those related to immigrant absorption and population dispersal. The small core of regular army officers was recognized as highly specialized, highly prestigious, and highly professional. With the increased sophistication of the army's weapon system, there was a perceived need to enlarge the core. Reserve duty was not seen as sufficient for many professional jobs in the armed forces or in intelligence. As a result, and in particular after the 1973 war, defense costs zoomed.

The defense industry

The high level of national priority assigned to defense, fuelled by political and security considerations, have provided the Ministry of Defense (MOD) with funds necessary to create a 'military-industrial' complex. This complex has grown particularly since 1967. In reaction to the embargo imposed by President Charles De Gaulle on French military sales to Israel in 1967, the then Director General of the Ministry of Defense embarked on an ambitious policy of achieving autarky in military supplies. This embargo convinced Israel's decision makers that a high degree of self-supply of arms is essential to the country's security. As a result, nearly all budgetary constraints on the expansion of the Israeli defense industrial companies were lifted. In addition, during this period the Ministry of Defense made its first decision to give extensive development and production orders to non-Ministry-owned firms. The result has been a large increase in the production of defense-related items as well as rapid development of the metals, electronic and electro-optical industries. Israel produces its own tanks, military jet aircraft, missiles, and many other military needs. This decision of the Director General of the Ministry of Defense to increase self-sufficiency in many of these lines was also the major reason for the growth of high-technology branches of the Israeli economy.

The defense sector has always been the most sophisticated one in Israel. The four major elements of government-owned arms industry are Israel Military Industries (IMI), specializing in small arms, artillery and ammunition; Israel Aircraft Industries (IAI), specializing in aircraft, missiles and naval vessels; the Authority for Development of Combat Means (*Rafael*), specializing in research and development and in missile systems, and the Army tank production. In the early years of Israel's existence, its high-tech industry was confined mainly to the manufacture of arms. In response to IDF's wartime needs, many products were developed and the Israel defense industry established a reputation for reliability. In fact, the local production of weaponry predates the establishment of the state and even the establishment of the military industry. As early as World War I, hand bombs were being made and afterwards thousands of hand grenades were cast. The 1929 riots instigated accelerated efforts to produce weapons, bombs and mines. The Israel Military Industry (IMI) was officially established in 1933 and manufactured grenades, bombs, mines, and later also explosives. Resulting from the Haganah's developments in communication systems, the Israel Military Industry also manufactured heliographs (signalling devices), and at a later stage 3-inch mortars and explosives. The Ezel, exhibiting a great deal of ingenuity and development efforts, also manufactured mines and explosives. The Lehi's armament industry produced explosives and roughly 600 Sten sub-machine guns.

Following the establishment of the state, the various underground plants became legitimate and expanded their activities. The modest workshops were transformed into a multi-faceted network of industrial plants producing advanced weapons and ammunition, including rocket systems and engines for missiles, as well as guns, rifles and the Israeli invented 'Uzi' sub-machine guns. The first armament plant not owned by the defense network was established in 1950: the collaboration between 'Solel Boneh' and the Finnish Tampalah Company resulted in the founding of the Soltam Company, specializing in the manufacture of heavy mortars.

In the early 1950s, this sector began exporting. After the Sinai Campaign of 1956, a great deal of captured weapons fell into the hands of the IDF and arms reinforcements were received from France. IMI was faced with a severe crisis. The army reduced its orders drastically (from IL 20.5 million in 1956 to IL 14 million in 1957). To avoid dismissing workers, IMI instituted a 3-4 day work week, and at the same time began extensive efforts to solicit export orders. In addition, IMI began to supply goods to the civilian market. Since then the military industry has made many attempts to export — at first to Europe (for example 'Uzi' sub-machine guns to Holland, Belgium, Germany and Austria) and then to Burma. The export was possible to a large extent because of IDF's reputation, acquired during the Suez Campaign. For the first time, the military industry's total export exceeded $1 million. By 1972, IMI exports were ten times their 1966 level, and by 1978 they accounted for more than 55 per cent of its total output. According to the *New York Times* (December 7, 1986), in the mid-1980s IMI exported 80 per cent of its production.

The Defense Ministry also established the Israel Aircraft Industry, that started out as a 'maintenance workshop' and evolved into a wide-scoped industry developing various planes and aeronautic systems. The Ministry merged two companies — one dealing in batteries and the other in crystals — 'Tadir' and 'Ran' — forming the Tadiran Corporation for the manufacturing of batteries and communication systems. At a later stage the Ministry of Defense sold half of the company's shares to the American GT&E in the hope that the US company would not only contribute to Tadiran's technological know-how and management but also (and mainly) to its market opportunities. The second half is owned by Koor. Later, GT&E sold its shares, and Koor became the sole owner.

Israel Aviation made its first sales abroad in 1954 to Burma. In 1955 it carried out maintenance work for France and in 1962, for the United States. Employment increased from 670 in 1956 to 21,000 since 1979. Exports constituted 23 per cent of output in 1975, 60 per cent in 1980 and 59 per cent in 1985.

The Ministry of Defense developed other networks: *Rafael* — the Authority for the Development of Combat Means — is the largest research and development organization in Israel and evolved out of the Science Forces, established in February 1948 by Prof. Ernst Zeev Bergman, one of the Weizmann Institute's leading scientists, who dealt in the design and development of weapons, explosives and electronic systems. By 1952, the Science Forces had become a design and development division of the

Defense Ministry (*Emet*) and in 1958 were named *Rafael*.

As early as the 1950s, *Emet* had developed the first Israeli-made computer (1956), solid and liquid rocket engine fuel (1956), and anti-tank artillery (1958). During this period, various missiles were being developed at *Rafael* (sea-to-sea, such as Gabriel, which was later moved for design and manufacturing by the Israel Aircraft Industry, and the Shafrir air-to-air). *Rafael* also had extensive operations in the field of electronic warfare, precision armaments and computers. *Rafael* made its first exports in 1974, and since then increased these exports significantly. In 1986, its exports were valued at more than $100 million.

The lion's share of development engineers in Israel were employed by the defense network which contributed immensely to the accumulation of knowledge in diverse areas — from the production of planes to the production of computers and missiles.

These companies have confronted serious difficulties in the late 1980s. Reduction in local military demand, the decline of the dollar in the world market and, for some, the cyclical downturn in the international electronics market combine to require substantial downward changes in this sector.

The rapid growth of American military aid since 1973 has had various effects on the Israeli defense industry. In the first phase, when military aid was approximately $1 billion, the Ministry of Defense maintained the objective of developing the industrial base in Israel. In this phase, the Israeli industry became exposed to the high technology of American weaponry, became familiar with state-of-the-art armaments and started subcontracting for the US industry. All of the above provided many opportunities for Israeli industry's rapid development. In later phases, changes in the structure of the military budget had a negative effect on the Israeli industry. The IDF significantly accelerated the purchase of US military systems in order to make use of the US dollars while simultaneously decreasing purchases from the Israel industry. As a result, within a very short span of time, not only did the Israeli defense industry lose a considerable share of the home market and had to look elsewhere for export opportunities, but R&D resources became limited. The firms found it extremely hard to adjust to the new environment.

The size of the industrial production catering to Israeli defense needs is not published. However, based on available figures, it can be stated that the defense sector has become an important and growing part of Israel's industrial production and exports. Defense Ministry sources (quoted by the *New York Times*, December 7, 1986) estimate that Israel exports $1.2 billion in arms and security services each year — more than a quarter of its total industrial exports. The defense sector is subject to competition from developed economies in which the competitive advantage is based on political considerations. (The same is true for trade with China and Eastern Europe).

Defense production in Israel has been characterized by: security restrictions, regarding export as well as the publication of figures; political impediments to marketing; inability to recruit capital abroad; increasing reliance on retained earnings to cover development costs, as a result of defense budget cutback; products geared to military needs, not to civilian markets; easy access to major Israeli political decision-making; increasing exports. Although the defense industry sees its major objective as serving Israel's defense needs, it holds that products for export must also be used by the IDF.

Some implications

Because Israeli-designed and produced military equipment and other military accessories such as telecommunications are, unfortunately, battle-tested, Israel enjoys a competitive advantage in weapons systems. Israel belongs to a small 'club' of countries (USA, USSR France, UK, Federal Republic of Germany, Spain, Italy, Brazil, Sweden and China) that produces large military equipment. Israel has apparently increased its exports of this equipment, much of which is based on original Israeli development. Halperin estimates the Israeli defense R&D effort to be equal to 4.5 per cent of GNP in 1984, compared to 0.7 per cent civilian industrial R&D (excluding university R&D). Given the apparent size of the defense sector, and its obvious competitive advantage, some strategic implications follow.

One such implication is the trade-off between the use of engineers and scientists in different sectors. Without reliable figures, it is difficult to estimate the ratio of engineers in the defense industries out of total engineers employed by industry, but it is certainly no less than 50 per cent.

The secrecy engulfing the defense sector does not allow a close examination of the allegation that too many engineers are employed by it. It is also alleged that technological manpower can achieve higher returns and greater exports per dollar spent on R&D in civilian products. This may mean that the massive induction of technological manpower into the military sector has arrested the development of conventional civilian industry. If this is so, another cost has to be taken into account on calculating the defense burden.

The ratio of R&D to sales in Israel's military sector was, according to Halperin, about 1:3 in the first half of the 1980s, with a clear upward trend. These ratios are similar to those found in the USA and the UK, so that they are not caused by relative inefficiency of Israel's defense sector. In fact, there are grounds to believe that Israel is more efficient. However, the R&D/sales ratio in Israel's civilian high-tech industries is 1:15-1:20. Excluding the chemical and pharmaceutical industries from the calculation (they are less comparable to military industries) brings the ratio down to around 1:8.

By its very nature, defense-related equipment cannot be sold to all markets. Thus, it may well be that Israel may find it more difficult to develop new markets. Moreover, the higher the cost of the equipment, the more difficult it may be to increase sales.

The defense-related industry in Israel has to be state-of-the-art. Its knowledge frontier is, at least partially, determined by exogenous factors. If it produces jet planes, missiles or tanks they should be at least equal, and preferably much better, than those produced by the big powers. Since the magnitude of R&D needed for the development of a weapon is equal for all producers, the *relative* burden on Israel is much higher, no matter how efficient Israeli engineers and scientists are as compared to their counterparts in other countries. For example, Israel Aviation Industry estimated the development costs of its proposed Lavi jet aircraft to have been $2.5 billion. Even if one assumes that such a development would cost $5 billion in the USA, the cost represents 10 per cent of annual Israeli GNP, while for the larger USA, the respective figure is only 0.0013 per cent. In GNP terms — the US can therefore develop a hundred planes for the same relative cost of one in Israel. Admittedly, the development of the Lavi would have taken more than one year, and its development costs in each year would not have been 10 per cent of GNP, but still, the more expensive (and indivisible) the development costs of a certain project, the less is the ability of a small country to develop such a system without suffering from serious side effects and a high portfolio risk. Indeed, after long debates, the Israeli government decided to halt the development of the Lavi.

Israel's defense-related industry develops and produces a whole gamut of equipment and components. Israel's vast military needs and the availability of a test ground certainly give the military industrial complex a competitive edge. It seems that this competitive advantage can be utilized best when the total size and cost of a project is limited to a given maximum. In terms of portfolio risk, the development of a jet aircraft is several times riskier than the development of small avionics parts. (In addition, it may be more difficult to export a jet plane than to export components. First because of the visibility, second, because of the investment needed: no air force purchases one jet plane. It either buys at least a whole squadron or none. Third, because such sales are dependent on explicit US permission, which may be suspect of being withheld to prevent Israeli firms from competing against US producers.) Military hardware includes not only jet aircraft and engines or tanks, but also electronic warfare systems, artillery, ammunition, electro-optic systems, communications equipment or avionics and other components, such as rotor blades. In all of them, project size is relatively small.

Military build-up has several positive spin-offs — from training of technicians by the army to technology transfer. The defense sector helped create a national infrastructure and exerted a strong impact on the entire industrial system, at least by demanding higher standards of production and quality control. The defense industry has been used as an engine of growth and of shifting the economy to more modern technologies and management techniques. It has also made considerable exports.

At the same time, the defense burden implies competition for resources with private investments, and increased taxes. Its imports must be financed by additional exports, by military aid or by reduced imports of other kinds. Despite its importance, a problem rarely referred to is the substitution effect between civilian and defense-related investments in technology (and therefore trade-offs between defense and economic development).

Unfortunately, problems in this area are more visible than the solutions. American experience suggests that commercial exploitation of defense technology is very difficult to accomplish. American investment in military and space technology in the 1950s and 1960s provided a great stimulus to industrial growth in the 1960s and 1970s, but relatively little of the commercial benefit was realized by the organizations that developed the technology. Large firms seldom succeed in efforts to 'transfer' technology from defense divisions to commercial operations. Defense contractors in the USA, to the extent they work for civilian market, let the two businesses run quite independently of each other with relatively little crossover of technology.

The mentality of the successful defense contractor is not compatible with the requirements of finding suitable commercial application. Successful transfer of defense technology in Israel, as in the USA, may be done by people leaving defense-related firms to start their own civilian venture. Previously acquired skills help them only when they realize that its survival depends on finding a commercial business.

The large defense firm, however, seems to create an environment that does not encourage transfer of technology. In a detailed study of thirty-four knowledge-based Israeli firms, Kusiatin (1986) found that almost none of the entrepreneurs came from the defense sector.

Survival under extended conflict

It was shown that the defense burden, both in economic and in social and psychological terms, has been very heavy. The way Israel survived, given the burden, is therefore very important.

In economic terms Israel was able to survive largely because of the influx of capital that made it possible to maintain the import surplus. In social terms, Israel did not become a militaristic society. Israel continued to be a parliamentary democracy, subject to the rule of law and the army is clearly subject to civil control. The army officers are promoted based on strict professional standards, although political involvement is rampant. As Perlmutter (1969) demonstrates, Israel is not a praetorian state. In fact, Israel was able to avoid any boundaries between its defense and its civilian sectors. The two sectors converge in terms of their non-authoritarian organizational modes, the power politics orientation and the democratic-coalescent political culture. To be sure, since 1967, the extent to which the democracy and the rule of law extend to the occupied terrorists has been a problem.

At least insofar as the Jewish state is concerned, despite the allocation of massive resources to defense and despite the prominence of national security issues, Israel did not become a 'garrison state', à la Laswell, ruled by 'experts in violence.' Militaristic values did not shape the way of life in Israel. Instead it developed a pattern of action in which civilization of the military system balances militarization of the civilian one. This pattern has been described as follows:

> The pattern of civil-military relations in Israel is structured and yet flexible to a degree, due to its tolerance of inconsistencies legitimized by public consensus. In such a framework, inclinations toward militarization of society are controllable even under conditions of national security as the

fusion of the military and civilian subsystems is restricted to one sphere. In this context, it is possible to suggest a tentative answer to the central question referred to in the introduction in this chapter: the survival of multiparty democratic politics under conditions of centrality of military institutions, values and elites. The answer is threefold: (1) the differentiation between dimensions of civil-military relations facilitated the simultaneous occurrence of processes of militarization and civilianization balancing one another. (2) the differentiation between value contents in terms of their relevance to either national security or domestic politics facilitated convergence between military and civilian elites. (3) the differentiation between national security and other spheres of public policy facilitated the control of civil-military fusionist tendencies on the basis of a fragmented rather than 'permeable' or 'integral' boundary.

(Horowitz, 1982, p. 98)

Security considerations, widely defined, have always been of the utmost importance in Israel. Israelis are divided on many crucial issues, varying from the relationship between the religion and the state to the best means of financing the municipalities. Even on such issues as the proper future borders of Israel or the relationships of Israelis and Arabs, Israelis are extremely polarized. If one issue unifies all Israelis, it is the need to achieve maximum security and the willingness for personal sacrifices at times of danger, or for anything seen as important for the defense of the state. Israelis are haunted by memories of the Holocaust, the grief and the bereavement. They are determined to make sure that Massada will not fall again, and that the Third Commonwealth of Israel will be secured. Israelis feel they have no other choice, they have nowhere to run away and they therefore cling to their security stubbornly.

Finally, despite the universal consensus on the need to maintain a strong army and a large military-industrial complex and although army generals have been held in high esteem, in particular after the sweeping victory of the Six Days War in 1967, the military did not become alienated from the policy and was never used in contest for political power. The army also did not take advantage of its strength to become a dominant pressure group or to seize control.

Unlike many other newly established countries, the Israeli army has always been subservient to civilian political leaders. Israel's first Prime Minister went a long way to establish a unified control of the political leaders on all factions of the

271

military and to isolate the military from party politics. In the first decade or two, the defense establishment was occasionally used for patronage by the ruling political party, most of the high ranking officers were loyalists to that ruling party, and those who came from the dissident underground organizations felt they had less chance of promotion. Still, even then and more so in the 1960s, the army has been seen as an apolitical, professional and national instrument of the country's policies. It has also been a place where young, ambitious persons could achieve relatively fast promotion and social mobility. Many of those achieved national status and a few became ministers immediately after leaving the army. Ten ex-generals served at one point or another as government ministers.

To a large extent, the existence of a common external conflict is one source of a strong need to solidify the ranks and for cohesion. The longer the conflict, and the larger the number of persons who see its management by political leaders as not just, the more difficult it is to endure it. Israelis until the 1980s did not question the basic needs for the defense burden, as well as the need to be strong and resolute. The outbreak of the 1973 Yom Kippur War took the country by surprise, and was a watershed, changing many perceptions. The Lebanon war in 1982 was considered by part of the population as wrong and immoral.

The way Israel seems to be able to survive the extended periods of what Yitzhak Rabin called 'dormant war' which, like a dormant volcano, is apt to erupt at any moment, is of interest. Baruch Kimmerling proposed this was possible because Israelis developed a mentality which perceives the conflict as a permanent condition. They also created a built-in social mechanism, an institutional arrangement, to cope with the conflict with minimum cost and maximum efficiency. He posited:

> that Israeli society is divided into two completely different yet substantially interconnected phases of activity: the first may be called "routine" and the second "interrupted". During the interruption phase, the main societal processes are suspended . . . The system's institutional arrangements are reorganized to focus upon implementation of a predominant goal, together with a complementary goal. The predominant societal goal is to ensure the very existence of the society in question from a perceived actual or potential threat . . . The feasibility of swift achievement is a primary importance: Israel can mobilize its entire military capacity within approximately 72 hours. This has not only military but also

far reaching social consequences, one of which is obligatory compartmentalization between routine life and social processes at the phase when society as a whole must cope with the conflict.

(in Lissak, 1984, p. 14.)

Conclusions

The geopolitical situation of Israel and its protracted conflicts with the Arabs had a strong impact on the Israeli economy and society. Despite the heavy defense burden, however, Israel never experienced military takeovers. The military in Israel does not reflect on group or class: the IDF is a 'people's army.' Unlike some developing countries, the Israeli army is not alienated from civil society.

Israel sees its political future as dependent first and foremost on its achievements in the battle field. The need to ensure military supplies dictated to a significant extent the foreign policies of the government and was a major consideration of Israeli diplomacy. An increased degree of independence in the production of a jet aircraft or a tank is perceived by many of the leaders as being of utmost importance in reducing international political pressures and providing a greater breathing space in international relations. All of the above means a major emphasis on defense needs and an automatic priority to the Israel Defense Forces' requisitions over any dream of economic independence or even solution of social problems. A state perceiving itself as fighting for its basic physical survival, a nation suffering from a complex of solitude and seclusion, seeing around it political discrimination, isolated from its neighbors, and remembering not only the Nazi Holocaust but also the memory of most nations ignoring their political commitments to Israel, cannot afford the assumption that free market forces can be allowed to determine the economic and therefore political capacity of Israel. In fact, market forces were deemed as impossible to apply if Israel wants an autarky in defense-related production or emergency inventory of fuel. Thus, anything remotely related to defense considerations — including, for example, problems related to the Arab economic blockade on Israel — receives a high priority and urgent consideration.

7 Foreign trade and the balance of payments

Introduction

The threat to the very existence of Israel from its neighboring countries resulted in a decision to create an integrated military machine that consumes a much larger proportion of the GNP than that of practically any other country in the world. The breakdown of economic relationships by its neighboring countries deprived Israel of considerable exports and of cheaper sources of imports. Israel pays higher insurance rates and shipping tariffs and its tourism is affected by the absence of peaceful relationships with most of its neighbors and by terrorism. One major cost of the 'no war, no peace' situation, however, has been that it saps strength necessary to build a strong civilian economy.

Yet, being a small country, Israel is heavily dependent on foreign trade. It has had to import all of its oil (except for a short period, when it owned the Sinai oil wells), almost all of its raw materials, most of its inputs for production goods. Israel also needs to import goods for final consumption or for investments. The tiny size of the market means that there is a wide variety of goods for which the total domestic demand is not large enough to allow domestic efficient production by serving the home market alone. Israel imports of goods and services since 1973 have been more than two-thirds of its GNP (Table 7.1). Indeed, most small countries have high ratios of imports to GNP. The ratio of imports to GNP has been growing, having been in the 30-40 per cent range in the 1950s and 40-50 per cent range in the 1960s. This basic fact means that Israel is very dependent on world trade and world trends, and that it must export a significant share of its production to earn the foreign exchange it needs to pay for the imports. Further, because of her geopolitical situation, Israel must export its goods and services to distant countries.

Table 7.1 Imports, exports and import surplus

Period	% of real growth p.a.			% of GDP in current prices		
	Imports	Exports		Imports	Exports	Surplus
1950-5	3.5	26.8		33.6	10.2	23.4
1956-60	9.8	20.4		34.6	14.4	20.2
1961-5	11.8	12.4		41.0	20.7	20.3
1966-70	14.2	13.0		45.2	26.2	19.0
1971-5	10.0	9.6		62.0	31.0	31.0
1976-80	0.0	8.2		64.6	43.1	21.1
1981-5	3.4	4.9		60.7	42.6	18.1
1988	-0.2	-2.3		72.3	54.0	18.3
1989	1.8	6.8				

Source: Z. Zusman: 'Exchange Rate Elasticity, Inflation, Structural, Changes,' *Economic Quarterly* (Hebrew). CBS Monthly Bulletin of Statistics, Supplement 5/1982; 5/1986. CBS Statistical Abstract. Bank of Israel Annual Report, various years.

Note: Excluding imports and exports of factors of production.

Israel attempted in the past to produce goods in which it did not have any competitive advantage with the dire consequences of high costs to Israeli consumers. One extreme example is the attempt to grow sugar beets in Israel and to refine the sugar locally despite the climate and the scarcity of water. Another, more recent example, is the attempt to assemble color televisions in Israel. The local cost of imported components was equal or even more expensive than the imports of the fully assembled sets. Local assembly lines were only profitable because of the high level of government protection.

Israel is a latecomer to many of the industries in which it would like to achieve export growth. Israeli firms now must export into markets that have become global, in which an increasing role is played by giant, multi-unit multinational enterprises. In a world in which experience, based on large-scale operations, is an important basis for competitive advantage and strategic options are determined by technologies of production and distribution on a world scale, small firms from a tiny country with very few natural resources find it extremely hard to compete. An additional set of difficulties stems from the growing trend towards protectionism. In addition, Israeli firms, and any firm trading with Israel, face an Arab economic blockage. As a part of their animosity to Israel, the Arabs have established an elaborate economic boycott. The organization responsible for the boycott seeks to intimidate companies and individuals trading with or investing in Israel, usually by threatening economic reprisals. The exact economic repercussions of the Arab boycott are not easy to quantify.

Since its inception, Israel has made great progress in covering a large per cent of its imports by exports. While in the 1950s Israel could not cover even a quarter of its imports, in 1961, it could already cover 41 per cent of its imports, and by the mid-1980s, three-quarters. By the end of 1989, exports covered 81.1 per cent of total imports and 87.4 per cent of civilian exports (in other words, total imports less direct military imports). Throughout this period, exports grew, but imports increased also. Thus, in the twenty-five years between 1961-86, imports of goods (as defined in foreign trade statistics) per capita increased from $269 in 1961, to $2,128 in 1986. Exports per capita increased from $110 to $1,586 respectively. In 1989, imports of goods per capita were $2,738, while exports per capita reached $2,394. Despite many efforts, Israel still is unable to balance its balance of trade, and a persistent deficit in the current accounts of the balance of payments ('import surplus') has always been the most distinctive feature of Israel's economy (Table 7.1). This deficit was one way to finance investment despite the absence of net domestic savings: the government dissavings in Israel have been much higher than the level of private savings. The import surplus allowed Israelis to raise both their private and public consumption and still maintain a high capital formation.

In this chapter we shall consider the trends related to the import surplus, the means by which it is financed, and the magnitude of the foreign debt. We shall then look at the volume and composition of Israel's international transactions and the magnitude of trade with Israel's major trading partners. We shall start with imports, move to exports of goods and then exports of services. Next we shall survey the balance of payments (and effective rate of exchange) policies and consider the terms of trade. Finally, we shall briefly analyze the comparative advantages of Israel's firms and possibilities of increasing manufacturing exports. This part of the chapter is based on a study made by Jerusalem Institute of Management in 1987, in which the author was a senior investigator.

Import surplus and its financing

Israel is unique in the size of the trade deficit (or import surplus) relative to GDP (Table 7.1). In other words, the country has persistently imported more than it has exported. Moreover, the size of the import surplus has been growing. It was lowest in 1954 ($232 million), reached a level of $400-$550 million in the 1960s and exceeded $1 billion in 1970. In the mid-1970s, the import surplus in Israel reached a level of about a third of GNP (or 20 per cent of total resources). Since then, the import surplus relative to GNP has gone down, but the absolute amount has reached very high levels. In 1988, the total import surplus was $5,326 million, down from the peak of $5,807 million in 1987. In 1989, it was sharply reduced to $3.7 billion. The civilian import surplus (for example when defense imports are excluded) in 1989, was $25 million compared to $3,220 million in 1988 and $3,335 million in 1987. The additional resources the economy had for use as a result of this import surplus have fluctuated from between one-fifth and one-third of GNP. This quite sizeable amount of additional resources has allowed the economy to have a high rate of investment while maintaining simultaneously high levels of both private and public consumption. In fact, the import surplus is so high that most Israeli economists measure many ratios from the total net available resources (GNP + import surplus or GNP + imports - exports) rather than GNP.

Of course, the deficit has had to be financed, and the means of financing the import surplus has changed. Israel was able to finance a significant share of its import surplus by unilateral transfers (that do not have to be repaid, being grants or gifts). In most years, Israel mobilized unilateral transfers to cover between 60 to 75 per cent of the deficit in the goods and services account. Net long-term capital flows (including foreign investments and long-term debt, but mainly the latter) have always been smaller than the amount of funds received by unilateral transfers. When these two sources were not sufficient, the remainder of the deficit had to be financed by increased short-term loans, by reduced foreign exchange reserves or (technically) by larger 'errors and omissions.'

The three major sources of unilateral transfers (and long-term lending) were world Jewry, the government of the Federal Republic of Germany and the government of the United States. World Jewry gave Israel financial support mainly through contributions to various institutions. The amount of these contributions has gone down in real terms. The nominal amount in the 1980s was about $500 million. Other individuals' transfers include money or goods sent by individuals (mainly new immigrants) or transfers of non-profit organizations. The total private transfers, net of transfers abroad, was $1,112 million p.a. in 1978-83, around $760 million in 1984-85, $1,198 million in 1986, $1,587 million in 1987, $1,452 million in 1988, and $1,817 million in 1989. World Jewry contributions, although nominally growing, declined in real terms. By 1983, World Jewry financed only 10 per cent of Israel's import surplus, compared to 28 per cent in 1970. Ben Gurion initiated, in 1951, the idea of selling Jews Israeli government bonds in addition to the United Jewish Appeal contributions. Since then, the bonds have continued to be sold at an interest rate much lower than the market rate of interest. In the 1980s, the sale of these bonds amounted to about $500 million, and redemption of earlier bonds was about the same amount. Israel's bonds are recorded as long-term debt, but they are considered by many as a quasi-contribution. In the 1970s, about half of the national foreign debt was in Israeli bonds with very low rates of interest and in direct investments — mainly by new immigrants.

The agreement on German reparations gave Israel an important new source of foreign currency. Israel was able to reduce drastically its short-term loans. The German government gave Israel a total of about $850 million in the form of goods between 1953 and 1965. In addition, individuals received personal restitution, some in lump sum settlements, and some in the form of pensions. The lump sum restitution payments were received mainly in the period 1954-74, but pension payments still continue. Personal restitutions from the Federal Republic of Germany were $426 million in the period 1978-83, about $325 million in 1984-5, $424 million in 1986, $531 million in 1987, $557 million in 1988 and $584 million in 1989.

By far the most important source of capital since 1973, financing more than 70 per cent of Israel's trade deficit, has been US government grants and loans. Technically, this aid was reflected in a rise in unilateral transfers in the second half of the 1970s and mainly in the 1980s. The majority of this US aid was granted for defense purposes, and consisted of imports of US-produced military equipment. In the second half of the 1980s, these amounted to $3 billion per annum in nominal dollars, of which $1.8 billion was for military aid and $1.2 billion for civilian purposes. The civilian aid in that period was about equal to the debt servicing costs on the earlier loans given to Israel by the United States. (In 1988, for example, debt servicing costs to the US were $1.24 billion.) In 1985 and 1986, the US added emergency aid of $750 million each year. The larger this aid as a per cent of the available resources, the greater has been the dependence of Israel on the United States.

Balance of payments

Table 7.2 gives a year-by-year account of Israel's balance of payments. The War of Independence was a drain on resources, and so was the large influx of new immigrants that the young State of Israel endeavored to absorb. In 1950, total imports of goods and services were $327.6 million, but exports were only 15 per cent of that amount ($45.8 million). The import surplus was covered partially by contributions received from the Jews in the Diaspora through the United Jewish Appeal (UJA) to the tune of $95 million and by loans. Because of an acute shortage of foreign currency, Israel had to dwindle the accumulated foreign exchange reserves of the British Mandate period, which were held in London as backing of the Palestine Pound. As mentioned, it also started selling bonds, mainly to Jews, abroad. In 1952, total imports were $393.2 million while the exports were $86.4 million. The import surplus was covered by immigrants' imports ($105 million) and a grant from the United States government ($86 million). The rest was financed by loans and a further reduction of reserves. Many felt at the time that from a strict economic point of view, the Israeli situation was nonviable. The government had to take short-term loans from well wishers, and was unable to finance even the most high-priority needs.

Between 1952 and 1965, imports grew by an average annual rate of 9.5 per cent and exports rose by 18 per cent per annum. During that period, the import surplus fluctuated between $232 and $564 million in current US dollars. From 1958 until the Yom Kippur War in 1973, unilateral transfers and long-term capital flows fully financed the deficit and even allowed short-term assets to be built. The total import surplus, from the beginning of 1949 to the end of 1965, in current dollars was $6,011 million. During that period, Israel received net unilateral transfers of $4,208 million. At that time, Israeli leaders aspired to achieve economic independence, that is to cover imports by exports. Needless to say, it was hoped that Israel's trade imbalance could be resolved by growing fast rather than by reducing the standard of living.

The foreign aid and the bonds were used mainly for investment and development of the economy. To be sure, not all the projects turned out to be successful and the funds were not always spent in what seems in retrospect to be the best allocation of resources. However, the investments did create growth. By 1964, when the German reparations to the government ended, Israeli exports reached more than half of its imports.

Since 1973, the increased absolute size of the deficit meant

Table 7.2: Summary balance of payments, 1952–1988 (millions of dollars)

Year	Goods and services[a] Exports	Goods and services[a] Imports	Import surplus	Unilateral transfers, net credit	Long-term capital Credit	Long-term capital Debit	Long-term capital Net credit	Short-term capital, net credit
1952	86	393	-307	191	137	30	107	9
1953	102	365	-263	173	90	23	67	4
1954	141	373	-232	263	135	57	78	-77
1955	145	432	-287	210	80	7	73	2
1956	178	536	-358	241	145	66	79	28
1957	223	558	-335	249	157	88	69	18
1958	235	573	-338	264	189	116	73	-6
1959	216	561	-345	251	174	89	85	-23
1960	267	586	-319	311	207	100	107	-39
1961	336	682	-346	343	291	110	191	-91
1962	397	840	-443	326	348	129	219	-112
1963	472	933	-461	340	483	214	269	-123
1964	577	1,017	-440	327	485	178	307	-78
1965	619	1,183	-564	321	415	187	228	-46
1966	711	1,234	-523	289	420	236	184	19
1967	834	1,283	-449	521	526	221	305	-274
1968	911	1,447	-536	438	468	274	194	54
1969	1,150	1,806	-656	464	528	311	217	265
1970	1,290	2,175	-885	650	982	300	682	-12
1971	1,402	2,664	-1,262	792	1,001	369	632	-268
1972	1,875	3,096	-1,221	1,059	1,217	482	735	-745
1973	2,222	3,316	-1,094					

1973	2,812	5,376	-2,564	2,190	1,443	503	940	-548
1974	3,559	6,754	-3,195	1,718	1,108	532	576	1,254
1975	3,687	7,536	-3,840	1,770	1,591	558	1,033	616
1976	4,400	7,469	-3,069	2,210	1,907	660	1,247	57
1977	5,479	7,850	-2,380	2,071	1,778	745	1,033	-556
1978	6,621	9,741	-3,120	2,246	2,060	969	1,091	-386
1979	8,030	11,687	-3,657	2,784	2,221	1,027	1,194	549
1980	9,791	13,567	-3,776	2,967	2,467	1,260	1,207	206
1981	10,439	14,768	-4,329	2,926	2,563	1,330	1,241	587
1982	10,165	14,885	-4,720	2,606	2,450	1,219	1,147	330
1983			-4,742	2,865	2,824	950	1,873	-414
1984	10,823	15,590	-4,655	3,266	2,387	1,083	1,304	505
1985	11,245	15,092	-3,847	4,997	1,221	1,227	-5	-230
1986	12,126	15,954	-3,827	5,382	1,884	1,488	397	-781
1987	14,288	20,503	-5,807	4,839	2,000	1,627	373	852
1988	15,796	20,977	-5,181	4,564	6,650	6,576	-529	492
1989	17,151	20,877	-3,726	4,876	7,205	2,298	-13	-395

Note: ªUntil 1958, the goods and services were based on c.i.f. recording of merchandise imports. Since 1958, recording has been based on f.o.b. The insurance and freight carried out by Israeli firms were recorded as exports, thus inflating both sides. In addition, there were all sorts of schemes that allowed import without payments if a relative sent an Israeli citizen the foreign currency or many other such schemes. Both imports and exports were carried out in literally hundreds of different effective exchange rates, and many activities were not recorded. From 1964, the expenditures abroad of the National Institutions were shown as imports, making the deficit in 1964 somewhat overstated.

a growing need to find other sources of financing it. Increasingly, the deficit (and the country's higher standard of living) were financed by increasing the size of foreign debt.

The worsening deficit was caused by several factors. The Yom Kippur War caused a leap in the size of defense imports that reached $1.85 billion in 1975. The 1973 war also disrupted exports and production. The war was followed by the first round of international oil price rises which pushed Israel's oil bill up, from $93m in 1972 to $628m in 1975. By 1980, Israel had handed back the Sinai oil fields to Egypt under the terms of the Peace Treaty between the two countries and oil prices were increasing again. Oil imports, in dollar terms, reached nearly $1.8 billion p.a. in 1976-9 and an estimated $1.5-$2.1 billion p.a. in 1980-85. At its peak the oil bill equalled about 8 per cent of GNP. The jump in the oil prices increased the size of imports dramatically. OPEC's quota system broke down in 1986, and the world price per barrel shrunk from $28 in 1985 to $15 in the third quarter of 1986. By the end of 1986, a quota system was reconstructed and the price went up to $18. Israel's oil imports for 1986 went down to $924 million. Rising prices in 1987 increased Israel's oil imports to $1,148 million in 1987, and decreased prices in 1988 meant an oil bill of $1,062 million. In 1989, oil imports were $1,247 million and in 1990, oil prices jumped to $30 per barrel following the Iraqi invasion of Kuwait.

Between 1981 and 1984, government policy caused a deterioration of the balance-of-payments situation: in an attempt to reduce inflation (and to be re-elected in 1981), the government reduced taxes on many imported luxury goods and reduced the general level of purchase taxes. This created a boom in domestic demand which increased imports and reduced exports. At the same time the exchange rate was held against foreign currencies in order to reduce imported inflation. This made Israeli exports less competitive at a time when world trade was growing slowly and further encouraged imports and travel abroad. The effect of these policies was to cause a rapid worsening of the current account deficit between 1981 and 1983 and a massive increase in external debt.

The magnitude of defense imports and their financing has a very large impact on the import surplus and on the current balance. Defense related imports (which have grown consistently after each war) depend on policy decisions rather than on efficient market considerations. Supply of such items fluctuates from year to year, causing wide fluctuations in the import surplus. Until 1960, defense imports were about $50 million a year. They then reached $100 million in the first half of the

1960s. In the period 1958-61, they were 2.2 per cent of GNP and 3.9 per cent in 1962-6. These imports grew during the 1967 war ($286 million) and again during the War of Attrition in 1970 ($624 million). By 1972, defense imports were down to $490 million. As a per cent of GNP, direct defense's supply was 8.6 per cent in 1968-72 and 12.4 per cent in 1974-80 (Berglas, 1983, appendix). In the 1980s, direct defense imports fluctuated between $1.8 and $2.4 billion per annum (but decreased to $1.2 billion in 1989).

In 1988, the Israeli government reached an agreement with the US government: it redeemed US government loans, given earlier with an interest rate of up to 13 per cent. The funds for redemption were tapped by issuing Israeli government bonds in the New York market for redemption, 90 per cent guaranteed by the US treasury. For the rest of the 10 per cent Israel bought US government treasury bonds and deposited them in US banks as a partial guarantee of the loan. The yield to maturity on these bonds was 9.5 per cent, allowing the Israeli government to save about $150 million of interest per annum. This conversion was concluded in 1989.

The result of all the developments described above has been a growing, even alarming, dependence on the United States government and an accelerated rise of the total foreign debt by more than $2 billion per year through 1985. In 1982, the foreign debt grew by $3,685 million. In the 1970s, capital imports consisted of about 30 per cent transfers by private individuals; an additional 27 per cent came from various Jewish philanthropists, 20 per cent from international organizations and foreign governments and 22 per cent were commercial loans. In the 1980s, more than a half of the capital imports came from the US government. Israel has moved from dependence on its Jewish brethren to a dependence on the US government, that some see as an unreliable ally. In addition, the foreign debt zoomed. In the period 1974-84, the deficit in the current balance reached about 6 per cent of GDP. By the end of 1984, Israel's total liabilities to foreigners were $30,366 million or $7,230 per capita! To be sure, some years (for example 1976-8, or 1984) showed improvements, but the trend showed a continuous increase in the deficit until 1985.

An integral part of the new economic policy, in July 1985, was the freeze of the rate of exchange to control inflation. The new policy was partially successful also in reducing the balance-of-payments deficit, and Israel received a substantial increase in grants from the US. As a result, the balance of payments current accounts registered a surplus in both 1985 and 1986 (and in 1989, the surplus was equal to 2 per cent of GNP). In 1988, there was a deficit of $20 million — about 0.5 per cent of GNP. Imports continued to grow faster than exports.

In 1987, a study by the Jerusalem Institute of Management, using the economic model of the Israeli Finance Ministry, had projected the level of export growth which would be required to achieve a balance in Israel's external account (assuming a continuation of US military assistance and of private transfers from abroad) by 1995. Based on certain assumptions about the growth of domestic consumption, the service sector, and exports to the territories, the model indicated that exports of goods must increase at a rate of 8.9 per cent per year in constant 1985 dollars (excluding exports to the territories of Judea, Samaria and Gaza). If US military assistance were to stop and all military imports were to be funded from local source, a positive balance of payments would require Israel to increase industrial exports by 18 per cent p.a. — a task probably beyond the capacity of the economy.

If the 8.9 per cent per annum growth could be achieved, the model projected that GDP would grow by an average of 5.0 per cent per year and GDP per capita by an average of 3.1 per cent per year. Substantial productivity improvements would have to be made to achieve this goal — not an easy task since Israel's productivity growth stagnated during the 1980s. In reality, this growth has not yet been achieved. Exports prices of goods grew by 2.8 per cent in 1986, 7.1 per cent in 1987, 13.2 per cent in 1988, and 4.4 per cent in 1989. The quantities for these years rose by 7.0, 10.3 (-2.4) and 3.5 per cent respectively.

Foreign debt

When debt is used to finance the deficit, the result is an increase in the country's foreign debt. Until 1970, most transactions were long-term and were carried out or guaranteed by the government. The government is still the major debtor, and it borrows mainly from the US government. In 1972, unilateral transfers were $1,053 million and this amount almost totally covered the import surplus ($1,114 million). Since then, Israel has resorted much more to debt to finance the import surplus. At least under some Likud finance ministers, the willingness to finance increased private and public consumption from rising debt was certainly not very responsible. As a result of the deterioration in the balance of payments since the mid-1970s, the short term debt, mainly at the beginning of the 1980s, increased.

From 1980 to 1985, Israel resorted to large-scale short-term borrowing. The result, of course, was an increased foreign indebtedness (Table 7.3). An increasing share of Israel's exports of goods and services had to be devoted to covering debt servicing. In the 1980s, net debt servicing was about 30 per cent of exports, 18-22 per cent of exports and unilateral transfers and 10-13 per cent of GNP. The new economic policy in 1985 and additional US aid arrested the deterioration. In 1989, net debt servicing was 7 per cent of GNP, compared to 13 per cent in 1985, 11 per cent in 1986, 10 per cent in 1987, and 8 per cent in 1988.

Immediately after the 1967 Six Days War, the net debt was less than $1 billion. In 1976, as a result of war, an energy crisis, but also zooming social expenditures, the net debt reached $7.6 billion. After two terms of the Likud government it was $20 billion (and more than $30 billion gross). In 1983 the import surplus reached more than $5 billion, and the unilateral transfers were only $2,855 million. This led to increased debt servicing problems which in turn worsened the deficit. The cost of financing has risen because of the increased size of the debt and its composition. In 1967, net interest payment abroad equalled about 1.7 per cent of GNP plus unilateral transfers. In 1974, the figure was 3.2 per cent and in both 1984 and 1985, 6 per cent. In 1987, 1988 and 1989, the interest payment was 3.4 per cent of total resources as defined above and 7-10 per cent of GNP. Moreover, in 1987, the net servicing of the external debt took 25 per cent of exports. (In 1988, because Israel converted some of its loans to the US government, the number is totally out of line — 44 per cent. Without this conversion the figure is 24 per cent. In 1984-6, the figure was 29-30 per cent.) In absolute terms, interest payments on the foreign debt in 1988 were about $2.5 billion and payments on principal (when the conversion is ignored), $1.8 billion.

By the end of 1988, Israel's gross liabilities to foreigners were equal to about 80 per cent of GNP. Sixty-three per cent of the debt was owed by the public sector, and 37 per cent by the private sector, equally divided between the nonfinancial sector and the banking system. Luckily, the creditability of Israel among foreign banks has usually been very good. The Israeli banks (including the Bank of Israel) have more financial assets abroad than money received from foreign banks. To be sure, the debt varies in terms of the rigidity of its repayment. Thus, in some years, deposits of foreign residents in Israel were shown as a part of the foreign debt. Some also feel that the holders of Israel's bonds would be more willing to accept an extension of

Table 7.3 Foreign exchange assets and obligations, 1953-1988 (millions of dollars)

Year	Obligations Long-term (1)	Obligations Short-term (2)	Total (3)	Foreign assets (4)	Net obligations (3-4)=(5)	Net assets (4-2)=(6)	Reserves held at the Bank of Israel (7)
1953	329	81	410	41	369	-40	—
1954	382	49	431	80	351	31	—
1955	419	47	466	89	377	42	51
1956	452	62	514	86	428	24	56
1957	483	58	541	82	459	24	53
1958	519	66	585	130	455	64	94
1959	569	66	635	168	467	102	124
1960	599	121	720	270	450	149	383
1961	700	126	826	365	461	239	503
1962	820	161	981	506	475	345	416
1963	940	174	1,114	626	448	452	515
1964	1,076	192	1,268	666	602	474	540
1965	1,214	273	1,487	779	708	506	634
1966	1,298	304	1,602	756	846	452	612
1967	1,580	273	1,853	968	885	695	695
1968	1,772	334	2,106	916	1,190	582	647
1969	2,110	413	2,523	729	1,794	316	381
1970	2,698	609	3,307	849	2,458	240	350
1971	3,203	1,558	4,761	1,585	3,176	27	548
1972	3,737	1,885	5,622	2,762	2,784	953	1,116
1973	4,997	1,795	6,792	3,890	2,902	2,095	1,761

Year							
1974	5,578	2,208	7,786	3,129	4,657	921	1,040
1975	6,751	3,301	9,782	3,496	6,290	465	1,040
1976	8,874	2,389	11,263	3,842	7,421	1,453	1,359
1977	9,235	3,804	13,039	4,783	8,256	979	1,359
1978	9,996	5,519	15,515	6,961	8,554	1,442	2,242
1979	11,359	7,538	18,897	8,471	10,426	933	2,570
1980	12,460	8,988	21,448	10,119	11,329	1,131	2,781
1981	13,435	10,276	23,711	11,142	12,569	866	2,847
1982	14,653	12,790	27,443	12,467	14,976	-323	2,993
1983	16,331	12,584	28,915	11,401	17,514	-1,183	1,873
1984	17,376	12,135	29,511	10,620	18,891	-1,515	2,601
1985	17,670	11,871	29,541	10,985	18,556	-886	3,190
1986	18,487	12,272	30,759	12,479	18,280	207	4,153
1987	19,347	12,559	31,906	13,641	18,265	1,082	5,329
1988	18,989	12,130	31,119	12,501	18,618	371	3,433
1989			31,137		16,408		4,430

Sources: 1953-1972 Ben-Porath, 1986, The Israeli Economy: Maturing Through Crises, p. 259. 1971-1989 *Statistical Abstract of Israel*, pp. 228-9.

Note: As of 1973, foreign currency deposits of residents were not counted as part of foreign liabilities.

the debt than some other lenders. To some extent, the foreign obligations, in particular the short-term ones, reflect speculative cycles related to devaluations. When the public expects a devaluation, there is a tendency to hold more foreign currency. Thus, in the last quarter of 1988, capital exports reached $1.8 billion. The New Israel Shekel was devalued by 5 per cent in the last week of December 1988, and by an additional 8 per cent in the beginning of January 1989 — and capital imports in the first quarter of 1989 were $1.7 billion. Note that the operations of the private sector in foreign currency are subject to a wide ranging control. Still, the foreign exchange controller cannot prevent wide ranging speculative short-term movement of capital. This can be made as a derivative of foreign trade, and the volume of this trade is very high in Israel. Despite declarations of encouraging foreign investments, direct foreign investments have not played a major role in Israel.

Imports

One hears many exhortations in Israel about waste in imports because the country buys what some persons insist are 'luxuries.' These arguments, of course, do not make much economic logic. Increased imports to Israel have resulted from the increased size of the population, the rising standard of living, the increased domestic production (that necessitates imports of more raw materials) and the higher prices of many import items, such as oil. As to 'luxuries,' it is debatable whether or not a refrigerator or an air conditioner is indeed a luxury item in a hot climate like Israel's. Whatever one's point of view is on that issue, the lion's share of imports consists of inputs for production and exports. Without the imports of raw diamonds, one cannot export polished diamonds! Hence, the Israeli economy is strongly affected by changes in world economy.

An efficient economy cannot reduce imports of raw materials for exports or for essential needs of the population. The imports to Israel grew because of a combination of the needs of a larger population, increased standards of living, larger defense needs, price rises in world markets, and increased exports (necessitating more inputs of raw materials and components). The major imports to Israel are investment goods, production inputs, fuel, and consumption goods. In the import of services, the major items are investments, transportation, travel and insurance.

Total demand for imports to Israel depends on the import components of the various sectors of the economy. In 1988, for example, Israeli imports were $20,982 million. Out of that total, $11,861 million were goods, and $6,187 million, services. Direct defense imports were $2,106 million and imports from the occupied territories were $827 million. Production inputs were $8,936 million (including $1,062 million for fuel and lubricants and $2,429 million for raw and polished diamonds), investment goods imports were $2,071 million. Consumer goods for direct consumption were $1,549 million, from which $734 million were durables, such as cars. There were also some adjustments. Clearly the lion's share of imports are for production or for defense purposes. The composition of imports has not changed much over the years, except for the oil bill, largely influenced by price differences. Imports of consumption goods have been around 10-12 per cent of total imports since 1960. Almost all imports were investment goods or inputs for production. Imports of investment goods have always fluctuated as a result of the economic climate. As we have already noted, defense imports also fluctuate dramatically.

Rising prices are the leading factor in dollar value import increases: in particular, oil prices jumped 12.5 times between 1973 and 1979. In both 1986 and 1988, prices of oil went down. Raw diamond prices increased 3.3 fold in the 1970s. Between 1970 and 1979, investment goods prices increased 2.5 fold and consumption goods, 2.7 fold. A very dramatic increase in defense imports, partially as a result of changing concepts of strategy, also took its toll and has already been discussed.

Finally, based on input-output tables, imports can be allocated to their final use. The share of civilian imports going to exports grew steadily, reaching 31 per cent in 1982, but then reduced to 29 per cent in 1987 and 1988. Since 1984, the share going to private consumption has increased, reaching 25-6 per cent. Public consumption took 4-5 per cent, and direct defense imports, 9-12 per cent. Investments were 13-14 per cent of imports, and capital services and miscellaneous, 17-25 per cent.

The main service imports are freight and transportation ($1,258 million in 1989), Israeli tourism abroad ($1,288 million in 1989), and insurance ($86 million in 1989). The transportation imports grew from $50 million in 1955 to $120 million in 1965, $600 million in 1975, $947 million in 1985 and $1,216 million in 1988. This item includes payments for port services, leasing etc. Israeli tourism abroad has become a significant item since the 1960s, as a result of rising prosperity and easing of controls, and has been growing fast ever since. Israeli tourism, it was $2.2 million in 1950, when 35,000 Israelis went abroad. In 1965, 100,000 Israelis went abroad and the amount spent was $45 million. In 1975, outgoing Israelis tripled to 300,000 and the cost was $160 million. In 1985, Israelis spent $549 million as tourists abroad and in 1988, $1,130 million. The craving to go abroad is partially a result of the need to leave, for at least a time, the tiny country. The fastest-growing item was investment income ($2,646 million in 1989). This item represents interest on foreign loans and dividends accruing to foreign investors. Increased foreign debt (and higher interest rates) made this item the largest in the service account.

The geographic distribution of Israel's international transactions has changed considerably. During World War II, the Middle East supplied over half of Palestine's imports. In the 1930s, it had supplied about 15 per cent. In 1948, all neighboring countries severed relations with Israel and all foreign trade stopped.

In the early 1950s, direction of trade was affected to a large extent by the lack of foreign currency. Israel maintained strong economic ties with the United Kingdom. However, the ability to finance a transaction was even more important. Israel signed clearing agreements with different countries. Clearing agreements provided that imports will be paid for by exports and not by Israeli currency. Using a clearing agreement, Israel could not buy the cheapest imports, but had to base its trade on barter transactions. Once foreign exchange shortage became less acute, these transactions were discontinued. Imports not made by barter were financed by US grants and loans in 1949-53. Then, the growth of German reparations in financing the imports increased the share of that country as a source of imports. In 1955, the share of goods imported under clearing arrangements was 19.1 per cent. In 1962, this share dropped to 4 per cent.

Beginning in the 1960s, imports came largely from the United States: about one-fifth to one-quarter of the imports. Two-fifths of Israeli imports came from the EEC. Germany and the United Kingdom each accounted for about 10 per cent of all imports. Japanese exports to Israel were only 0.5 per cent of Israel's total imports. By the latter half of the 1980s, the EEC and EFTA supplied a total of 56-64 per cent of imports, excluding raw diamonds, oil and direct defense (in 1989, 54 per cent). Imports from North America were 22-31 per cent (in 1989, 23 per cent), and from the rest of the world, 11-15 per cent (1989, 23 per cent).

Export of goods

No country can indefinitely import raw materials and industrial components without exports. Moreover, Israel is too small to achieve an efficient production scale in a wide variety of products by serving home markets alone. Attempts to protect production of such items against foreign competition result in higher prices and inefficiencies. In the long run, growth must come from increased exports.

To understand why Israel has economic problems, it is instructive to look at the pattern of its exports. The economy can be thought of as a portfolio of industries and of firms. The portfolio of Israeli exports of goods has changed radically several times since 1948. In the 1950s the main export commodities were citrus and polished diamonds. In 1949, these two items consisted of over 80 per cent of all Israel's exports. At that time, total exports were only $28.5 million, covering only 10 per cent of imports. In 1955, it was $90 million, covering 25 per cent of imports. From then until 1967, the exports grew in real terms by 15.7 per cent p. a. In the period 1968-72, the real growth in exports was 11.4 per cent, and until 1977, 9.6 per cent. In the 1980s, exports did not grow, and even declined in real terms. Israel started exporting by exploiting its natural resource advantages: its climate allowed it to produce high-quality citrus fruits, and later, other agricultural products; the Dead Sea gave it potash and bromine; and the Negev, phosphates. Special relations with other Jews abroad (and the problems faced by the Belgian industry during World War II) allowed it to excel in diamonds. Later, Israel developed exports based on special advantage at home: its own needs for sophisticated defense equipment, and the fact that this equipment was battle tested, gave Israel an advantage in military arsenal, from which it could export more than $1 billion. Israel also developed expertise in agricultural techniques for arid climates. It could export its drip irrigation systems and similar products. Again, home market requirements gave the impetus. Jewish firms abroad gave Israel a market outlet for some food and textile products.

Diamonds are still the largest export branch. It began in 1939, when several diamond cutters from Belgium and entrepreneurs from Nathanya started to come together. Contacts between South Africa and the centers of polished diamonds in Belgium and Holland were cut off by war in 1940. As a result, Israel was able to establish itself as a major production center. After the war, the Israelis were able to maintain relations with the Diamond Syndicate. Exports, valued at $12 million in 1950, increased to $56 million in 1960, more than $200 million in 1970, $550 million in 1975, and $1.41 billion in 1980. During the early 1980s, the market and prices collapsed, causing a rapid decline in Israel's exports. Since 1982, the market has recovered and Israel has captured some share from Belgium. The value of these exports began to return to the 1980 level and then surpassed it. Diamond exports were $1.26 billion in 1985, $2.55 billion in 1988 and $2.74 billion in 1989. The industry has close to 85 per cent import contents, reducing its significance to the nation's exports earnings. Its value added per employee, however, is higher than in the other manufacturing branches. In 1987, value added per employee at product prices in diamonds was NIS 42,000 while the average for manufacturing industry excluding diamonds was NIS 35,000. Value added per employee was lowest in textiles: NIS 17,000; and in food, drinks and tobacco, NIS 27,000. Because of these characteristics the share of diamonds in industrial production is only 4 per cent, compared to 27 per cent in value of production and exports. The competition of new polishing centers (India, USSR) has been intensifying. This competition was strong in particular when the world demand was mainly for small stones, a more labor intensive process than the cutting of large stones. Today, Israel is specializing in bigger stones, and is the second-largest exporter of polished diamonds. Note that this extremely successful export branch has been much less subject to government control than any other economic branch in Israel. In fact, for many years the diamond industry was effectively exempt from maintaining books and keeping other records for income tax purposes. Note also that diamonds are traded as commodities: there are no brand names in diamonds.

The second item of exports was citrus products, with very high value added. Citrus exports were $17 million in 1950, $47 million in 1960, $86 million in 1970. In 1980, it was $237 million, but since then the value of citrus exports has gone down. By 1989, it was only $131 million. With time, the exports have diversified, and value added has been reduced: many items were manufactured or only assembled in Israel with their value added lower than the extremely high one achieved in citrus products. By the mid-1950s, import substitution policies helped create some local industry. Industrial exports also increased, aided by multiple exchange rates, clearing agreements and barter. In 1958, for example, only 35 per cent of exports were paid for in foreign currency, 60.5 per cent were done on clearing agreements and 4.5 per cent through barter. In that year, total exports were $90.9 million, of which $34.1 million were agricultural, $22.6 million diamonds, $32.8 million industrial, and $1.4 million others.

Industrial exports were not always the kind that brought benefit to the local economy. Exporters acquired dollars at one rate and exported at another. As one example, Kaiser Frazer's assembled cars were purchasing components acquired for foreign currency and selling the cars in all sorts of barter deals (for example for Colombian coffee).

In the 1950s and the 1960s, a significant percent of industrial exports was less than profitable from the national point of view, and was based to a large extent on the availability of subsidies. In 1958, a study made by Michael Bruno showed the average effective cost of a dollar of agricultural exports to be IL1.57 to $1 US. Diamonds were IL1.73 = $US, but textiles were exported at a cost of more than IL4 = $US (the official rate of exchange was IL1.8 = $US). These kinds of distortions continued for many years.

In the 1960s, the diversification of Israeli imports came by increasing manufacturing exports with much lower value added than that enjoyed by agriculture. The exporters were in the main import substitutors. Production was carried out to meet the requirements of the domestic markets. Goods were exported only when they could not be sold at home on the basis of individual transactions and a surplus mentality, not on a long-term strategy. In 1965, traditional industries accounted for two-thirds of total exports. Some exports came from natural resources: potash and phosphate.

In the late 1960s, it was clear that import substitution policies would not create major growth in exports. An office of the Chief Scientist was created in a number of ministries, the most important of which was that in the Ministry of Industry and Trade. Chief Scientists received a special budget for encouraging knowledge-based industries by investing in industrial R&D projects with export potential. The emphasis on defense and knowledge-based industries led to a rapid realization of this purpose. Exports from knowledge-based industries have grown rapidly. Total exports in current dollars increased three fold between 1966 and 1973; those of the sophisticated sectors increased ten fold. In 1989, high-tech exports accounted for half of all exports of goods.

In the state-owned sector, the military industries rapidly developed export markets (chapter 6). Other industries that grew fast on the basis of exports were textiles and clothing: despite many failures, a series of mergers created larger and dominant firms. This was also a period of increased influence by financial institutions. Other important developments were the creation of the Corporation for Industrial Financing and the establishment of Israel Chemicals for all chemical industries in 1968 (since 1971, the company has dealt only with inorganic chemicals). Chemical exports, only $3 million in 1955, increased dramatically, reaching $850 million in 1980 and about $1.3 billion in 1989. Moreover, a growing per cent of the export was of Israeli innovations and developments.

Since 1973, industrial exports have grown at a much higher rate than domestic industrial production. Sectors which fared best were those which increased their exports most. The major exporters are metal products, electronics, transportation equipment, chemicals, clothing, foods, beverages and tobacco, as well as mining and quarrying. The two last branches are raw material based. Food products are largely based on local vegetables (citrus, tomatoes, frozen vegetables). Most firms are small, compete against each other, are seasonal and sell through large distributors on a private label basis. Mining is capital intensive, and made up of mainly government-owned companies (phosphates, potash, bromine, salt).

Total industrial exports (excluding diamonds), in current dollars rose more than eighteen fold from $389.3 million in 1970 to $7,023 million in 1989. Those of the textile and clothing industry increased six times, from $98.2 million in 1970 to $626 million in 1989. Those of transport equipment rose from $15.1 million in 1970 to $649 million in 1989, and of electrical and electronic goods from $12.8 million in 1970 to $1,429 million in 1989. Moreover, in 1965, modern science based industries such as electronics, chemicals, transport equipment, metals and machinery accounted for 37 per cent of output. By 1985, they accounted for 56 per cent. Their export growth rate between 1965 and 1984 was 16 per cent in real terms, compared to 9 per cent in the traditional industries (food, textiles, clothing, wood, paper, printing, rubber and plastics), which accounted for the rest of output.

Since 1970, an increasingly larger per cent of Israeli exports came from high-technology industries and was based on Israeli designs and original research. These are the products in which Israel has a strong comparative advantage. However, these are also the areas of endeavor that by their very nature are less susceptible to a central direction of governmental planners. The simplistic division of the Israeli economy into 'traditional' and 'sophisticated' is largely insufficient to analyze international trade. High value added per employee can be gained in exporting fashion design (classified as 'clothing') while parts of the electronics industry are based on low wages per employee.

In 1970, diamonds, agricultural products and clothing and

textiles made up 69 per cent of exports. By 1985, these three sectors represented only 41 per cent of the nation's exports. Over the same period, electronic products, chemicals and minerals, metals and machinery and transport equipment grew from 23 to 49 per cent of exports. Since 1980, the export of the first group shrank in terms of constant dollars (when constant means deflated by the US GNP deflator) by over $1 billion. The new export branches were not growing fast enough to compensate for this loss, so that total exports in the period 1980-85 declined by $815 million.

The share of exports of industrial products increased three fold between 1958 and 1988, thus making a major contribution to the internationalization of the economy. In 1958, only 15 per cent of industrial products were exported. In 1965, the percentage rose to 20 per cent of all products; in 1985, it was 48 per cent. By 1988, the weight of exports in industrial production reached 50 per cent. These figures are based on input-output analysis. Therefore they take account of the final destination of the intermediary products used in the production process. For example, the value added of industrial inputs to exported agricultural output is included in exports. This change in the structure of exports was a result of a few strategic decisions made decades before.

The diversification of exports was pronounced in all branches. Agricultural exports increased first in cotton, then in more eccentric products such as avocados and mangoes. However, the growth of agricultural products was constrained by water availability.

In terms of geographical distribution, the largest market for Israeli exports used to be the United Kingdom. In the early 1950s, it took 30 per cent of exports. By 1970, this share had fallen to 10 per cent. The largest buyer, particularly of diamonds, has been the United States. Israel signed a preferential agreement with the EEC in 1964 (and this agreement was replaced in 1975 by a free trade agreement). Yet the EEC's share in Israel's exports has not increased since the mid-1960s. In 1988, Europe took 44 per cent of Israeli exports, North America 26 per cent and the rest of the world 30 per cent.

Much of the macroeconomic work is concerned with industries. From a public policy perspective, it is also useful to look at firms and their ability to achieve a competitive advantage. This point of view is in particular relevant in Israel, in which only a few major firms export. In fact, in 1985, fully 50 per cent of Israel's manufacturing exports were made by 18 firms, some of which are a part of the same holding company (such as the different subsidiaries of Israel Chemicals). Further, the corporate concentration of industrial exporters is increasing. In 1982, 4 firms exported 25 per cent of industrial exports. In 1985, only 3. It took 23 firms to export 50 per cent of industrial exports in 1982. In 1985 the number was 18. More than 188 firms exported 75 per cent of industrial exports in 1982; in 1985 the same was done by 71 firms. Industrial exports tend to be concentrated in other countries, too, but the concentration in Israel is higher. For Israel to increase its exports, it needs more firms that are able to compete in the world market. Obviously, steps should be taken in the short run to ensure that more firms will export in the long run.

Many existing firms cannot be expected to export, at least not on any important scale. They are predominantly sheltered from foreign competition. Some of them were established for import substitution reasons. Their ability to compete in Israel stems from barriers to entry for imports: either because of high transportation costs as a per cent of total price (limestone, cement, disposable diapers, building materials); or because of the need for proximity to the markets because the products are perishable (bread, milk, produce); or because of the importance of quick local service (industrial cranes, repairs); or because they are difficult to transport (sulphuric acid). Others are sheltered because of customs, duties, or other government protection, having been created for employment reasons. Some of them are capital-intensive and cannot compete with the much larger firms operating in the world markets (for example steel and paper). Growth generated by the development of these firms is restricted by the size limitations of domestic demand. Many of these firms can defend their domestic position in an open economy, even though they cannot necessarily export.

In the event some of these sheltered firms *did* export marginal production (in fact, even cement was exported), they did so only because of the large subsidies given to them directly or indirectly (investment grants related to exports). Furthermore, exports were often a condition for an 'approved enterprise' status. As a result, some industrial exports have been carried out at a loss in order to receive the benefits. The vast majority of Israeli exporters are import substitution firms, not export-oriented companies.

Non-sheltered firms are those that produce world-traded products and services. Many of these firms may be expected to export only marginally, mainly because the firm is large in Israel but small in world markets (cigarettes, paper, many food products).

Export of services

Service exports in 1989 were $6,233 million, about 56 per cent of the merchandise exports ($12,486) and not much less than industrial exports excluding diamonds ($7,023 million). Yet, the traditional adversarial reaction to services still affects the discussion of these exports. Most analyses of the exports concentrate solely on merchandise.

Some of the exports of services have to do with returns on flows of funds. When an Israeli bank holds financial assets abroad, and receives interest on those assets, this interest is technically exports of services. An important part of the services are the revenues from tourists coming to Israel. These revenues are very volatile, and depend on the security situation in the country. Israel's service exports also include transportation and communication. Transportation and communication are divided a follows: one-third for ground transportation; one-third for ocean transportation and ports; 17 per cent, communication; 17 per cent, air transportation; and 1 per cent storing and fuel transportation by pipelines. Some of the transportation exports grow as a function of industrial exports' growth. Much of this export is transportation of export goods, but about $500 million ($568 million in 1988) comes from transportation among foreign ports.

The plan for Israel's economy for 1985-90, issued by the Economic Planning Authority in June 1985, projected growth in incoming tourists of 5.3 per cent a year and increased revenues from tourism by 5.5 per cent p.a. in real terms, reaching $1,455 million in 1990. Tourism receipts, in 1989, were $1,468 million so the goal may be reached in nominal dollars, but not in dollars of 1985 value.

Clearly, tourism, transportation and other forms of services exports can make an important contribution in increasing Israel's foreign exchange earnings. Unfortunately, government policies do not help these exports, and often even impede their growth.

Table 7.4 shows the number of tourists entering Israel. Theoretically, Israel should have a very high inflow of income from tourism. First, the country has more sunny days than many other countries; second, it has great seashores. The gulf of Eilat is certainly a tourist attraction with its corals and the very good weather during the winter months. In addition, Israel is also the holy land to Christians and Jews. Pilgrims came to the holy land even before it was as convenient to do so as today. Still, the number of tourists to Israel, when compared to very similar tourist nations near the Mediterranean such as Spain or Italy, is not very high.

Table 7.4 Tourist arrivals by country of residence, and tourist revenues

Country of residence	1960	1970[a]	1975[a]	1980[a]	1985	1986	1987	1988	1989
					Thousands				
Arriving tourists	114.0	441.3	549.1	1,175.8	1,264.4	1,101.5	1,378.7	1,112	1,177
Asia	6.0	29.0	75.2	42.3	75.1	83.4 }	93.1 }	105	113
Africa	5.8	16.8	36.1	39.5	31.0	32.8	36.1 }		
Europe	40.9	185.9	839.8	718.5	677.0	665.3	839.8	712	696
America	59.5	202.2	380.1	355.3	456.0	297.0	380.1	315	293
of which USA:	49.7	166.9	293.5	284.7	367.0	211.7	293.5		
Oceania	1.5	7.0	23.9	16.1	23.0	18.7	23.9		
Not known	0.3	0.4	5.7	4.1	2.3[b]	4.3	5.7		
Revenues according to balance of payments ($ million)	55.0 (1965)	100.0	235.0	902.8	1,101.0	799.0	1,041.0	1,161	

Source: Bank of Israel, Annual Report, 1989, chapters 2, 6.

Notes: [a]Till 1984 through 1985 'not known' has been included proportionally in the countries. [b]In 1984 cruise passengers.

The government aided the construction of hotels, subsidizing the original investment. The number of tourists to Israel grew from very few to 44,600 on average in the 1950s. In 1960, Israel had for the first time 100,000 tourists. By 1965, the number reached 300,000. In 1970 the number of incoming tourists was 441,000. In 1979, the number of incoming tourists (excluding cruise passengers) exceeded 1,000,000 for the first time; in 1980, it was 1,175,000. The peak was in 1987 with 1,378,700 incoming tourists. In 1988, despite a growth in world tourism of 9 per cent and despite the festivities of the fortieth anniversary of the State of Israel, the number of incoming tourists decreased by 14 per cent to 1,112,000. It increased by 6 per cent in 1989 to 1,177,000, because of the political uncertainty and perhaps also as a result of higher prices: the revenue from tourism in 1988 were equal in nominal terms to that of 1987, despite the drop in tourists numbers, reflecting increased prices. In 1989, revenue from tourism rose by 9 per cent to $1,470 million.

Government policies and the ability of firms to export

Israel's ability to export enough in the 1990s to cover its import needs depends on the competitiveness of Israeli firms in the world market. This, in turn, depends on changes in the market place as well as changes in government policies and firms' strategies. A detailed analysis of Israel's export potential clearly shows that without major changes in the economic environment the country will not be able to achieve economic independence. Structurally, exports are based in the long run on firms that enjoy competitive advantage in the world market. Government policies are of utmost importance, too.

To be sure, Israeli firms export not only to get the highest return. Many export to preserve the level of employment, to develop resources free of local constraints or to utilize surplus capacity. The defense sector, for example, often exports to preserve employment and remain in its state of readiness for a possible increase in domestic needs. State-owned and Histadrut enterprises, in particular, preferred continued export drive, even at a loss, rather than facing a need to fire a large number of workers. This policy is sometimes rationalized by the need to maintain a position in the market. Exports also continue simply because contracts were signed months, even years, in advance and cannot be changed because of an abrupt change in government policy. In these cases, firms adjust to the new reality by not taking export orders for future delivery; and the result of the fixed rate of exchange is felt two or three years later, as evidenced by the gloomy export situation at the end of 1988. In 1986, several large firms continued to export at a loss caused by the frozen rate of exchange, hoping for better times in the future. Firms also continued to take orders on which they barely broke even to avoid reduced employment.

Moreover, a number of kibbutz industries are capable of product development or enjoy already clear competitive advantages, mainly in products for agricultural uses — from irrigation to PVC sheets for hot houses. That could lead to enhanced export, but this would be taking its toll in terms of ideological beliefs of the individual kibbutz. Because ideology calls for avoiding hired labor, each individual kibbutz attempts to maintain a size commensurate with its limited manpower supply — or, in some cases, to enter into partnership with another kibbutz — but is reluctant to grow even if it has market potential. The central kibbutz organizations were depicted as 'insurance companies, not charging premiums. They help or guarantee plants in trouble, but have no say in the decision to erect the plant.' Kibbutz voluntary organizations attempt to learn how to use their combined strength, cooperating in R&D or marketing. Thus, although kibbutz industry has highly motivated workers and very high capital intensivity, they may work in one shift because kibbutz members refuse to work second or third shifts, and do not expand the plants (and exports). A kibbutz movement promotional tract explains:

> We make some unusual demands of a factory. It should be small and efficient so that our members can work it alone without the need of hired laborers. We don't want to grow into rich bosses making money off the labor of others; we want to be independent and we want every worker to know that he is an owner, not a salaried hand making money for the boss.
>
> Sometimes, though, our factories are too successful and too demanding of labor and some kibbutzim have decided to hire outside workers. Many of us think that bringing outside workers to the kibbutz contradicts our values.

Almost any government policy — be it monetary, fiscal, aid to R&D or regional development policy — affects the environment in which the firm operates and the competitiveness of the firm. In this sense, all government policies have an impact on the balance of payments. In Israel, as we have repeatedly pointed out, the government has always played a major role in economic development. It created a complex network of programs, taxes, subsidies, domestic and international agreements and many *ad hoc* decisions. All of these components affect the traded sector of the economy and its ability to compete internationally. Further, macroeconomic theory tells us that if a country does not want to increase unemployment, it can reduce the import surplus only by a reduction of one of the domestic uses (and in a case of export-led growth — relative reduction in the uses). Therefore, if a country simply devalues without making sure that other policies will simultaneously reduce local demand to free resources for export, it may simply create inflation, not additional exports. In the specific case of Israel, the country has been unable to achieve a real devaluation since 1954. Real devaluation means a rise in prices received by exporters *relative* to the local prices or relative to local costs.

In this chapter we deal with the international transactions of the Israeli economy. Therefore, we shall analyze only those government policies that directly pertain to balance of payments. It is well to remember, however, that this distinction is rather an artificial one. Thus, encouragement of capital investments in specific regions reduces the cost of capital to the investors (and in Israel, this cost was negative for many years) making these endeavors more profitable. Exports are based on relative profitability. In other words, if the firm can get a higher return in the domestic market, it may decide not to export.

In point of fact, in the specific case of Israel, decisions made in the 1950s and 1960s to develop the Negev (including expensive searches for minerals), disperse population and provide employment in remote areas resulted in many failures. But it also added to the development of the mining and later the chemical industry by the public sector, which then also developed defense-related industries.

During the late 1950s and 1960s, the government increased its investment in and allocation of funds to industry emphasizing import substitution. This resulted in the relative (but not absolute) decline of agriculture. Industrialization of the kibbutzim reinforced this trend. Attempts to disperse population led to investments in development towns, and the erection of plants in these towns — mainly textiles — as a major source of employment. As shown in chapter 5, these textile firms were heavily subsidized. Later, the government had to bail out textile companies in order to maintain the basic economic infrastructure in some development towns, but several strong firms emerged, acquiring many of the less successful ones.

The 1967 French embargo led to a decision to reduce

dependence on military equipment imports — and to a fast growth of these industries (see chapter 6). The Katchalsky Katzir Committee (1968) recommendation led to the introduction of R&D subsidies to build up Israel's knowledge-based industry. Defense and defense-related production has however dominated total national expenditure on R&D.

These decisions, in retrospect, created a major structural change in Israeli manufacturing employment and mainly in the composition of its exports. The time required for a firm, in particular one new in technology business, to develop into a major export company (and in the case of high tech, the rate of failure) has to be appreciated. Thus, since 1961, only ten new technology-driven entrepreneurs' start-up companies have reached over $15 million in export sales. Only three of them reached that level in less than ten years.

Furthermore, out of sixty-six start-ups funded by the office of the Chief Scientist in the Ministry of Industry in 1980 and 1981, two firms achieved unqualified success exceeding $10 million in annual export sales by 1986. Nine were modest successes, reaching $1–5 million in export sales by 1986. Thus, a total of 17 per cent had succeeded to some degree by 1986. Fully 52 per cent had failed entirely, and 32 per cent remained in question in 1986, with less than $1 million in annual sales.

The final verdict on many start-ups can take more than the five or six years. A 17 per cent success rate after five years is an estimable achievement. This record is not as impressive as that of Silicon Valley at its peak, but it is close to the rate achieved by the United Kingdom between 1950 and 1975. One may conclude that thousands of new entrepreneurs should start operations in the hope that a minority of them will be very successful.

Strategic decisions were, of course, very important, but government policy encompassed more than just these decisions. First, the government has played a major role in directing available credit and subsidizing capital investments. Second, the government attempted to compensate for the overvalued exchange rate by levying import taxes and by giving special premiums (later, exchange-rate insurance) to exporters (and also by granting them import tax and duty rebates). The government also encouraged exports by a program of export-risk guarantees and by negotiating a duty-free access to the EEC and the US. The government did not choose to have a high enough exchange rate.

The policies to be discussed here are the foreign exchange controls, the policies pertaining to the effective rate of exchange, the international agreements, export risk guarantees and tax rebates. Imports and exports in a specific year were of course influenced by the gap between the actual exchange rate and its equilibrium level as well as the effective rate of exchange for each specific item. For certain short periods, the Ministry of Finance gave priority to balance-of-payments considerations over fear of inflation. In other times, domestic economic problems directed a freeze of the exchange rate. Almost always, the government used a variety of subsidies to give exporters a higher rate of exchange. This was based on specific decisions for each particular item.

Since the establishment of the State of Israel, the country has faced foreign exchange problems. The Palestine pound was fully convertible to the British sterling. The Israeli newly created currency did not enjoy that automatic convertibility to an international means of exchange. Further, the country could not export enough to gain sufficient foreign exchange to meet demand. The Israeli government had to design policies to decrease the demands for foreign exchange and to enhance its supply.

The Israeli government has always been concerned that a free market for imports at an equilibrium exchange rate would result in the importation of luxuries, while low income persons would remain without basic necessities. The government opted for a system of foreign exchange controls, rationing all expenditures by requiring licenses and requiring all receipts to be sold to an authorized foreign exchange dealer, and through it, to the central bank. Foreign exchange controls have also been used as a barrier to the import of consumer goods that were made in Israel — irrespective of the cost of production in Israel compared to world price. Very often, inflationary pressures widened the gap between the official and the market equilibrium rate of exchange. In some periods, balance-of-payments considerations took priority. In others — domestic policies were considered more important.

Until the end of 1975, Israel adhered to a fixed exchange rate system. Devaluation under this system has always been overdue, usually taking place after the system deteriorated, when the gap between official and black market rate had become very large and an increasing number of international transactions were being made outside the official system. One reason for these delays was that a devaluation was interpreted as a sign of weakness. Thus, the first devaluation, in February 1952, came about only after foreign exchange reserves were completely exhausted. It took until mid-1954 to reach what was considered then an equilibrium rate of IL1.8 = $US. This rate was held until February 1962, when it was changed abruptly to IL3 = $US with dire consequences. One of the results of this large devaluation, it will be recalled, was that the government had to agree to an abolition of the linkage of its loans. It was unable to reintroduce linkage of its loans until 1979.

In 1975, a system of crawling peg was introduced, allowing a monthly devaluation of 2 per cent. This change had become necessary because of the much higher inflation levels in the period after the 1973 war. In October 1977, the system was replaced by an ostensibly free fluctuating exchange rate, that could change daily either by going up or by going down. In reality, the Bank of Israel intervened in the market heavily. To be sure, for a few months the new system did fluctuate almost freely with a minimum intervention, resulting in major fluctuations in short-term movements. In particular since March 1979, however, the Bank of Israel has determined the rate. Given the basic fact that the private sector sells less foreign exchange than it buys, the Bank of Israel could easily determine the daily rate. Thus, in effect the exchange rate is determined by government fiat, not market forces.

The regulation and control of all foreign exchange transactions adds more complexity to the work of a business firm. The firm has to get a license or a special permit for any one of many different transactions. Thus, without Bank of Israel approval, an Israeli firm cannot establish a subsidiary abroad, nor can it close its exchange position by forwarding shekels against dollars. As in any other situation requiring a special permit, there is a great deal of room for bureaucratic discretion. Furthermore, the need to get approval when one wants money for travel abroad is a nuisance that adds to the costs of operations.

Israel's reliance on extreme foreign exchange controls was relaxed in October 1977, when the government announced a major reform, eliminating or easing certain controls, in particular on travel. Israelis were also allowed to keep up to US $3,000 or its equivalent in foreign currency. However, the framework of controls, specifically on capital movements, remained and most of the regulations were tightened again later.

The *official* rate of exchange in Israel was rarely equal to the *effective rate of exchange*. The latter is the rate actually received by sellers of foreign exchange, or paid by the buyers. The effective rate of exchange has been changed much more frequently than the official rate, and has always been different for different transactions. On the selling side, exporters have always received a much higher than official effective rate of exchange and the effective rates were different among different groups of exporters. Thus, an exporter of services, for example someone receiving royalties from abroad, rarely received any premium over and above the official rate, while exporters of manufacturing goods received a bigger premium. Premiums for some goods, such as textiles, were often much higher. On the buying side, importers had to pay a much higher than formal rate of exchange because of levies of customs, tariffs, evaluation of the imported good at a higher than invoice price, purchase taxes and so on. Exporters received rebates on import taxes they paid on imports used for exports.

In the 1950s, premiums for exporters were granted on the selling price of the goods. This system allowed many manipulations based on an arbitrage among effective rates of exchange more than on economic profitability of the export. Later the premiums were granted on the basis of the value added in exports or on the basis of the so-called 'cost of a saved dollar.' Thus, if the value added in exports (export less both direct and indirect import components — all denominated in a foreign currency) is the denominator and the total direct and indirect costs of the export denominated in local currency are the numerator, the fraction shows how many units of domestic currency have to be spent for local resources in order to get one unit of foreign currency of value added in exports. This fraction is thus the cost of the saved dollar, and since the mid-1950s it has been an important method of calculating the economic viability (or the cost to the economy) of different exports. Premiums to exports were given only for the value added. Yet, the calculation itself still left quite a lot of maneuvering ability. Indirect costs were those for the economy. Thus, the cost of fuel oil in producing electricity is shown as an indirect cost for each firm using electricity. The calculation in each specific case could involve haggling between the economists of the Ministry of Trade and Industry and those of the firm. Thus, although subsidies were given according to the value added level, the value added level itself was a subject of bargaining between an exporter and a government civil servant.

In the 1960s, the government took several additional steps to assist exports and improve the balance of payments. It created state-owned export firms or organized government-sponsored export cartels for canning, cotton yarn, metal products, raincoats and edible oils, as well as regional export firms (to Africa, Latin America, Far East) and later a holding company (Alda). The Israel Company for Insurance of Foreign Trade Risks was created, as well as an agriculture export firm (Agrexco) and many other exporting firms. These exporting firms were expected to aid small firms' exports.

The government signed trade agreements with the EEC in 1975 (which apply mainly to industrial commodities), and with the US in 1985. These agreements have been part of a long-term liberalization of the economy, moving away from import substitution towards reliance on exports as the engine of growth. Israel is the only country enjoying trade agreements with both the US and the EEC.

Since 1981, the government has also provided exchange rate-consumer price differential insurance. This is designed to protect exports from the ravages of domestic inflation. The measure has not been cut, despite budget stringency in 1985-6. This example illustrates the importance ascribed to exports in government policy. Exports also enabled manufacturing to grow. The rate of direct and indirect exports in manufacturing output including diamonds was 19 per cent in 1965-6, 36 per cent in 1980-81, and 40 per cent in 1986-8. In human capital intensive branches, these shares were 18 per cent, 40 per cent and 46 per cent respectively.

From the point of view of the businessperson, a most important ingredient of any government policy is its consistency and continuity. The uncertainty created by the frequent changes in government policies, some of which have been applied retroactively, is one of the entrepreneur's major problems. A related concern is that of a lack of universal rules: too many factors are 'negotiable,' depending on the whims of a civil servant. This, in turn, makes government 'largesse' perceived, at least somewhat, like a windfall.

As the businessperson sees it, government officials fail to understand the difficulties of the export market. Moreover, the government assumes a first claim on the nation's resources, leaving to the business sector only what is left. Taxes are levied according to perceived government needs, without any consideration of the devastating effect on incentives or productivity. In addition, they claim, public employment has been growing (although public consumption has decreased) despite several decisions to reduce the public sector's work force.

The development of an export market is a long and costly process, and shifting exports from one country to another is complicated. Yet government economists say if the fall in the value of the dollar makes Europe a more promising market, then exporters should shift to the latter. Although they agree that industry should respond to market signals, businesspersons note that the response takes time. In the interim, exports to the dollar area began to fall or stagnate before those to Europe had increased. Exporters feel that the complexity of such adjustments is not appreciated by the authorities.

Israel's economy is closely linked to the dollar, and between 1980 and 1984, this partial linkage worsened the economy's competitiveness in Europe. On the other hand after the introduction of the new economic policy in 1985, Israel's exporters to the US had a difficult time because of the frozen rate of exchange, despite increased costs. Exporters to the EEC fared better because of the devaluation of the dollar. In 1988, the New Israel Shekel (NIS) had been effectively revalued *vis-à-vis* the dollar: the domestic price increase was higher than that abroad, but the rate of exchange was frozen. At the end of 1988, the government saw no option but to back down from its policy of a frozen rate of exchange. The NIS was devalued. Several additional devaluations followed in 1989 (in January and June).

Terms of trade

Since 1973, as a result of large changes in prices and world-wide inflation, foreign trade figures in nominal dollars have been liable to lead to serious misinterpretation of the figures. There are a number of ways to measure real export or import growth. None is perfect. One possible means is to deflate the figures by the US GNP deflator. This has the advantage of making international comparisons possible but the disadvantage of being affected by the differences in US dollar exchange rates with other currencies.

An index constructed by the central bureau of statistics measures the changes in a basket of export commodities. This index captures real quantity changes in exports, but less so changes in prices. Some series are calculated in constant NIS, others in nominal dollars.

Commodity prices increased dramatically after 1973, and then again in 1979-80, largely as a result of the two oil shocks. In 1980, commodity import prices were three times higher than in 1972. These changes affect, of course, the welfare of the people. Yet estimates of gains or losses are based on somewhat arbitrary assumptions. One such estimate was calculated by Nadav Halevi. His results are reproduced as Table 7.5. The gains or losses from changes in terms of trade are computed in column 1 by asking 'What could last year's exports have bought this year, given that import and export prices did not change in the same way?' The second column estimates the losses resulting from the

Table 7.5 Estimated gains and losses from changes in terms of trade, 1973-82[a]

Year	Gain or loss from export (1)	Loss from long-term transfers (2)	Gain from interest payments A (3)	B (4)	Total annual gain or loss A (5)	B (6)	Total annual gain or loss (-) as % of imports A (7)	B (8)
1973	-104.0	-751.2	34.8	34.8	-820.3	-820.3	-0.15	-0.15
1974	-127.8	-628.6	63.3	110.4	-693.1	-646.0	-0.10	-0.10
1975	-70.7	-169.5	20.3	182.3	-219.9	-57.9	-0.03	-0.01
1976	61.7	-58.8	7.8	200.9	10.7	203.8	0.00	0.03
1977	177.1	-257.6	11.4	231.8	-69.1	151.3	-0.01	0.02
1978	115.1	-418.3	63.0	374.3	-240.2	71.1	-0.03	0.01
1979	-289.2	-716.0	103.1	557.7	-202.1	-447.5	-0.08	-0.04
1980	-219.5	-706.3	154.5	1,168.8	-771.3	243.0	-0.06	0.02
1981	75.9	145.9	-29.2	958.9	192.6	1,180.7	0.01	0.08
1982	269.9	223.4	-63.8	1,137.4	429.5	1,630.7	0.03	0.11

Source: Halevi in Ben-Porath, 1986, p. 253.
Note: A includes gains from interest payments from price changes during the year; B includes gains from interest payments from cumulative price changes.
[a] Columns 1-6 are expressed in millions of dollars.

fact that the unilateral transfers and long-term capital transfers sums were determined before the rise in import prices. Inflation means gains on fixed interest payments, and these are calculated in columns 3 and 4.

The Bank of Israel shows in its annual reports the changes in the terms of trade in various ways. One is Israel's export prices versus those of the OECD; another is terms of a basket of five currencies, weighted by the composition of Israel's international trade. In addition, the index of raw material prices is shown. This is important in the case of Israel, since much of her exports is raw materials intensive, and thus sensitive to changes in the prices of the raw materials. An analysis of the impact of each of these factors is too technical for the purpose of this book.

Comparative advantages of Israeli firms

Non-sheltered businesses can be divided according to the nature of their assumed competitive advantages. One means of doing so is to categorize businesses according to the portion of the cost structure that is most significant in determining competitive position. This can include raw materials purchasing, manufacturing processes, marketing and distribution, research and development or applications engineering. These components are parts of the cost structure of every business, but usually only one or two are decisive in determining success in a particular business segment.

When Israeli manufacturing exports are analyzed in terms of their sources of competitive advantage, 70 per cent are raw material based, defense-oriented, or based on special relations, as in the case of the diamonds, or on unique knowledge, as in the case of agricultural technology. The rest of the industrial exports come from many small export quantities. Since the late 1960s, a new breed of Israeli business has begun to develop products solely for international markets, based on niches that had not been developed by larger firms in other countries. By the mid-1980s, there were several hundred firms that aimed primarily at the export market. Most are in the area of advanced engineering, although the list includes also textile, clothing and plastics firms. Nine of these firms, each exporting $20 million or more, accounted in 1985 for half of the exports of the export-oriented business. The rest of Israel's exports came from import substitution firms. The exports of these firms are, by definition, limited: most of these firms export limited quantities on a marginal cost basis and often as a private label.

309

Unless a major structural change increases dramatically the number and variety of the Israeli exporters, it is difficult to see how Israel can achieve a goal of an export-led growth aimed at reduced balance-of-payments deficits. Israeli raw material based exports have either declined or reached a plateau. They are unlikely to revive significantly. In agriculture, the water constraint makes it difficult to increase exports without a major structural change in production. In addition, Brazil has emerged as a formidable competitor in the concentrated citrus market and Spain in the fruit market. Citrus sales declined in both volume and prices, due not only to competition but also to fluctuating exchange rates and adverse weather conditions. Earnings from exports of citrus fruits reached a peak of $247 million in 1981-2, but declined to $115 million in 1983-4. By 1986-7, they were $200 million. In 1988, the quantity exported declined by 21.6 per cent, and prices went up by 12.4 per cent, resulting in lower export revenues. In 1989, quantities went down by an additional 21.9 per cent and prices decreased by 4.7 per cent — resulting in revenue of more than $131 million. In raw materials based chemicals exports, it is difficult to increase the level of extraction. Unless the firms integrate forward to special chemicals and a higher value added, a major increase in exports is unlikely. Defense companies have confronted serious difficulties in the mid-1980s, but since then have been showing much more resilience. The export of defense products, however, is subject to wide fluctuations. In addition, Israel is inherently limited in the countries to which it can sell. Even though there are many possibilities to increase these exports, it may not be wise to raise the share of these exports out of the total because of the portfolio risk.

Usually, small firms find it hard to export. In Israel, most large firms do not export at all, being either public utilities or banks, or export less than a third of their output. In this category are firms in food, clothing, petrochemicals, paper and civilian communications. Many of these import substitutors have become highly diversified in order to grow, but their production is subscale in international terms in all areas. They are protected by natural and by artificial import barriers

Many of these companies achieved limited export penetration, in the 1960s and 1970s, by opportunistically establishing relationships in selected countries and exporting to them, often by covering only their marginal costs. In some cases, exports were pursued only in the short term in order to gain an 'approved enterprise' status. The exports of many of these firms declined when lower-cost competition intensified. Often, the exports were unprofitable for the economy. These companies do not have the long-term perspective nor the desire to make the major investment of time and money required to gear up for the sustained export growth. Many of these firms have a reputation for going into markets when demand exceeds supply with high prices and pulling out when competition intensifies and prices drop. They are sometimes viewed as unreliable in supply, sometimes breaking commitments in a tight market if another customer offers a higher price. They are also seen as unresponsive to specific market tastes, and lacking product quality needed for significant export penetration. Most of these firms are provincial rather than international in outlook. Their managers learned to lean on the government and to achieve various subsidies in return for helping in promoting certain goals such as more employment. For these firms the transition to sustained exports is an extremely difficult one. This transition might become easier if exports became a national priority, not unlike the pioneering of the Yishuv period and the military in the first two decades of the state.

There are four main potential sources of increased exports (1) growth of established major exporters; (2) the emergence of new firms of substantial scale by growth of export oriented small rapidly-growing companies; (3) existing exporters pursuing higher value added segments; and (4) the formation of new (small) firms entering the export market.

In the short run, very few additional firms can be expected to export on a large-scale basis. The majority of Israel's exports will continue to come from a relatively small number of firms. In the long run, if exports are to grow significantly, national policy must seek to facilitate the development of thousands of new firms of smaller size. Start-ups and small firms provide the seeds from which more exports can be accomplished, even though this takes a long time. Thus, in 1985, 75 per cent of Israeli industrial exports was accounted for by the 71 largest exporters. Only 9 of them were established after 1971. Further, in 1985, there were 22 firms exporting $40 million or more. Only 3 of them were established in the 1970s, and only 1 of them in the 1980s.

Understanding the comparative advantage of Israeli firms in the world market highlights important reasons for Israel's declining industrial export performance. It also points to the policy changes needed. In order to achieve a high level of exports, many new entrepreneurs would have to flourish. The surplus mentality shown by many Israeli firms would have to change completely; the government policies would have to be designed to foster this large number of start-ups. Therefore, the government would not be able to continue its centralized operations, controls and regulations. It would also have to reduce its grip on the capital market.

If no major changes occur in either the international relations of Israel or in the domestic economy, existing firms cannot be expected to achieve the rate of exports required for Israel to be economically independent. To achieve economic independence, major changes will have to occur in people's beliefs, firms' strategies and government policies. A national effort to change this situation both at the firm and the government level will be possible only with public recognition of the necessity of exports.

Conclusions

Israel's foreign trade is large and growing: since 1970, the long-run trend has been for exports to increase their share of GNP by 25 per cent, while imports increased theirs by only 18 per cent. The difference in their base levels has meant that the serious balance-of-payments problem has persisted. Most financing of the import surplus depends on political factors, for example the friendship of the US government. Even if one assumes an indefinite continuation of defense aid, it would be only prudent to base the economic policies on an attempt to achieve a balance in the external accounts by increasing exports in order to cover import needs, in particular if Israel's defense burden remains at the same level.

There are only very few new major exporters in Israel, and, in several of its major export businesses, Israel has reached a plateau. In the past, Israeli exports were based on obvious competitive advantages, for example potash or phosphates and later defense-related items. These businesses cannot grow as they did in the past without a change in direction — either in products or in markets. For such a change to occur on a large scale, Israel will have to transform its attitudes toward profitability. It will also have to relax government controls over the economy. Israeli firms will have to transform their culture, and the country will have to adapt its institutions, decision-making modes and criteria for operations.

The question of the capital inflow and the import surplus is directly related to some political rather than economic factors. Clearly, one way of solving many of the economic woes of Israel is to reduce the huge defense burden, and tourism may be invigorated by peace with Israel's neighbors and less threat of terrorist activities. This question is related to one's belief system about the future of the occupied territories and the ability to rely on formal agreements with the Arabs.

Under existing institutions, there is an inadequate motivation to achieve export growth, both at the government and firms level. The ability of Israel to increase economic efficiency is impeded. One prerequisite is a voluntary, cooperative regulation of conflicts over economic and social issues. Only by convincing civil servants, labor union leaders and business managers to impose strict limits on domestic quarrels and conflicts can one hope to make export-led growth a national goal. It must be recognized that all segments of society are in the same boat and everyone must help to pull the oars if a national goal is to be achieved. Such a national consensus has been reached in the past on issues such as defense needs, absorption of immigrants and the struggle to achieve economic independence. If successful exporters are to be seen as 'national heroes' and export success to be a source of pride, not envy, there is a high probability of increased exports.

8 Israel as a moving target

Introduction

In many ways, Israel is no different from other small countries, attempting to define and maintain for themselves a place in a world increasingly becoming globally integrated. It is one of the few states founded by a migration of settlers, implanting new settlements and forging new institutions in virgin territories perceived to be uninhabited. In such new societies, the founders create a new social order, and do not have to take into account the traditions of an entrenched population. To be sure, the land to which the pioneers came was not totally empty (nor were other new countries). However, they built new institutions, ignoring any indigenous social order, be it the 'old Yishuv' or the Arabs. The frontier experience, the ideological motivation, the creation from scratch of new institutions, the revolutionary nature of the society and the transplantation of ideas from homeland to the new environment are all common to all new societies: Australia, Canada, New Zealand, the Republic of South Africa, or the United States.

Israel is unique among new societies both by being developed on the basis of socialist principles and in being created by immigrants from Eastern Europe, not by settlers from Britain or Western Europe. Later, Israel was to be unique because of its move from a dominance of socialist thinking to a strategic alliance with the US. This shift was a result of a decline of the importance of ideology concomitant with an increase of Soviet antagonism toward Israel, but also a growing evidence that socialist orthodoxy did not work. Stalin's assassination of almost all Jewish writers in 1952, and the persecution of Jewish doctors in 1953, certainly did not make it easy even for the hardened ideologues to see the USSR as a friendly nation. Israel is also unique in the magnitude of the foreign unilateral transfers it was able to receive. The uncertainty regarding the continuation of these flows is a major factor in evaluating Israel's future political

314

economic problems.

Israel can boast of some great achievements but also some equally large problems. It is also a country with a very dynamic, ever-changing texture. Understanding Israel is like trying to catch a moving target. Its institutions keep modifying their shape and the society undergoes metamorphoses. Modifications have been a result of the confrontation with reality, often a cruel reality. To understand Israel, it is important to analyze the political, economic and cultural continuities and discontinuities. To understand what has been endured and what has been revamped, one should look for the informal relationships, not the formal systems. Israel is a tiny country, and a very informal one. The crucial question to be confronted is not what were the formal changes, but how did the informal system work? In previous chapters, the gap between the formal and informal was demonstrated. Thus, chapter 3 demonstrated how various payments were made, not through the pay slip to maintain the formal egalitarian rule, but to pay more to some. Even today, certain high-level civil servants and officials, and members of the Knesset get much higher pension rights (4 per cent for each year of work, starting almost immediately, or at age 40, rather than 2 per cent for each year with payments of pension starting at the age of 65 for most of the population). In many cases, titles of individuals do not reveal their real importance. A title of Deputy Prime Minister may mean that its holder is an extremely important individual, or it may simply be an empty title. The President of Israel has only symbolic power. These characteristics were detailed in chapter 4.

Israel is an extremely complex society, full of contradictions, and including a wide variety of entities, associations and polities. The Israeli society is a diversified body, insurgent to paternalistic authority, and rebellious against government authority. It is full of tensions, oppositions and bitter well-intentioned controversies. This book has attempted to portray a general picture of the political economy of Israel. In doing so, it was necessary to supply many details and many partial analyses. The danger of such a narration is that the main themes become obscure. The main purpose of this chapter, therefore, is to recapitulate some of the major themes and elaborate upon them. It summarizes the major trends and picks up the major threads.

Getting a perspective

We analyzed the interrelationships between economics, social fabric and political structure throughout the book. The buds of Israel's political economy may be found in the period immediately after World War I. The few immigrants who came to Eretz Israel in the first Aliyah did not have any central political institution. The World Zionist Organization started its 'Palestine office,' headed by Dr Arthur Ruppin, only in 1908. A Zionist leader, Menachem Ussishkin, convened an 'assembly of the Yishuv' in 1903, but the central political organization created there lasted only a year. The two main political bodies of the Jewish colonization movement in Eretz Israel — *Ha'va'ad Ha'leumi* (the National Council) and the Jerusalem Office of the World Zionist Organization (whose functions were transferred to the Jewish Agency in 1929) — were both created in the 1920s, under the British Mandate. The Balfour Declaration served as a recognition of the international community in the legitimacy of the Zionist vision to resettle the land of their forefathers and as an opportunity to implement that vision. By 1948, when David Ben Gurion, an immigrant of the second Aliyah, read the declaration of independence, stirring every Jewish heart all over the world, two millennia of a Jewish stateless situation ended. In a period of a few decades, the dreamers saw at least one facet of their dream materialize. The revolutionaries became the rulers of a sovereign state.

Israel's economic problems cannot be discussed without taking into account the heavy and growing burden of the defense toll on the economy. One result is the relatively large power of the Defense Ministry and its almost unlimited ability to get funds. The need for security was coupled with two other needs, dictated by the basic values of the state's leaders. The first was the burning belief, stemming from many generations of Jewish tradition, in the super importance of mutual aid and mutual responsibilities, and therefore in the necessity of immediate forging and implementing of social tools generally identified with a welfare state. The second stemmed from a utopian point of view of the Founding Fathers on the necessity of strict ideals of equality, socialism, and the superiority of the collective decision to what was perceived as a wild pursuit of affluence and private welfare.

The importance of mutual aid dictated a widely agreed increase in the level of economic intervention of the state and a rise in the size of the government budget. It also resulted in an inability of the economy to adjust to external shocks or to cope with the need to change the industrial structure even at a price of a temporary high unemployment. The second belief meant a general preference for societal requirements over those of the individual. Any theory based on Hedonism was perceived as improper for the special needs of the Israeli society and of building a Jewish Home Land. These problems do not stem simply from erroneous policies nor are they the result of bad luck. In fact, they are entwined in the social fabric of the country and its political structure.

The combination of these three factors with the gloomy reality of a less developed country, the general perception of inadequate sources of private capital and only a handful of private entrepreneurs all aided to reinforce the belief that the state alone could achieve security, social goals and accelerated economic growth. A widespread consensus that government should intervene, regulate and direct the economy developed. It was shown in previous chapters that the very high degree of governmental intervention in Israel and its deep involvement in decisions almost to the level of an individual firm had deep ideological roots. It is a consequence of the way the political economy had been developed during the Yishuv period and reached its apex in the 1920s. It is strongly based on deep ideological beliefs coupled with pragmatic political power considerations. As we shall see, the political leaders did not rely on ideology alone.

The government was also able to tap large sources of capital and therefore could decide on the allocation of that capital. If the government had been able to master political will and create the consensus required to avoid a mass protection of the domestic production, the collectivist type of decisions would not have necessarily caused severe misallocation of resources. The Israeli government, however, was very reluctant to open the economy to full-blown foreign competition.

Israel was able to achieve so many of its objectives simultaneously in part because it had at its disposal massive capital inflows that allowed a high rate of capital formation. The attempt to achieve simultaneously so many national objectives was also made possible by a willingness to sacrifice current consumption for later needs coupled with a high level of economic growth. Later, when growth stopped and private consumption continued to grow, the multiple goals were financed by a significant increase in both domestic and foreign debt. Total unilateral transfers increased dramatically in the 1970s and the 1980s, largely as a result of the jump in US aid. Yet the needs seem to have been insatiable. More importantly, Israelis shared a sense of common destiny, stemming from a long and tight struggle to survive and a strong feeling that there was no alternative. In the 1980s, this consensus was shattered, at least to some extent.

Throughout our analysis, we have stressed the major problems that have troubled the economy. First among these is the extreme dependence of the country on the continuation of a large inflow of capital to finance the very large import surplus. Almost since the first decade of Israel's existence, its economists have repeatedly warned that 'sometime in the next few years, the capital inflow will decrease substantially' (Halevi and Klinov-Malul, 1968, p.11). Economists were worried about the dislocations and the costs that would result from the necessary transformation of the economy to accommodate a lower level of capital inflows. Both because of luck and political astuteness, capital continued to flow, and the structural adjustments continue to be postponed. In 1952, Israel's net foreign debt was $375 million; in 1988, it was $18.6 billion. Between 1952 and 1964, the GNP tripled; and exports already covered about 50 per cent of imports. Between 1965 and 1972, GNP continued to grow by 8 to 15 per cent a year, except during the recession of 1966-7. Since 1974, growth has stopped and Israel's increased living standards have been paid for by a deterioration in the balance of payments, heightening the dependence on foreign sources of capital. One result was that foreign debt has reached record levels. Still, in the tables of world indicators, published by the World Bank, Israel's GNP per capita in 1986 ($6,210) ranked number 22 among the 117 countries listed in the World Development Report for 1988. It was surpassed by the rich oil countries, by 17 out of 19 'industrial market economies' (except Spain and Ireland) and by Singapore and Hong Kong.

Another major change in the 1970s was the first rejection of a sitting government in Israel's history. The election results of May 17, 1977, were the first setback for Labor since its victory against its major opponents in the Yishuv period and its ascendancy to the control of the Jewish National Institutions in 1931. This major upheaval, again, was interpreted in different ways by different sociologists and political scientists. Some stressed demographic trends relating to age and ethnicity that undermined Labor's base of traditional electoral support. Others saw the problem more in the public scandals that rocked the party and undermined public confidence.

In the 1988 elections, the ultra-Orthodox parties gained a bigger share of the votes, an outcome unpredicted by any of the experts that were carrying out public opinion polls. Anti-Zionist religious parties today hold the power to decide the form and structure of the Zionist state.

By 1970, Israel was no longer a closely knit society of

idealists and revolutionaries, nor were most of its citizens dependent on the government so that it could make them docile and obedient. The revolutionaries became leaders or bureaucrats. Their solidarity was not always extended to include the new immigrants, who came from totally different ethnic origins, cultural molds, and traditions. Their previous emphasis on obligations sometimes turned into a stress on entitlements.

These changes are a few of many that show the basic continuous changes in a dynamic society such as Israel. Israel is a moving target, in which things are still shaping out. They took place amid a constant threat to the very existence of the State of Israel. The increasing sophistication of weapons systems made it more and more difficult to rely on soldiers 'on 11 months' leave.' The army has become increasingly more professionalized, with professional soldiers devoting decades of their lives to military service, and leaving the service with very little that would prepare them for non-military life. Equity problems of the sharing of reserve duty burden were becoming important issues.

Israel was created as a Jewish state, and most of its citizens want to see it as a Jewish state. Unless Israel finds a way to attract many more Jews to live within its borders, the question of the relations between Israel in its pre-1967 borders and the Palestinians of the area (that used to be called the West Bank) would become more than a question of military needs, secured borders or ideological attachment to the land of the forefathers. There will be a need to discuss how to maintain the Jewish majority without becoming a garrison state or an apartheid-like regime. Different possibilities may be examined, including exchange of populations. The relations with Jews in the Diaspora are also going through a major transformation.

These themes are largely interrelated. They are in turn related to the ability of Israel to survive and finance its swollen current account deficit. The solutions to all these problems will have to come from within the nation. These solutions cannot be based only on economic science. Based on economic considerations in their narrowest sense, Israel cannot survive, and most of the elite can become much richer by moving to other countries. The forefathers of Israel, who created the *mythos* of the pioneer, understood that point very well. In the much more heterogeneous society that is the Israel of today, it is crucial to be able to reach new consensus, in which economic efficiency considerations will be taken into account. Otherwise, Israeli firms could not compete in the global arena. Such a consensus does not necessarily mean that Israel must adopt a liberal type free enterprise economy. It must, however, change the *mythos* to allow the new entrepreneurs to become the heroes of the future. While it is almost natural to emphasize the problems and difficulties, it is important to do so with some perspective.

Some dreams that turned into achievements

This book started by comparing the dreams and the reality. The dreams were mainly the creation of a new Jew, the build-up of a new and egalitarian society, the molding of a new culture, and the creation of a new, but based on the old, comprehensive model of social, economic and political structure — Herzl named his utopian description, 'the old-new land' (*Altneuland*). For the socialist Zionist, the new society was to be imbued with the contemporary socialist ideologies, but permeated with the Jewish social traditions and the mystique of the Jewish people. The nonsocialist leaders and the socialist pioneers collaborated to create new institutions and build a new economy. They, in effect, constructed a homeland for the Jews. They also forged central political institutions that maintained a large degree of quasi-state power and authority.

These dreams were assumed to be achievable by the sheer will power of the pioneer. Economic laws, it was believed, could be ignored as irrelevant. Those pointing out economic constraints were never well received in the Yishuv society nor in the Israeli one. The pioneers aspired to liberate the Jew from the Diaspora mentality by insisting on physical labor. They also aspired to expand the capacity of the country to absorb more immigrants. They attempted to achieve this revolutionary transformation, not to follow laws of economic profitability. Shimshoni (p. 224) points out that Israeli leaders are skeptical of experts. They would still remind anyone that when the Jezreel Valley was acquired in 1920, it was swampy and fallow. Foreign Zionists and experts opposed the deal based on what they felt was an objective cost-benefit analysis. Today, this valley is the heartland of Israel's flourishing agriculture.

The Zionist revolution that transformed persecuted Jews to proud farmers and soldiers in their own sovereign state started only a hundred years ago. To achieve its many dreams, it had to mystify the reality and to demand many sacrifices in the name of ideological beliefs. The core values were regarded as sacrosanct. The tiny community did not have enough of an economic base for the home market to develop its own industry and the new zealots refused to become simply a colonial minority living on the toil of the Arab worker.

As to reality, that depends on the period we are looking at and on the perspectives taken. Israel is a country characterized by sharp swings, abrupt changes and dynamic movement. Further, scientific research has begun to show some inconsistencies between official ideologically biased proclamations and reality, even during the Yishuv period. Thus, it was shown that the egalitarian ideal was not always a basis for actual pay, or that the pursuit of political power was a better explanatory variable than ideological announcements, or that Ben Gurion did not mold the army to be free of any political meddling.

In 1882, 20,000 Jews lived in Eretz Israel. In 1919, the Jewish population of Eretz Israel was 57,000. Between 1919 and 1932, the Jewish population grew by 8.0 per cent per annum. During the period 1932-1947, it increased by 8.4 per cent p.a. In the quarter century ending in 1948, the Jewish population in Eretz Israel grew eightfold. In 1948, when the state was proclaimed, there were 650,000 Jews in it; in 1988 — about 3.5 million. After 1948, the rate of immigration accelerated. By the end of 1951, the Jewish population had more than doubled again. The next doubling of Jewish population took two more decades, and since the 1970s the growth through immigration practially stopped, to be renewed in 1989.

Only 70 years ago, the area that is now Israel was a deserted land, neglected for generations and extremely poor. Its soil was largely washed to the sea, its forests were destroyed, and its rivers turned into marshes that had to be drained. The land did not have any electricity, road conditions were poor and small villages faced months of virtual isolation. In less than a lifetime, a group of dreamers worked diligently and hard to form a new nation, to restore a virtually dead language (one that was neglected and used only in prayers for more than two thousand years), to create some of the finest universities in the world, and to establish a network of political and economic institutions.

The country was certainly not one of milk and honey. However, it was turned from a weary and neglected place, infested by swamps and eroded by desert climate, to a mosaic of green and to a place where world records in milk production per cow or yields of several crops per dunam of land (and even more important — per cubic meter of water) were achieved by the obstinate devotion of many hard-working pioneers and by massive capital flows. Between 1922 and 1932, the GNP in the Jewish sector of Eretz Israel grew by 17.6 per cent p.a. (7.8 per cent p.a. per capita). Between 1932 and 1947 the growth was 11.2 per cent p.a. or 3.0 per cent p.a. per capita. The total stock of capital increased fifteen fold (Sicron, 1957; Szereszewski, 1968).

Moreover, in the first decade of Israel's existence GNP tripled; it doubled in the second decade. Finally, in terms of per capita product, the growth was 4.7 per cent annually in the British Mandate period, 5.2 per cent annual average from 1952 to 1972, and less than 1 per cent per annum since then. Thus, Israel enjoyed one of the highest rates of immigration *and* product growth in the world for about fifty years (from 1922, in the Yishuv period, to 1972). Since then, economic growth has come to a halt. Business firms have moved from stressing growth to emphasizing survival, from willingness to take business risks to hesitation, vacillation and irresoluteness.

The reasons for the arrest in growth have been studied by many of Israel's leading economists. It has been proposed that the growth stopped because of the escalation of oil prices, the worsening terms of trade, the zooming defense burden and the slowing down of immigration. Another reason for the changing fortune of Israel may have been its inability to adjust the institutions and the political weal to allow a return to growth, led by exports. This type of a growth strategy must be carried out by firms able to compete successfully in the world market. In the domestic economy, the government can protect industries, allow monopolies or procure products at higher than world prices. For example in order to achieve regional distribution of industries, certain firms may be favored. In the world arena, however, firms must compete in a free market and achieve competitive advantages. Moreover, export success is a moving target: competitors may increase their productivity, enhance their technological capabilities, or develop new products, making competition fiercer. Israel does not have many natural resource endowments, but does enjoy the availability of a highly motivated and well-educated labor force. This human capital should enable the country to compete in high-technology markets.

In the relatively short period of its existence, Israel's history is marked by many more notable great achievements. First, the country was not only able to absorb into its ranks a large influx of immigrants from more than a hundred countries, but also to mold them into a multifaceted culture of one nation, and more or less integrate them into both the economic and the social fabric of the country. Second, Israel was able to survive despite continuous threats from her neighboring countries and from Arab terrorists of different kinds. It successfully built a massive, strong and efficient military force that protected it in several and very frequent wars. It also developed an impressive array of military and security-related manufacturing industries, producing among others tanks and armored vehicles, jet aircraft, RPVs (remotely controlled pilotless vehicles), missiles, sophisticated communications equipment and some of the best and most reliable small weapons produced in the world. Israel also developed a network of agricultural training centers, that transformed persons with no knowledge or tradition in farming to skilled workers achieving some of the world records in agricultural production. Until 1974, Israel was also able to expand income per capita at a rapid rate.

In addition to these achievements, Israel developed a fine and notable network of social services. A large-scale program of social legislation was set in motion in 1953, when the National Insurance Institute was created, and more social legislation was introduced in the beginning of the 1970s. This second round has come about largely because of effective political pressures of the Jews of Asian and African origins but also because of guilt feelings of the old timers. One result has been the sharp decline in net taxation. While gross taxation increased, the transfer payments increased even faster. Gross taxation zoomed from 28 per cent of GNP in 1960-65 to about 50 per cent in the first half of the 1980s. Net taxation was 19 per cent of GNP in the 1960s and about the same ratio in the 1980s. Moreover, the activities of the National Insurance Institute mushroomed. The Institute levied high payroll taxes and increased the gap between the cost of labor to the employer and the net wages, but financed more social services and a free high school education. Further, there is a very strong sensitivity to human problems of adjustment. More often than not, the government was unable to implement a policy designed for economic recovery for fear of its impact on human misery and therefore on the probability of emigration. The threat of emigration is a very powerful tool that does not let the government apply too strong an economic medicine.

Agricultural experimental stations, after many trials and errors, found the most suitable crops for the land. Manufacturers, faced with innumerable difficulties, erected and developed factories producing extremely sophisticated products invented in Israel and sold in dozens of foreign markets. To be sure, not all investments were very wise. In fact, there is ample evidence that much of the investment resources have been consistently misallocated. A whole generation of medical doctors with great zest and indefatigable energy eliminated the many diseases, mainly malaria, and made Israel a model of health services, of hospitals provisions and of medical research. The rate of infant mortality per 1,000 live births, still 54.3 in the mid-1950s, was reduced to 8.8 by the end of 1987. The country enjoys an incredible diversity of newspapers and periodicals, theatres and concerts. The independence of judges and democratic institutions are zealously guarded.

Some dreams were simply achieved. Zionists spent many nights arguing on the differences between a national home and a state. Since 1948, the Jewish state has been a fact. The sovereign rights of the state are fact, as are the rule of law and the democratic regime. Now that the existence of the State of Israel is taken for granted despite its neighbors' rejection of its very right to exist, Israelis are groping to define a place for themselves and a new vision for their nation. Most of them came (or were born) after the state was established; not as pioneers believing in an ideology. They have to find a way for a tiny nation to continue to survive without being an integrated part of a larger trade block. They have to create, design and structure a new set of institutions, commensurate with changing economic reality and shifting ideologies. They also look for the best ways to define the unique bonds that tie them together as a Jewish state and, based on these bonds, the relationships between them and the Jewish people living outside Israel.

Once their dreams became a reality, some dreamers found themselves without new dreams. It is not easy to define the role of a Zionist outside Israel. It is also not clear that such national institutions as *Keren Kayemet* should continue to exist. Other dreams are moving targets. The State of Israel is a creative entity, changing continuously. It is a dynamic entity that has taken many forms in the relatively short period of its independent existence. Before discussing the many changes in the reality of Israel, some continuities should be mentioned.

Some continuities: the dynamic rhythm of unchanging trends

There are several processes that have been true throughout and are permanent characteristics of the Israeli political economy. First, Israel has always been seen as an alien wedge by its neighbors. One result was that since the beginning of Jewish new settlement, there was a need for armed vigilance and for self-protection. The high priority allotted to basic security needs had enormous repercussions to the whole way of life in Israel — as was shown in chapter 6.

Second, and often taken for granted, the very existence of Israel allowed Jews, for the first time after two thousand years, to live in their own sovereign state, free from oppression, enjoying the inalienable rights of free citizens in a democratic society, subject to the rule of law of their own making, free from any threat of cultural extermination. A new Jew, with a free upright walk, was created. Resisting any threat of physical annihilation, the Jews have become for the first time after two millennia responsible for their own destiny. Israelis strongly believe, based on the recent experience of the Holocaust period, that Israel must protect itself; that no other country would necessarily help them and certainly no other country will let all of them emigrate. Because of Jewish anxiety over the fate of Israel, some of them believe Israel is less secure than the dreamers believed it would be.

Third, Israel may be seen as a collection of successive waves of immigration. The Ingathering of the Exiles was always a major theme, and the successive waves brought into the country new human resources, new cultures, new ethnic groups — all of which had to be molded together — not always successfully.

The absorption of a very large influx of new immigrants also led to an increase in the income differentials among different ethnic groups of the population. The veteran Ashkenazi population has certainly increased its lead over the newcomers, and this problem has caused many difficulties. On the social front, the aspirations for the creation of a 'melting pot' and the integration of all the different Jews of all sorts of traditions and variety of heritage has turned out to be illusory. The tensions caused by the ethnic gap began to appear in the 1960s, once the major preoccupation of the new immigrants was not only to get basic shelter and food. Since then, the ethnic gap has become a major, and almost chronic, political and social issue that had strong impact on the economy.

Fourth, despite being in a state of siege, Israel kept its democratic institutions intact. The army was always subject to the civilian control. The courts were beyond reproach, and the mass media made sure that any ill-doings would be published rather than remain covert. To be sure, the fact that Israel has always been a liberal, pluralistic democracy does not mean that there were no informal ties between political leaders and army officers, or that pressure groups did not attempt to lobby and influence party oligarchies. However, it is certainly a true democracy in the West European tradition, very much unlike neighboring states.

Fifth, Israel aspired to be not simply another small country, but a light to the nations, a great cultural center and an outstanding scientific bastion for perspicacious scholars, artists and religious teachers, that will persistently educate the Diaspora Jews, making Israel a light beam of wisdom to the world. She has also been driven by a strong belief in social justice and the need for solidarity of all persons. Because these values were very strong, and came with dearly held beliefs in an egalitarian society, and because of the core belief in the Ingathering of the Exiles; the gap between income, wealth and status levels of Ashkenazi and Sephardi Jews was viewed with great anxiety. More importantly, Israel is often judged (and judges itself) according to much more severe moral standards than other countries. Thus, when Israel decided to expel eight Arabs convicted of many atrocities against Jews and Arabs, this decision was appealed several times, up to the Supreme Court. After about a year and a half, the Supreme Court rejected the appeal; the eight were expelled. This incident was reported on the front page of the *New York Times* and the UN Security Council met to discuss the expulsion in June 1989. In the same week, Bulgaria expelled 64,000 of its citizens of Turkish origin. Turkey protested, and the *New York Times* devoted a few lines to the Bulgarian cabinet decision in its inside pages.

Sixth, Israeli leaders were concerned that the individual citizens may be too weak, too greedy or too egotistical to work for the community and be subservient to the community rules. They therefore created strong central institutions that would limit the liberty of the individual to work for selfish objectives, and attempted to make sure that all individuals are obedient to the rules. This was achieved in the non-sovereign period of the Yishuv by centralized mobilization and allocation of resources. Moreover, the resources were mobilized from outside the constituents, therefore the problem of willingness to pay was less severe. It was also achieved by making individuals and individual organizations subject to rules of the game, designed to make the center decide for all of the members.

These rules of the game were naturally transformed when the sovereignty of the state became a reality. Yet the individual citizen was still expected to be subservient to the national needs, the government mobilized most of the resources and allocated more resources than it collected from the citizens. Most of the time, leaders totally disregarded economic calculations on deciding on what was perceived as a 'heroic' national project. Despite myths, the reason for this behavior was not that there was no other way to achieve such lofty national goals as the defense of the country and the absorption of the immigrants. The reasons were ideological and political. These beliefs led to another, perhaps most important to the topic of this book, distinguishing characteristic of the Israeli economy — the exceptionally large and prominent role of the government, and the dependence of citizens on government.

Government's role in the economy

The history of the Israeli economy points to continued increasing political influence on the economic system. Such political intervention occurred with preferences given to selected economic sectors, while ignoring market forces. Later, preferences were given to certain old timers in an extraordinary network of interdependence and mutually agreed central direction. Israeli governments, irrespective of their ideological leanings, never pursued policies leading to economic efficiency or to the operation of a free market economy. Political leaders believed that capital and labor markets were inadequately developed. They thought that given the infant state of Israeli industry, these markets could not be relied upon to achieve economic development on their own. Moreover, most political leaders perceived private wealth as theft and private greed was seen as anathema. The economy of Israel is very much politically dominated, in which total dependence changed into interdependence and to a government which is prisoner of its close relations with and past promises to different interest groups, with a national consensus calling for the achievement of too many tasks without any attempt to decide on priorities.

The leaders of the Zionist movement were in the main indelibly East European intellectuals. They spoke several languages fluently, possessing great eloquence and a high degree of intelligence. Most of them held several university degrees. They were all men of ability in their particular professions. They were not religious, and also had lost hope for the possibility of assimilation. The center of the organization was in Europe and its leaders only visited Eretz Israel once in a while. Only a few were West Europeans, and even fewer were Americans. Many of these leaders had a note of worldiness and elegance about them, always fashionably dressed, even with frock coats.

A cleavage between 'east' and 'west' appeared several times in the history of the Zionist movement, since the time Herzl proposed to substitute Uganda for Palestine, failing to understand the fixation of Jews on Eretz Israel and their inability to transfer their longings and dreams to another country, even as a temporary palliative measure. As already discussed (chapter 2), the American Zionist leaders, headed by Judge Brandeis, disagreed with the East European Jews on the role of *Keren Hayesod*. Both sides realized that the country had been neglected for generations. They were fully aware of the fact that its good soil had been washed into the sea and the valleys, and the reconstruction of the land to regain what had been destroyed, or the draining of the marshes could not be done unless they could be financed by national capital. They differed on the means of achieving these shared objectives.

We have seen that Weizmann was able to overcome Brandeis' resistance to a centralized organization. The synergy between leaders like Dr Chaim Weizmann or Dr Arthur Ruppin and the leaders of the labor movement created a cooperation system in which the pioneers were those expected to carry out the national development policies. Those opposing this cooperation were against the basic paternalistic and centralist system, created at that time and continued to this very day.

The covenant between the labor pioneers and the Zionist leaders meant that direction and intervention would increase. First, in order for the Zionist Organization to help the pioneers, who had zest and indefatigable energy but no funds and skills, the organization had to direct these persons, teach them and guide them in minute detail. Second, for the experiment to have any probability of success, people had to accept the preference granted to the labor communal settlements and the undaunted denial of funds to the private sector. Third, they had to accept that Jewish labor, despite its higher costs, should receive preference, and Jewish produce, again despite its higher costs, should be preferred to the cheaper Arab produce. These types of preferences are far from possible if one believes in the superiority of a free market economy.

For Ruppin, solitary settlers or a small village could not have survived in the face of the innumerable difficulties in Palestine. As he saw it, only the communal settlers could maintain themselves in the unsettled and remote parts of the country and their apostolic devotion could compensate for the lack of skills. The soil, neglected and abused for centuries, could be restored only in such a communal and unselfish effort. Since he (and others) believed that an agricultural base was the only way to create a new Jewish culture, he needed the pioneers to do the job. Other leaders were advocating development of towns and manufacturing, but their way was not accepted. This is not to say that cities were not built. In fact, city populations were always the majority.

The labor pioneers were able, because of their superb political organization and their agreements with Weizmann and the religious parties, to achieve a hegemony position in the Yishuv political structure. Ben Gurion became the leader of the Zionist Organization in 1935, and Labor continued to lead the movement (and the government) until 1977. For Mapai leaders, intervention was not only acceptable, but ideologically sanctioned. With time, the bureaucracy learned to enjoy the power of intervention and to behave as if they knew best what was good for the citizen.

The question of the degree of government involvement or that of the possibility to rely more on market forces was never allowed to be tested empirically. A national economy, unlike a chemical laboratory, is not an entity on which people like to make experiments when they believe the probability of success is extremely low. One important junction from this point of view was when the Federal Republic of Germany agreed to pay Israel reparations. At that time, as discussed in chapter 4, Israel again opted for a centralized political system, not for market allocation. The ramifications of this intervention on the degree of dependence of individuals and therefore on the ability of entrepreneurs to flourish was never widely appreciated. The leaders of that time distrusted the market and viewed profits as rewards to parasitism. The Histadrut pension funds refused to invest their reserves in land, always considered an inflation hedge, because this was considered 'speculation.'

The Israeli government controls the intermediation between private savers and investors, using domination to make investment decisions, despite a long history of constant misallocation of investment resources. The first finance ministers — Eliezer Kaplan, Levi Eshkol and Pinhas Sapir — enjoyed a significant level of political power and were totally autonomous in the determination and execution of economic policies. These three created a system of almost total identity between political and economic power, that reached its apex in the system of improvisation and a detailed and particular intervention on an *ad hoc* basis perfected by Pinhas Sapir. When Yehoshua Rabinowitz became a Finance Minister he used more independent experts in planning economic changes such as a tax reform system. Yet the political control of the economic system continued and the structure of the economy remained intact. This high level of political involvement was a major characteristic also of the governments created by the Likud parties. One result of government dominance has been a total dependence of most business firms on the government. The many who found the system intolerable (and some of them may have been potentially great entrepreneurs) did not invest in Israel, or moved to other countries, in which they sometimes were extremely successful. With time, some large business firms became less dependent on government funds, having accumulated more capital through retained earnings. One-sided dependence was gradually altered to a system of interdependence and of give and take within wide boundaries of an establishment.

The establishment includes not only the government but also the managers of the large firms in the three major sectors of the economy — having a sort of old-boy network. There are very high barriers to entry into that group and the economic system has remained highly politicized, keeping the newcomers, the small entrepreneurs and those unknown to it outside the establishment. One result is that it is extremely difficult for persons with new, daring and innovative ideas to get these ideas accepted. Since a free market does not exist, these persons cannot try the new ideas on their own, and civil servants are quite wary of trying unconventional ideas. Even consumers' protection institutions were financed (and their managers were nominated) by the political leaders in the government or in the Histadrut. Israel does not have independent non-civil service regulatory bodies, and too independent persons would not be nominated as directors in the state-owned enterprises. These positions are held as a source of political patronage and as means to repay political debts.

Despite a wider recognition that market forces may be a better means for resource allocation decisions, government bureaucracy and politicians found it extremely hard to give up even a little bit of their cherished power. Despite much preaching, government intervention deepened; and the diverse methods of the intervention continued, irrespective of the party of power. Government intervention shifted from rationing, *ad hoc* decisions and administrative controls to the control of virtually all sources of capital and their administrative allocation at varying rates of subsidy.

To a large extent, it is inappropriate to use a term like intervention when one considers the Israeli situation. The Israelis have always believed in cooperation and in mutual assistance. The seeds of the Israeli political economic system were sown during the 1920s. Since then, the system has been characterized by an extremely high degree of centralization and political arrangements and agreements on the allocation of public capital. The system was also based on a pluralistic economic system in which public, private and Histadrut sectors (and in the Yishuv period — a separate religious sector) coexist. The criteria for the existence of an economic entity were never its efficiency or its competitive strength. Rather, it was the ability of the unit to create employment. Israel also attempted to shield business firms from competition, thus creating a business culture in which export based on competitive advantage is neither nourished nor preferred.

In addition, the Israeli managers have learned that the success of the firms they head depends more on governmental decisions than on their success in navigating the firm to the right strategy in the marketplace. The government has learned that it depends on the business activities of some firms in attempting to achieve its goals and thus the two sides became interdependent. The Israeli economist dealt mainly in macroeconomic problems and both the business managers and the government failed to understand the meaning of these models. There was also a strong belief in the superiority of egalitarian society and in the desirability of avoidance of a class system. This avoidance was achieved to some extent by rotating managerial jobs.

In this type of an economic system, many entrepreneurs have always been institutional rather than individualistic, working for increased power, for the glory of their sector and for the expansion of the size of the firms they managed. Finally, the system had a heavy dose of political and security dimensions. In fact, political parties controlled the economic resource allocation.

For such an economic system to work, there were several important prerequisites. First, individuals had to be willing (or to be coerced to accept) to pay higher than world market prices for domestically manufactured goods. These goods could then be produced even at inefficient or non-world competitive prices, allowing the owners to pay the workers comparatively high wages. During the Yishuv period, this was achieved by an ideology emphasizing the importance of building a new economic base, and therefore strong social pressures to prefer more expensive Jewish-made products. Second, there was a need for a large influx of capital that would allow enough resources to be used — and in which uses did not have to be equal to domestically produced sources. As long as the additional resources came from grants that did not have to be repaid, the question of the efficient allocation of resources could conveniently be ignored. Once the deficit had to be financed from loans, the ability to repay these loans had to be considered, but politicians could always conveniently postpone this consideration. Third, the political system (and later the government) had to hold a tight grip on all sources of foreign funds and the intermediation between savers and investors. Fourth, the system necessitated a homogeneous population of persons willing to sacrifice private gains for the achievement of national goals, and ready to deprive themselves of all sorts of benefits in order to achieve various ends.

Since much of the funds at the disposal of the government came from outside, and since there was a widespread feeling that the government would bail out those who might fail and help each individual to get a higher standard of living, the system could continue even though the new generation believed in a very different ideology. This new generation readily and willingly got used to government clientele. In fact, individuals learned to expect the government to supply them with many services. Since those living in Israel today are not the pioneers but their descendants or newcomers, there is very little role left to the ideology. Individuals have very high expectations regarding the level of services they can expect from the government. Many escalated their demands for both more and wider array of government services. Every year, these demands intensified, and the ability of the government to supply all these needs with total disregard to costs have shrunk. Still, to this date the intervention of the government in every aspect of economic life in Israel is greater than in any noncommunist country in the world.

Being a coalition, the government was turned into a set of feudal estates of the different ministers, each one attempting to get and increase the largesse for those who voted for him or in whose value he believed. In this system there was no economic planning or strategy. Ministers generally believed that it was only the finance minister who should worry about the budget and its balancing. None of them were willing to cut the budget they were responsible for or even to reduce the many duplications among many ministers by giving up a function or a department. The legislative body has had very little influence on the resource allocation. The absolute control of the capital market and its ability to tap foreign funds allowed the government to achieve at one and the same time political-economic objectives, security goals, social justice missions and absorption of immigration. Most political leaders ignored any economic constraints and refused to take into account any economic reports that may have cast doubt on the economic justification of their cherished activities. They were unwilling to decide on priorities. The general consensus has been that Israel must achieve all goals simultaneously. At least until mid-1985, the driving force was the vision and the political will, not the cold economic calculations and the budget constraints.

A guilt complex

The final persistent theme related closely to that of the government's role is that of shame in any desire to have a better quality of life. Perhaps because of the long reign of the ideology, Israelis often suffer from a guilt complex. Throughout the period of modern settlement in Israel — starting with the Yishuv period and continuing uninterruptedly in the years of the state — political leaders, leading economists and influential newspaperpersons joined in giving the average citizen a guilt complex. Citizens were told they should be ashamed for wanting to consume more, that only such an irresponsibility causes the country to be in a bad economic state. The citizen should not prefer an imported and much cheaper Australian butter to the more expensive Tnuva butter lest Jewish farmers should go bankrupt. The citizen must refrain from even dreaming of owning such luxury items as a washing machine or a refrigerator. The definition of what is or is not a luxury item came, of course, from a government official, who also tried to explain to the North African Jews that they should change their eating habits and move to eat what so appropriately was called 'uniform' bread. Items such as furs were for some reason not considered luxury. Portnoy's Jewish mother set the pattern, and most leaders continued in building up the guilt complex. Newspaper articles accused the public of being too greedy and too consumption conscious. The failures of the political leaders were less well recorded. Yet most of the reasons for the scarcity of certain goods or for the continuation of a large import surplus or for the zooming of the country's foreign debt were not that the citizens were irresponsible. If anything, the Israeli citizens were both responsible and docile. They paid one of the highest rates of taxes in the world, they served in reserve duty an endless number of days, they were willing to work hard for relatively low wages (and were constantly told by economists that their wages were too high!). They also saved. In fact, private savings in Israel have always been high, increasing from 22 per cent of GNP in 1955-62, to 28.8 per cent in 1963-72, and 35.3 per cent in 1973-7. Since then, savings have been reduced to 30.6 per cent in 1978-82 and to 20-27 per cent later.

To be sure, Israeli citizens attempted to find small means to protect themselves from a constant barrage of governmental directives and to anticipate the next (and frequent) change in these policies before it occurred. In short, they attempted to be rational human beings. The government, in turn, behaved as if it was omnipotent. The government also designed a hundred and one ways to discriminate among its citizens. The Ministry of Housing did not simply help a citizen to acquire a house. It had regulations on the location of the house, the size of the flat, and the materials used in the construction. These were related to the number of children, the income of the parents and many other variables. New immigrants to Israel were allowed to bring many household goods exempt from customs. They were not exempt from going through all kinds of bureaucratic mazes in order to implement these rights. Even in the middle of the 1980s, the Ministry of Housing attempted to allow a new immigrant to receive government participation in rent only if the flat were less than a certain size. The general rule has always been: the leaders know best, the political party has all the wisdom, the private citizen should be disciplined. Certainly, he should not look for even legitimate loopholes. Anita Shapira, an historian of the period, often emphasized that the leaders despised the masses. The government also dissaved. Until 1966, its deficit averaged less than 4 per cent of GNP. Between the 1967 war and 1972, it was 15 per cent. After the 1973 war, it jumped to over 30 per cent in 1973-5. Between 1975 and 1984, it ranged from 20-27 per cent. The government deficit only saw a serious drop in mid-1985.

While the ordinary citizen suffered from excessive bureaucracy, high taxes and need for licenses for almost anything, some privileged individuals were exempt from taxes or the need for licensing and often received government largesse. One can give many examples of largesse: allowance of a larger per cent of construction rights out of the land if a construction firm agrees to sell a certain number of flats to young couples, subsidies to public transportation, a cartel for the marketing of fuel, taxi licenses, import licenses, a large number of unrealistic rates of exchange, and so on.

As one small example, in the summer of 1983, the Knesset enacted a law forbidding deceit in Kashrut. Of course, no one lied on Kashrut before, and fraud has always been illegal. But the law allowed the religious parties many more patronage jobs. This law gave the Chief Rabbinate monopoly power to grant Kashrut certificates. Places of business had to pay for Rabbinical supervision, so that the certificate would be granted. The irony of the law was that the extremely pious ultra-Orthodox Jews would not recognize the supervision of the Chief Rabbinate and have their own supervision organizations. The costs are paid by the secular individuals.

While these trends have been persistent, there were also important changes. The 1977 elections results were to many the first sign of the political change. This change, however, had long roots in many ideological, social and cultural changes.

The Six Days War, which left Israel in control of a million and a half Arabs, led to many questions. The unification of the various political centers of power under Mapai hegemony was replaced by multiple political power centers after the upheaval of 1977. The rapid pace of economic growth ceased and was replaced by stagnation. It was recognized that, being a tiny open economy in a global setting, Israel could not continue its existence based on a constant flow of capital grants. If the country were going to pay its own way, it would have to mold new institutions capable of competing in the world market, and to promote a belief system recognizing the need for global competitiveness. Such a system may simply be based on unfettered market operations. It could also retain the spirit of cooperation as long as the need for world class efficiency is recognized. This system may be possible because of the many gradual changes and some of the major discontinuities that can be identified in Israel.

Some discontinuities: the changing reality

The generation of pioneers who came from Eastern Europe was united in its ideological proclivities. Their ideology was nurtured from the socialist beliefs of Eastern Europe. In the Yishuv period, leaders and other pioneers spent their years in endless debates among various points of view on the vision of the nation they were to build and the meaning of their life. They had a strong and continuous sense of mission. For them, those who had different views were arch-enemies, who should be ostracized from any duty, and boycotted with contempt.

The Zionist movement called on individuals to place themselves at the disposal of the community in order to serve national goals, sacrificing private interests. Some of the movements extended this requirement to all walks of life; others emphasized the importance of national goals only on issues related to defense or to political objectives. For them, the allegiance to the nation did not include the economic sphere. Later, the disappointment with the anti-democratic manifestations of the USSR moved Israel to create a western state, an ally of the United States. The ideology shifted, and its base was deteriorating. It was not shared by the second and third generation, who have been great believers in pragmatism. The power of the search for a new Jew has dimmed. Now Israelis look for a higher standard of living or a higher social status.

Many of the new generation in Israel look to North America for inspiration. Most economists in Israel are trained by the Chicago school tradition and believe passionately in the superiority of the free market system. Often, this belief is mingled with socialist slogans, still remembered from earlier participation in the Youth Movement's activities. The institutions of Israel, however, are those molded and shaped by the forefathers according to their ideological beliefs and needs. As one example, moshavim in Israel are subject to a law that gives all power and prerogatives to the moshav association, with very little discretion to the individual member. Many of the young generation feel this is wrong, but none were able to rebel effectively to force a change in the law or the regulations. Another example is the system of elections — both in the country and within the political parties. Already elections within parties have begun to be made under different, more democratic and participative, rules from the 1980s. Young Israelis would also hope to see changes in the proportional representation system.

Many Israeli social scientists emphasize the central position of ideology as an engine moving the first generation. Many leaders in Israel were portrayed as preoccupied with ideological controversies. Many of the economic achievements are attributed to a high level of motivation, stemming from ideology. Medding (1972), who studied the operations of Mapai, concluded that its control was based on consensual agreement, that is, on its ability to mediate among various social groups achieving consensus. Yonathan Shapiro (1984) emphasizes the role of a ruling elite, believing this oligarchy gained control of the political party and the Histadrut and used this control to achieve dominance.

Second, and perhaps the most misunderstood shift, is that of the ethnic composition. In 1948, Israel was a country composed mainly of Eastern European Jews, with a few coming from Asian and African countries and a minority of North American Jews. By 1970, the majority of Israelis were of Asian and African origin.

Despite swift progress in terms of their educational and economic statutes, Jews of ethnic origin still perceive themselves as deprived persons. Therefore, Israel may be about to go through a whole series of changes not only in terms of its economic institutions but also in terms of the ethnic origin of its leaders. The majority of positions of supreme power in Israel are still largely held by Jews of Eastern European origin.

The ethnic revolution is still in process. It first looked like a major rift. The oriental Jews were described as human dust, that would have to be re-educated to be absorbed into the existing culture and the existing predominantly Ashkenazi society. These efforts were clearly ill directed, and obviously failed. Oriental Jews, feeling deprived, voted mainly for Likud. Labor was perceived as being a secular, arrogant, elitist, intolerant, and paternalistic establishment. It was remembered that Labor tried to get the new immigrants' votes through material inducements. Once the new immigrants learned more about the political system, and once they were less dependent on the establishment for their means of livelihood, they shifted their votes in protest to the Likud, in particular since Mr Begin was perceived as more appealing to religious Jews, being himself an observant Jew. Note that most Sephardim Jews are religious or at least maintain the tradition. Indeed, the elections of 1988 have shown that many Sephardim would vote for ultra-Orthodox religious parties.

These considerations lead us, thirdly, to the role of religion in Israel. The country started as a secular society. Herzl and many of the Zionist leaders were anti-religious. The ultra-Orthodox did not recognize the State of Israel. Formally, Israel (unlike other Middle Eastern countries) is a secular state, with no 'official' religion. At the same time, religious feelings and traditions are of utmost importance in Israel, and the Chief Rabbinate has a very elevated status. One paradox of Israeli life is that, in 1990, the anti-Zionist ultra-Orthodox persons may be those who will determine the future of the state. Clearly, neither the Labor nor the Likud are able to create a government without these ultra-Orthodox representatives; many of those come from the Sephardi side, and their power has grown tremendously.

The fourth consideration is the changing culture. The first Aliyah, the Old Yishuv, attempted not only to create a new Jew, but also a new culture: different from the second and third Aliyah and their Russian-inspired culture, which clashed often not only with the culture of the first pioneers, but mainly with Polish-inspired symbols of Betar, the Revisionist youth movement. It created the ideal and mythos of the 'Working Eretz Israel' (*Ha'Ovedet*). The first generation of immigrants looked with awe at the growing Israeli born. The native born embraced pseudo-military careers with much zeal. They had a different way of speaking and developed their own lingo and their own culture, known as the Palmach culture (ironically, one of the main creators of this culture was born in Poland as Tehilim-Zeiger, and changed his name to Dan Ben Ammotz). Most Israelis changed their names to sound both Hebrew and Biblical. Israel's diplomats had to change their names to Hebrew sounding ones before they took a foreign assignment.

The old timers attempted to impose their culture on the newcomers, but the oriental-inspired culture is totally different. Today, a unique Israeli culture is still in the process of creation. It is also a very heterogeneous one. The ultra-Orthodox Habad movement attempts to 'market' to the secular Jews a new religious culture. Each Jewish community tends to have its own traditions, symbols and culture — cherished for many years in the country from which the community had emigrated.

Three more metamorphoses should be analyzed in detail. They are the question of intergenerational relations, the changing relations between Israel and the Diaspora, and the changing relations of Israel and the Arabs. There are also other forces that seem to divide Israel and cause people to fight and argue. However, there are more unifying forces, overriding the dissimilarities. These consist of the roots of the country that give it strength and preservation. Although the ethnic differences are very important and traditions are dissimilar, all Israeli Jews share a common religious heritage. Second, all Israelis share a passionate belief in nationalistic objectives. Third, Israel has enjoyed a dominant political culture based on an extreme confidence and a sense of belonging.

Intergenerational relations and conflicts

The family atmosphere of the Yishuv period has changed as a generation grew who saw the existence of the state as obvious as opposed to miraculous. This generation was born into an atmosphere of sovereignty, and the Zionist yearnings for redemption did not stir them. They preferred an organized country, with a high quality of life, to pioneering simplicity, the pioneer ethos and the weight of extreme equality. This new generation was nicknamed before the Six Days War 'the espresso generation.' They did not accept the socialist heritage of the Founding Fathers. Instead, they believed in free enterprise and in market determined competition. As they saw the situation, the old politicians were corrupted and defiled. The majority of the young generation either did not want or was not allowed by 'the old guard' to be contaminated by politics. They made their mark in a military career, in scientific achievements or in being successful lawyers or in other professional pursuits. This generation was shocked from the political oversights that became clear in the 1973 Yom Kippur War. It then tried to achieve change, but since seems to have lost patience.

The domination of the strong leaders of the Founding Fathers generation left the country without successors. The leaders born in Eretz Israel learned from childhood to conform and to obey, not to think independently. By the end of the 1960s it was already clear that none of the political parties was able to replenish and raise a new generation of leaders from within. The main place from which new political leaders were sought was the army. Ex-generals were 'parachuted' into high-level government positions by both major parties. The Likud was fused by an ex-general, Ariel Sharon. These generals, however, were unable to give the country a new vision.

Those born in Israel are known as Sabras. Like the desert cactus fruit whose name they bear, Sabras are said to be a bit prickly and tough on the outside but tender and sweet in the inside. They were adored by many as the manifestation of the new Jew: strong, athletic, and generous. Yet, the Sabras were unable to create the new leaders of the nation.

As a result, one of the most difficult problems is that of the successors to the existing national leaders. Yonathan Shapiro of Tel Aviv University claims that:

> In Israel the Zionist socialist leaders exploited during the formative period of the creation of the political-party system the severance of the new immigrants from their society and culture. They erected a political, economic and cultural structure that aided in the social and cultural absorption of the immigrants and in so doing were successful in imposing their party on the system and to achieve a spiritual dominance and political control.
>
> (Shapiro, 1984, p. 155)

The problem, however, is that the first generation of leaders enjoyed complete totalitarian control. The second and third generation still have not found their place. The Israeli-born generation is sometimes confused. It certainly looks for new meaning in life. The ideology of the Founding Fathers generation may be dead, but it is recognized that one must make sure that some norms for communal life are maintained.

The native-born generation excelled in the military, in scientific endeavor and in the management of large administrations. They also attempted to take over various parties, but all these attempts ended in failure. The native-born generation was able to penetrate the power elite and to reach its summit only after the old generation leaders died or were forced to resign their posts as a result of the Yom Kippur War. The first native-born prime minister was Yitzhak Rabin, ex-Chief of Staff of the Israeli IDF. He was also the first to lose the seat of government. The upheaval brought as a prime minister another of the first generation — Polish-born Menachem Begin.

In many walks of life, one can detect a third-generation crisis. The third generation is now managing the factories created with a great vision by their grandparents, and leading the political parties. Many of them were unable yet to shape their own world view and to be able to take the reign of power successfully. In the 1980s, the Israeli political culture shifted into populism. As in other countries where populism was used, it catered to deprived groups. The native-born elite did not know exactly how to deal with these deprived groups.

Last, but not least, for the new generation there is very little that is sacrosanct. Many are having great fun in attempting to demystify the Zionist revolution. 'Young historians' are looking for evidence of wrong-doings of the Israelis, of any flaws however minor in the behavior of the first generation, and question the basic assumptions of the Zionist cause and its core values. Others look for ways to cut any links between Israelis and the Jews abroad, claiming a direct link to the land of Canaan, not to the Jews of the Diaspora.

Israeli relations with the Jewish Diaspora

The relationships between Israelis and their kin in the Diaspora have also gone through many transformations and are changing constantly. The Diaspora Jews do not rely on Orthodox Judaism as a basis of their congruence. Their relationships with Israelis are complex. The problem is also the changing identity of the Israelis as Jews and their relationships with Jews abroad.

Israelis of the founding generation were mostly secular. Yet they fervently believed they were to create a Jewish state, a Kingdom of Priests and a Sacred Nation. The Israeli schools teach the Jewish history, devote much time to the study of the Bible, and are run according to the Jewish calendar, having vacations during Jewish holidays. This creates a problem of identity conflict among the non-Jews in Israel. It also creates a problem of identity among Jews. Some Israelis — albeit the minority — see themselves as the descendants of the Canaanites, not as Jews. Most Jews, however, share a common religious heritage and forty centuries of a common past, along with adversity and suffering, are interwoven with triumph and exaltation.

Israel was proclaimed as a place of refuge for all Jews. It

came about because of long and arduous work by many who believed passionately in the need to change the trend of Jewish history. This history has been full of events in which Jews had to fly away from one country to another because of persecution. The suffering seemed unending. Time and again, Jews were lured to a country by those who needed their skills to establish a middle class of bankers, physicians, craftsmen and men of commerce — trades in which Jews were known to excel. Time and again, they were later persecuted. Time and again, Jews were burned at the stake for rejecting the dubious opportunity offered them to convert to Christianity. Kings and noblemen repeatedly unleashed blood orgies and riots against Jews in the hope of turning the anger and the general discontent of the poor people into venom against Jews as scapegoats. The long history of torment, persecutions, and other agonies is a part of the soul of any Jew. Jews were also banned from ownership of land and were excluded from many professions. In Russia, millions of Jews were forbidden to live outside the Pale of Settlement. They faced a constant barrage of suppressive laws, were restricted from entering universities by a *numeros clausus*. They were also boycotted from most professions. Jews have through time kept their longing for the return to the old land. Toward the end of the 19th century, many Jews left Russia for Western Europe or the United States. Many of them attempted wholeheartedly to assimilate themselves into the culture of the host country. Jews in Germany called themselves Germans with Moses religion, exerting themselves frantically to efface their own identity in order to be accepted as equal Germans, thus gaining a security that turned out to be illusory. Only a tiny minority of Jews were Zionists. The obstinacy and persistence of the Zionist movement cannot be explained except in terms of innermost feelings and faith.

The Nazi Holocaust taught Jews that anti-Semitism has not ended in an enlightened period, that skilled medical doctors do not hesitate to use Jews as guineapigs for their atrocious experiments, and that even in modern times and in enlightened cultures, they may be turned into soap and ashes in state-run and operated kilns of death. Jews also find it hard to forget that the countries fighting the Nazis refused to spare a few bombs in order to bomb the concentration camps and perhaps decelerate the pace of the killing machines, even though the leaders of these countries were fully aware that Hitler was attempting a total obliteration of the Jews. Nor is it easy to forget that England was keeping the gates to Palestine closed against the unhappy men, women and children who were making the last desperate effort

341

to reach the safety of their promised land, wandering over the Mediterranean in coffin boats. The incredible starkness of these tragedies has intensely affected Jewish thinking.

The proclamation of an independent Jewish state in the land of the Patriarchs has been the seal of a long line of aspirations, prayers, and the fulfillment of dreams and of hopes. Indeed, on November 29, 1947, when the United Nations decided on the partition of Palestine, and even more so on May 14, 1948, when the Jewish state was officially proclaimed, a great wave of rejoicing spread throughout the Jewish world. Since then, Jews showed both pride and anxiety as to the existence of Israel. Many worked long and hard to help the State of Israel defend itself or to survive and remain effective. The solidity of the Jewish people indeed helped Israel in many ways, mainly in money contributions. Israel, however, was regarded as a 'night shelter,' not as a place in which one lives, leaving the affluence and convenience of the Western democracies. In one sense, Israel is perceived as an insurance policy. Its very existence is important not only as a source of pride, but also 'just in case' it is ever needed because meaningful Jewish life ceases to be possible in the Diaspora (or if anti-Semitism raises its ugly head again). Israel's existence is thus a contingent asset, important in case of emergency, in which one can find refuge. As long as the refuge is not needed, life outside Israel is certainly easier, maybe even more rewarding.

Jews outside Israel felt that their bonds to their relatives in Israel gave them moral responsibility to aid Israel, but most of them preferred to continue living outside the state. American Jews learned to help Israel but also not to intervene in its internal politics. This, too, has been changing. First, more and more American Jews believe that they have the right to intervene — and many of them disagree with the official Israeli line on the territories or on economic policies. A growing number of them choose to stop their contributions to the United Jewish Appeal or to direct these contributions to other causes, not to funds that can be used by the Israeli government.

In 1988, for the first time in Israel's history, United States Jews intervened openly (and successfully) in Israeli politics: the attempt of the large political parties to draw the small religious parties to a narrow coalition made each promise a change in the Law of the Return that would make a Jew defined by Orthodox Jewish laws. These developments have caused a vehement reaction from many non-Orthodox Jews who openly gave dire warnings that Israel would cause itself irreparable harm by changing that law. It is said that it was this intervention that forced the two large parties to again create a national unity government.

This intervention was indeed a major change in the pattern of relationships between Jews in Israel and in the Diaspora. Since the Yishuv time, the community in Israel has been dependent on the Jews in the Diaspora for sources of capital and manpower. It was also dependent on the Jews in the Diaspora for political support. Yet the very essence of the Zionist movement has been the negation of the diaspora and the belief that Jews should immigrate to the land of their forefathers. At the same time, the financial resources and the political support was claimed and mobilized from Jews who remain living outside Israel. Jews living in Israel have seen themselves as both morally and spiritually superior to those staying abroad. For many, the tiny community of Israel's major *raison d'être* was to become a spiritual center for all Jewish people. Jewish creativity was seen as flourishing under the skies of the Holy Land and coming to a full efflorescence in Israel after being stifled in the Diaspora. The Zionist movement was also largely a secular one, revolting against the many years of Rabbinical control. It was to create a new Jew in Israel. Was that Jew still a kin of the old Jew in the Diaspora?

Paradoxically, the more the two communities became different the more the Israelis, grudgingly perhaps, implicitly legitimized the Diaspora. The negation of the Diaspora does not go hand in hand with the need for its help. As early as 1929, when Weizmann's proposal for an enlarged Jewish Agency was accepted, it was also at least implicitly accepted that Jews could continue to live in the Diaspora as long as they contributed money to the Yishuv. The Revisionists at that time may have been correct in seeing the participation of the non-Zionists as a major betrayal of the pristine Zionist vision. Since then, they have all come, hat in hand, and asked for financial and other aid.

Some of the young Israelis, devoid of many of the characteristics of the Diaspora Jew and having much less emotional ties to their brethren in distant lands, are becoming irritated by the changing attitudes of Jews abroad and by their refusal to immigrate. These young persons serve many months in reserve duty, they have to make many sacrifices, and they pay a very dear price for the continued existence of the safe haven called Israel. They feel the division of the burden is unfair. They begin to examine the very belief that Israel should continue to be a state of all the Jews — even those who do not want to come to it. One result of such an introspection, not widely shared at the time of writing, is the proposal to announce in advance that the

Law of the Return will be abolished some years ahead. Those who would be willing to come will be welcome to do so, but only within so many years. If they do not want to take advantage of that opportunity, they of course have the full rights and privileges of so doing — but not to enjoy forever the right of return without any price.

Another problem of the relations between Jews and the state of Israel is perhaps a more dangerous one in principle. This is the problem of the relations between the laws of the secular state and the laws of the religion. For some extremely ultra-Orthodox Jews, the man-made laws of the state should not be obeyed, when they are perceived as contradicting the divinely revealed laws. Fortunately, this problem has not developed into a crisis, but could in the future. As one example, students of religious places of learning (Yeshivot) are exempt from army conscription. This exception was agreed by the then Prime Minister Ben Gurion, who was convinced by the religious leaders of the need to maintain the continuous study of the religious scripts, in particular since so many of the students in Yeshivot in Europe were slaughtered. At that time, it was a question of a few hundred students. Today, there are tens of thousands exempted, and many young Israelis resent the fact that so many of their religious friends do not have to serve in the army.

Israelis and Arabs

As a Jewish state, Israel is expected by its own citizens and by the outside world to have much higher moral standards than any other country. The Jews, who were a persecuted minority for two thousand years, find it extremely difficult to forget the feeling of being a minority when they are now a majority in their own sovereign state. This made them very ambivalent as to the best ways to deal with Israeli Arabs, and even more so — the ways to achieve peace with their neighbors. By the end of the 1980s, the issue of the future of the occupied territories may be one on which Israelis are more divided. The links between Israeli Arabs and the PLO are growing stronger, and the way Israel should deal with Israeli Arabs is far from clear.

As long as the country operated under a wide consensus that its defense policies stemmed from lack of any choice, since its Arab neighbors do not want to tolerate it or recognize its existence, much of the hardship of the defense burden was accepted as stemming from no choice. Clearly, the Arabs did not accept the November 19, 1947 UN resolution and attacked Israel, invading upon the proclamation of its independence. Nasser closed the international waterway of the Suez Canal to Israeli shipping and blocked the Red Sea from Israeli shipping. Certainly, many and frequent terrorist attacks were tolerated if not organized by the neighboring countries. These countries also organized the PLO. Certainly, the Arabs refused to recognize Israel's legitimacy; they blockaded it militarily and economically. Israel has had to defend itself and to respond with armed vigilance. The sweeping victory in the unwanted war of 1967, however, created new problems of being a country holding occupied territories and ruling occupied persons. To some, these were not occupied but liberated territories, promised by God to the Jewish people. How can one give away the burial place of the Patriarchs in Hebron, or other places of a deep religious significance? To others, these territories were held as bargaining chips in the hopefully soon-to-come peace negotiations. When President Anwar El Sadat pierced the veil of hatred and came to Jerusalem to negotiate, he was accepted with open arms. The Israelis made very painful decisions, returning to Egypt all of the Sinai even though the border was nothing more than an agreement from 1906 between two defunct empires: the British and the Turkish.

The 1982 Lebanon war was the first breach in a wide consensus. Many Israelis found the war uncalled for and not one of 'no choice.' The long period of occupation of hundreds of thousands of Arabs that clearly do not want to be subject to Israeli occupation has caused some more soul searching and debates on the best process to achieve lasting peace. This problem may create a torn country and split the Israelis into camps. Today, Israel behaves as if these problems could be kept in abeyance. The future of the occupied territories has polarized Israel, and the degree of that polarization continues to widen. For some, there is no question but that Israel should declare sovereignty over these territories. These are also often the people who believe that there is no way to reach an agreement with the neighboring Arab states, that Israel should never negotiate with the Palestine Liberation Organization (PLO) and that the land belongs to the Jews by a divine promise given to the Patriarch Abraham. On the other side of the argument are those who believe passionately that annexing these areas will destroy the Jewish nature of Israel (or force it into a kind of apartheid-type policy), that Israel should negotiate with the PLO and that any attempt to add more settlements in these territories is detrimental to the future of Israel. There are no easy answers to these questions. Certainly, even mentioning the problem provokes strong feelings and intense reactions.

Attempting to forecast its future is even more difficult. The problem is not only what kinds of adjustments one can assume will happen in the existing system; the question is the type of general vision the country will be able to put before her citizens. Much depends also on changes in the environment: in the confrontation states as well as the major powers. Thus, more and more persons believe that Jordan should be made the Palestinian state, since the majority of the population there are Palestinians. Some also propose moving Palestinian Arabs from the West Bank east of Jordan, perhaps as a partial compensation for the 800,000 Jews from Arab countries that moved to Israel. Others see the solution in a unilateral retreat from the West Bank.

Conclusions

Israel, toward the 1990s, is not a country with a free market liberal economy rather a state in which much of the resources are allocated by the government in different ways. Israel's economy is subservient to its political system and to its national objectives. Much of this is a heritage of the voluntary system created in the pre-state period, that was carried over to the state. In the formative years of the state, the first priority had to be given to physical survival in the face of constant infiltration by Arab guerrillas and a frontal attack in every possible international forum attempting to undermine the very existence of the country and destroy it. In addition, the wide opening of Israel's gates to the 684,000 new immigrants that arrived between May 1948 and December 1951 strained all resources. These resources had to be concentrated on an attempt to supply the massive influx of people shelter, food and employment and prevent major health hazards. There was no way to achieve all these goals without a decisive governmental intervention and direct action.

The economic policy of 1985, while badly needed to stabilize the economic system, also injected for the first time in Israel's history some market discipline. The belief system of most economic leaders did not change fast enough to allow them to read the change and adjust to it. By the end of 1989, many business firms in Israel, in particular in the Histadrut sector are facing many difficulties and struggling to survive. The young generation of Israel has different ideals and does not identify with the old symbols. More than 50 per cent of those under 24 voted for the Likud. The labor leaders failed to implement or even to initiate the fundamental changes called for, perhaps because they did not fully understand the factors that led to their failure. Yet without major changes it would be extremely difficult to invigorate Israel and put the country on a growth path. The political contest between the Likud and Labor has become one of a major disagreement on the shaping of the social fabric of Israel. Many of the old values, even that of the importance of work, has been delegitimized. New values have yet to emerge.

Economists in Israel preach the supremacy of a free market. Yet, the economy is strongly influenced by a centralized political control, and social institutions are geared more for consensus via compromise than to the competition of the free market. Civil servants who enjoy their high level of power attempt to control the economy. Israel still has to adapt itself to the new environment and achieve a new consensus. Hopefully, this will be one that will recognize the very important need to achieve competitive advantage in the world arena in order to achieve some degree of economic independence.

Israel, in the 1990s, needs to make some important strategic choices. It cannot afford to continue operations based on the assumption of 'things as usual' and rely on foreign donors to supply a significant per cent of its resources. To achieve economic growth coupled with social equity, Israel must increase its exports, and reduce the level of government intervention in its economy. The magnitude of the task would be more manageable if the defense budget could be drastically reduced, or if many more affluent immigrants would flock to the country's shores.

Israeli society was transformed, and some of its institutions are now somewhat outmoded. To survive into the 21st century, Israel will have to revamp the institutions created by the founding generation and move to an economy in which only firms able to compete in the world market will survive. Alternatively, a new consensus may be achieved that firms must be internationally competitive, that all segments of society are in the same boat and everyone must help to pull the oars for economic, and therefore political, independence to be achieved.

A cooperative resolution of conflicts over economic and social issues is more in line with the history and belief system of Israel. In the past, Israel emphasized employment creation and tolerated the existence of firms that could not compete in a world market. Israel also allowed a large level of disguised unemployment to continue. In the 1990s, cooperation will be needed to achieve a major structural change, allowing firms to exist only if they can compete in the world arena. Some institutions, forged in earlier periods to fit the needs and the prevailing ideology of that time, are ill suited to cope with new conditions and may have to be razed.

Israeli politics has been governed by splits, the tendency for divisiveness, rifts and personal quarrels. At the same time Israel is also to a large extent a monolithic body. The fear of a total cataclysm and utter destruction pushed the Israelis to be always prepared to devote themselves to achieve national goals, to sacrificing their own personal needs and to a considerable space of solidarity and decisiveness in anything related to the national survival. Despite many debates and controversies, Israelis have a clear set of agreed national goals, and the public interest and community needs are perceived as having priority over any individual benefits.

One major lesson of Israel's experience is that a nation can create for itself dynamic competitive advantages in the world markets by a high level of investment in human capital. The Israeli experience seems to show that raw materials or cheap labor are not the only means of achieving economic growth. In fact, much of the growth can be achieved if a nation invests in the creation of new knowledge and skills, and if firms are innovative in designing strategies which introduce to the world economy new products and new processes. Israel exports today a myriad of sophisticated products based on its own R&D efforts. Such economic growth can be achieved without a major social upheaval and while maintaining a democratic regime if there is a widely-held national consensus on the importance of certain goals and the willingness to work hard to achieve these goals.

Another important lesson of Israel is the limit to the ability of a rational individual to transform large communities to new ideals. Such transformations do not seem to hold in the third generation. Israel's pioneers were extremely optimistic. They believed community life could and should transform the basic nature of human beings by creating new economic and social arrangements. For these arrangements to work effectively, individuals must sacrifice private interests, placing themselves at the disposal of the community. Individuals should forget their desire for private property, suppress their greed and ignore their inclinations to work hard solely for themselves as individuals and for their close families. Instead, they should be committed to a collective growth. Israel's experience shows that such a commitment is possible for special reasons and for a limited time. Yair Stern, who created *Lehi*, wrote that 'we have enlisted in the cause for our entire life, only death will release us from the ranks.' A few hundred followed him to the underground. Those surviving the underground period were released from their solemn oath by the state's independence and went their own way to take care of themselves as individuals. Private interests were sacrificed for some time by a few. The founders of the kibbutz felt such a metamorphosis was possible, even desirable. They also believed that rational behavior would win over any impulses. They believed they could precipitate matters, suppress individualism and compel themselves to serve only the nation and the class. The two commitments were considered complementary. Most Israelis are motivated in their daily life by looking after their own good. The commitment to live only for nationalistic ideals has waned now that Israeli adults are into the third generation. The inability of Israeli society to maintain the same level of zeal toward national economic matters can be seen as the first omen, predicting the clamor in Eastern Europe in 1989. Even the Soviet Union had to move to reconstruct its economy despite the resistance of the old guard. To be sure, Israel has always been a democracy, and many would continue to live in a kibbutz and enjoy its unique model of community life. The third generation of Israelis, however, would rather see themselves in a market economy and with less dependency.

References

Note: * before a title means the publication is in Hebrew.

*Aharoni, Yair (1970), *The Working of Boards of Directors in Israel*, Tel Aviv: Israel Institute of Productivity.

*Aharoni, Yair (1977), *Structure and Conduct in Israeli Economy*, Tel Aviv: Gomeh.

*Aharoni, Yair (1981a), *State Owned Enterprises in Israel and Abroad*, Tel Aviv: Gomeh.

Aharoni, Yair (1981b), 'Managerial Discretion in State-Owned Enterprises,' in Raymond Vernon and Yair Aharoni (eds.), *State Owned Enterprises in the Western Economies*, London: Croom Helm, pp. 184-93.

Arian, Asher (1985), *Politics in Israel: The Second Generation*, Chatham, N.J.: Chatham House.

*Arnon, Ya'akov (1981), *A Spiraling Economy*, Tel Aviv: Kibbutz Meuhad.

Aronoff, Myron J. (1977), *Power and Ritual in the Israel Labor Party: A Study in Political Anthropology*, Amsterdam, Netherlands: Van Gorcum, Assen.

Aronson, Shlomo and Dan Horowitz (1971), 'The Strategy of Controlled Retaliation – The Case of Israel,' *State and Government*, Summer, pp. 77-99.

*Avineri, Arie (1977), *Sapir*, Jerusalem: Peleg.

Avineri, Shlomo (1981), *The Making of Modern Zionism: The Intellectual Origins of the Jewish State*, London: Weidenfeld and Nicholson.

Bank of Israel, *Annual Report*, various years.

*Bank of Israel (1965), *The Reparations and Their Impact on Israel's Economy*.

Barkai, Chaim (1954), *The Public, Histadrut, and Private Sectors in the Israeli Economy*, Jerusalem: The Maurice Falk Institute for Economic Research in Israel, 6th Report, pp. 13-90.

*Barkai, Chaim (1981), 'Defense Costs in Retrospect,' Jerusalem: The Falk Insitute for Economic Research in Israel, Research Paper 115.

*Beilin, Yossi (1987), *The Hebrew Manufacturing Industry*, Jerusalem: Keter.

Bein, Alex (1952), *The Return to the Soil: A History of Jewish Settlement in Israel*, trans. by Israel Schen, Jerusalem: Young and Hechalutz Department of the Zionist Organization.

Ben David, Joseph (1965), 'Professions and Social Structure in Israel,' *Industrial Relations*, 5, I, October, pp. 48-66.

*Ben Gurion, David (1951), 'The Uniqueness of the Worker,' *Israel's Government Yearbook.*

*Ben Gurion, David (1959), *The Sinai War*, Tel Aviv: Am Oved.

*Ben Gurion, David (1967), *Meetings with Arab Leaders*, Tel Aviv: Am Oved.

Ben-Porath, Yoram (1966), *The Arab Labor Force in Israel*, Jerusalem: The Maurice Falk Institute for Economic Research in Israel.

Ben-Porath, Yoram (1975), 'The Years of Plenty and the Years of Famine – A Political Business Cycle?' *Kyklos*, 28, pp. 400-3.

Ben-Porath, Yoram (ed.) (1986), *The Israeli Economy: Maturing Through Crises*, Cambridge, Mass.: Harvard University Press.

Ben-Porath, Yoram and Michael Bruno (1977), 'The Political Economy of a Tax Reform: Israel 1975,' *Journal of Public Economics*, 7, June, pp. 285-307.

Ben-Shahar, Haim, Saul Bronfeld and Alex Cukierman (1971), 'The Capital Market in Israel,' in P. Uri (ed.), *Israel and the Common Market*, London: Weidenfeld and Nicolson.

Berglas, Ethan (1983), *Defense and the Economy: The Israeli Experience*, Jerusalem: The Maurice Falk Institute for Economic Research in Israel, Discussion Paper 83:01.

Bonne, Alfred (1943), *The Economic Development of the Middle East*, Jerusalem: Economic Research Institute, Jewish Agency for Palestine.

*Bregman, Arie (1983), 'The Slowdown of Industrial Productivity – Causes, Explanations, and Surprises,' *Bank of Israel Economic Review*, 55, pp. 48-60.

*Bregman, Arie (1986), *Industry and Industrial Policy in Israel (1965-1985)*, Jerusalem: Bank of Israel Research Department.

Bregman, Arie (1989), *Technological Progress, Structural Change, and Productivity in Industry: The Case of Israel*, Bank of Israel Discussion Paper 89:10, August.

Caiden, G. (1970), *Israel Administrative Culture*, Berkeley, CA: University of California Press.

*Dayan, Moshe (1976), *Milestones*, Tel Aviv: Adanim.

Divrei Ha'Knesset (Knesset Protocols), various issues.

Don, Yehuda (1977), 'Industrialization in Advanced Rural Communities: The Israeli Kibbutz,' *Sociologia Ruralis*, 17:59-72. Reprinted in Ernest Krausz (ed.), *The Sociology of the Kibbutz*, New Brunswick, N.J.: Transaction Books, 1983, pp. 371-84.

Dubin, Robert and Yair Aharoni (1981), 'Ideology and Reality: Work and Pay in Israel,' *Industrial Relations*, vol. 20, no. 1, Winter, pp. 18-35.

Dun and Bradstreet (1981 and 1985), Dun and Bradstreet 100: *Israel's*

References

Leading Enterprises, Tel Aviv: Dun and Bradstreet.

Easterlin, Richard A. (1961), 'Israel's Development: Past Accomplishments and Future Problems,' *Quarterly Journal of Economics*, LXXV, February.

Eban, Abba (1977), *An Autobiography*, London: Weidenfeld and Nicholson.

Eisenstadt, S.N. (1954), *The Absorption of Immigrants*, London: Routledge and Kegan Paul.

Eisenstadt, S.N. (1967), *Israeli Society*, London: Weidenfeld and Nicolson.

Elon, Amos (1971), *The Israelis: Founders and Sons*, New York: Holt, Rinehart and Winston.

Etzioni-Halevi, H. (1977), *Political Culture in Israel* (with R. Shapira), New York: Praeger.

Gansler, J.S. (1983), *The Defense Industry*, Cambridge, Mass.: M.I.T. Press.

Goldstein, Yaa'kov (1975), *Mapai – Factors in its Establishment*, Tel Aviv: Am Oved.

Gottleib, Avi and Ephraim Yuchtman-Yaar (1983), 'Materialism, Postmaterialism, and Public Views on Socioeconomic Policy: The Case of Israel,' *Comparative Political Studies* 16, 3:307-35. Reprinted in Ernest Krausz (ed.), *Politics and Society in Israel: Studies of Israeli Society*, 1985, pp. 385-412.

Gurevich, D. and A. Gretz (1947), *Statistical Yearbook of Jewish Palestine, 1947*, Jerusalem: The Jewish Agency.

Halevi, Nadav and Ruth Klinov-Malul (1968), *The Economic Development of Israel*, Jerusalem: Bank of Israel and Praeger, Praeger Special Studies in International Economics and Development.

*Halevi, Nadav and Yaakov Kop (eds.) (1975), *Issues in the Economy of Israel*, Jerusalem: The Maurice Falk Institute for Economic Research in Israel.

Halevi, Nadav, Maurice Teubal and D. Tsiddon (1983), *The Development of Israel's Industrial Exports, 1970-1980*, Jerusalem: The Maurice Falk Institute for Economic Research in Israel.

*Halperin, A. (1986), *Military Buildup and Economic Growth in Israel*, Jerusalem: The Hebrew University.

Horowitz, Dan (1982), 'The Israel Defence Forces: A Civilianized Military in a Partially Military Society,' in Roman Kolkowicz and Andrei Korbonski (eds.), *Soldiers, Peasants, and Bureaucrats*, London: George Allen and Unwin, pp. 77-105.

Horowitz, Dan and Baruch Kimmerling (1974), 'Some Social Implications of Military Service and Reserve Systems in Israel,' *European Journal of Sociology*, 2, pp. 64-89.

Horowitz, Dan and Moshe Lissak (1973), 'Authority Without Sovereignty: The Case of the National Center of the Jewish People in Palestine,' *Government and Opposition*, 8, pp. 48-71.

Horowitz, Dan and Moshe Lissak (1978), *Origins of the Israeli Polity*,

Chicago: University of Chicago Press.

*Horowitz, David (1948), *The Economy of Israel*, Tel Aviv: Massada.

Israel, Central Bureau of Statistics, *Statistical Abstract of Israel*, various years.

Israel, Committee on Income Distribution and Social Inequality (1966), *Report*, Tel Aviv: The Committee.

Israel, Committee on Income Distribution and Social Inequality (1971), *Report*, Tel Aviv: The Committee.

Israel, State Controller, *Report on Audit of State Corporations*, various issues.

Israel, State Controller, *Annual Reports*, various years.

Klinov-Malul, Ruth (1984), 'The Industrial Structure of Product in Israel,' Jerusalem: The Maurice Falk Institute for Economic Research in Israel, Discussion Paper 84:10.

*Kochav, David and Yaakov Lifschitz (1973), 'Defence Expenditures and Their Influence on the National Economy and the Industry,' *Economic Quarterly*, 20, no. 78-9, pp. 256-70.

*Kusiatin, Ilan (1986), *The High-Tech Entrepreneurial Process in Israel 1968-1983*, Ramat Aviv, Israel: JIM – Jeruslam Institute of Management.

*Lavski, Hagit (1980), *The Foundation of Zionist Financial Policy: The Zionist Commission, 1918-1921*, Jerusalem: Yad Ishak Ben-Zvi Publications.

*Lifschitz, Gabriel (1988), *Socio-Economic Differences among Development Towns*, Jerusalem: The Jerusalem Institute for Israel Studies.

Lissak, Moshe (1961), *Social Mobility in Israel*, Jerusalem: Israel University Press.

Lissak, Moshe (ed.) (1984), *Israeli Society and Its Defense Establishment: The Social and Political Impact of a Protracted Violent Conflict*, London: Frank Cass.

*Livtin, Uri and Liora Meridor (1982), 'The Grant-Equivalent of Subsidized Investment in Israel,' *Bank of Israel Economic Review*, 54, pp. 3-24.

Medding, Peter Y. (1972), *Mapai in Israel*, Cambridge: Cambridge University Press.

Meridor, Leora Rubin (1985), 'Financing a Government Expenditure in Israel, 1960-1983: A Macroeconomic Analysis,' PhD thesis submitted to the Hebrew University of Jerusalem.

Metzer, J. (1979) *National Capital for a National Home (1919-1921)*, Jerusalem: Yad Izhak Ben-Zvi Publications.

Metzer, J. (1983), 'The Slowdown of Economic Growth in Israel: A Passing Phase or the End of the Big Spurt?' Jerusalem: The Maurice Falk Institute for Economic Research in Israel, Discussion Paper 83:03.

Michaely, Michael (1971), *Israel's Foreign Exchange Rate System*, Jerusalem: The Maurice Falk Institute for Economic Research in Israel.

353

References

Michaely, Michael (1975), *Foreign Trade Regimes and Economic Development in Israel*, New York: National Bureau of Economic Research.

Michaely, Michael (1983), 'The Floating Exchange Rate in Israel: 1977-1980,' in D. Bigman and T. Taya (eds.), *Exchange Rate and Trade Instability: Causes, Consequences and Remedies*, Cambridge, Mass.: Ballinger.

*Nachmani, D. (1981), *The Distribution of Imports to Israel Among Final Uses, 1971-1979*, Jerusalem: Bank of Israel Research Department.

Ofer, Gur (1967), *The Service Industries in a Developing Economy: Israel as a Case Study*, New York: Praeger and the Bank of Israel.

Pack, H. (1971), *Structural Changes and Economic Policy in Israel*, New Haven and London: Yale University Press.

Patinkin, Don (1960, 1967), *The Israeli Economy: The First Decade*, Jerusalem: The Maurice Falk Institute for Economic Research in Israel.

Peres, Y. (1971), 'Ethnic Relations in Israel,' *American Journal of Sociology*, 76, pp. 1,021-47.

Peri, Yoram (1982), *Between Battles and Ballots: Israeli Military in Politics*, Cambridge: Cambridge University Press.

Peri, Yoram (1984), 'Civilian Control During a Protracted War,' in Zvi Lanier (ed.), *Israel's Security in the 1980's*, New York: Praeger.

Peri, Yoram and Moshe Lissak (1976), 'Retired Officers in Israel and the Emergence of a New Elite,' in G. Harris-Jenkins and J. van Doorn, (eds.), *The Military and the Problem of Legitimacy*, Beverly Hills, Calif.: Sage.

Perlmutter, Amos (1969), *Military and Politics in Israel: Nation Building and Role Expansion*, London: Frank Cass.

Perlmutter, Amos (1985), *Israel: The Partitioned State: A Political History Since 1900*, New York: Charles Scribner's Sons.

Perlmutter, Amos (1989), 'Israel's Dilemma,' *Foreign Affairs*, vol. 68, no. 5, pp. 119-32.

*Rabin, Yitzhak (1979), *Service Book*, Tel Aviv: Maariv.

Radian, Alex (1984), 'The Policy Formation Electoral Economic Cycle, (1955-1981),' in D. Caspi, A. Diskin and E. Gutmann (eds.), *The Roots of Begin's Success*, Kent: Croom Helm.

*Roeter, Raphael and Nira Shamai (1971), 'Distribution of Personal Income in Israel – the Trend During the Sixties,' *Social Security*, January 1, pp. 58-62.

Rubner, Alex (1960), *The Problems of Israel Economy: The First Ten Years*, London: F. Cass.

Sacher, H.M. (1982), *A History of Israel – From the Rise of Zionism to Our Times*, New York: A. Knopf.

Safran, N. (1978), *Israel: The Embattled Ally*, Cambridge, Mass.: Harvard University Press and The Belknap Press.

Sanbar, Moshe (1984), *The Political Economy of Israel, 1948-1982*, Jerusalem: Jerusalem Institute for Federal Studies, Center for Jewish Community Studies.

Sarnat, Marshal (1966), *Saving and Investment through Retirement Funds in Israel*, Jerusalem: The Maurice Falk Institute for Economic Research in Israel.

*Shapira, Anita (1989), *Visions in Conflict*, Tel Aviv: Am Oved.

*Shapiro, Yonathan (1984), *An Elite Without Successors: Generations of Political Leaders in Israel*, Tel Aviv: Sifriat Poalim.

Sharkansky, Ira and Alex Radian (1982), 'Changing Domestic Policy 1977-81,' in Robert O. Freedman (ed.), *Israel in the Begin Era*, New York: Praeger, pp. 56-75.

*Shefer, Eliezer (1983), 'The Arms Race: Israel and the Confrontation Countries,' in Z. Sussman and M. Felber (eds.), *Studies in Economics 1981*, Jerusalem: The Israel Economic Association.

Shimshoni, Daniel (1982), *Israeli Democracy: The Middle of the Journey*, New York: The Free Press.

Sicron, Moshe (1957), *Immigration to Israel: 1948-1953*, Jerusalem: Falk Project and CBS.

Simon, Merrill (1989), *God, Allah, and The Great Land Grab: The Middle East in Turmoil*, Middle Village, NY: Jonathan David Publishers.

Simpson, Sir John Hope (1930), *Palestine: Report on Immigration, Land Settlement and Development*, Cmd 3686, London: HMSO.

Smooha, S. (1977), *Israel Pluralism and Conflict*, London: Routledge and Kegan Paul.

Szerszewski, Robert (1968), *Essays on the Structure of the Jewish Economy in Palestine and Israel*, Jerusalem: The Maurice Falk Institute for Economic Research in Israel.

Teveth, Shabtai (1972), *Moshe Dayan*, London: Weidenfeld and Nicholson.

*Toren, Benjamin (1979), 'The Industrial Subsidy for Location of Textile Mills in Development Towns in Israel', Ph.D. dissertation, The Hebrew University of Jerusalem.

Ulitzur, A. (1939), *The National Capital and the Construction of the Country: Facts and Figures*, Jerusalem: Keren Hayesod.

Weizmann, Chaim (1966), *Trial and Error*, New York: Schoken Books.

*Yanai, Nathan (1982), *Political Crises in Israel*, Jerusalem: Keter.

Index

Index